Wildlife Management

A Series of Books in Animal Science

G. W. Salisbury, Editor

Wildlife Management

Robert H. Giles, Jr.

*Virginia Polytechnic Institute
and State University*

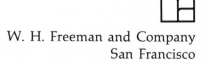

W. H. Freeman and Company
San Francisco

Library of Congress Cataloging in Publication Data

Giles, Robert H
  Wildlife management.

  (A Series of books in animal science)
  Includes bibliographies and index.
  1. Wildlife management. I. Title.
SK353.G53   639'.9   78-15700
ISBN 0-7167-0082-4

Printed in the United States of America
1 2 3 4 5 6 7 8 9

Contents

Preface

This is a book about wildlife and people. It describes people's potential role in using, benefiting from, preserving, and managing the wildlife resources of the world. At its center is the professional wildlife manager. Throughout, the need is expressed for rational management of natural resources in general, but particularly of wildlife, for wildlife is a synthetic indicator of how well we are managing all of our resources.

I have tried to present an overview of wildlife management, placing more emphasis upon naming the parts of the problems than upon detailing processes and solutions. Some readers are likely to judge the book long on diagnosis and short on prescription. Their perception is accurate. It is no more proper for a person having read an introductory text on wildlife management to prescribe a land treatment for wildlife than for a pre-med student having read an introduction to medical science to prescribe for a friend's ailment. To prescribe without *mastery* of the wildland sciences is to engage in land-health quackery.

The book is designed to assist instructors of introductory college and university courses in wildlife management. No course prerequisites are assumed. Courses in basic statistics and ecology will enhance the usefulness of the text. The text is intended to accompany creative college and university presentations, and some topics may require an instructor's assistance. Boxes demonstrating computations are included for more advanced students. Depending on the instructor's emphasis, sections of the text may be omitted without loss of continuity.

This text is also expected to be helpful in career guidance, in improving citizen involvement in environmental projects, and in increasing appreciation of the wildlife resource and its social and environmental milieu. I trust it will be useful to commissioners and public decision makers, land use planners, and, in general, people who love the outdoors.

Part I, Chapters 1 through 5, presents the basic principles of wildlife management, progressively integrated. In Part II, general case approaches are taken for an individual species, a species group, a habitat group, and a managerial function. Part III discusses people, both as users of the wildlife resource and as makers of wildlife management policy. Within these chapters are discussions of research, decision making, and future orientations. The intent of the chapters in Parts II and III is to expand on the basic concepts, to give examples, to show how the material of the first five chapters can be integrated, and to provide insight into the approaches that have been or may be taken to wildlife management.

Specific career information is not included in this book because of (1) the breadth of wildlife management described, (2) the changing status of agencies and requirements, (3) the uncertainty of licensing and certification, and (4) the strong dependence of wildlife management employment on government-funded programs and organizations.

Study questions and references are provided at the end of each section to guide the student and to stimulate further thought and reading. The selected references show the source of the concepts and research conclusions and suggest gateways to a vast literature. No attempt is made to provide an inclusive set of references on any topic.

This book is mostly about terrestrial wildlife, but fish are often grouped with other vertebrate fauna as wildlife. Fisheries management and wildlife management share many principles and problems and are often cooperatively performed by the same people. There are great similarities and parallels between fish management and wildlife management. However, there are significant differences in the factors of the environment, regulations, control, and management practices. All of these differences cannot be treated adequately in one brief introductory book. Chapter 8 highlights the similarities and introduces major unique fishery concepts.

I have concentrated on North American wildlife management, but I believe that wildlife principles are basically the same regardless of the country or the species. Governments, agencies, laws, and international policy greatly influence wildlife populations, which are usually far removed from the sites, the time, and the people participating in forming policy. Through awareness of the consequences of such decisions and attention to reducing undesirable consequences, world wildlife will be better preserved and managed.

I appreciate the assistance in many ways of the wildlife and fisheries faculty of Virginia Polytechnic Institute and State University. However, I take full responsibility for the presentation. It must be recognized that wildlife management is a relatively young and dynamic field, approached from many perspectives by many professions, and therefore there is no universal theory. There is dogma, of course, but even this changes.

I am grateful to some of my students who daily teach me and who dampen my pessimism about the fate of humankind and wildlife in the world today. I have appreciated the advice and assistance of Harvey C. McCaleb, Gunder Hefta, and Patricia Brewer of W. H. Freeman and Company. Joan Westcott's editorial work was masterful and invaluable. I am very grateful to my wife for editorial assistance and for typing much of the final manuscript. She and my daughters deserve more than my thanks and acknowledgment for their support, encouragement, and sharing of burdens related to this book.

June 1978

Robert H. Giles, Jr.
Blacksburg, Virginia

PART I
PRINCIPLES AND CONCEPTS

Chapter 1

The Resource and
Its Management

What is wildlife? This is a good question without a good answer. There are no clear taxonomic or even behavioral boundaries defining wildlife, so a dictionary will be of little help. Wildlife certainly must include game animals and songbirds. Some people argue about whether fish are wildlife. Past the seldom-debated anchor points, wildlife may also include, depending on local policy and purpose, wild horses, urban rats, introduced zebras, salamanders, porpoises, and butterflies. The often fruitful debates over the definition of wildlife center on such practical questions as who is willing and sufficiently competent to work with a species, which agency has responsibility under the law (or desires it), and what species fall within the purview of various disciplines and universities. In effect, then, society determines what constitutes wildlife. In view of the changing definitions of wildlife, it is not surprising that debate continues about the proper body of knowledge and the principles of wildlife management.

Some years ago a bill was introduced into Congress to change the name of the U.S. Biological Survey to the U.S. Wildlife Service. The encompassing word had fared well until a fisheries commissioner, apparently fearing loss of visibility and thus congressional support, succeeded in getting the name amended in the final hour to the U.S. Fish and Wildlife Service. This political ploy has resulted in wildlife connoting terrestrial animals.

Wildlife usually refers to wild or semidomesticated terrestrial vertebrates. The species most often mentioned are those that provide benefits (or detriments) for human society, notably game animals. Recently, vertebrate pests have been included as major wildlife forms, largely because of lagging research and professional involvement in this area. Butterflies may also be included, but it is to be hoped that applied entomologists will assume responsibility for their management. Wildlife is not wildflowers or lichens, nor is it nematodes. Viruses are quite wild but they are hardly wildlife. There is a danger of opening a conceptual umbrella so wide that it covers all biology and then discovering the topic of interest has been defined away. Wildlife is always what some individual or group with a purpose decides it to be. In other words, the definition of wildlife is a decision. It is best conceived as a contextual definition: *that population is wildlife, manage it!*

In this book wildlife and fisheries management are separated because (1) wildlife has grown through usage to connote terrestrial forms and (2) there is a major literature, as well as professional group, that finds sufficient difference in problems and solutions to discriminate between the two. Special fisheries concepts are treated in Chapter 8. Elsewhere, the reader will, I hope, allow me to use wildlife loosely, usually to denote terrestrial forms, but also to imply that the topic is relevant to managing both aquatic and terrestrial forms of wild animals. Where major differences exist in their management, I shall specify "fisheries."

The Concept of Wildlife Management

Wildlife management is
>the science and art
>of making decisions and taking actions
>to manipulate the structure, dynamics, and relations
>of populations, habitats, and people
>to achieve specific human objectives
>by means of the wildlife resource.

This long and cumbersome definition has many implications.

Wildlife management is evolving from an art form to a science. Perhaps it will never become a science, but every effort should be made to encourage this evolution. The art of wildlife management is observable in a few areas around the country where a manager's unique touch shows through. There are agency meetings and political encounters in which one feels in the presence of an artisan, so adroitly are discussions and decisions handled. There are wildlife areas similar in character to others that produce quite different social benefits under the managerial control of a special manager. All managers are more or less artful. The emergence of wildlife as a science does not destroy managerial artistry but increases the predictability of systems, reduces risks, allows the transfer of knowledge and exchange of techniques, and enables resource benefits to be experienced widely, rather than only on those areas where there are managers of genius or of more than 20 years of experience.

Wildlife management is a decision science. Its appropriateness is measurable by the rightness of decisions that are made. Managers earn their wages by making decisions. Weather may change, animals may escape, or a laborer may do a poor job, but these all occur after a decision is made. The goodness of a decision bears little relation to whether, or how well, it was carried out. Of course, wildlife managers do actively work afield, and their actions need to be judged to decide whether they are actually wildlife management and, if so, how well executed.

The object of this decision making is *control*. Management is a cybernetic or control function, guiding systems toward objectives. It requires analyzing, designing, and tending systems. Unless change results that is significantly different from that which would occur without the presence of the manager, no management has occurred. Wildlife managers are not paid to watch the grass grow or populations change. They must strive to be in control of systems. Whatever obstacles are placed in their paths, whether drought, poachers, or the constraints of a shortsighted law, they must work to increase their effectiveness in meeting the objectives set forth. In most wildlife systems nature is provident. Game will be produced. The managerial function is measured in the difference between the benefits the system would produce naturally and those it produces under the wildlife manager's guidance.

There are essentially two kinds of management: *active* and *passive*. Active management manifests itself in positive measures such as *increasing* pheasant populations through planting food patches, or elk populations through making prescribed burns of rangelands to produce food; *stabilizing* some populations through specifying harvest dates and methods while stabilizing food production; *decreasing* some populations by harvesting deer, for example, deer that are damaging orchards, using chemosterilants to reduce disease-carrying fox populations, and poisoning selected flocks of blackbirds or sugar cane rats.

Passive management is the prevention of certain actions or letting natural developments take their course. Wilderness preservation provides opportunities for rangelands and forests to reach mature stages essential for some wildlife species. No overt act (other than legal designation, boundary marking, and surveillance) is needed. In fact, attempts to speed up the maturing of a forest by irrigation or fertilizers may produce results undesirable for the species being managed.

No matter what kind of wildlife management is being practiced, consideration must be given to three fundamental and mutually exclusive characteristics of animal populations, habitats, and people—namely, structure, dynamics, and relations. *Structure* refers to the classes and hierarchies used to describe systems and name their parts. It includes sex, age classes, and weight groups. *Dynamics* are always expressions of rates, changes, and differences and include growth, mortality, birth, and range expansions. *Relations* are cause-and-effect pathways or changes and interactions, including, for example, social breeding behavior, soil-moisture relations, competition for light, and student-teacher responses. These three fundamental characteristics provide an organization and checklist for managerial actions.

The manager works with populations, habitats, and people. Populations are typically emphasized, for the manager deals with wild animals, often uncounted, over large areas. While knowledge of individual animals is essential, the manager works to generate benefits from the group, not the individual animal. Individuals are the subject of veterinary science and zoo keeping.

Habitats are emphasized. Wildlife is almost ubiquitous, so there is a fine line between general environmental management and habitat management. The difference is in the emphasis and in the intent. The wildlife manager is not working to alter environments in general, but to alter the homes of animals to achieve certain pre-stated wildlife-related objectives. Unless this difference in the objectives is known at some level (although it may not be apparent to everyone), it is impossible to distinguish a wildlife manager from a forester, range manager, or farmer.

The third part of the wildlife system is also subject to manipulation. People may be manipulated, as they are daily, by advertising, teaching, and laws. The wildlife manager may change perceived levels of importance of game, may get people to vote or support a cause, or may concentrate hunting to eliminate range problems resulting from high population densities.

Modern wildlife management is objective-oriented. Unless a set of objectives is specified *before* actions are taken, then there is no way to evaluate them. For actions to be adjudged "wildlife management" these actions must be seen to achieve wildlife-related objectives. They must pertain specifically to the wildlife resource. Objectives are stated in terms of specific desired benefits that should result from decisions. There may be many benefits and losses from any action on the land, such as building a hunter access trail or a fishing pond. Those that are produced by or derived from the wildlife resource are the interests of the field of wildlife management.

A Short History

Although the history of wildlife management goes back hundreds of years, as attested by Marco Polo's reports from the thirteenth-century court of Kubla Khan, the first textbook on game management was published in 1933 by Aldo Leopold. Leopold came from a forestry background, and his terminology and concepts have strongly influenced the development of wildlife management. In the United States, game management emerged from a mixture of protectionist law enforcement, foresters with a European gamekeeper orientation, range and agricultural interests, professional soil conservationists, and a host of perceptive naturalists and early ecologists. U.S. wildlife management has from the first reflected the old Magna Carta provision that made wildlife the property of the state and not of the landowner.

Fisheries and game interests have proceeded along intertwining pathways, fisheries science beginning long before the game production sciences. They meet where field personnel must enforce both game and fish laws, stock fish in one season and develop habitats in another, and educate the public, which includes hunters and fishermen. Yet funding, environments, and techniques of research and management are different in the two fields, and thus the divergences are also quite real. Intertwining pathways, with overlaps and occasional points of identity, give the best picture of the relations between the two. The differences are emphasized, or not, by the approach taken to the subject.

The Wildlifer

There are university-educated wildlife management experts employed to do wildlife management. These people typically hold master of science degrees. They are called wildlife managers, wildlife technicians, wildlife biologists, wildlife conservationists, or some specialist title such as wildlife researcher or waterfowl biologist. This terminology largely results from civil service differences in the various states. I typically refer to these paid practitioners of wildlife management as *wildlifers*.

There are real problems with such a word because there are many people interested in and working in wildlife management—enforcement personnel, lobbyists, administrators, fiscal experts, enthusiastic students, educators, very well-informed and supportive citizens who actively manage their yards, and sportsmen who manage their lands and farms to enhance wildlife populations. There are research lab technicians, field workers, and media specialists. There are legal, organizational, and administrative reasons to develop a tighter terminology and to certify various levels of education and managerial competency for these practitioners in the field of wildlife management. There are few other reasons for doing so; therefore a wildlifer is any person who aspires to achieve increased knowledge or mastery of wildlife management (as defined previously).

Approaches to Wildlife Management

There are many viable approaches to the study of wildlife management. Adoption of any one will aid the neophyte, but a multidimensional approach is strongly recommended for the maturing student.

The *species approach* is particularly useful for the manager who is responsible for a management unit and can compile a list of wildlife species. With the list in hand, the manager can proceed to study each species and its special management problems. In large areas or those with very long lists, however, this task is practically impossible. Table 1-1, an outline of the subgroup "big game species," shows how immense the task can become. Studying representative forms is sometimes a practical alternative, especially for managers in agencies or companies that transfer employees frequently from one territory to another.

Some agencies persist in grouping species under such blanket categories as "upland game," "waterfowl," and "big game." Is not a deer upland game as well as big game? Where do songbirds fit within such a species-habitat-taxonomic aggregate? The problem may seem trivial on the surface, but once the categories are fixed by use in budgets or embedded in university course structure, they can influence thinking about wildlife management, as well as allocation of funds. In the long run, the name can result in inefficiencies and failure to achieve maximum benefits from the available wildlife resource.

The *biome approach* stresses the similarities of processes and principles in the major, globally recognizable ecological communities. There are eight major biomes: deciduous forest, coniferous forest, tundra, grassland, desert, chaparral, tropical savanna, and tropical forest. Studies focus on the differences between these areas, on comparisons of ecological processes and their rates, and on unique or overlapping species groups. Mastering the structure and dynamics of more than one biome in a lifetime is unlikely. In practice, managerial study and techniques are rarely biome-specific. However, biomes provide a powerful organization for ecological studies and descriptions.

The *techniques approach* takes a particular tool or technique and seeks out ways it can be used with various species, in various biomes, or for particular problems. Examples of techniques that have been profitably employed are the eye-lens weight method of aging animals, the use of anesthetizing drugs on animals, and the sonar detection of fish populations. The techniques approach may result in great redundancy, but it tends to be very practical. Its primary drawback is not emphasizing objectives. When one is working with a hammer, there is a temptation to treat everything as if it were a nail.

The *land health approach* derives from an analogy, suggested by Leopold (1949), between the wildlife manager and the medical doctor. According to this analogy, the manager is a sophisticated general practitioner, who, aided by experts and research, diagnoses, prescribes, and treats the ills of the land. These diseases may be inherent as well as caused, latent as well as overt or symptomatic. Techniques are needed for improved diagnosis as well as for cures. Education and prevention are as important as curative action. The analogy is very rich, and the student is encouraged to explore it and to discover where it, like all analogies, fails.

TABLE 1-1

The immensity of the task required for a species-specific approach is suggested by this outline of the subgroup called big game species.

Class Mammalia
  Infraclass Eutheria (Placentals)
    Cohort Ferungulata
      Superorder 1 Ferae
        Order Carnivora
          Suborder Fissipedia
            Superfamily Canoidea
              Family Canidae (Dogs)
                Genus *Canis* Example: *Canis lupus,* the wolf
              Family Ursidae (Bears)
                Genus *Ursus* Example: *Ursus americanus,* the black bear
            Superfamily Feloidea
              Family Felidae (Cats)
                Genus *Felis* Example: *Felis concolor,* the mountain lion
          Suborder Pinnipedia
            Family Odobenidae (walrus)
      Superorder 2 Protungulata (First ungulates)
        (The condylarths and others)
      Superorder 3 Paenungulata (The near ungulates)
        (The elephants, conies, and sea cows)
      Superorder 4 Mesaxonia
        Order Perissodactyla (Odd-toed ungulates)
        (The horses, tapirs, and rhinoceroses)
      Superorder 5 Paraxonia
        Order Artiodactyla (Even-toed ungulates)
        (The pigs, camels, and ruminants first appearing in the lower Eocene)
          Suborder Suiformes
            Infraorder Palaeodonta
            Family Suidae
              Genus *Sus* Example: *Sus scrofa,* the wild boar
                   Pecari Example: *Pecari angulatus,* the peccary
          Suborder Ruminantia
            Infraorder Pecora
            Family Cervidae
              Genus *Cervus* Example: *Cervus canadensis,* the wapiti or elk
                   Odocoileus Example: *Odocoileus hemionus,* the mule deer
                   Rangifer Example: *Rangifer arcticus,* the barren ground caribou
                   Alces Example: *Alces americana,* the moose
            Family Antilocapridae
              Genus *Antilocapra* Example: *Antilocapra americana,* the prong-horn antelope
            Family Bovidae
              Genus *Oreamnos* Example: *Oreamnos americanus,* the mountain goat
                   Bison Example: *Bison bison,* the bison or American buffalo
                   Ovibos Example: *Ovibos moschatus,* the musk-ox
                   Ovis Example: *Ovis canadensis,* the bighorn sheep

Source: Adapted from J. Z. Young 1952:554–556.

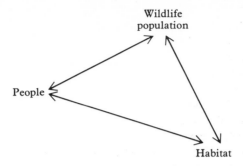

FIGURE **1-1**
The wildlife population-habitat-people triad
shows the three major aspects of wildlife
management as equal and interactive. With
appropriate allocation of time, money, and skills
to each, a desirable dynamic balance can be
reached.

The *population-habitat-people approach* emerges directly from the definition
of wildlife management. This triad is pictured in Figure 1-1. Like the three-
legged milking stool, this system requires all three parts to serve its function.
Furthermore, the three major parts must be equally balanced. This approach
represents a conscious effort to redress the imbalances in funding, research,
public education, and university instruction that continue to arise.

An *energetic approach* advocated by Odum (1971) and Moen (1973) is one of
the most promising of the modern approaches to wildlife management. In
general, it describes all earth systems as energy systems, dependent upon the
sun. According to the first and second laws of thermodynamics, energy is (1)
limited and (2) undergoing dispersion (entropy) or being lost. All systems from
animals to agencies can be analyzed as entropy-minimizing systems and energy
flow-maximizing systems. All behavior and system processes can be studied
relative to these two criteria. The animal is seen as an energy budgeter, re-
sponding sensitively to its total environment to achieve a desirable long-term
balance between energy intake and losses. Moen's *Wildlife Ecology* is recommended for further study and development of this invaluable approach.

The *systems approach* I perceive to be the most useful approach over the long
run. (See Von Bertalanffy 1968, Beer 1959, Donald 1967, Emery 1969, Rabow
1969, Laszlo 1972a, 1972b, Churchman 1968.) This approach starts with the
concept that all systems are subsystems of larger wholes. Every system has a
context, as illustrated in Figure 1-2. A rabbit has the context of other rabbits,
field, shrubbery, brush piles, foxes, hawks, and climate. A systems approach
thus permits a holistic view of wildlife problems. It can effectively embrace

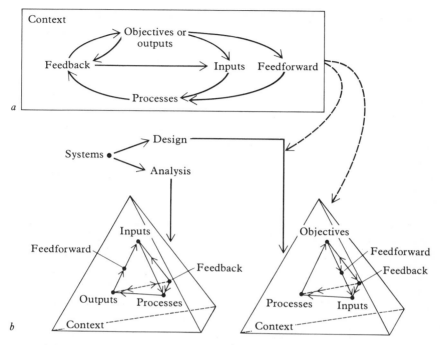

FIGURE **1-2**

(*a*) The configuration of the general system can be applied universally to all analysis and design problems. (*b*) The same concept seen as an equilateral tetrahedron is a volume that can be packed with others, indefinitely. It symbolizes how all systems are subsystems. In practice, the context is specified, the system analyzed or designed, and then, under the influence of feedback, the next larger (or smaller) system is attached.

every topic within wildlife management and provide the tools and concepts for integrating the contributions of other disciplines into wildlife management, and wildlife management into the larger whole of society.

When one adopts a system approach, one sees almost everything, including, of course, wildlife management, as a general system (Figure 1-2) with the components of *context, inputs, processes, outputs* or *objectives, feedback,* and *feedforward.*

Context is the naming of a relevant subsystem, the delineation of a problem, the identification of a unit on which work will be done. It narrows management problems to a workable size and at the same time provides a structure for fitting smaller units into larger ones as problems are solved.

Inputs are the energy or matter that come into systems, such as sunlight, rain, money, or ideas, depending on the type of system.

Processes are the actions, arrangements, and transformations employed with inputs to produce outputs. A decision maker takes data (inputs) and processes them (arranges, synthesizes, computes indices, compares) to arrive at a conclusion (output).

Outputs are the value-free end products, including energy, which result from the processing of inputs. Some may be waste, some may be stored, some may be highly valued.

Objectives are desired, and consequently valued, outputs. All systems are either *analyzed* or *designed* (see Figure 1-2). Of course, the two are interrelated. When systems are analyzed, typically only outputs are described. They are reported and no particular value or importance is attached to them. An objective description is the end product of systems analysis. In systems design, however, objectives are pre-set and things done to achieve them. Design is value-laden. In a designed system, objectives are more or less achieved. There are outputs of the system, but these are translated as objectives-achieved. There may be much action and much output of a system, and yet few objectives achieved poorly. The difference is the ineffectiveness of the system, which feedback may reduce.

Feedback in wildlife management systems includes inspections, progress reports, and monitoring devices. Feedback should operate on all parts of the system including the objectives themselves. There should even be continual improvement of the feedback processes themselves. Feedback operates on the basis of the difference between a state of perfection, defined by objectives, and the state of the present system. If the difference is zero, there is no need for feedback, but when there is any difference, then feedback, if operating properly, will find the least costly ways to make the greatest change toward the objectives.

Feedforward means shaping the future design of a system. Not merely predicting or forecasting, it is a system-forming concept, one intended to make a system most right over the long run, even if sometimes very wrong. In practice, it is much like a hunter leading a fast-moving target. Feedforward does not appear to occur in nonhuman systems.

Much more will be said about the systems approach throughout the rest of the text. Not only does it make available to wildlife management the methods of the fields of systems analysis and operations research, but also it challenges managers to go beyond the "which is best?" (either-or) questions and ask the more encompassing questions of which mix or configuration is best.

Micro- and Macro-Habitat

The three components of the wildlife management triad—population, habitat, and people—can all be approached at either the *micro* or the *macro* level (see Figure 1-3). Habitat provides the best illustration of these different scales, but it

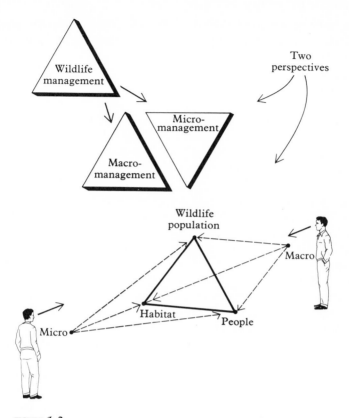

FIGURE **1-3**

Wildlife management may be conceived on two scales, micro- and macro-management, for habitats, wild animal populations, and people. Most wildlifers work at the micro scale; many work part-time in both scales. A few work full-time in macro-management.

should be kept in mind that they apply to the wildlife population and people, as well. (For example, population management at the micro level might mean direct removal of a problem population, and at the macro level, legislative action to achieve alternative control. Management of human behavior at the micro level might entail teaching a group of farmers about wildlife habitats, and at the macro level, changing national farm subsidies that result in habitat destruction.)

Micro-habitat is all of the on-site factors influencing a wildlife population. These factors may include the trees affecting squirrels, terraces affecting range vegetation used by deer, or willow thickets used by moose; the temperatures of the den; the wind velocity in a field hedgerow; or the extra energy made available as food by a platform of crusted snow. In general, there are site-specific factors over which a manager with sufficient resources can exert a reasonable degree of control.

Micro- and macro-habitat exist along a continuum. The difference between them is almost artificial, but there are good reasons for emphasizing it. Macro-habitats refer to the larger contexts, whose forces the manager is unaccustomed to being able to control. The macro-habitat includes land use patterns, wind velocities, light intensity and spectra reaching animals and plants, composition of the air, and radiation levels.

These are factors over which the manager may indeed have relatively little control. But relative is an insidious word. A change of 0.001 hectare in a food plot is not very much, but in a million food plots it is a massive area. Extensive micro-habitat management may improve 1000 hectares for wildlife in the same year that utility lines destroy 1000 hectares. Habitat work may increase game populations 2 percent in a state in which air pollution decreased survival rates by 3 percent.

Most wildlifers now work at the micro level. Many work part-time at both micro and macro levels. Too few work full-time in macro-management. Both kinds of wildlife managers are needed. Some managers must plow ground, while others must lobby; some must seed, while others develop computer systems. Neither is more important than the other; *both* are important. Perhaps macro-management—by citizen and professional—must be done until a better balance is struck.

Management Objectives

A resource, by definition, supplies specific benefits to people. It is people, in other words, who decide what is a resource. *Animals* exist, with or without humans; but the *wildlife resource* is a human construct. If humans disappeared, or for some reason stopped utilizing animals, the resource would no longer exist.

A resource need not provide the same benefits to all people. Few do. Resources are perceived differently by each person, with regard to both supply and demand. It is very improbable that any entity—whether coot, coal, condor, or car—is perceived identically as a resource by any two people.

In analyzing the wildlife resource, the first step is usually to specify the animal or animal group being discussed. It may be relatively useful to speak of "forestry," inasmuch as trees are often treated as integrated communities, but it is almost impossible to talk about "the wildlife resource" as a meaningful entity. What, for instance, is the impact of a powerline right-of-way on wildlife? It is very hard on squirrel and woodland warbler habitat but great for deer forage and sparrows. The species or set of species *must* be specified.

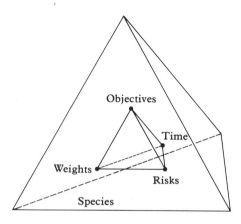

FIGURE **1-4**

The species-specific wildlife resource as a
human concept with four interactive dimensions.

The second analytical step is to identify the major objectives that can be
satisfied by a resource. A resource, remember, is a means for achieving objectives. The next step is to assign priorities to those objectives. After that, a
statement of risk is attached to each objective, indicating what undesirable
consequences might be experienced as a result of failure to achieve the objective.
The last step is to consider some appropriate period of time in which the
resource may be meaningful. This assessment takes into account subtle interactions of age, life expectancy, health, time since last experience, and planning
horizons. Figure 1-4 summarizes these dimensions of the wildlife resource
concept.

Wildlife managers work for different clients. Some work for private estates
directed by a single decision maker. Others work for companies, where they are
responsible to a board. Still others work for state, province, or national agencies.
The latter work for the "public," a very difficult body to define, both because of
people's mobility and because of a widespread feeling that the work should serve
future generations as well as those paying the present salaries. Practically
speaking, however, the wildlife manager works for particular wildlife users,
whether private individuals or the public. The rightness of managerial decisions
can only be judged relative to the employer's objectives. If the manager acts on
a personal set of objectives incompatible with the employer's, mismanagement
may be charged. The manager, of course, may seek to change the employer's
objectives and thus the benefits obtained from a given wildlife population.

Wildlife Benefits. The primary objectives of wildlife management, and thus the classes of benefits obtainable from the resource, are: (1) metaphysical goals, (2) preservation for its own sake, (3) recreation, (4) physical utility, (5) contributions to the ecosystem, (6) gene pool potentials, (7) monitoring of environmental quality, and (8) monetary benefits. Some overlap. Whether anyone holds one or more of these objectives is irrelevant. Some one does. Everyone is likely to weight them differently. If specific objectives can be listed for each user, then weighted and assigned acceptable risk levels, the wildlifer can escape from the debates of "good" or "bad" and proceed with systems that best satisfy human needs and desires.

How to create such systems and how to resolve conflicts among objectives or between groups of people is the essence of management. Most individuals have multiple objectives, some of which are in conflict. Wildlife-interested groups definitely conflict (for example, the hunting and anti-hunting groups). The means of resolving such conflicts, discussed throughout this book, include simple trade-offs, scheduling benefits from different areas, satisfying the most people, satisfying the most intense desires, achieving minimum costs or risks, maximizing production, allocating something to satisfy, at least partially, all participants in a conflict, and many others.

Metaphysical goals. The wildlifer, steeped in a science and technology education, may not comprehend that certain people hold private, nondiscussable and nondescribable objectives for the wildlife resource. The reasons for desiring wildlife and requiring its management are given simply as "just because." It is likely a wildlifer would have to have the same metaphysical awareness as the client to manage actively to achieve such an objective. Usually managing to achieve other objectives satisfies this objective.

Preservation for its own sake. Wildlife managers, as well as the public, take pleasure just in knowing that animal species are being preserved. There may be other reasons for preserving a species, but discriminating this objective helps direct managerial action. Animals are seen an essential part of the land's character and vitality. A forest is not the same without a bobcat, nor a mountain without a goat. The world without the whooping crane will be a less complete world. Quantity is almost unimportant; *presence* is the key. The representation of wildlife in the arts, from primitive cave paintings to modern photography, attests to the importance that humans have always attributed to wildlife.

Recreation. Wildlife-related recreation includes the sports of hunting and fishing; other active recreational pursuits such as following tracking trails, taking bird walks, looking for game, and taking cross-country ski census routes; and passive recreations such as watching birds at feeders, reading about wildlife, and watching televised wildlife programs.

For the hunter or fisherman, the recreational experience is measured by more than just the take. Also important are the pre-hunt preparations, including practice with dogs and equipment, the trip to the hunting site, the exercise, the challenge of stalking, killing the prey, the hunting camaraderie, the escape from everyday chores, and the emotional and social satisfactions, later, of recalling the hunt.

A wildlife-oriented recreational event, whether for the purpose of taking a trophy head or gaining a new animal for a life list, may have either beneficial or detrimental effects on the physical, social, and mental state of the resource user. Attention must be given to *net* recreational benefits. The negative aspects of law violation or a lost crippled animal are rarely included in the recreational benefit talley, but should be for each resource-user population.

Physical utility. Perhaps the oldest reason for managing wildlife is that wildlife provide meat, fur, hides, horns and bone, hair, and other products to meet human needs, either directly or through sale or barter. There are entire herds of big game managed largely for meat, not recreation. Management of fur-bearers, once exclusively done for fur production, now includes a recreational objective in some areas.

Contributions to the ecosystem. The ecological values of wildlife are usually asserted and then passed over. The vast interactions of animals with their environments are poorly understood, despite years of investments in research. Nevertheless, enough is known to command caution about wildlife losses or extreme abundance. Wildlife is a vital part of a complex, fluctuating system. Major changes in wildlife can lead to dangerous lows and highs in the performance of the system.

Gene pool potentials. Losses of wild species through domestication can also result in losses of certain heritable characteristics, perhaps essential for long-term survival in new dynamic environments. Such losses reduce the opportunities for genetic manipulation. Wildlife can provide the genetic resource, the gene pool, for studying and developing useful hybrid forms.

Monitoring of environmental quality. By observing wildlife, the status of the ecosystem within which humans live may be appraised. Wildlife becomes the index to environmental quality, an early-warning system that may suggest when action is needed to prevent deterioration of the human life style or decline in longevity. Raccoons (*Procyon lotor*) are studied to assess heavy-metal buildups along streams; starlings (*Sturnus vulgaris*) are collected to assess pesticide buildups.

Wildlife may also provide a human health analog. Experimental populations of animals show the effects of crowding and other phenomena to be potentially analogous to their effects on humans. With increased crowding of vertebrates occurs increased disease susceptibility, homosexuality, and resorption of embryos, as well as reduced care of young, reduced nest tending, and reduced infant survival. It seems likely that wild populations can provide, if humans will look, the models for human population self-regulation at carrying capacity.

Additionally, experiments for the well-being of human society may only be possible on experimental, nonhuman populations. Occasionally humans cannot see themselves clearly. They are deluded by self-importance. Wildlife can provide an alternative view of the structure, function, and relations of them and their systems.

Monetary benefits. It has been said, erroneously, in many wildlife conference halls that a monetary value cannot be placed on wildlife. It can, and many wildlife populations are managed to increase monetary returns, or reduce losses, from wildlife. These include hunting activities and equipment, fees, fur sales, crop and livestock damage, and differences in land value due to the presence of wildlife.

Valuation of Wildlife. It was a sad day when "economic value" of wildlife was allowed to be translated as "monetary value." Economics deals with more than money. It is a study of resources, their values and how they are assigned, and allocations. The modern student of wildlife management will be discriminating and force the question out into the open: monetary or economic?

There is little question that a monetary value can be placed on wildlife. The following list of 25 ways to do so should suggest at least that it can be done. Whether the value is appropriate will remain, as with all values, debatable. The student should recognize that (1) there are legitimate reasons for assigning monetary values to wildlife, as well as illegitimate ones; (2) any value is an estimate; and (3) even dollars (or other currency) are imprecise, fluctuate in value, and vary in importance depending on how many are possessed. The market system is not very precise and exhibits lags. Still, it is society's dominant means of measuring value. In fact, often money seems the only game in town.

If the wildlifer must play the valuation game, here are some ways. A combination of methods will often be needed to arrive at a value. Methods vary in their theoretical strength, data requirements, and propriety. There are no simple answers for a question as complex as the value of wildlife.

1. *Benefit lists.* By listing the benefits to be derived from wildlife it is possible to compare the values of areas or periods by the number of species present. The assumption is that the more species there are, the more benefits. This method can be refined to species-specific benefit lists. The result is a relative value, useful for some purposes. Ordinal (order), not cardinal (actual numerical), value may be adequate for some decisions.

2. *Maximum benefits.* Assume a very large number of benefits can be obtained from a population. These are so difficult to measure that it is reasonable to say that each animal taken represents a very large but unquantified amount of value. The greater the take or number of sightings,

the greater the benefits obtained. Harvest serves as a proxy for benefits produced. Trends in harvests or reported use represent trends in resource benefits.

3. *Gross tax-base increase.* The change in taxation after wildlife populations are managed is a measure of wildlife value. Tax increases from visitors and new commercial and real estate development or from increased crop production, once wildlife damage is removed, are ways to express a minimum worth of wildlife. It is a monetary expression. Some countries manage wildlife to attract tourists and to add to the tax base.

4. *Gross land-value increase.* Like landscaping, wildlife enhances land value for some people. The difference between land value with and without wildlife reflects a minimum value of wildlife and can be expressed in monetary terms. The fact that people place different values on wildlife does not negate the measure. Items are variously priced and may or may not be sold. The pricing of any commodity is difficult. It should be no surprise that pricing wildlife is especially difficult, though not impossible. The major difficulty is that there is no real marketplace for wildlife.

5. *Added value.* Although it is often asserted that birds add value to crop or forest yields as a result of their pest control or other allegedly beneficial activities, attempts to demonstrate this added value have so far been unsuccessful. This remains a fruitful area for very careful research.

6. *Direct worth.* The shooting preserve provides a known market for wildlife. Prices charged, once other services are deducted, give a direct worth of a particular type of wildlife. Permits to hunt and club memberships are also sold. The total price is the worth of a hunting opportunity—a rental of space and time, but one that is wildlife-dependent. It is very easy to lose sight of whether wildlife, hunting success, or hunting opportunity, or nonconsumption use of wildlife is being evaluated. There is no right answer or methodology. It requires clear thinking, assistance from broad-based economists, and careful analysis of each problem.

7. *Parallel worth.* There may be commodities enough like wildlife in the purposes they serve that an assumption is tenable that they are of nearly equal value. Examples might be of beef prices and game meat or park visits and hunting area visits. The value of wildlife lands is often assumed to be that of surrounding lands used for farms or forestry. An hour of wildlife recreation might be compared to the price paid for an hour spent in an alternative recreation. Ratio preferences (or practices) for individuals who engage in multiple forms of recreation can be obtained by questionnaire. When at least one form has a monetary value (for example, bowling), the preference ratios can be used to estimate the worth of the other forms.

8. *Assigned gross monetary value.* Expert appraisers, either in groups or bargaining sessions, assign a direct value to a person-day of wildlife activity. This is also called "assigned user charges" and is a simulated market value. The appraisers may also assign a percentage of income spent as attributable to wildlife. This is also a minimum value. The benefit people actually receive generally is stated by them to exceed what they are willing to pay to achieve it.

9. *Management cost.* Wildlife managers over the years have spent money on wildlife management. Assuming they were operating rationally, they must have thought the wildlife worth at least as much as they invested. Thus, the managerial expenditures can be computed as a minimum wildlife population value. Returns must be weighed against the gains that would be realized from an alternative investment, such as putting an equivalent amount of money in the bank. Production costs usually bear little relation to the value, making this a weak measure. The worth of a shot of an antibiotic has almost no bearing on the worth of the resulting years of a person's life. This method of wildlife valuation suffers the same limitations. The method requires that potential production of animals (realized or not) be utilized in the computations.

10. *Destruction value.* For an endangered species, replacement costs may be meaningless. However, land destruction costs can be computed. If a dam will destroy a pheasant recreation resource valued at $10,000 per year, then the recreational value, capitalized at 6 percent assuming no increase in pheasant hunting value, will be about $167,000 ($P$ = annual value/interest rate). A hectare marsh is said to be worth between 120 and 150 thousand dollars, based on the functions society must replace if the marsh is destroyed. Every land use change affects adjacent lands (and landowners). Society or adjacent owners may one day require that a developer pay a destruction penalty equal to the ecological losses resulting from development. Computer simulations can aid in assessing these consequences and costs.

11. *Replacement value.* The worth of wildlife equals the costs to replace it in the open market. The market criterion serves wildlife managers well, for the replacement costs will be very high for most forms, incalculably high for others. Costs for zoo and game farm animals provide starting prices. Wildlife lands lost to dams, highways, nuclear sites, and other developments should be valued according to replacement costs for areas equally as productive of the same species over time as the lost area. It is a policy decision whether production will be measured as animals or as benefit-hours. Courts sometimes assign replacement costs (as for game taken by law violators).

12. *Damage and control costs.* A bear that kills a sheep is valued by society as the negative capitalized value of the sheep. Control costs are a wildlife value. The value of bears or blackbirds at the zero damage threshold is the net cost to society to achieve this level. How much damage a farmer or livestock owner is willing to tolerate before taking action tells how much the wildlife is valued in the context of other resource allocation decisions. There is a peculiar dimension to the control cost concept known as the bounty hunter syndrome. No rational bounty hunter will destroy the population that provides income. Instead, the bounty hunter may play the role of manager, for example, by releasing females, thereby stabilizing or increasing bounty income through quasi-exploitation of the resource.

13. *Gross expenditures.* The gross expenditures of wildlife resource users on guns, ammunition, motels, food, clothing, archery, cameras, bird seed, books, binoculars, and so forth are sometimes taken as the value of wildlife. Large numbers result, such as $23 million for Pennsylvania, $53 million for Wyoming, and $2.1 billion for the whole United States in 1970. Though this approach is much used, it raises a number of questions: (1) How are wildlife expenditures to be isolated from total trip expenditures? (2) How should equipment costs, such as the cost of a rifle or a camera, be allocated over time? (3) If there were no wildlife, would the money be redirected or removed from the local market? (4) Are *net* benefits estimated? (5) What is the relative order of magnitude of secondary and primary benefits by area and population? (6) With what other businesses are such data comparable?

14. *License fees.* About 43 million Americans spend $270 million a year on licenses. They are a very small part of hunting or fishing expenses and probably do not influence demand. A license may buy a day or a season, a trophy buck or several squirrels. The license fee is administratively fixed in ways that bear no relation to cost of production of game or the value of a hunting opportunity. It is one way to get at a value limit, however.

15. *Vacation time loss.* The worth of an hourly wage or a day's work is generally known. Vacations and weekend time are scarce commodities. To take part in some wildlife pursuit one must usually miss days of work. (Unpaid leave or foregone salary may be involved.) The minimum worth of wildlife to a population can be estimated as the worth of time spent in using the wildlife resource. Willingness to spend time is an important economic base. This may later be adjusted to reflect a person's *perceived* worth of a work hour.

16. *User fees.* Also called "primary willingness to pay" or "monopoly revenue," the user fee is the price a person is willing to pay for admission to a wildlife area. It is arrived at by varying the fees to determine when people

are turned away. This is the price that maximizes total revenue, but it, too, is a minimum wildlife value. There are few pay-to-hunt or pay-to-use wildlife areas. A study of existing ones and experimental use of others might be instructive.

17. *Willingness to pay.* Rather than fees, total costs may be counted. Willingness to travel and spend money is an expression of the worth of a potential wildlife-related experience. Travel time has been widely used as the cost index. The visitor hour spent on-site per round-trip travel hour seems highly relevant as a modifier of classical willingness-to-pay estimates. Other adjustments should be made for mean camp set-up time (a capital investment), probability of an early kill, and searching time.

18. *Competitive willingness to pay.* Computations of willingness to pay may be made to see how much wildlife adds to the competitive attractiveness for travelers of areas in the same vicinity.

19. *Willingness to exchange.* Exchange value of wildlife land (and thus wildlife produced per unit area over time) is the amount of money society, through its agents, is willing to pay to acquire land.

20. *Consumer surplus.* In the methods described so far it has been implied that the benefits exceed those that are quantified. How to quantify the additional amount, called consumer surplus, remains a problem. Consumer surplus is what the public is *not* willing to pay, nevertheless values highly, and theoretically might be willing to pay. Even when consumer surplus is estimated and added to the price paid (for travel, fees, and so on), giving total benefits, this figure cannot be used as equivalent to the monetary value or market price of tangible goods since it is an inflated value. It can, however, be used in comparisons when consumer surplus is computed for other goods. The estimates are user-specific; alternative sites may have different users and different fixed costs.

The concept is shown in Figure 1-5. The wildlife manager will find it particularly useful as a measure of agency performance since "enhancement of wildlife," an obscure objective at best, can be translated into "maximizing the consumer surplus."

Pearse (1968) studied 3.8 percent of 14,000 resident big game hunters in an area of British Columbia. Fixed costs of hunters were the cash costs of round-trip travel, time spent in travel transformed to dollars based on income, and expenses of licenses, guides, and so on. These fixed costs for each hunter were subtracted from the highest observed fixed cost for all hunters in each income class. This was a minimum estimate of each individual's consumer surplus. The weighted average consumer surplus over all income classes was $197. Multiplying this by the total number

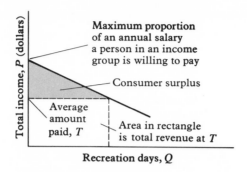

FIGURE **1-5**

Consumer surplus is shown as shaded area. The rectangle represents the maximum revenue obtainable by a nondiscriminating seller of access. To fail to count consumer surplus is to underestimate by this amount the value enjoyed by users under free access. (After Pearse 1968 and Coomber and Biswas 1973:24.)

of hunters yielded an aggregate consumer surplus of $2,826,162. See Box 1-1 and Box 1-2, pages 24–26.

Consumer surplus needs further development for wildlife management, but it seems to provide a powerful methodology, particularly for recreationally oriented wildlife objectives.

21. *Option demand.* Some economists say option demand is merely a variation on consumer surplus. But under certain conditions it acquires a distinctive meaning. Option demand is the amount a person is willing to pay to be able to exercise an option to use a resource in the future. The less willing a person is to take risk, the greater are the values he assigns his options. Even though a person never uses a facility, he may be willing to pay something to insure that if he changed his mind, it would still be available to him. Memberships in certain clubs or organizations fit the concept.

Option demand is particularly relevant to species preservation, rare and endangered species management, and wilderness preservation. Many people seem to derive benefits from knowing rare species exist. They may never see one, but they have retained, through their taxes effectively spent on preservation, the option to see the species.

Option demand, like consumer surplus, deserves further creative development. At present, questionnaires, simulations of what the total cost of preservation will be to society, and direct tax costs are the only means for estimating option demand.

Box 1-1. Computing the Consumer Surplus for a Wildlife Recreational Experience

$$\text{Consumer surplus} = T_s$$
$$\text{Total benefits} = T_s + \text{Total revenues.}$$

Estimating total benefits is the problem. Total revenues are the relatively standard costs of a wildlife recreational experience. They should be as refined as possible (e.g., Food cost = Cost of restaurant meal − Cost of average meal), and they typically include meals, lodging, equipment costs (prorated over years of expected use), guides, licenses, and round-trip travel costs. Time spent in travel is converted to dollars by the formula:

Worth of an hour = Annual income ÷ Reported working days in a year
÷ Reported working hours per day.

This may be further refined to disposable income or income minus perceived fixed expenses at each individual's present standard of living. These computations are readily handled by a computer.

Total benefits for an income class (e.g., those making $4000 to $6000 per year) are estimated as the highest total revenues that any individual, i, in an income class, n, paid. This is symbolized as $C_{\max}$. The equation is:

$$T_s = \frac{k \sum\limits_{j=1}^{n} \sum\limits_{i=1}^{k} (C_{\max} - C_i)/k}{H},$$

22. *Opportunity cost.* The amount of benefits a person is willing to forego to enjoy another set of benefits is opportunity cost. What a hunter says he would have to be paid to give up a day of hunting is called expressed opportunity cost. Horvath (1974) found that in the Tennessee Valley 269,094 hunting households would have demanded $323.5 million to give up 6.3 million hunting days in 1971. To give up watching and photographing wildlife, 76,328 households would have demanded $329.6 million for forfeiting 13.8 million days of participation. The actual relation between expressed willingness to forego an experience and actual willingness remains unknown.

Another potentially productive use of opportunity cost, which establishes a minimum wildlife value, involves estimating the financial sacrifices made to preserve wildlife. For example, to have squirrels, forests

where k = the number of hunters in each income class j,
   n = the total number of income classes,
   i = each individual hunter in the sample,
   C_i = the total revenues paid by each ith hunter, and
   H = a coefficient that inflates the results of the computations for the sample to the total hunter population and equals sample size/sample as a proportion of total hunters.
(See Box 1-2 for an explanation of statistical symbols.)
   Representative data are shown in the following table:

Consumer surplus computations for resident big game hunters in an area in British Columbia, 1964.

Income group (dollars)	Number of hunters	Highest fixed cost (dollars)	Average consumer surplus (dollars)
Less than 2000	25	66	47
2000 to 4000	67	183	149
4000 to 6000	219	287	224
6000 to 8000	109	320	221
8000 to 10,000	32	267	152
Over 10,000	33	355	196
Total	485		Weighted 197

Source: Pearse 1968:96.

must be retained. To protect squirrels means to forego the harvest income from the forest. See Box 1-3. To have antelope, one must be willing to forego the likely monetary returns from rangeland modifications. This method assumes that in a generally rational market wildlife has to be worth *at least* X dollars. Like other methods, it is not perfect, for it estimates a market value for a nonmarket commodity.

Another approach useful in environmental impact analysis is to compare the lowest possible cost for a project that might affect wildlife—say, a dam or a powerline that would impact wetlands, wildlife refuges, or critical nesting areas—with the cost of moving the site or selecting an alternative in order to avoid the wildlife problem. The cheapest powerline may cost $40 million. An alternate route that avoids a heron rookery may cost $42 million. If society (or the decision maker) chooses the second route, it is

Box 1-2. Statistical Symbols

Most college students now have some familiarity with statistical symbols, but for those needing a refresher and those yet unfamiliar, the following is presented. Statistical symbols are used for efficiency. An observer may say:

Please subtract a constant that I call k, which is equal to 1.3, from each observation. This was my bias in estimating tree diameters. I have diameters for 130 trees. Then add the results and divide the sum by 130 to get the average tree diameter.

All of the above can be symbolized as

$$\bar{x} = \frac{\sum_{i=1}^{130} (x_i - k)}{n}.$$

It reads: x-bar is equal to the sum of the x's, each minus k, starting from i as the first observation and continuing through all 130 observations, all of which together is divided by n, or 130.

$\bar{x}$ is a conventional symbol for the average or the arithmetic mean.

Σ is upper-case sigma of the Greek alphabet, conventionally meaning "the sum of" or "add all of the following."

$i = 1$ means to start with the ith value and sum through 130 values or the number of values specified above the symbol Σ, such as n.

130 is the total number of units to add.

The wildlifer may only want to take weights of animals older than one year, that is, start with the second year. This would be symbolized underneath Σ as $i = 2$. Data on exceptionally old animals may not be sought because they are unique. In that case, the wildlifer may not want to study all n observations but only those in age class $i = 2$ to some specified age class, s; or maybe to age class $n - 1$. The *sum* is to be divided by n, not each $x_i - k$.

Once the language is learned—and it is very simple, for there are relatively few symbols or conventions—the communication can become very efficient. Statistical "spaghetti" that seems confusing to many, is a simple coding system that can be readily mastered with a minimum of effort. Its use is minimal in this text. A teacher or advanced student can help any student over any barrier it may seem to present.

Box 1-3. Using Opportunity Cost to Estimate the Monetary Value of a Squirrel

An 80-year-old upland oak forest has 18,000 bd ft per acre. At a stumpage value of $30 per thousand board feet, it is worth $540 per acre. ("Stumpage" means bidding price for wood or expected gross return minus reasonable profit minus costs of removal minus labor and other costs.) Anyone who insists upon having squirrels must be willing to forego other possible benefits. To cut the forest is to forego squirrels; to have squirrels is to forego dollar returns. The opportunity cost can be developed in a similar fashion for other resources.

An alternative is: If stand growth is at 200 bd ft per year per acre and other land value and terminal harvest value are included to suggest profits of $10 per acre per year, and the acre can yield (in the hunting sense) one squirrel per acre, then the squirrel, by the landowner's decision not to cut because of needed squirrels, is worth at least $10.

Following the pattern of McKean (1966:52-53) I would argue that the imputed worth of a squirrel, say $10, is reasonable. This figure may be questionable on several accounts, but it will be helpful to managers and decision makers wrestling with land use problems. How useful the figure is cannot be demonstrated, but the figure itself is likely to be worth much more than it costs to obtain it.

saying that the wildlife from that rookery over the life expectancy of the line is worth at least $2 million to present and future societies.

Habitat management for wildlife often conflicts with forest and rangeland objectives. One use of opportunity cost is to ask: What timber profit must I forego to allow wildlife habitat practices? The amount is the minimum worth of the wildlife computed as net increase in animals as a result of the investment. The extra animals per dollar foregone give a measure of the minimum worth of wildlife in that situation. Sizes of clearcuts as a habitat management practice can similarly be studied. Forestry costs decrease with the size of clearcuts. Many wildlife benefits decline as the size is increased. How much wildlife is worth in a timber operation can be expressed as how many dollars of profit an operator is willing to forego, or costs incur, to receive additional wildlife benefits.

23. *Secondary opportunity costs.* Sportsmen set fires, leave gates open, destroy fences, and incur other landowner costs. They create health problems with

waste and litter. They compact the soil at recreational sites and reduce timber growth in such areas. By accounting these lost benefits, a clearer concept of net wildlife-related benefits can be achieved. This has not been done. It is unlikely that the value of these lost benefits would be held to be the sole value of wildlife.

24. *Energy.* Wildlifers may see a new day in environmental economics in which values are measured in terms of energy. All systems may be analyzed as energy inputs, energy storage, and conservation and final comparisons made of energy budgets or net energetics. A leading proponent of this concept is H. T. Odum (1971). (See also Odum and Odum 1976.) The practical aspects of wildlife energy systems are given by Moen (1973). Primary production in natural communities is a function of sunlight, the energy required to do work. The rate of production is an index to the work a system can do. All systems are energy systems, and transformations among them made possible by the common unit of energy (the kilocalorie = 3.97 BTU = 0.0012 kwh = 4186 joules) permit the substitution of market prices, as for gasoline, coal, or oil, or the kilowatt-hour. It has been determined that 13,632 kilocalories of energy are required to produce one dollar of GNP. Energy value is likely to be a dominant concept in ecosystem management and economic theory. It does not now equate 100 grams of eagle to 100 grams of elephant. Perhaps it will one day as citizen-preference-weighted kilocalories.

25. *Assigned proxy values.* The U.S. Wildlife Refuge System has assigned proxy values to wildlife. Individual animals are assigned a value relative to all other species. These values are based on scarcity and use and are assigned by a national committee and periodically revised. The value scheme provides a means to communicate better within the agency and to improve on allocations of funds. Dollars are spent to achieve Refuge Benefit Units (RBU), or the greatest wildlife value per tax dollar spent. Depending on their use, the RBU or other proxy values may fit several of the foregoing methods of wildlife valuation.

Constraints

It may appear that the wildlife manager, as presented so far, is merely a tool of society, a means to any end. This is true only to the extent that employee is subject to employer. The wildlifer may retain dominance for several reasons. First, there are specific objectives to be achieved. Second, there are legal and ethical constraints. In most states the law governing wildlife includes the requirement that no animal shall become extinct. Third, there are economic constraints. The manager's emphasis must be on objectives. However, the wildlifer is one citizen with one vote, and with objectives no more important than any other citizen's in a democracy. The wildlife manager's professional responsibility is to achieve employer objectives, subject to constraints. A manager who exercises personal ethical constraints must recognize that these are personal and be prepared to take the consequences associated with them. The manager can modify objectives, weights assigned to each, risk-taking attitudes, and the means of evaluation. However, employer, rather than personal, objectives must be pursued, at least until it is possible to change those objectives, risk the consequences of a decision to perform suboptimally (relative to the objectives), or move on.

Of course, education of the public or employer *is* possible and is usually a specified part of the job. The wildlife manager, with extensive education and experience in the field, knows more about wildlife than the general public. The point is that only the public, or employer, can say what constitutes benefits, and therefore what the wildlife management objectives should be. When these concepts break through clearly upon wildlife managers and their profession, major conflicts will disappear and a new era of improved resource use for society will begin.

The past era has been inglorious. There have been political favors paid in stocked game and fish, wildlife land exchanges made that were only possible through great pressure from politicos, elections won or lost on the stands taken by candidates on hunting seasons and bag limits, hatcheries and game farms built and closed as if pawns moved on a playing board, whole commissions replaced by newly elected governors, entire professional wildlife staffs made to resign, and various jobs in wildlife agencies, both state and federal, used as the rewards for political campaign contributions. Wildlife refuges or projects have been acquired as politically conspicuous area-development moves rather than contributions to balance wildlife production systems. Expressed hatred for an entire wildlife agency, stemming from some conflict, has led people into politics for revenge.

Within the wildlife agency, similar politics are played. Wildlifers favor certain species because of their personal values, education, or expertise. Wildlifers disagree over the appropriateness of bucks-only or either-sex deer hunts in certain areas. Agency directors favor wildlifers by promotions, assignments, and rewards, based in part on the mutuality of their species interests. Willingness to fight a habitat-destroying dam or highway project is strongly influenced by a wildlifer's values, perceived personal risks, and impacts to the individual's preferred species. Research funds and programs, such as those for songbirds and rare and endangered species are direct reflections of the wildlife leader's experience and knowledge and thus the estimated risks or benefits to be derived. Sincere efforts to act on behalf of the people have been taken by many wildlifers.

Only recently has the difference been quantified between what they thought the public wanted and what the public said it wanted. With such evidence, there is no wonder that there have been such hot spots of public disapproval of wildlife management action. All such disapproval will not go away, even with perfect knowledge of the public's objectives. It can be reduced by increasingly sophisticated research and manipulation, simultaneously, of wild animal populations, habitats, and people, particularly their objectives, values, and perceived risks.

Study Questions

1. Define wildlife.
2. Define wildlife management.
3. What are the major approaches to wildlife management?
4. Describe a general system.
5. What is the major wildlife management triad?
6. Differentiate, with examples, between macro- and micro-management.
7. What is the difference between designing and analyzing systems?
8. In what sense is management a cybernetic function?
9. Differentiate between active and passive management.
10. What is a resource and how is it related to objectives?
11. Sketch the resource tetrahedron.
12. List the major categories of benefits provided by the wildlife resource.
13. List as many as you can of the 25 ways by which wildlife are valued. Do you feel that the value of wildlife can be ascertained?
14. With which primary objectives will the following valuation methods be most useful: willingness to pay, consumer surplus, option demand, opportunity cost?
15. What does your professor think about the ethical constraints on a wildlife manager? What do you think? What do the wildlife managers in your area think?
16. Is it appropriate to attempt to manipulate human values associated with wildlife? What are your criteria for deciding?
17. How many references can your class collect about energy valuation and resource energetics published since 1970? Summarize them and relate them to wildlife.

Selected References

Beer, S. 1959. *Cybernetics and management.* John Wiley and Sons, New York. 214 p.
Churchman, C. W. 1968. *The systems approach.* Delacorte, New York. xii + 243 p.

Coomber, N. H. and A. K. Biswas. 1973. *Evaluation of environmental intangibles.* Genera Press, P.O. Box 336, Bronxville, NY. 77 p.

Donald, A. G. 1967. *Management, information and systems.* Pergamon Press, New York. 169 p.

Emery, F. E. 1969. *Systems thinking: selected readings.* Penguin Books, Baltimore. 398 p.

Giles, R. H., Jr. (Ed.). 1971. *Wildlife management techniques,* 3rd ed., revised. The Wildlife Society, Washington, DC. vii + 635 p.

Horvath, J. C. 1974. *Executive summary: economic survey of wildlife recreation.* Environmental Research Group, Georgia State University, Atlanta.

Laszlo, E. 1972a. *The systems view of the world.* George Braziller, New York. viii + 131 p.

Laszlo, E. 1972b. *Introduction to systems philosophy: toward a new paradigm of contemporary thought.* Harper Torchbooks, Harper and Row, New York. xxi + 328 p.

Leopold, A. 1933. *Game management.* Charles Scribner's Sons, New York. 481 p.

Leopold, A. 1949. *A Sand County almanac and sketches here and there.* Oxford University Press, New York. 226 p.

McKean, R. A. 1966. The use of shadow prices. In *Problems in public expenditure analysis, Studies of government finance,* ed. S. B. Chase, Jr. The Brookings Institution, Washington, DC, pp. 35–65.

Moen, A. N. 1973. *Wildlife ecology: an analytical approach.* W. H. Freeman and Company, San Francisco. xviii + 458 p.

Odum, H. T. 1971. *Environment, power, and society.* Interscience Publishers, John Wiley and Sons, New York. ix + 331 p.

Odum, H. T. and E. C. Odum. 1976. *Energy basis for man and nature.* McGraw-Hill, New York. x + 397 p.

Pearse, P. H. 1968. A new approach to the evaluation of non-priced recreational resources. *Land Economics* **44**(1):87–99.

Rabow, G. 1969. *The era of the system: how the systems approach can help solve society's problems.* Philosophical Library, New York. vi + 154 p.

Von Bertalanffy, L. 1968. *General systems theory.* George Braziller, New York. xv + 289 p.

Chapter 2

Population Analysis

Wildlife managers typically work with *populations* of animals—that is, groups of animals in specified areas at specified times (for example, the 1979 King Mountain elk herd). They may either analyze populations or design them. For rational population decisions, analyses must come first. Analysis connotes describing, breaking down units into subunits, discriminating, factoring, and employing valid taxonomies. Analysis is a creatively destructive process. *Design,* on the other hand, is a synthetic process. It is the process of creating, building, assembling, manipulating, and shaping—*for a purpose.* To design a population is to set in motion a system that just as precisely as possible directs the structure, dynamics, and relations of a population toward a set of objectives. Analysis tends to be as value-free as possible. Design is loaded with value, since it is engaged in to achieve specific human objectives.

Populations are resources. All definitions of resources include the primary dimensions shown in the tetrahedron in Figure 2-1. These four dimensions—energy, time, space, and diversity—give a useful picture of a resource. They provide a checklist for analyzing the state of the resource, or its parts, and focus attention on the topics that must be addressed in developing a design or plan for changing the resource.

Any system can be analyzed in terms of three exclusive categories—structure, dynamics, and relations. Structure is the substance, the components, the named

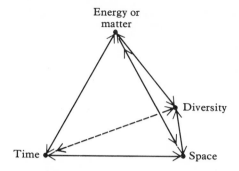

FIGURE **2-1**

All resources can be conceived as having four
basic characteristics. The tetrahedron provides
a means for emphasizing the interactions of
these characteristics.

elements of a system. Dynamics are the changes and processes, usually expressed as rates. Relations, difficult to define, include causal pathways,
behavioral interactions, breeding, antagonism, competition, time sequences,
and spatial arrangements. These three fundamental analytical categories of
wildlife populations are shown in Figure 2-2.

Population Structure

Species Lists. *Range maps* show where individual species occur (see Figure 2-3).
Time-lapse maps (Wetherbee et al. 1972) can show how species' ranges change
over time. An area *species list* can be conceived as the results of examining a
series of overlapping range maps for an area.

Knowledge of the species in an area is essential for doing population analyses. Imagine trying to study the interactions among specified components of
an ecosystem! The more complete the list, the fewer risks the analyst runs. The
interactions (I) in systems are related to the number of items (N) in such
systems:

$$I = N(N - 1).$$

Failing to list one game species in a list of 10 can lead the wildlifer, as applied
ecologist, to consider only 72 interactions, instead of 90 interactions. The
hazards of not listing a particular insect may not be very great in a list of 300
species [$I = 300(300 - 1) = 89,700$ versus $I = 299(299 - 1) = 89,102$], but if
that species is a disease vector, then it may represent a serious omission.

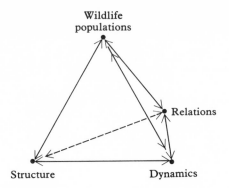

FIGURE **2-2**

The analysis of wildlife populations is best done in three interactive categories.

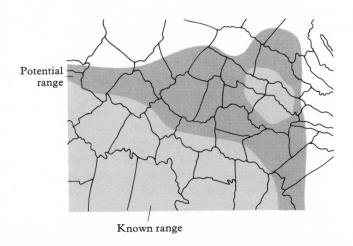

FIGURE **2-3**

A hypothetical range map. Known range is typically based on observed animals. Where identical habitats are contiguous to known range, a potential or possible range may be shown in order to indicate sampling has not been done.

The list of animals in an area can be changed by introductions. *Primary stocking* is the releasing of animals from one area into an area in which the species has never occurred. *Secondary stocking* is releasing animals into an area from which the species has been exterminated. *Primary transplanting* means

Wildebeest
(*Connochaetes
taurinus*)

Greater Kudu
(*Tragelaphus
strepsiceros*)

FIGURE **2-4**

Examples of exotics stocked into the United States. (From "Horns and Antlers" by
Walter Modell. Copyright © 1969 by Scientific American Inc. All rights reserved.)

capturing native wildlife in the field and moving the animals directly to another
site (whether previously occupied or not). *Secondary transplanting* is the
movement of the offspring, taken in the field, of primary or secondary stocking
efforts into another area. *Released game* is simply the game released in an area
prior to a hunting period. These animals typically do not survive long enough to
add significantly to residual populations.

Hundreds of animal species called *exotics* have been employed in primary
stocking experiments around the world. (Figure 2-4 shows some representative
species.) Stocking exotics is a conspicuous wildlife management activity. Exotics lend variety, their benefits appear high per unit cost, and several success
stories can be cited. However, there is a long list of reasons for *not* stocking
exotics. The wildlifer should present this list to the layman stocking enthusiasts
who arise annually:

1. Of the thousands of efforts that have been made to stock exotics, there have
    been few successes. The ring-necked pheasant has not been successfully
    stocked in the South, nor has the cotournix quail been successful.

2. The species may become a pest or a failure, for no one can predict how an animal will act under the stresses of new environments or population interactions. The house sparrow and starling are examples.

3. It is impossible to do pre-stocking research on either area suitability or pest hazards. Only deduction is possible.

4. The ecological community can be disrupted, and it may not be restored by simply subtracting the problem animals. Rabbits and goats can so alter a habitat that it may not return to its original state in centuries.

5. Foreign diseases and parasites of wildlife can be transmitted and may become epidemic (as in Hawaiian birds).

6. Stocking efforts tend to be newsworthy and thus tend to detract from the needed management of native species problems. The result is a net reduction in public wildlife management involvement.

7. Importations are an admission of defeat in managing native populations to meet existing needs.

8. Stocking exotics is usually a public agency response to a few people with a loud demand, rarely representative of the will of most of the people.

9. The total selection, transportation, quarantine, and supervision costs are very great. There is a high probability of subsequent costs.

10. The costs are usually relayed to the public. Such risk-filled enterprises are rarely appropriate for public funds expenditures.

11. Exotic wildlife may not stay where it is put.

12. Recreational quality of a hunt may be reduced for a significant number of sportsmen since they can no longer choose, after successful stocking, to go into an area of only native wildlife. There is no way to protect the historical-use rights of various segments of the public.

13. An evolutionary natural legacy will be lost, a population complex that is in harmony with a set of environmental properties and constraints. Do people have the *right* to change such legacies for future generations?

Because there have been some successes, stocking of exotics is likely to continue, despite the many reasons why it can rarely be justified. In such cases, the wildlife biologists will insist upon the following *minimal* analyses, prior to releases:

1. Criteria for selecting and collecting vigorous animals.

2. Appropriate minimum stocking numbers.

3. Proper sex ratio.

4. Efficient, stress-minimal transportation.

5.   Quarantine hazards.

6.   Parasite and disease loads.

7.   Possible role of the species in the new environment.

8.   Behavior (relative to objectives of stocking).

9.   Reproductive capacity.

10.   Resistance to native diseases and predators.

11.   Possible actions as pest or predator.

12.   Gaminess, or elusiveness, and ability to withstand user pressures.

13.   Possibilities of hybridization.

14.   Probabilities of movement out of the target area.

15.   Suitable control methods, if they are needed.

16.   Biostatistical methods for properly evaluating success or failure of the effort.

These studies should be conducted over sufficient time by disinterested scientists at the stocking advocate's expense and should maintain a guilty-until-proved-innocent orientation. Illegal importations should be discouraged, and all costs of damages associated with such importations should be assigned to the advocate's estate.

The list of wildlife present in an area only partially reflects the genetic makeup of that population. The wildlifer will know of certain population differences that are conspicuous, but must keep in mind that there are subtle, genetic differences in populations due to mutation-rate differences among areas, isolation of populations by terrain, and human actions. It is likely that most genetic differences are strongly tied to energy flow and energy budgeting within populations (see Moen 1973). These must be studied and appreciated to enable, through separation of effects, improved prediction of the effects of habitat changes on animals. Of course, the likely consequences of exotics and hybridization must be fully analyzed. As wildlifers become more sophisticated, they will attempt to analyze and manipulate genetically identifiable populations. By such emphasis they will genetically stratify populations, thereby improving on sampling efficiency and the conclusions based on sampling. They may, thereby, (1) better interpret pesticide and pollutant effects on wildlife, (2) categorize populations by harvestability or vulnerability, (3) explain limits to habitat manipulation effects on birthrates and antler or horn size, and (4) define improved management regions.

Three misconceptions about wildlife genetics are commonly harbored by the public. (1) Many people believe that wildlife populations need "new blood," or stocking. There is no evidence that extensive inbreeding occurs or that, where it does, it has deleterious effects on populations. Population demise is most usually correlated with habitat demise, but there can be many causes. (2) Unusual or "freak" animals, because they are conspicuous and often make the news, are thought to be more prevalent than they really are. There are no deer-goat crosses. What appear to be such creatures are piebald deer. Animals with anomalies usually die in early life. (3) It has been held that trophy heads are selected against by hunters. But the genetic characteristics of the big trophy bulls are amply preserved in female and also young animals. The demise of big trophies is typically a problem of excessive populations per unit area or shortages of food. There is very little evidence in any population, wild or otherwise, of inheritance of behavioral traits (for example, ability to avoid hunters or tendencies not to migrate).

A special class of wildlife listed in some areas is *rare* or *endangered species.* The precise meaning of these terms is currently being debated in the law courts, so I shall not attempt definitions. Sufficient to say that an *extinct* animal is one lacking survivors. An animal may become extinct through the evolutionary process of *extinction,* in which one species evolves into another, with no loss in total species. Or it may become extinct through *extermination,* the actual loss of a species as a result of natural or human actions. Over billions of years, many life forms have become extinct. Extinction is actually a far more natural state over geologic time than survival.

There have been accelerated species losses since the mid-1800's. The causes and causal theories for these losses vary widely. They include:

1. Reclassification; erroneously classified organisms or groups are now lumped into a single taxon.
2. Hybridization.
3. Overspecialization.
4. Improved data collection and recording.
5. Natural evolution.
6. Catastrophe (for example, floods, volcanic activity).
7. Habitat conversion and destruction by human beings.
8. Poisoning.
9. Pollution.
10. Hunting, particularly with firearms in primitive areas.
11. Egg collecting.
12. Natural competition.
13. Disease and parasites.
14. Introduction of exotics.

15. Introduction of predators.
16. Human error.

Whatever the causes, whatever the history, there are over 100 mammalian species and 150 avian species in great danger of extermination. Over three-fourths of these are threatened by humans.

Few, if any, people are bent upon the destruction of the last remaining individual of a species. No one sets out to destroy an endangered turtle. Its habitat is ruined by a highway. The cause is human action, but no purpose need be ascribed. Lack of knowledge of the turtle's presence and unwillingness to avoid the area both have the same results. Most wildlife are threatened by human ignorance, apathy, and the species' own impoverished hereditary legacy.

The whooping crane (*Grus americana*), pictured in Figure 2-5, is one endangered species (represented in 1977 by only about 90 known birds) with the odds stacked against its survival (Allen 1952). The following reasons are cited: (1) The whooping crane is large and migratory and a gunner's target on its flight over hundreds of miles where law enforcement is impossible, (2) vast areas of wild land are needed for its breeding, (3) the birds are noisy and lively on nesting grounds and thus readily detected by predators, (4) they are monogamous, (5) they do not breed until several years old, (6) only two eggs are laid, (7) adults are flightless during molt, (8) young are flightless for several months after hatching, (9) young depend on adults for food for months, and (10) if one member of a family is shot, others stay with it, making themselves vulnerable.

The management of rare and endangered species is discussed in the next chapter.

In addition to morphological criteria for listing wildlife there are value criteria. Rareness is one such criterion. Another is ownership. Wildlife in the United States, in the tradition of English common law, is the property of the state. It is owned by the landowner only when "reduced to possession" (for example, taken by hunting). Other forms of wildlife, notably waterfowl, are international property, as prescribed in the Migratory Bird Treaty between Canada, the United States, and Mexico.

Other concepts of wildlife valuation have been listed in Chapter 1. Relative species importance, whatever the criteria used (that is, money, energy, or citizen weightings from questionnaires) is essential for analysis and later for management. Each animal or population segment is translated by users into some resource unit such as opportunity-days or pounds of meat. The population is not necessarily correlated with the value or resource benefits, experienced or potential. For the fisheries manager in particular, the emphasis needs to be shifted from fish available or produced to the important resource concept of quality-weighted fishing opportunity. Many studies demonstrate that fish available and days spent are poorly correlated.

FIGURE **2-5**
The whooping crane is one example of about 180 endangered species of birds. There are approximately 90 survivors (1977).

Density. Density is the number of animals of a species per unit area. Density is often expressed as animals per hectare (1 hectare = 2.471 acres) or 100 hectares (1 km²). There are no standard density expressions, so conversions of units are often needed (Table 2-1). For example, where a deer density of one per square mile exists (row 6, column 6, in Table 2-1), there is one per 258.998 hectares (row 7, column 6 or 1 divided by 0.003861 row 6, column 7). Two rabbits per hectare (row 7) is equivalent to 0.81 per acre (2 × column 4, row 7). Density is rarely known exactly; it is estimated. Estimating wildlife populations is difficult because large areas are involved, numbers of animals are often low, animals may be inconspicuous or hide, and they may move or hibernate. Sampling is difficult and expensive, and funds are rarely adequate to achieve the sample sizes determined by computation to be necessary for reaching suitable conclusions.

Except for the purposes of developing techniques or doing preliminary surveys, there is no justification for engaging in costly sampling programs unless the researchers have reasonable expectations of obtaining *pre-computed* required sample sizes. At the end of a study with inadequate samples, the only statements possible are: (1) no conclusions could be reached due to inadequate sample size, and (2) more research is needed. Both conclusions were known before the study began!

TABLE 2-1

Conversion coefficients for population density estimation. Multiply or divide the animals or biomass per unit area in the left column by the number in the column corresponding to the desired unit.

Animals or biomass per unit area	Expressions of unit area (numbers correspond to rows in left column)							
	1	2	3	4	5	6	7	8
1. 100 sq ft	1.0	9.0	10.7639	435.60	43.56	278,784	1,076.3911	107,639.1069
2. 100 sq yds	.111111	1.0	1.19599	48.40	4.84	30,976	119.5990	11,959.9018
3. 100 sq meters	.092903	.836127	1.0	40.4686	4.04686	25,899.906	100	10,000
4. Acre	.0022956	.020661	.0247105	1.0	0.1	640	2.47105	247.105
5. Sq chain	.022956	.20661	.247105	10.0	1.0	6,400	24.7105	2,471.05
6. Sq mile	.000003587	.000032283	.00003861	.0015625	.00015625	1.0	.003861	.3861
7. Hectare	.00092903	.0083612	.01	.404686	.0404686	258.998	1.0	100
8. Sq kilometer	.00000929	.000083613	.0001	.00404686	.00040404686	2.58998	.01	1.0

There are alternatives to these approaches. One is to work more diligently to obtain required funds and manpower to do the job. Saving, pooling funds, and forming cooperative programs may help. Until funds are available for well-planned, long-term studies of population densities, research should be directed toward analysis of population responses to environmental factors and toward more deductive methodologies, including those using computer simulations. Another approach is to re-evaluate the needs for accuracy and confidence in conclusions reached from a density estimate. What difference will it make to anyone if the true value is off 1 percent from an estimate of 12 animals per 100 hectares? If the estimate is for an endangered species, accuracy may be critical; if for Norway rats (*Rattus norwegicus*), perhaps not so important.

Often a density is not needed—only knowledge that the density, whatever it was, is about the same as last year. Indices to relative density will often suffice, such as regional game harvest figures. Population *trends* may be all that must be analyzed.

Wildlife populations can be estimated. There are few good examples, but they are sufficient to support that conclusion. Once the needs are seen; adequate statistical advice obtained; funds, manpower, and equipment secured; and the field work skillfully carried out, important advances will be made in wildlife management.

To solve the problems just cited, a variety of techniques for estimating density have been created (Overton 1971). Wildlife managers must converge on the question of density from several directions, bracketing it in, narrowing its possible range.

One method is to use population *indices* such as track counts, calls of birds, and lodges. Observers themselves must be "calibrated," for they will often not see or hear all of the animals that are present. For example, where field work identifies 100 beaver (*Castor canadensis*) lodges in an area and aircraft patrols observe only 85, then it may be appropriate to inflate all flight counts over similar terrain by 1.18 (that is, 100/85).

Direct counts of wildlife, such as from along a road or path, may be useful. These transects, run at the same time each year, can be used to estimate animals per observed area or to determine trends. Helicopters and fixed-wing aircraft have been used in waterfowl and big game counts. Drives by teams of people are also made. These involve people walking through an area counting animals seen or driven past a point. In some experimental work, extermination of populations in fenced areas or selected areas has been done to obtain insight into the relations of animals observed and progressively changing animal density under constant conditions.

Time-area counts add to the methods of direct counts a limited observation period, say 30 minutes. An observer counts all the animals seen in an area from

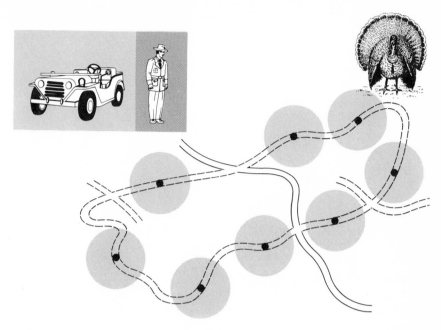

FIGURE **2-6**

Trend counts fall between the direct and time-area counts. A density estimate is not sought, only an index to the density trend. At sunup on a series of spring mornings an observer drives a pre-planned (usually constant) route, stopping at markers or at regular odometer readings, listening for 5 minutes, and recording the grouse drumming or turkey gobbling. The totals for different years are then compared.

one point. The distance to the farthest animal determines the radius (*R*). The population index, *I*, is computed:

$$I = \text{Animals counted}/\pi R^2,$$

and the procedure repeated at several sites until the index stabilizes. See Figure 2-6. The approximate radius within which the animal can be heard is needed to determine the area being sampled by the listener. It can be determined with an artificial call sounded by an assistant at increasing distances from an observer. This determination is only made once.

By capturing, marking, and releasing as many animals as possible, eventually 100 percent might be marked. In practice, however, this would be nearly impossible, and prohibitively expensive. An alternative is to construct a

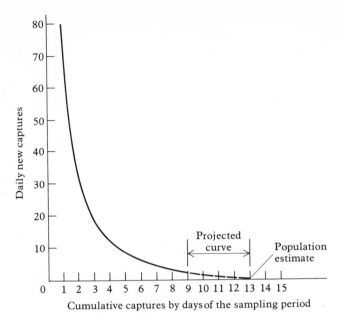

FIGURE **2-7**

From a Leslie graph or cumulative capture curve, a population estimate based on the likely condition of no new captures can be obtained
by projecting the known curve to the horizontal axis. (Changing the
vertical axis to a logarithmic scale will aid in determining the horizontal intercept more precisely.)

cumulative capture curve, also known as a Leslie graph, which, if projected to the
horizontal axis, will yield a population estimate (see Figure 2-7).

The *outer-bound* approach (Robson and Whitlock 1964) is based on the
rationale that an observer will see more animals on some days than on others and
that the highest count can be used to compute an estimate according to
probability theory. See Box 2-1.

Fecal counts, or counts of the pellet groups of big game, rabbits, and birds,
have been used for years as indices to populations and area-use levels. Various
studies show that deer and elk defecate about 12.5 pellet groups per day
(Overton 1971:431). By counting groups in one-fiftieth acre (0.0081 hectare)
plots, days of use per acre can be obtained. Although these counts have been
used to estimate populations, it is best that they be confined to making estimates
of use and foraging because groups-per-day vary with forage and animal age.
Other reasons for not estimating populations by this method are that groups are
clustered, making sampling difficult; movement patterns confound results; and

Box 2-1. The Outer-Bound Method of Population Estimation

Observe or trap animals, or make counts repeatedly. Eventually there will appear a highest value (n_k). The next highest value is n_{k-1}. Then N, the population estimate, is

$$N = 2n_k - n_{k-1}.$$

An upper confidence limit to the population estimate is N_H, given by

$$N_H = n_k + \frac{1 - \alpha}{\alpha}\ (n_k - n_{k-1}),$$

where α is the confidence limit, say 0.05 (or the 95-percent level). If $n_k = 30$ and $n_{k-1} = 25$, then $N = 35$ and $N_H = 125$.

pellet groups from previous years can cause counting problems for unskilled observers.

Capture-recapture is an ingenious method of population estimation. It is often called the Petersen-Lincoln method. A wildlifer captures animals (for example, by net, box trap, snare, drugs, dart gun, foot-hold trap, or baffle trap), marks them (for example, with band, ring, tags, collars, toe or ear clip, hair trim, or dye), and releases them. The estimation of populations from animals captured and released rests on certain critical assumptions; if they fail, elaborate mathematical adjustments may be needed. These assumptions are that (1) animals do not lose (or gain) markers, (2) there are no recruitments or losses to the population, (3) there are no differences in mortality between marked and unmarked animals, (4) marked and unmarked animals are equally easy to catch, and (5) animals tend to be distributed randomly and redistribute themselves at random after capture. The total population (N) is related to the total marked population (M) in the same way that the total sampled population (n) at some later date is related to the marked animals in the sample (m). Thus,

$$N/M = n/m \qquad \text{and} \qquad N = Mn/m.$$

Overton (1971) summarized various modifications of this approach. The modern wildlifer uses a computer and will tend to use Jolly's approach (1965) to the technique, with its adjustments for various factors such as mortality.

A concept of *theoretical maximum density* (also called saturation point) provides the manager with a standard for management efforts. Density is influenced by so many factors that it is conceivable that no area has yet achieved its maximum. There is a direct relation between this concept and the outer-bound approach to density estimation previously discussed. The longer the wildlifer looks and experiments, the more likely it is that evidence will converge to support a population density higher than has ever been observed. It is a useful quest. Theoretical maximum densities should be regularly studied and carefully reported. As for the perfect motor, we may never see one, but the concept of 1.0 efficiency is very valuable. The maximum density for bobwhite quail (*Colinus virginianus*) is 3.1 per acre (Kellogg et al. 1972:15). The outer limit seems to be set by crowding or competition within a species, but is probably determined by available utilizable energy (see Moen 1973). This will be discussed later.

Sex Ratios. The sex of most animals is readily determined from their external genitals, mammary glands, color, weight, shape of the pelvis, presence of penis ligaments, and, of course, internal sex organs.

Wildlife managers must know the sex ratio of their populations. The ratio is the best indicator of procreation potential. It also influences mean population body weight (see Table 2-2) and thus food requirements. A fixed food supply will support more young female animals than adult males. Trophy animals are produced at the expense of total animals produced. Sex ratio may determine the potential harvestable animals or those subject to an environmental pollutant. Sex ratio is expressed, by convention, as males per 100 females. (See Box 2-2 and Table 2-3.)

The importance of sex ratio varies with the breeding behavior of a population. It is most important for monogamous species. *Monogamy* is the pairing for mating of a male and female for at least one complete breeding season and often longer. It is a strong social bonding. *Polygamy* is a less restricted mating behavior and among wildlife is difficult to distinguish from *promiscuity*. Polygamy is the mating of one male with more than one female and the establishing of recognizable social ties with these females. A harem of females is maintained by defense and other behavior for one complete breeding period, usually several months. The number of females reproductively serviced by one male is limited. In *promiscuity*, no ties or only temporary social ties are established, and tendencies to herd or congregate are terminated after estrus (heat, or the period of female sexual receptivity). In monogamous species, the productive strength of the population is limited by the lowest proportion of males or females. The manager of monogamous species must be more sophisticated than the manager responsible for promiscuous species.

Wildlife managers and population analysts usually speak of a *cohort* of animals. This represents a standard number of 1000 or 10,000 animals. When a

TABLE 2-2

Average weights of animals (in pounds) in a population as influenced by three representative sex ratios (50, 70, and 90 percent female).

Percentage of females in population = 50

Mean weight of males (pounds)	Mean weight of females (pounds)																
	90	100	110	120	130	140	150	160	170	180	190	200	210	220	230	240	250
90	90	95	100	105	110	115	120	125	130	135	140	145	150	155	160	165	170
100	95	100	105	110	115	120	125	130	135	140	145	150	155	160	165	170	175
110	100	105	110	115	120	125	130	135	140	145	150	155	160	165	170	175	180
120	105	110	115	120	125	130	135	140	145	150	155	160	165	170	175	180	185
130	110	115	120	125	130	135	140	145	150	155	160	165	170	175	180	185	190
140	115	120	125	130	135	140	145	150	155	160	165	170	175	180	185	190	195
150	120	125	130	135	140	145	150	155	160	165	170	175	180	185	190	195	200
160	125	130	135	140	145	150	155	160	165	170	175	180	185	190	195	200	205
170	130	135	140	145	150	155	160	165	170	175	180	185	190	195	200	205	210
180	135	140	145	150	155	160	165	170	175	180	185	190	195	200	205	210	215
190	140	145	150	155	160	165	170	175	180	185	190	195	200	205	210	215	220
200	145	150	155	160	165	170	175	180	185	190	195	200	205	210	215	220	225
210	150	155	160	165	170	175	180	185	190	195	200	205	210	215	220	225	230
220	155	160	165	170	175	180	185	190	195	200	205	210	215	220	225	230	235
230	160	165	170	175	180	185	190	195	200	205	210	215	220	225	230	235	240
240	165	170	175	180	185	190	195	200	205	210	215	220	225	230	235	240	245
250	170	175	180	185	190	195	200	205	210	215	220	225	230	235	240	245	250

TABLE **2-2**, *continued*

Percentage of Females in population = 70

	Mean weight of females (pounds)																
Mean weight of males (pounds)	90	100	110	120	130	140	150	160	170	180	190	200	210	220	230	240	250
90	90	97	104	111	118	125	132	139	146	153	160	167	174	181	188	195	202
100	93	100	107	114	121	128	135	142	149	156	163	170	177	184	191	198	205
110	96	103	110	117	124	131	138	145	152	159	166	173	180	187	194	201	208
120	99	106	113	120	127	134	141	148	155	162	169	176	183	190	197	204	211
130	102	109	116	123	130	137	144	151	158	165	172	179	186	193	200	207	214
140	105	112	119	126	133	140	147	154	161	168	175	182	189	196	203	210	217
150	108	115	122	129	136	143	150	157	164	171	178	185	192	199	206	213	220
160	111	118	125	132	139	146	153	160	167	174	181	188	195	202	209	216	223
170	114	121	128	135	142	149	156	163	170	177	184	191	198	205	212	219	226
180	117	124	131	138	145	152	159	166	173	180	187	194	201	208	215	222	229
190	120	127	134	141	148	155	162	169	176	183	190	197	204	211	218	225	232
200	123	130	137	144	151	158	165	172	179	186	193	200	207	214	221	228	235
210	126	133	140	147	154	161	168	175	182	189	196	203	210	217	224	231	238
220	129	136	143	150	157	164	171	178	185	192	199	206	213	220	227	234	241
230	132	139	146	153	160	167	174	181	188	195	202	209	216	223	230	237	244
240	135	142	149	156	163	170	177	184	191	198	205	212	219	226	233	240	247
250	138	145	152	159	166	173	180	187	194	201	208	215	222	229	236	243	250

TABLE **2-2**, *continued*

Percentage of females in population = 90

Mean weight of males (pounds)	Mean weight of females (pounds)																
	90	100	110	120	130	140	150	160	170	180	190	200	210	220	230	240	250
90	90	99	108	117	126	135	144	153	162	171	180	189	198	207	216	225	234
100	91	100	109	118	127	136	145	154	163	172	181	190	199	208	217	226	235
110	92	101	110	119	128	137	146	155	164	173	182	191	200	209	218	227	236
120	93	102	111	120	129	138	147	156	165	174		192	201	210	219	228	237
130	94	103	112	121	130	139	148	157	166	175		193	202	211	220	229	238
140	95	104	113	122	131	140	149	158	167	176	185	194	203	212	221	230	239
150	96	105	114	123	132	141	150	159	168	177	186	195	204	213	222	231	240
160	97	106	115	124	133	142	151	160	169	178	187	196	205	214	223	232	241
170	98	107	116	125	134	143	152	161	170	179	188	197	206	215	224	233	242
180	99	108	117	126	135	144	153	162	171	180	189	198	207	216	225	234	243
190	100	109	118	127	136	145	154	163	172	181	190	199	208	217	226	235	244
200	101	110	119	128	137	146	155	164	173	182	191	200	209	218	227	236	245
210	102	111	120	129	138	147	156	165	174	183	192	201	210	219	228	237	246
220	103	112	121	130	139	148	157	166	175	184	193	202	211	220	229	238	247
230	104	113	122	131	140	149	158	167	176	185	194	203	212	221	230	239	248
240	105	114	123	132	141	150	159	168	177	186	195	204	213	222	231	240	249
250	106	115	124	133	142	151	160	169	178	187	196	205	214	223	232	241	250

50

TABLE **2-3**

Sex ratios and percentages of sexes in populations.

Sex ratio males to females	Percent females	Percent males	Sex ratio males to females	Percent females	Percent males
1 to 100	99.0	1.0	47 to 100	68.0	32.0
2 to 100	98.0	2.0	48 to 100	67.6	32.4
3 to 100	97.1	2.9	49 to 100	67.1	32.9
4 to 100	96.2	3.8	50 to 100	66.7	33.3
5 to 100	95.2	4.8	51 to 100	66.2	33.8
6 to 100	94.3	5.7	52 to 100	65.8	34.2
7 to 100	93.5	6.5	53 to 100	65.4	34.6
8 to 100	92.6	7.4	54 to 100	64.9	35.1
9 to 100	91.7	8.3	55 to 100	64.5	35.5
10 to 100	90.9	9.1	56 to 100	64.1	35.9
11 to 100	90.1	9.9	57 to 100	63.7	36.3
12 to 100	89.3	10.7	58 to 100	63.3	36.7
13 to 100	88.5	11.5	59 to 100	62.9	37.1
14 to 100	87.7	12.3	60 to 100	62.5	37.5
15 to 100	87.0	13.0	61 to 100	62.1	37.9
16 to 100	86.2	13.8	62 to 100	61.7	38.3
17 to 100	85.5	14.5	63 to 100	61.3	38.7
18 to 100	84.7	15.3	64 to 100	61.0	39.0
19 to 100	84.0	16.0	65 to 100	60.6	39.4
20 to 100	83.3	16.7	66 to 100	60.2	39.8
21 to 100	82.6	17.4	67 to 100	59.9	40.1
22 to 100	82.0	18.0	68 to 100	59.5	40.5
23 to 100	81.3	18.7	69 to 100	59.2	40.8
24 to 100	80.6	19.4	70 to 100	58.8	41.2
25 to 100	80.0	20.0	71 to 100	58.5	41.5
26 to 100	79.4	20.6	72 to 100	58.1	41.9
27 to 100	78.7	21.3	73 to 100	57.8	42.2
28 to 100	78.1	21.9	74 to 100	57.5	42.5
29 to 100	77.5	22.5	75 to 100	57.1	42.9
30 to 100	76.9	23.1	76 to 100	56.8	43.2
31 to 100	76.3	23.7	77 to 100	56.5	43.5
32 to 100	75.8	24.2	78 to 100	56.2	43.8
33 to 100	75.2	24.8	79 to 100	55.9	44.1
34 to 100	74.6	25.4	80 to 100	55.6	44.4
35 to 100	74.1	25.9	81 to 100	55.2	44.8
36 to 100	73.5	26.5	82 to 100	54.9	45.1
37 to 100	73.0	27.0	83 to 100	54.6	45.4
38 to 100	72.5	27.5	84 to 100	54.3	45.7
39 to 100	71.9	28.1	85 to 100	54.1	45.9
40 to 100	71.4	28.6	86 to 100	53.8	46.2
41 to 100	70.9	29.1	87 to 100	53.5	46.5
42 to 100	70.4	29.6	88 to 100	53.2	46.8
43 to 100	69.9	30.1	89 to 100	52.9	47.1
44 to 100	69.4	30.6	90 to 100	52.6	47.4
45 to 100	69.0	31.0	91 to 100	52.4	47.6
46 to 100	68.5	31.5	92 to 100	52.1	47.9

TABLE **2-3,** *continued*

Sex ratio males to females	Percent females	Percent males	Sex ratio males to females	Percent females	Percent males
93 to 100	51.8	48.2	122 to 100	45.0	55.0
94 to 100	51.5	48.5	123 to 100	44.8	55.2
95 to 100	51.3	48.7	124 to 100	44.6	55.4
96 to 100	51.0	49.0	125 to 100	44.4	55.6
97 to 100	50.8	49.2	126 to 100	44.2	55.8
98 to 100	50.5	49.5	127 to 100	44.1	55.9
99 to 100	50.3	49.7	128 to 100	43.9	56.1
100 to 100	50.0	50.0	129 to 100	43.7	56.3
101 to 100	49.8	50.2	130 to 100	43.5	56.5
102 to 100	49.5	50.5	131 to 100	43.3	56.7
103 to 100	49.3	50.7	132 to 100	43.1	56.9
104 to 100	49.0	51.0	133 to 100	42.9	57.1
105 to 100	48.8	51.2	134 to 100	42.7	57.3
106 to 100	48.5	51.5	135 to 100	42.6	57.4
107 to 100	48.3	51.7	136 to 100	42.4	57.6
108 to 100	48.1	51.9	137 to 100	42.2	57.8
109 to 100	47.8	52.2	138 to 100	42.0	58.0
110 to 100	47.6	52.4	139 to 100	41.8	58.2
111 to 100	47.4	52.6	140 to 100	41.7	58.3
112 to 100	47.2	52.8	141 to 100	41.5	58.5
113 to 100	46.9	53.1	142 to 100	41.3	58.7
114 to 100	46.7	53.3	143 to 100	41.2	58.8
115 to 100	46.5	53.5	144 to 100	41.0	59.0
116 to 100	46.3	53.7	145 to 100	40.8	59.2
117 to 100	46.1	53.9	146 to 100	40.7	59.3
118 to 100	45.9	54.1	147 to 100	40.5	59.5
119 to 100	45.7	54.3	148 to 100	40.3	59.7
120 to 100	45.5	54.5	149 to 100	40.2	59.8
121 to 100	45.2	54.8	150 to 100	40.0	60.0

population, no matter what its size, is described as a cohort, it can be more readily compared with other populations. A cohort with a sex ratio of 25:100 has a *productive component* of 800 (for example, $[100/(25 + 100)] \times 1000$). By harvesting males, the productive component is increased. Where a limited food supply or range carrying capacity exists, and population increases are desired, managing to keep the proportion of females high is a typical managerial strategy. To reduce a population that is doing crop damage, just the reverse is needed. Where bucks-only hunting laws exist, it is almost impossible to reduce or stabilize a population with an expanding female component. Whatever the average female birth rate, that number, multiplied by the females, is the annual production of young.

Box 2-2. How to Compute Sex Ratios

Males: 100 females

From raw data: 1063 bulls, 2784 cows.

$$\frac{1063}{2784} = \frac{x}{100}$$

$$x = 38$$

Therefore, 38:100 is the conventional sex ratio.
From female percentage: 60% females.

$$\frac{60}{100} = \frac{100}{x + 100}$$

$$x = 66$$

Therefore, 66:100 is the conventional sex ratio.
From male percentage: 60% males.

$$\frac{100 - 60}{100} = \frac{100}{x + 100}$$

$$x = 150$$

Therefore, 150:100 is the conventional sex ratio.

Percentages

Percent females from raw data: 1063 bulls, 2784 cows.

$$\frac{2784}{1063 + 2784} = 0.724$$

Therefore, the percentage is 72% females.
Percent males from raw data: 1063 bulls, 2784 cows.

$$\frac{1063}{1063 + 2784} = 0.276$$

Therefore, the percentage is 28% males.
Percent females from sex ratio: 60:100

$$\frac{100}{60 + 100} = 0.625$$

Therefore, the percentage is 62.5% females.

Age Ratios. Of equal importance with sex ratios are age ratios. Ages of wildlife are determined by body size, weight, hair and feather color and texture, stage of feather molt, development of the genitals, tooth wear and eruption, annual rings in teeth, eye lens weight, bone cartilage development, and other indicators. There is yet need for improved aging techniques, particularly for small wildlife. By banding and marking juveniles, wildlifers have obtained known-aged animals to work out these methods. Some species can only be divided into young, subadult, and adult classes; some into only young and old.

By grouping animals into age classes, determining proportions, and graphing them (Figure 2-8) as age pyramids, some knowledge of population change or dynamics can be obtained. Dynamics derives from structure. Alone, age ratios are inadequate for evaluating dynamics. Only when the age ratio is combined with a life expectancy statistic (to be discussed later), the sex ratio, and the production of young per female can a reasonable appraisal be made.

Populations are constantly turning over or replacing themselves. The percentage of young in a population determines its turnover rate. See Box 2-3.

Age ratios suggest population productivity since all ages are not equally productive. Age ratios tell of vulnerability and hunting pressure on herd segments. Age ratios are related to trophy quality of a population and to forage required (for age is related to size and size is related to metabolic requirements and to hunter preferences).

The age ratios can be interpreted on the basis of the following generalizations:

1. A youthful age composition indicates that births exceed deaths.
2. Age affects the number of young produced per year.
3. Age affects germ-cell maturity and breeding capability.
4. Reproduction is generally concentrated in a certain age group.
5. Age is an expression of the environment since animals tend to reproduce to the limit of the environment.
6. Mortality varies with age in each species.
7. Age ratios reflect the population's experiences over its life span. Limiting factors have a sculpturing effect on a pyramid. The age ratio or pyramid reflects the nature of hunting as a mortality factor by showing (a) differential vulnerability, (b) differential hunter selectivity, and (c) effects of past exploitation and yields.
8. Past exploitation is generally inversely related to the width of the pyramid base (the youngest age).
9. Exploitation of young or middle-age animals is generally directly related to the width of the base of future pyramids; that is, intensive exploitation of these segments of the population will cuase an expansion of the age base in the immediate future.

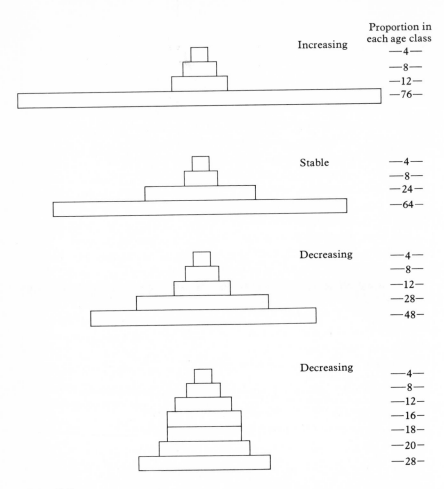

FIGURE **2-8**
Shapes of age pyramids can indicate the trends of population change. (After Alexander 1958:128.)

10. Exploitation of old animals is generally inversely related to the width of the base of the future pyramid; that is, the more intensive the exploitation, the narrower the pyramid age base.

11. Age ratios have their greatest utility in combination with data on sex ratios and reproductive vigor.

The wildlifer may work with populations for which there are no good aging techniques or for which classification into ages is easily biased. There is no universal age-class theorem except to collect data based on well-designed ex-

Box 2-3. Calculating the Average Turnover Period for Populations

If a population is relatively stable, the number of young equals the mortality. Mortality can be otherwise determined. The turnover period, T, for a population can be computed as

$$T = \frac{\ln N_t - \ln N_o}{\ln(1 - d)} + 1,$$

where N_t = the terminal cohort size (5),
$\quad N_o$ = the original cohort size (1000), and
$\quad d$ = the annual mortality rate (estimated as young in a stable population).

In a population of 1300 animals with 700 young, or $d = 0.538$,

$$T = \frac{\ln 5 - \ln 1000}{\ln(1 - 0.538)} + 1$$

$$= \frac{1.610 - 6.908}{-3.832} + 1 = 2.38.$$

Source: Petrides 1949.

periments and to keep the ages as "pure" as possible. Do not aggregate data; let the computer do that later after statistical analyses justify lumping or discriminating. Use coefficients developed in later studies to improve or correct data for biases. Do computer analyses, simulating how conclusions about populations might change under different assumptions for classifying the ages of animals. Apply corrective feedback at each step. At least, do not dismiss the need for collecting age data just because the data gathered last year were not used.

Sex and age ratios can be combined into a sex-specific age pyramid (Figure 2-9) as a useful analytical aid.

Population Dynamics

Rates of Change. All living populations are dynamic. The analysis of the change in population over time is the study of population dynamics. The basic

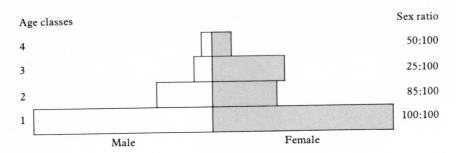

FIGURE 2-9

An example of a sex-specific age pyramid showing the results of differential mortality within a population.

concepts of population dynamics are depicted in Figure 2-10. The rate of change in the population during the period T in Figure 2-10 is simply the population at T_2 minus that at T_1, divided by that at T_1. If there are 100 animals at T_1 and 150 at T_2, then the rate of change is 0.5 (that is, $(150 - 100)/100$). This is the simple rate of change.

An average population can be calculated and plotted as the *equilibrium*, as in Figure 2-10. This shows a zero rate of change and expresses the central tendency during the period studied.

A straight line, called a *regression*, can be eye-fitted through all of the points of the curves to show the central tendency of the population over time. See the line in Figure 2-10. By various algebraic techniques an equation (called a simple linear regression equation) can be derived that tells all mathematicians precisely what line should be drawn to fit the points. An equation for the line is:

$$\text{Total population} = a + b(\text{Time in years}).$$

In this equation a specifies where the line crosses the vertical axis and b specifies the slope of the line. The slope of the line is another way to express rate of change. A slope or b value of 1.0 indicates that even though there are fluctuations, the population is increasing at a rate of about 45° or 50 percent of a vertical or infinitely great expansion per year. A slope of 0.05 indicates that the population increases 5 units for every 100 units of time. A slope of 3.0 implies that the population is expanding very rapidly. The percentage increase is not the same as the slope. It must be expressed based on the original population, the time, and the end population.

When there are many years and large fluctuations, it is best to use a computer to obtain the slope. An alternative is to take the natural logarithm (logarithm to the base e, $e = 2.71828$) of the numbers, plot these, and fit a line by eye through

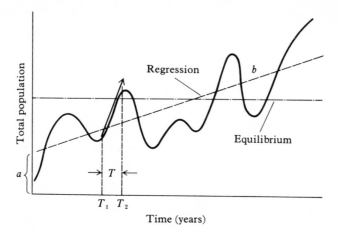

FIGURE **2-10**

Population fluctuations can be graphed to show rates of change over
the short and the long run. The population may increase rapidly during
some period *T*, starting at T_1 and ending at T_2. The average population
size in a specified period is usually called the equilibrium. The regression is a line that best fits all of the observed population levels. A
simple equation can be substituted for the graph, that is, Total population = *a* + *b* (Time in years). The line intercepts the vertical axis at
a; *b* specifies the rate (or slope) of the line.

the points. Table 2-4 lists the natural logarithms (denoted $\log_e$ or ln) of the
numbers from 10 to 2400 in increments of 10. The natural logarithm of 100 is
4.605. To find the antilog of a number, look in the logarithm column for the
closest number. The corresponding number (interpolate if necessary) is the
antilog. The antilog of 7.600 is 2000. Where natural log tables are not available,
common logarithms ($\log_{10}$) can be used and the logarithm multiplied by
2.30259. (To convert $\log_e$ to $\log_{10}$, multiply by 0.43429.)

The wildlifer grows to expect the variation in population densities shown in
Figure 2-10. Part of this is due to sampling error and the problems previously
discussed with estimating densities. The further one goes with statistics, the
more likely one is to pay attention, not to the line (as an expression of the central
tendency of the population) but to the *distribution* of the probable population
(Figure 2-11).

These are simple, or linear, rates of change. They are a *convenient* way to
analyze populations. Populations tend to change exponentially. Demonstrate
this for yourself by plotting the results of matings of a pair of quail twice a year
for 3 years, 6 chicks per clutch, and assume that all birds survive and themselves
mate in one year. The results are identical to compound interest rate equations

TABLE **2-4**
Naperian logarithms ($\log_e$ or ln) for a representative set of populations of size x.

x	ln x	x	ln x	x	ln x	x	ln x
10	2.302585	310	5.736572	610	6.413459	910	6.813444
20	2.995731	320	5.768320	620	6.429719	920	6.824373
30	3.401196	330	5.799092	630	6.445720	930	6.835184
40	3.688879	340	5.828945	640	6.461468	940	6.845880
50	3.912023	350	5.857933	650	6.476972	950	6.856462
60	4.094344	360	5.886104	660	6.492239	960	6.866933
70	4.248495	370	5.913503	670	6.507277	970	6.877295
80	4.382026	380	5.940171	680	6.522092	980	6.887552
90	4.499809	390	5.966146	690	6.536691	990	6.897704
100	4.605169	400	5.991464	700	6.551080	1000	6.907755
110	4.700480	410	6.016157	710	6.565265	1010	6.917706
120	4.787491	420	6.040255	720	6.579250	1020	6.927557
130	4.867534	430	6.063785	730	6.593044	1030	6.937314
140	4.941642	440	6.086774	740	6.606649	1040	6.946976
150	5.010634	450	6.109247	750	6.620072	1050	6.956545
160	5.075173	460	6.131226	760	6.633318	1060	6.966023
170	5.135798	470	6.152732	770	6.646390	1070	6.975413
180	5.192956	480	6.173785	780	6.659293	1080	6.984715
190	5.247024	490	6.194405	790	6.672032	1090	6.993933
200	5.298317	500	6.214607	800	6.684611	1100	7.003065
210	5.347107	510	6.234410	810	6.697034	1110	7.012115
220	5.393627	520	6.253828	820	6.709304	1120	7.021084
230	5.438079	530	6.272877	830	6.721425	1130	7.029972
240	5.480639	540	6.291569	840	6.733401	1140	7.038783
250	5.521461	550	6.309917	850	6.745235	1150	7.047517
260	5.560681	560	6.327936	860	6.756932	1160	7.056175
270	5.598421	570	6.345635	870	6.768493	1170	7.064758
280	5.634789	580	6.363028	880	6.779922	1180	7.073269
290	5.669881	590	6.380122	890	6.791221	1190	7.081708
300	5.703782	600	6.396929	900	6.802394	1200	7.090076

for banking. Table 2-5 shows the results of using a compound interest equation as follows:

$$N_t = N_0(1 + r)^t,$$

where N_t = the population at some future time t,
  N_0 = the population at some starting period, as at transplanting (in Table 2-5 it is 60),
  r = the rate of increase, and
  t = time in years.

Like the turnover period previously discussed, another rate statistic has

TABLE **2-4,** *continued*

x	$\ln x$	x	$\ln x$	x	$\ln x$	x	$\ln x$
1210	7.098375	1510	7.319864	1810	7.501081	2110	7.654443
1220	7.106606	1520	7.326466	1820	7.506591	2120	7.659171
1230	7.114769	1530	7.333022	1830	7.512071	2130	7.663877
1240	7.122867	1540	7.339538	1840	7.517520	2140	7.668561
1250	7.130898	1550	7.346010	1850	7.522941	2150	7.673223
1260	7.138866	1560	7.352441	1860	7.528332	2160	7.677863
1270	7.146771	1570	7.358830	1870	7.533693	2170	7.682482
1280	7.154614	1580	7.365180	1880	7.539026	2180	7.687079
1290	7.162397	1590	7.371489	1890	7.544332	2190	7.691656
1300	7.170119	1600	7.377758	1900	7.549608	2200	7.696212
1310	7.177782	1610	7.383989	1910	7.554858	2210	7.700747
1320	7.185387	1620	7.390181	1920	7.560080	2220	7.705262
1330	7.192934	1630	7.396335	1930	7.565275	2230	7.709757
1340	7.200424	1640	7.402452	1940	7.570443	2240	7.714231
1350	7.207859	1650	7.408530	1950	7.575584	2250	7.718685
1360	7.215240	1660	7.414573	1960	7.580699	2260	7.723120
1370	7.222566	1670	7.420578	1970	7.585789	2270	7.727534
1380	7.229838	1680	7.426549	1980	7.590852	2280	7.731930
1390	7.237059	1690	7.432484	1990	7.595889	2290	7.736306
1400	7.244227	1700	7.438383	2000	7.600902	2300	7.740664
1410	7.251345	1710	7.444248	2010	7.605889	2310	7.745003
1420	7.258411	1720	7.450079	2020	7.610852	2320	7.749322
1430	7.265429	1730	7.455876	2030	7.615790	2330	7.753623
1440	7.272398	1740	7.461640	2040	7.620705	2340	7.757906
1450	7.279319	1750	7.467371	2050	7.625594	2350	7.762170
1460	7.286191	1760	7.473068	2060	7.630461	2360	7.766417
1470	7.293017	1770	7.478734	2070	7.635303	2370	7.770645
1480	7.299797	1780	7.484368	2080	7.640122	2380	7.774856
1490	7.306531	1790	7.489970	2090	7.644918	2390	7.779048
1500	7.313220	1800	7.495542	2100	7.649693	2400	7.783223

meaning in some situations. It is *doubling time.* How long it takes for a population to double is determined from

$$t_d = \frac{\ln 2}{r} = \frac{0.6931}{r}.$$

If a population's exponential growth rate is 10 percent, then the doubling time is 7 years. The annual growth is the same as the exponential growth rate for all practical purposes ($e^r = (1 + r)$; in the above example, $e^r = 1.10$ and $r = 0.09531$).

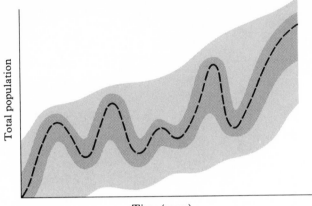

Time (years)

<small>FIGURE **2-11**</small>
The curve in Figure 2-10 is a summary or best estimate of population changes over time. Less emphasis should be placed on the line and more emphasis on the probable distribution of the population estimate in each year. The population has a high probability of actually occurring in the more densely shaded area.

As a basis for evaluating how well a population is performing, the wildlife manager will want a measure of a maximum rate of increase. This is determined by

$$r_{max} = (\ln m)/t,$$

where m is the net reproduction rate and t is the average age of females in a population when they first give birth or lay hatchable eggs (Southworth 1966:288). See Table 2-6. A net reproduction rate of 1.5, as in some deer populations, may be associated with early fawning ($t = 1$) and a capacity rate of increase of 0.41. In less fertile areas where fawning is delayed until the second year the maximum is 0.20.

Natality. The concept of net reproduction rate is variously used in the literature of wildlife management, so anyone employing this concept in population analysis should take care to define it quite explicitly. For our purposes, net reproduction is the number of young surviving until some pre-specified time of the year. It is the total young born minus the deaths in the first year of life (or up to some specified time). The rates associated with population increase are called *natality*. Natality is occasionally called "birth rate," but this term introduces the

TABLE 2-5

The changes in an initial population of 60 animals over time when the population is increasing at various rates.

Time (years)	Rate of increase									
	0.1	0.2	0.3	0.4	0.5	0.6	0.7	0.8	0.9	1.0
1	66.0	72.0	78.0	84.0	90.0	96.0	102.0	108.0	114.0	120.0
2	72.6	86.4	101.4	117.6	135.0	153.6	173.4	194.4	216.6	240.0
3	79.9	103.7	131.8	164.6	202.5	245.8	294.8	349.9	411.5	480.0
4	87.8	124.4	171.4	230.5	303.8	393.2	501.1	629.9	781.9	960.0
5	96.6	149.3	222.8	322.7	455.6	629.1	851.9	1133.7	1485.7	1920.0
6	106.3	179.2	289.6	451.8	683.4	1006.6	1448.3	2040.7	2822.7	3840.0
7	116.9	215.0	376.5	632.5	1025.2	1610.6	2462.0	3673.3	5363.2	7680.0
8	128.6	258.0	489.4	885.5	1537.7	2577.0	4185.4	6612.0	10190.1	15360.0
9	141.5	309.6	636.3	1239.7	2306.6	4123.2	7115.3	11901.5	19361.2	30720.0
10	155.6	371.5	827.1	1735.5	3459.9	6597.0	12095.9	21422.7	36786.3	61440.0
11	171.2	445.8	1075.3	2429.7	5189.9	10555.3	20563.1	38560.9	69893.9	122880.0
12	188.3	535.0	1397.9	3401.6	7784.8	16888.4	34957.3	69409.5	132798.6	245760.0
13	207.1	642.0	1817.2	4762.3	11677.2	27021.5	59427.4	124937.1	252317.1	491520.0
14	227.8	770.3	2362.4	6667.2	17515.8	43234.3	101026.5	224886.6	479402.6	983040.0
15	250.6	924.4	3071.1	9334.0	26273.6	69174.9	171745.1	404795.8	910864.7	1966080.0
16	275.7	1109.3	3992.5	13067.7	39410.4	110679.8	291966.6	728632.0	1730642.0	3932160.0
17	303.3	1331.2	5190.2	18294.7	59115.7	177087.6	496343.2	1311537.0	3288220.0	7864320.0
18	333.6	1597.4	6747.3	25612.6	88673.5	283340.1	843783.3	2360766.0	6247616.0	15728640.0
19	367.0	1916.9	8771.4	35857.6	133010.3	453344.1	1434431.0	4249376.0	11870470.0	31457280.0

TABLE 2-6

The maximum rate of population increase determined by the average age of females when they first give birth (t) and net reproduction rate per generation (m).

							m							
t	0.1	0.2	0.3	0.4	0.5	1.0	1.5	2.0	2.5	3.0	3.5	4.0	4.5	5.0
1	−2.30	−1.61	−1.20	−0.92	−0.69	0.00	0.41	0.69	0.92	1.10	1.25	1.39	1.50	1.16
2	−1.15	−0.80	−0.60	−0.46	−0.35	0.00	0.20	0.35	0.46	0.55	0.63	0.69	0.75	0.80
3	−0.77	−0.54	−0.40	−0.31	−0.23	0.00	0.14	0.23	0.31	0.37	0.42	0.46	0.50	0.54
4	−0.58	−0.40	−0.30	−0.23	−0.17	0.00	0.10	0.17	0.23	0.27	0.31	0.35	0.38	0.40
5	−0.46	−0.32	−0.24	−0.18	−0.14	0.00	0.08	0.14	0.18	0.22	0.25	0.28	0.30	0.32
6	−0.38	−0.27	−0.20	−0.15	−0.12	0.00	0.07	0.12	0.15	0.18	0.21	0.23	0.25	0.27
7	−0.33	−0.23	−0.17	−0.13	−0.10	0.00	0.06	0.10	0.13	0.16	0.18	0.20	0.21	0.23
8	−0.29	−0.20	−0.15	−0.11	−0.09	0.00	0.05	0.09	0.11	0.14	0.16	0.17	0.19	0.20
9	−0.26	−0.18	−0.13	−0.10	−0.08	0.00	0.05	0.08	0.10	0.12	0.14	0.15	0.17	0.18
10	−0.23	−0.16	−0.12	−0.09	−0.07	0.00	0.04	0.07	0.09	0.11	0.13	0.14	0.15	0.16

problem of whether hatching is birth, as well as the more important problem of the specific time period for measuring the rate. Will natality be determined immediately post-partum? After seven days? On the opening day of the hunting season? At issue is the definition of net reproduction.

In birds, for example, the analytical decisions are between eggs laid, eggs fertile, eggs hatched, young at the end of one week, and young at the end of summer. Even the base for expressing the percentages of success is in question—eggs laid, eggs fertile, eggs hatched? *Fertility* typically refers to the population's ability (expressed as number per cohort, or rate) to produce viable sex cells; *fecundity* is the ability to conceive or produce viable zygotes; and *natality* is the ability to produce viable offspring.

The best time criterion for analysis will depend on the objectives of the analysis. Once again is evident the intrusion of human goals and values into the most objective of analytical processes.

The typical types of reproductive rates are:

1. Primary natality = fecundity = *in utero* young/total female adults.
2. Net natality = total female young/total female adults.
3. Refined natality = total young/total female adults.
4. Gross natality = total female young/total adults.
5. Crude natality = total young/total adults.
6. General natality = (pregnancies) (mean litter size) (total adults).

Note the decreasing precision and that 1 through 3 are female-specific. Sex ratios are important statistics for the analysis of reproductive rates. There is much difference in reproductive potential between a population with a sex ratio of 10:100 and refined natality of 1.8 and another population with an unknown sex ratio (but assume 55:100 and see Table 2-3) and crude natality of 0.8. The first population cohort is known to produce 1634 young. The second produces 800 at an unknown rate (but one which, by our assumption, is 1.2 or 0.8/0.645).

A *male:female:young* expression has been used by some wildlifers to combine the information on sex ratio with an expression of natality. A bull:cow:calf ratio for example, presents at a glance the natality of the cows, sex ratio, and potential herd productivity.

As a result of changing natality, population growth rates change. Buechner (1960:79) used the equation

$$r = \ln(1 + Sm_r),$$

where r = the rate of population increase,
S = the proportion of adult females in the population, and
m_r = refined natality.

TABLE **2-7**

Likely rate of population increase given the refined natality (m_r) and the proportion of adult females in the population (S).

					S				
m_r	0.05	0.10	0.15	0.20	0.25	0.30	0.35	0.40	0.45
10.00	0.405	0.693	0.916	1.099	1.253	1.386	1.504	1.609	1.705
9.75	0.397	0.681	0.901	1.082	1.235	1.367	1.484	1.589	1.684
9.50	0.389	0.668	0.886	1.065	1.216	1.348	1.464	1.569	1.663
9.25	0.380	0.655	0.870	1.047	1.198	1.328	1.444	1.548	1.641
9.00	0.372	0.642	0.854	1.030	1.179	1.308	1.423	1.526	1.619
8.75	0.363	0.629	0.838	1.012	1.159	1.288	1.402	1.504	1.597
8.50	0.354	0.615	0.822	0.993	1.139	1.267	1.380	1.482	1.574
8.25	0.345	0.602	0.805	0.975	1.119	1.246	1.358	1.459	1.550
8.00	0.336	0.588	0.788	0.956	1.099	1.224	1.335	1.435	1.526
7.75	0.328	0.574	0.771	0.936	1.078	1.201	1.312	1.411	1.501
7.50	0.318	0.560	0.754	0.916	1.056	1.179	1.288	1.386	1.476
7.25	0.309	0.545	0.736	0.896	1.034	1.155	1.263	1.361	1.450
7.00	0.300	0.531	0.718	0.875	1.012	1.131	1.238	1.335	1.423
6.75	0.291	0.516	0.699	0.854	0.989	1.107	1.213	1.308	1.396
6.50	0.281	0.501	0.681	0.833	0.965	1.082	1.186	1.281	1.367
6.25	0.272	0.486	0.661	0.811	0.941	1.056	1.159	1.253	1.338
6.00	0.262	0.470	0.642	0.788	0.916	1.030	1.131	1.224	1.308
5.75	0.253	0.454	0.622	0.765	0.891	1.002	1.103	1.194	1.277
5.50	0.243	0.438	0.602	0.742	0.865	0.975	1.073	1.163	1.246
5.25	0.233	0.422	0.581	0.718	0.838	0.946	1.043	1.131	1.213
5.00	0.223	0.405	0.560	0.693	0.811	0.916	1.012	1.099	1.179
4.75	0.213	0.389	0.538	0.668	0.783	0.886	0.979	1.065	1.143
4.50	0.203	0.372	0.516	0.642	0.754	0.854	0.946	1.030	1.107
4.25	0.193	0.354	0.493	0.615	0.724	0.822	0.911	0.993	1.069
4.00	0.182	0.336	0.470	0.588	0.693	0.788	0.875	0.956	1.030
3.75	0.172	0.318	0.446	0.560	0.661	0.754	0.838	0.916	0.989
3.50	0.161	0.300	0.422	0.531	0.629	0.718	0.800	0.875	0.946
3.25	0.151	0.281	0.397	0.501	0.595	0.681	0.760	0.833	0.901
3.00	0.140	0.262	0.372	0.470	0.560	0.642	0.718	0.788	0.854
2.75	0.129	0.243	0.345	0.438	0.523	0.602	0.674	0.742	0.805
2.50	0.118	0.223	0.318	0.405	0.486	0.560	0.629	0.693	0.754
2.25	0.107	0.203	0.291	0.372	0.446	0.516	0.581	0.642	0.699
2.00	0.095	0.182	0.262	0.336	0.405	0.470	0.531	0.588	0.642
1.75	0.084	0.161	0.233	0.300	0.363	0.422	0.478	0.531	0.581
1.50	0.072	0.140	0.203	0.262	0.318	0.372	0.422	0.470	0.516
1.25	0.061	0.118	0.172	0.223	0.272	0.318	0.363	0.405	0.446
1.00	0.049	0.095	0.140	0.182	0.223	0.262	0.300	0.336	0.372
0.75	0.037	0.072	0.107	0.140	0.172	0.203	0.233	0.262	0.291
0.50	0.025	0.049	0.072	0.095	0.118	0.140	0.161	0.182	0.203
0.25	0.012	0.025	0.037	0.049	0.061	0.072	0.084	0.095	0.107

Table 2-7 can be used in the following ways. A manager given a long-term objective of increasing a grouse population at a rate of about 0.2 discovers that, assuming a 100:100 sex ratio, the natality must be between 0.25 and 0.50 to reach the objective. Another manager wants to know what harvest will be

TABLE **2-7,** *continued*

				S						
0.50	0.55	0.60	0.65	0.70	0.75	0.80	0.85	0.90	0.95
1.792	1.872	1.946	2.015	2.079	2.140	2.197	2.251	2.303	2.351
1.771	1.850	1.924	1.993	2.057	2.118	2.175	2.229	2.280	2.328
1.749	1.829	1.902	1.971	2.035	2.095	2.152	2.206	2.257	2.305
1.727	1.806	1.879	1.948	2.012	2.072	2.128	2.182	2.233	2.281
1.705	1.783	1.856	1.924	1.988	2.048	2.104	2.158	2.208	2.257
1.682	1.760	1.833	1.900	1.964	2.023	2.079	2.133	2.183	2.231
1.658	1.736	1.808	1.876	1.939	1.998	2.054	2.107	2.158	2.206
1.634	1.712	1.783	1.850	1.913	1.972	2.028	2.081	2.131	2.179
1.609	1.686	1.758	1.825	1.887	1.946	2.001	2.054	2.104	2.152
1.584	1.661	1.732	1.798	1.860	1.919	1.974	2.027	2.076	2.124
1.558	1.634	1.705	1.771	1.833	1.891	1.946	1.998	2.048	2.095
1.531	1.607	1.677	1.743	1.804	1.862	1.917	1.969	2.018	2.065
1.504	1.579	1.649	1.714	1.775	1.833	1.887	1.939	1.988	2.035
1.476	1.550	1.619	1.684	1.745	1.802	1.856	1.908	1.957	2.003
1.447	1.521	1.589	1.653	1.714	1.771	1.825	1.876	1.924	1.971
1.417	1.490	1.558	1.622	1.682	1.738	1.792	1.843	1.891	1.937
1.386	1.459	1.526	1.589	1.649	1.705	1.758	1.808	1.856	1.902
1.355	1.426	1.493	1.556	1.614	1.670	1.723	1.773	1.821	1.866
1.322	1.393	1.459	1.521	1.579	1.634	1.686	1.736	1.783	1.829
1.288	1.358	1.423	1.484	1.542	1.597	1.649	1.698	1.745	1.790
1.253	1.322	1.386	1.447	1.504	1.558	1.609	1.658	1.705	1.749
1.216	1.284	1.348	1.408	1.464	1.518	1.569	1.617	1.663	1.707
1.179	1.246	1.308	1.367	1.423	1.476	1.526	1.574	1.619	1.663
1.139	1.205	1.267	1.325	1.380	1.432	1.482	1.529	1.574	1.617
1.099	1.163	1.224	1.281	1.335	1.386	1.435	1.482	1.526	1.569
1.056	1.119	1.179	1.235	1.288	1.338	1.386	1.432	1.476	1.518
1.012	1.073	1.131	1.186	1.238	1.288	1.335	1.380	1.423	1.464
0.965	1.025	1.082	1.135	1.186	1.235	1.281	1.325	1.367	1.408
0.916	0.975	1.030	1.082	1.131	1.179	1.224	1.267	1.308	1.348
0.865	0.921	0.975	1.025	1.073	1.119	1.163	1.205	1.246	1.284
0.811	0.865	0.916	0.965	1.012	1.056	1.099	1.139	1.179	1.216
0.754	0.805	0.854	0.901	0.946	0.989	1.030	1.069	1.107	1.143
0.693	0.742	0.788	0.833	0.875	0.916	0.956	0.993	1.030	1.065
0.629	0.674	0.718	0.760	0.800	0.838	0.875	0.911	0.946	0.979
0.560	0.602	0.642	0.681	0.718	0.754	0.788	0.822	0.854	0.886
0.486	0.523	0.560	0.595	0.629	0.661	0.693	0.724	0.754	0.783
0.405	0.438	0.470	0.501	0.531	0.560	0.588	0.615	0.642	0.668
0.318	0.345	0.372	0.397	0.422	0.446	0.470	0.493	0.516	0.538
0.223	0.243	0.262	0.281	0.300	0.318	0.336	0.354	0.372	0.389
0.118	0.129	0.140	0.151	0.161	0.172	0.182	0.193	0.203	0.213

necessary to take the annual increase from a population of 2600 deer when the sex ratio is 25:100 and $m_r = 1.25$. There are 80 percent females. In the 0.80 column and 1.25 row, the rate of increase is a substantial 0.693. The harvest, therefore, must be 1800 deer (0.693 × 2600).

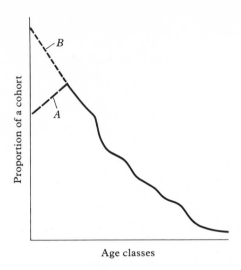

FIGURE **2-12**

An example of a mortality curve. Such curves are
usually negatively logarithmic. The data may be
from trapped animals, sightings of animals with
color or pattern markings specifying their age, or
from checking station data. In checking station or
harvest data some evidence of hunter selection or
differential vulnerability occurs (*A*). Parallel
studies or projections (such as *B*) can be used to
correct for part of this bias. When the proportions
in the harvest are assumed to be like those in
the population, these data can be used to graph
age pyramids.

Migration. Population increases are typically those of natality. The only other
ones are stocking and transplanting, previously discussed, and immigration.
Movements into an area occur as a result of *dispersion* from other centers;
horizontal or *seasonal* migration, such as waterfowl flights and caribou
movements over vast areas; and *altitudinal* migration, such as that which occurs
as animals move from winter to summer ranges (also seasonal), largely in
response to high-mountain snow depths. The time at which observations are
made of these spatial movements significantly influences the density estimates,
their changes, and thus estimates of natality or recruitment.

Mortality. Mortality describes the changes in populations due to suspected
causes of death. It is a rate of change. These suspected causes typically include
energy shortage and starvation, disease, predation, natural catastrophe (for

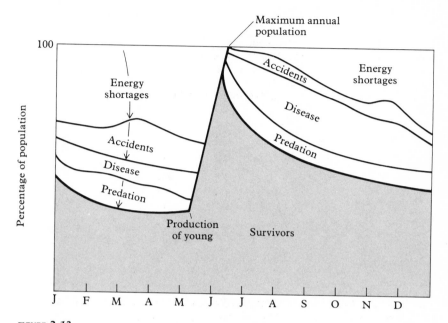

FIGURE **2-13**

The proportion of animals dying each month from various causes can be graphed for analysis. The detailed research needed for such graphs has seldom been done.

example, floods and fires), accidents (both natural and human-caused), hunting and trapping, pollution, and poisoning. Habitat loss usually acts through these same agents, as well as through reduced natality; it is rarely a direct mortality factor.

Evidence of mortality is very difficult to find. Sick or injured animals hide, they are naturally inconspicuous, and scavengers and decay work rapidly. In analyses of pollution effects, wildlifers should be on guard against charges of "no evidence." The evidence is only likely to be collected in changes in density or natality. Whether animals are killed or not born as a result of pollutants is a mere quibble. An example of a mortality curve is shown in Figure 2-12.

Efforts can be made to analyze mortality by time of year. Results can be graphed as in Figure 2-13. These can suggest where and when the efforts can be best allocated to reduce (or accelerate, depending on the objectives) such mortality. Where certain dominant mortality factors are not manageable, natural limits will be set on the manager's control. The manager should communicate these limits and the costs of achieving control effectiveness over various types of mortality.

TABLE **2-8**

Computation of d_x for a
hypothetical population of
90 animals in five age
classes:
$d_x = (\text{Harvest}/90) \times 1000$.

Age class	Harvest	d_x
1	40	444
2	20	222
3	15	167
4	10	111
5	5	56
Sum	90	1000

The proportion of the total population sampled in each age class is conventionally symbolized d_x. This is the actual number of animals in each class divided by the total sample. Either the actual proportion or the numbers in a cohort may be reported. In Table 2-8 the latter is used, that is, $d_1 = 40/90 \times 1000$. The animals in each age class can be determined from counts, harvest data, or any representative sampling. If the data are representative of the age structure, or can be adjusted so they are reasonably representative, then d_x can be determined. See Table 2-8. Of course, other analyses are needed when animals only live a few years (as do most small game and songbirds) or when aging techniques are not known.

Hunting mortality is a much sought and badly needed statistic. It can be converted into various units of benefit, for example, average person-hours or dollars spent per animal harvested. Hunting mortality can be measured or estimated by the following means:

1. Density estimates before and after the hunting season.
2. Hunters (or hunting pressure) and proportionate kill.
3. Band or tag recover rates.
4. Checking stations, compulsory or voluntary.
5. Spot checks of hunters' bags.
6. Kill tag returns.
7. Proportionate kill weighted by area.
8. Hunter questionnaires and interviews.

Box 2-4. A Means for Determining Crippling Losses of Deer

Every year a proportion of the animals seen and shot by hunters is not recovered. An estimate of this amount is needed, not only to help reduce it, but to add to the total legal kill to obtain an estimate of the total kill.

Method: Several workers walk through a hunted area immediately after the season and place out many burlap bags filled with leaves. These are simulated deer. Another crew, perhaps a sportsmen's club, walks through the same area on a well-coordinated dead-deer "drive." They record deer seen, both dead and simulated. It is unlikely they will see all dead deer or bags. Since the number of bags set out is known, a proportion yields an estimate of dead deer, D:

$$D = \frac{\text{(Total deer seen)(Total bags placed)}}{\text{Bags found}}.$$

Where areas and hunter pressure are known, results can be extrapolated, cautiously, area-wide.

9. Before-and-after comparisons of tracks, signs, calls, and sightings along cruise lines.

10. Spy blinds (watching, unobserved, hunter performance and comparing actual performance (for example, ducks shot) with reported performance.

11. Crippling loss analyses. See Box 2-4.

12. Comparisons of sex and age ratios before and after a hunt. See Box 2-5.

Survival. The surviving members of a population over time can be described in *survival curves.* Because both the population and time are changed into proportions, any populations can be more usefully compared. In Figure 2-14, curve 2 is much like that observed for bighorn sheep. After a high lamb mortality, most sheep live for a long time, then die. Curve 4 animals (some invertebrates) have a proportionate survival (or mortality). Insects, mollusks, and plants tend to have a curve of type 5. Most game species survival curves tend to fall between 3 and 5. Curve 1 is a theoretical curve, most closely approximated by very short-lived insects (ignoring egg and overwintering stages).

Survival is symbolized as l_x. It is best figured as progressive subtraction from a cohort ($l_1 = 1000$ and $l_{x+1} = l_x - d_x$) as shown in Table 2-9. Over half (556) of the animals in the first age class survive to age 2 and older.

Box 2-5. How to Estimate Hunting Mortality Based on Changes in Sex and Age Ratios

The proportion of the population killed is

$$Q = \frac{(B - A)}{(K - A)},$$

where B = the age or sex ratio *before* the hunt,
K = the age or sex ratio in the *kill*, and
A = the age or sex ratio *after* the kill.
If the percentage of females in a population before a trapping season is 0.60, the percentage in the kill is 0.10, and the percentage after the season is 0.70, then

$$Q = \frac{(B - A)}{(K - A)}$$

$$= \frac{(0.60 - 0.70)}{(0.10 - 0.70)}$$

$$= \frac{-0.10}{-0.60} = 0.17.$$

When a ratio is used,

$$Q = \frac{K(B - A)}{B(K - A)}.$$

If the sex ratio before a bucks-only harvest is 40:100 and 25:100 after the season, the hunting mortality was

$$Q = \frac{(100 + 100)(40 - 25)}{(40 + 100)(100 - 25)}$$

$$= \frac{3000}{10,500} = 0.29.$$

Source: Based on Petrides 1949, Selleck and Hart 1957.

For a population to survive, it must achieve a threshold density. Actual thresholds are only poorly known. Each is a function of genetics, behavior, and the probabilities of contact for breeding.

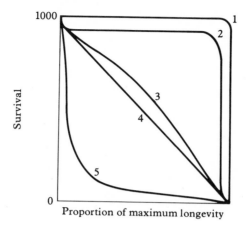

FIGURE **2-14**

Five types of survival curves described in the text.

TABLE **2-9**

Computation of l_x (survival) from d_x. $l_1 = 1000$ and $l_{x+1} = l_x - d_x$ (from Table 2-8).

Age class	d_x	l_x
1	444	1000
2	222	556
3	167	334
4	111	223
5	56	167

Survival data can be used to determine *life expectancy*. Do not confuse life expectancy with *physiological longevity*, the maximum longevity ever observed for a species (often in zoos), with *ecological longevity*, the maximum longevity observed for a particular population. Life expectancy means the probable years of life to be lived by individuals in an age class. A favorite exam question of population analysts is: What is the difference between the life expectancy of a 90-year-old man in ancient Rome and a 90-year-old man in modern America? The answer: none. They both have a probability of living less than a year. Environmental differences will be manifest in other age classes. Life expectancy

TABLE **2-10**

A life table for a hypothetical population.

Age class	Harvest	d_x	l_x	m_c	L_x	e_x
1	40	444	1000	0.5	778	1.78
2	20	222	556	1.2	445	1.80
3	15	167	334	1.5	278.5	1.67
4	10	111	223	1.5	195	2.50
5	5	56	167	0.9	83.5	0.50
Sum	90	1000	2280			

for wildlife, as for humans, is an index to total population life quality—both of environmental and social interactions.

Life expectancy is computed by the operations in Table 2-10. This analytical format is called a *life table*. Usually only x, d_x, l_x, and e_x are reported. Here, however, a column for m_c, or age-specific crude natality, is shown. It provides a means for integrating previous natality concepts with other concepts of population dynamics.

The average survival between age classes is L_x; that is,

$$L_x = (l_x + l_{x+1})/2,$$

and is an intermediate statistic needed to compute e_x, or life expectancy in any age class x. Life expectancy is

$$e_x = (L_x + L_{x+1} + \cdots + L_n)/l_x,$$

where n is the last age class. Note that even though animals were observed to live 5 years, the expectation of years of life for an animal of age 1 is less than 2 years. Having weathered all of the life storms, an animal of age 4, although there are few, has the longest expectancy. There is a fairly sharp drop-off at age 5. This may bear further study, either to confirm data or to explain phenomena operating.

By looking at age-specific natality, it is possible to compute a weighted mean natality (m_x) from

$$m_x = l_x m_c / \Sigma l_x,$$

which, in this case, is 0.47 (2153/2280). The large number of relatively unproductive animals in the first age class accounts for the apparently low mean.

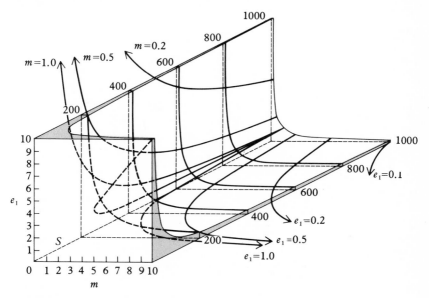

FIGURE **2-15**

A working model of population stability. The surface described by the curves represents population stability. When values of P fall on the surface, the population is stable; when they fall below the surface, a decreasing population is indicated; when they fall above the surface and not within the volume, an increasing population is indicated. (From Giles et al. 1969.)

Notice that if food and other factors could increase first-year natality, sizeable population natality gains could be made.

The population analyses of this chapter can be unified by Figure 2-15. This model is based on the concept that a population's productivity is a function of the number of years of expected life at birth (e_1), its producers or adult females (S), and its natality (m). A cohort in its lifetime must replace itself if the population is to be stable.

Where $P = e_1 \times S \times m$, stability exists when $1000 = 1000$. Figure 2-15 shows all conditions of stability on the ski-slope surface. When the three population statistics converge (that is, describe a point by three coordinates) above the surface, the population is increasing. When they converge below the surface (inside the volume), it is decreasing. The diagram is a conceptual aid. It moves beyond the oversimplifications of the age pyramids (which are now incorporated in the e_1 statistic) and embraces a general graphical model that holds for all species, from aardvarks to zebras.

Age data are often suspect. Some wildlifers reject the life table approach out-of-hand as unrealistic or faulty because of age data problems. The greatest use of the life table is in setting up a mental accounting system or matrix for

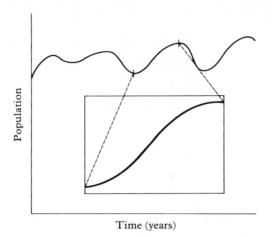

Time (years)

FIGURE **2-16**

The *S*, sigma, or sigmoid-shaped curve characteristic of most populations. It can be seen as an expression of the annual fluctuation of births and deaths, longer cycles, or growth past some point of introduction of a species.

what is going on in a population. That alone demands attention. As in population estimates, assumptions have to be made and diligence exercised to refine data. Good analyses of bad data will result in bad analyses; but with corrective feedback, continued refinement and data transformation and adjustments, the once-bad analyses can be converted to those that will serve the wildlifer very well—at least well within the confidence levels and accuracies required for reasonable solutions to most wildlife problems.

Relations Among Population Factors

Most biological populations can be graphed as a sigmoid or sigma-shaped curve (Figure 2-16). An exponential curve is intuitively unrealistic, whereas the flattened-*S* curve describes the course of most populations well, whether they be trees, turtles, or trout. The exponential curve levels out as a result of a host of factors, different in most populations. There are space limits, limits to available food, crowding and related hormonal imbalances, and disease. To discover the upper limit of a population, together with its causes, is a prime task of population analysis. It is at the bend or asymptote of the curve that the dominant relations between population factors occur. Many of these are not yet known.

Cycles. Very few populations have true cycles; most fluctuate. A cycle has an equal period (the time between peaks or troughs) *and* amplitude (the height of the peaks or depths of the troughs). Creatures that evidence a 3- to 4-year cycle are the snowy owl (*Nyctea nyctea*) and the Arctic fox (*Alopex lagopus*) as well as some European game birds and lemmings. Animals exhibiting a 9- to 10-year cycle are the northern ruffed grouse (*Bonasa umbellus*), sharp-tailed grouse (*Pedioecetes phasianellus*), willow ptarmigan (*Lagopus lagopus albus*), snowshoe hare (*Lepus americanus*), muskrat (*Ondatra zibethicus*), and Canada lynx (*Lynx rufus*). Cycles remain an enigma. Various hypotheses for their cause include: (1) random factors, (2) predators, (3) food, (4) atmospheric ozone, (5) sunspots, (6) disease, (7) stress or crowding, and (8) dispersion.

Stress. Still under investigation is the phenomenon of population stress or crowding. It seems that when animals reach a certain density they turn off their natality. This is behavioral-physiological and involves stimuli that operate to change the hormonal balances of the adreno-pituitary axis. This, in turn, can lead to death by adrenal failure, increased disease susceptibility, increased metabolism, and reduced fertility and fecundity. The result is population reduction. Stocking animals into naturally dense areas has resulted in *reduced* population densities, not increases, as intended by sportsmen. This has been a stress phenomenon, probably interactive with food available per animal. Disease is likely to have evolved in some populations as a density-regulating mechanism. Such a mechanism would be "healthy" over the long run for the population under natural conditions.

Stress occurs in red grouse when cover is removed between nesting sites. The nesting hens, seeing other hens, nest farther apart, thereby reducing densities. Hen pheasants, when population density becomes too high, are believed to leave about-to-hatch clutches of eggs and respond instead to the calls of newly hatched chicks nearby. Chicks do not hatch, thus reducing the natality. Male fighting, area defense, and various excessive displays are believed to reduce natality. Stress analyses are badly needed in the field and laboratory. These studies must be deeply rooted in biochemistry and extensively concerned with behavior, spatial analyses, time sequences, and cumulative stimuli. Nutritional status interactions with stressful conditions are largely unexplored. There is much speculation and generalization from laboratory studies. More of the latter, some field studies, and less speculation are needed.

Predation. Stress is intra-specific; predation is inter-specific. Predation, like browsing or grazing, is a feeding activity when looked at from the point of view of the predator population, a mortality factor when seen from the point of the view of the prey or a user of the prey (such as a sheepraiser). For some people, predation is a welcome message that ecological systems are still functioning; for others, it is an unquestionable evil to be eliminated. There is probably no problem in wildlife management that evokes more extremes of opinion. Concern with predators may range from raising control funds, to studying the energetics of predation, to seeking preservation of wild canids (dog family). The predator may be approached from various perspectives—recreational, esthetic, ethical, scientific, or economic. A particularly satisfying perspective is, broadly, the interaction of the population dynamics of the predator species and prey species.

Predator populations are dependent upon an energy resource. That energy resource is their prey, whatever it may be. The energy resource available is a function of (1) species-specific predatory behavior, (2) prey species richness, (3) prey species abundance (biomass), and (4) cover. Predator populations are limited by prey populations; prey populations are only limited by predator populations under (1) islandic conditions and (2) unnatural situations such as stocking, fencing, barriers to migration, concentrations such as during feeding, and unusually low densities of female proportions of a population.

It is known that predator populations respond to prey populations. Where prey populations are high, predator populations may increase through enhanced vigor, health, and reproduction. Where predators cannot obtain sufficient net energy per unit area per unit time, they migrate or die. The rises and falls of prey and predator populations have proved difficult to measure, and the costs of doing so may well exceed the benefits.

The greater the prey density, the greater is the biomass available to predators. From animals of approximately equal weight, the protein, water, and energy returns to a predator per unit of energy invested are greater in dense, rather than in sparse, populations. Contacts between predator and prey vary with wind, periods of activity, and cover.

Predator populations are subject to the ecological Rule-of-Ten, based on the second law of thermodynamics. The rule is that with each passage of energy from trophic (feeding) level to trophic level, there is only about 10-percent efficiency. The trend is, in general: 1000 kcal of grass energy is eaten and becomes 100 kcal of mouse energy. The mouse is eaten and becomes 10 kcal of owl energy, and so on. At the end of the pyramid, there can never be a large number of carnivores as predator populations. Animals that are omnivorous are more successful than carnivores.

Learning is one way by which energy is conserved. Predators, more than herbivores, are dependent upon stored information. Duplication of parental acts, avoidance mechanisms, and recognition of game trails reduce energy losses. Such losses are more critical for predators than prey. When animals (or people) use the same trails, feed in the same areas, or are otherwise repetitive or provide information to predators, then predation is likely to continue. The amount of predation is directly related to the stability of pattern in prey behavior.

Vulnerability is a misleading concept, for it can be as much a function of the predator as the prey. However, it usually is used as a prey concept. *Availability* and *utilization* of foods are more appropriate analytical concepts. Percentage frequency of occurrence should be related to actual feeding behavior to establish a "prey preference index." The concept implies that some species are more tasty, or more evasive, or more prone to flight (or defense, as in the case of the encircling musk-oxen, *Ovibos moschatus*). Herds act much like the compound eye of an insect, responsive to predation from all sides. The fact that predation is also influenced by occurrences of prey during predatory hours, or coincident behavior, illustrated by the habits of nocturnal mice and owls, is another reason for recommending against use of the word vulnerability except where very specifically defined or for informal public communications.

Whether predators prey on surplus animals or not is relevant only to an objective. There is no innate, inherently proper population for any area. Natural populations wax and wane and even disappear in local areas. Predators prey upon available animals. Whether the removal is excessive or not can only be judged relative to an objective.

Predators may consume weak, dying, and even dead animals. The energy required to take a diseased, parasitized, or starving animal will be less than the energy required to take a vigorous one. Through the concept that animals balance energy losses very carefully with inputs, explanations are available for why some animals take only sick young, whereas others attack mature bulls, and why these actions differ on the same range in different years. The same concept can be used to explain why under opportunistic circumstances abnormal predation is seen (a predator taking an otherwise unacceptable prey). The acts of individual animals, except for natural history interest, are almost irrelevant. Significant change in benefits from a *population* is the criterion of predation.

There are no long-term habitat studies done along with predator and prey studies that provide substantive evidence that predators significantly reduce wildlife prey populations (and, thus, eventually reduce themselves). In studies to date, changes in habitat could explain prey population changes reported as a result of predator removals.

There is no doubt, however, that predatory populations drain energy from prey populations by causing fright, chasing, and reducing feeding time. Predation can reduce the prey population's nutrient intake, reduce lactation or necessary feeding and care of young, cause home range shifts (and related forage energy resources), and cause changes in reproductive success through (1) impaired fertilization, (2) reduced implantation, and (3) abortion and pre-natal (and perhaps nonpredatory post-natal) death. Whether it does cause these changes or not must be decided in situation-by-situation analysis.

It should be noted that there is a major difference between *injury* and *damage* from predation. Predation is used loosely to mean the killing of any animal by another animal. But to the wildlife manager, the criterion is significant loss of human benefits from prey populations. If attacks result in loss of milk yield from a herd of cows or in sheep frightened over a cliff, then the act of predation has occurred. If rabbit population *harvests* (not populations) are significantly reduced, predation has occurred. If net monetary gains from an overcrowded and stressed chicken flock at the time of marketing are not reduced significantly by a weasel-caused 0.5-percent reduction in the size of the flock, no predation has occurred. Injury has occurred, but not damage. When real damage (not injury) is experienced, cost-effective control is justified.

Sometimes a "buffer species" is introduced to take predation pressures off game animals or animals of interest. One person's buffer is another person's prize, however. The more the biomass (or energy) for predators in a form equally or more readily taken, the more diffuse will be the predator pressure. If mice will remove predator pressure from hawks on quail, then mice are buffers. The management of buffer species is identical to the concept of managing a "faunal habitat" for predators. The objective is to increase the net energy available to an animal per unit time per unit area.

Few replications of predator-prey studies of wildlife have been conducted. Much predator-prey theory derives from laboratory invertebrate populations. The skilled manpower to conduct the needed studies daily over many thousands of acres in over 30 areas for at least 3 years is unlikely to be assembled or funded. In the meantime, controversy over predation is likely to remain both fierce and frustrating. Perhaps new research methods will enable economies sufficient to obtain answers. Computer simulation can provide new insights into feasible benefits, costs, and control techniques.

Behavior. Although all types of wildlife behavior are of interest to the wildlife manager, few are of direct managerial value. The manager's principal question regarding behavior, and all other population characteristics, is: If I had information about the phenomenon, how would it influence my decisions about how the population should be manipulated to achieve my objectives? The basic researcher will claim that facts have value in themselves. The wildlife manager will at least seek to reduce the time between research discoveries and applications.

The major topics of behavioral study for the wildlife manager will be: (1) time of migration and breeding, (2) maximum size of herds and flocks, (3) group formation relative to habitat, (4) flushing and flight distances, (5) avoidance behavior, and (6) territoriality and occupancy. Radiotelemetry (following animals with microtransmitters attached that signal their position) has been used to obtain movement data on stocked animals, normal home ranges, and flight patterns and distances.

Exciting research potential lies in elucidating the energy relations of behavior. Behavior can be usefully interpreted as success in achieving energy balance, either in the short run or in the long run. Migration, at great energy cost, may result in net savings. The cost of staying in an area may far exceed that of moving. Territorial display or defense of areas represents an inexpensive energy cost for a population, far less than direct assault, wounding, or killing the invaders. The energetic efficiencies of herding and covey huddling can be described and optimum herd sizes computed for the environmental regimens in a particular year. There is much more to be learned and energetics is likely to provide a unifying theme (Moen 1973).

In the area of feeding, energy is also becoming the unifying concept. Large animals require more food energy than small animals, but they utilize it more efficiently. Sex ratios, age ratios, reproductive stage, and lactation all interact to determine whether energy available from photosynthesis will be sufficient for a population of a particular weight distribution. Studies of some populations now show that energy requirements in summer are so great, that with the energy costs of processing masses of succulent summer vegetation, summer, not winter, is the critical period.

Production Curves. Animal production is a function of habitat. Animals have very specific habitat requirements. When these are well met, population density or natality is high. When they are poorly met, densities are low or unstable. All habitats tend to be dynamic. All tend to change progressively to some fairly steady state. This state is often called the climax vegetation. The dynamics of the environment is called *succession* and it is naturally in one direction—toward climax.

As succession occurs, there are different stages of plant and community development. In much of the eastern United States the pattern is from bare rock, to lichen moss, to grass, to forb, to broadleaf shrub, to pine, then to mixed hardwood. Each of these stages is particularly suited to several species of animals (invertebrates as well as vertebrates) and hostile to others. Each stage provides food (available energy) for only certain life forms. Each provides more or less protection from the wind (energy loss by convection) or more or less solar inputs (energy available from radiation or re-radiation). Succession creates, dynamically, an environment in which only some life forms can achieve an energy balance. As plant communities change, so do the animals present within them. Animals often contribute to the change. They may even cause changes that, through a series of complex relations, result in environmental destruction for them but a situation highly suitable to later successional stage (called seres or seral stages) animals.

These changes can be graphed as successional curves, or in the terminology of economics, production functions (see Figure 2-17). These curves may be categorized as *actual* or *potential.* Often the latter will be the most useful to the manager. A poacher or a feral animal (domestic animal gone wild) may cause a

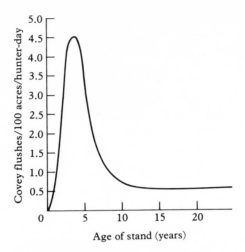

FIGURE **2-17**

An example of a production function. Here the production of bobwhite quail covey rises or flushes is expressed as a function of the age of a planted southeastern pine forest. Quail are abundant in the early field stages of pine growth, but disappear as the trees become dense and understory vegetation is shaded out.

temporary reduction of density, but the habitat potential remains. Action can be taken to eliminate the problem that is independent of the dominant, long-term habitat production potential. Different soil, moisture, elevation, slope, and aspect (the compass direction that a slope faces) can influence successional curves. These are representations of what the environment is doing (or not doing) for a species of wildlife (see Figure 2-18). Certain configurations and arrangements of habitat tend to increase wildlife. These can be seen as coefficients or multipliers of the successional curves. They are the synergistic relations upon which the wildlife manager capitalizes.

In analyzing wildlife populations over very large areas (for example, Figure 2-19a), which are the typical domain of the wildlife manager, the curves in Figure 2-19b are invaluable for integrating density and dynamics in time and space. The upper curve in Figure 2-19b is the sum of all the curves below it. It represents area-wide quail hunting opportunity over time.

Multiple-species curves can also be created. Assuming rabbits, grouse, and squirrels are being managed on the same area, the manager first obtains a relative weight for the importance of each species—that is, the human value attributed to each. The manager may personally assign weights or allow this job

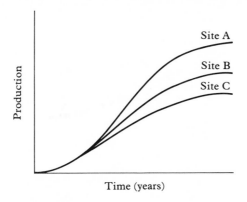

Time (years)

FIGURE **2-18**

Production functions may have any shape. For a
particular factor of interest, such as woodland
warbler populations or tree squirrels, site factors
may change the rate but not the shape of the
curve. Curves can de determined by (1) studying
areas through their change over time or (2) studying production on similar areas that are of
representative ages of succession.

to be done by supervisors, representatives, panels, juries, committees, sample
questionnaires, or public vote. The range in methods is from dictatorial to
democratic and varies according to country, political philosophy, and personal
professional ethics. Assume a sampled set of citizens were asked to weight the
species most preferred as 100 and the other two in relative numerical importance to that. The modal weights were 30, 95, and 40, respectively. The relative
weights then were adjusted to add up to 1.0 since management was directed at
one set of wildlife—a three-species complex as unity. These were then 0.13,
0.59, and 0.28. The curves are shown in Figure 2-20a. Every number along the
curve is multiplied by the above coefficients (Figure 2-20b). This converts all
curves to equivalent production units. The units are no longer grouse or squirrels but units of desired wildlife. As equivalent units, they can be summed
(Figure 2-20c) to represent the animal benefit units likely to be available per acre
in the same year (based on the best available knowledge of production in each
area of the country). The species are assumed to be largely independent.

The joint production of an area for the three species in the example is shown
in Figure 2-20c. This curve describes, explains, and allows prediction of
population changes over time in an entirely homogeneous area. Where data are
unavailable, wildlife managers would make their best estimates of the curves in
Figure 2-20. Where experts and experienced field personnel are available, their

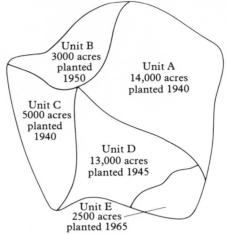

a

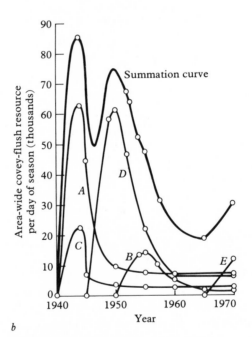

b

FIGURE **2-19**

The area-wide production of quail-hunting
opportunity on a managed forest (*a*). The curves
of the individual areas are plotted and the area
under them added (*b*). This can be done manually
for small areas, but for thousands of tracts of
different age, different site, and different acreage,
a computer is used.

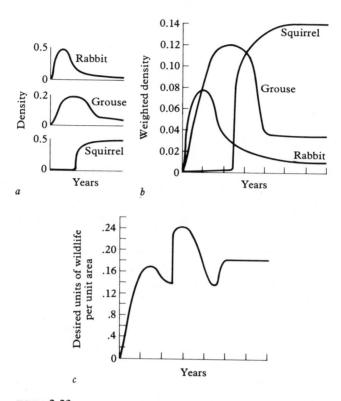

Individual species production functions (*a*), are weighted (*b*). Note the interaction of densities and species weights. An aggregate production function (*c*) expresses the likely production over time of wildlife benefits.

knowledge should be captured in the form of such curves. Representative areas of different ages should be studied to provide points along such curves. Through conscientious data collection, over time, wildlife managers can develop local production functions that provide them and future managers with splendid decision-making assistance.

Population density is determined not only by the age of a habitat but also by other site factors such as water, interspersion, edge, juxtaposition, and presence of people. These provide other dimensions to Figure 2-20c. Most populations are a function of many factors, probably at least 20 dominant ones. These would have to be graphed as an *n*-dimensional figure. Population can, therefore, be thought of as existing within an *n*-dimensional volume or hypervolume. The task of the population analyst is to discover these dimensions, their shapes and interactions, their thresholds and extremes. By doing so, the analyst gains predictive power over the population and thus the power to manipulate populations to achieve objectives—whatever or for whomever they may be.

Diversity. Diversity is a diagnostic measure of land health. It enables comparisons to be made between watersheds and management areas, between wilderness and managed communities, between polluted and nonpolluted ecosystems. It may also become an objective: to maximize diversity, on the assumption that stability is a function of diversity.

Diversity relates to many ecosystem properties: the more advanced a system's stage of development, the more diversity is exhibited; the more diverse the flora, the more diverse are the resources for fauna (and thus faunal diversity); the more species diversity, the less likely it is that a loss in one species will disrupt the entire system; increasing system production (of energy sources) increases potential diversity; higher biomass per unit area (for example, rice, sorghum) requires reduced diversity; long-term energetic efficiency is positively related to diversity; more diverse plant communities more completely utilize the sun's energy; species diversity is directly correlated with climatic stability, systems with low diversity are unable or slow to adjust to environmental changes or managerial treatment; diversity protects human populations against the risks associated with instability.

Diversity is often measured as the Shannon index of diversity, H, that is,

$$\overline{H} = -\sum_{i=1}^{q} p_i \log p_i,$$

where p_i = the importance probability for each species. Importance probability can mean, depending on management objectives, weighted importance, density, calories of required biomass, or productivity. The value p_i is computed as the importance value, n, of each species, i, for all q species, divided by the total importance values, N, that is, $p_i = n_i/N$.

Modified for use solely with animals (Odum 1971:144), the diversity index, D, is

$$D_1 = \frac{\displaystyle\sum_{i=1}^{q} \frac{s_i - 1}{\ln \Sigma \, s_i}}{\ln \Sigma \, s_i,}$$

where S_i = the cumulative number of species (also called richness) and s_i = the number of individuals in each species. Lloyd (1964) described a way of weighting species based on reproductive rates.

One index of diversity (Berger and Parker 1970) is simply

$$D_2 = p_{max},$$

where D_2 = diversity conceived as "dominance" and p_{max} = the maximum proportion of any one species in a sample. Another index of diversity (Simpson 1949) is

$$D_3 = 1 - \sum_{i=1}^{q} p_i^2$$

and is a measure of the probability that two specimens, picked at random from a large sample, belong to different species. Biomass and longevity differences make this index difficult to interpret.

Watt (1973:34) used

$$D_4 = K(B/P),$$

where K = constant, B = biomass, and P = productivity or net energy flow per unit time. As applied: If P is fixed, as in a lake, biomass can be increased by diversifying the species.

Diversity, although much used, is only recently undergoing theoretical development, and much more field work is needed to determine its real significance or to substitute concepts. The following conversation suggests how wildlifers might use the concept (or find it used against them):

Ned: My wildlife area is more diverse than yours. I have five species.

Kit: I have four species, but my area is most diverse since I have more individuals per species.

Ned: But I have a wider range of numbers per species than you do. In my species I have 4, 10, 60, 90, and 100 individuals. You have about 80 in each species.

Kit: But of my species, I have a greater range of animal volume (due also to sex and age differences) and thus I have a greater diversity of ecological efficiency.

Ned: You've gone too far. My species are more diverse simply on the basis of the proportion of individuals in the species with the most individuals.

Kit: But it is inappropriate to group black bear and 11 species of rodents into the same statistic.

Ned: Perhaps, but I know my species densities vary more through the years than yours do.

Kit: Yes, but my success is in having greater diversity of habitats. I have 40 different timber stands.

Ned: But they are all of the same size. I have 30 but they vary from 1 to 100 acres each. They have a mean of 60 and a standard deviation of 15 acres.

Kit: But they are not scattered; all of your small units are up north.

Ned: But your stands are mostly of the same age.

Kit: Even though I don't know why, my stands don't have a random distribution of species . . . *or* individuals.

Ned: But their shape increased my diversity; your stands are all elliptical or wander along with the contour.

Kit: But in the end I have greater diversity per individual than you do.

Ned: That's now meaningless unless we can agree on a basis for comparing general diversity.

Kit: We could use a three-dimensional concept of (1) species and individuals as simply "partitioned biomass," (2) spatial diversity or pattern, and (3) variance over time.

Ned: That's too complicated!

Kit: Compared with what?

Study Questions

1. What are the three primary categories for population analyses?
2. What is the basic analytical checklist under each?
3. Define a population.
4. Discriminate between analysis and design.
5. What are the possible interactions in a 16-species community?
6. Define "transplanting."
7. List ten reasons why introduction of exotics should be discouraged.
8. "Inbred" is the suggested diagnosis for a low game bird population. Discuss the possibilities.
9. What animals have become extinct?

10. Quail are said to have a maximum density of 3.1 per acre. How many is this per hectare?

11. Name at least five ways to estimate population density.

12. Having trapped and marked 62 rabbits, a wildlifer retrapped and caught 19, 10 of which had ear tags. What population estimate would be made?

13. Plot a Leslie graph from captures of 6, 5, 6, 4, and 2 animals per day over a 5-day snap-trapping period. Discuss your results and conclusions.

14. A wildlifer observed 2436 cows, 1003 calves, and 400 bulls on a helicopter flight over elk winter range. What were the appropriate reported ratios?

15. Compare the mean weight of populations, both with 110-pound does and 160-pound bucks, but one with 50 percent females, the other with 90 percent females. Which cohort will require the most food?

16. List techniques for determining animals' ages. Where can these techniques be learned?

17. Plot the regression of deer kill (K) over time (T, the year AD, for example, 1978): $K = 1063 + 0.83T$.

18. Locate harvest figures for your state or county. Transform to the logarithm. Plot an eye-fit curve, then compare it to a computed curve.

19. What is the doubling time of a population with rate of increase 6 percent? What is the rate of increase in a world human population with doubling time of 37 years?

20. A cohort has a crude natality of 2.0. What is the refined natality when the adult sex ratio is 25:100?

21. A cohort of 1000 females has a refined natality of 1.5. Assuming a sex ratio in the young of 100:100, what is the net natality? What happens to this statistic if the primary sex ratio is weighted toward males?

22. How can mortality be estimated?

23. Using hypothetical or real data for a population, compute a life table. Interpret it.

24. What are likely causes of wildlife cycles? Write a term paper, focusing on recent literature.

25. Define a buffer species.

26. Differentiate between injury and damage.

27. Debate the question: Knowledge of only a few types of wildlife behavior are of direct managerial value to the wildlifer.

28. Sketch production curves for one species in several areas. Add them. Plot the results.

29. What is a suitable source of species weights? Discuss. Review the literature on public participation in natural resource decision making.

30. Define "diversity" and compare several estimators of it.

Selected References

Alexander, M. M. 1958. The place of aging in wildlife management. *Am. Scientist* **46**(2):123–137.

Allen, R. P. 1952. *The whooping crane.* Res. Rep. No. 3. Nat. Audubon Soc. 246 p.

Berger, W. H. and F. L. Parker. 1970. Diversity of planktonic Foraminifera in deep-sea sediments. *Science* **168**:1345:1347.

Buechner, H. K. 1960. *The bighorn sheep in the United States: its past, present, and future.* Wildlife Mono. 4. 174 p.

Craighead, J. J. and F. C. Craighead, Jr. 1956. *Hawks, owls, and wildlife.* Stackpole Company, Harrisburg, PA. 376 p.

Errington, P. L. 1967. *Of predation and life.* Iowa State University Press, Ames. 277 p.

Giles, R. H., Jr. (Ed.). 1971. *Wildlife management techniques,* 3rd ed., revised. The Wildlife Society, Washington, DC. vii + 633 p.

Giles, R. H., Jr., C. D. Buffington, and J. A. Davis. 1969. A topographic model of population stability. *J. Wildlife Management* **33**(4):1042–1045.

Hornocker, M. G. 1970. *An analysis of mountain lion predation upon mule deer and elk in the Idaho primitive area.* Wildlife Mono. 21. 39 p.

Jolly, G. M. 1965. Explicit estimates from capture-recapture data with low death and immigration—stochastic model. *Biometrika* **52**:315–337.

Keith, L. B. 1963. *Wildlife's ten-year cycle.* The University of Wisconsin Press, Madison. 201 p.

Kellogg, F. E., G. L. Doster, E. V. Komarek, Sr., and R. Komarek. 1972. The one-quail per acre myth. *Proc. National Bobwhite Quail Symposium* **1**:15–20.

Lloyd, M. 1964. Weighting individuals by reproductive value in calculating species diversity. *American Naturalist* **98**(900):190–192.

Mech, L. D. 1966. *The wolves of Isle Royale. Fauna of the National Parks of the United States,* Series No. 7, 210 p.

Moen, A. N. 1973. *Wildlife ecology.* W. H. Freeman and Company, San Francisco. 458 p.

Odum, E. P. 1971. *Fundamentals of ecology,* 3rd ed. W. B. Saunders, Philadelphia. xiv + 574 p.

Overton, W. S. 1971. Estimating the numbers of animals in wildlife populations. In *Wildlife management techniques* (3rd ed., revised), ed. R. H. Giles. The Wildlife Society, Washington, DC, pp. 403–455.

Petrides, G. A. 1949. Viewpoints on the analysis of open season sex and age ratios. *Trans. N. Am. Wildlife Conf.* **14**:391–410.

Robson, D. S. and J. H. Whitlock. 1964. Estimation of a truncation point. *Biometrika* **51**:33–39.

Salyer, J. C. II and F. G. Gillett. 1964. Federal refuges. In *Waterfowl tomorrow,* ed. J. P. Linduska. Fish and Wildlife Service, USDI, Washington, DC, pp. 497–508.

Selleck, D. M. and C. M. Hart. 1957. Calculating the percentage of kill from sex and age ratios. *Calif. Fish and Game* **43**:309–315.

Simpson, E. H. 1949. Measurement of diversity. *Nature* **163**:688.

Southworth, T. R. E. 1966. *Ecological methods.* Methuen and Company, London. xviii + 391 p.

Watt, K. E. F. 1973. *Principles of environmental science.* McGraw-Hill, New York xiv + 319 p.

Wetherbee, D. K., R. P. Coppinger, and R. E. Walsh. 1972. *Time lapse ecology, Muskeget Island, Nantucket, Massachusetts.* MSS Information Corp., New York 173 p.

Whittaker, R. H. 1975. *Communities and ecosystems,* 2nd ed. Macmillan, New York. xviii + 385 p.

Chapter 3

Population Manipulation

Wildlife populations fluctuate naturally. The highs and lows of these fluctuations may bring either great benefits or great losses to society. High rat and poisonous snake populations are generally considered undesirable. Low game populations are cause for displeasure among hunters. Wildlife can be left alone to fluctuate naturally, but if this choice is made, the side effects must be anticipated and deemed acceptable. Managerial inaction is itself a decision, which implies that the costs or risks of taking action exceed the likely long-term benefits. The role of the wildlife manager is to manipulate populations by whatever means possible so as to stabilize or maximize their associated benefits—or at least minimize costs, risks, or undesirable effects. The concept of population manipulation is depicted in Figure 3-1.

Manipulating populations is not easily done under any circumstances. The interactions of people, species, and environmental factors make every project unique. That is why the task should never be submitted to a routine or "cookbook" approach. It requires the best-educated wildlife manager available, one who is a master of population analysis and who comes armed with a computer.

Objectives

The objectives of manipulating a population can be to increase the population; to stabilize it; or to decrease the total population, the density, or the rate of

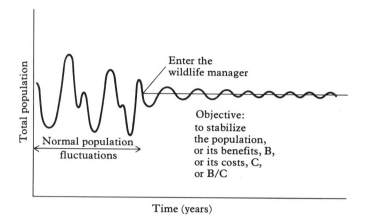

FIGURE 3-1

Normal population fluctuations can be reduced or controlled by managerial efforts. Here an objective of population stability has been articulated.

change to some desired point and then increase or stabilize it—for example, to reduce the population of a pest species to the 1960 level and stabilize it there.

The increase-stabilize-decrease pattern of stating objectives is more important than is intuitively evident. The population manager works with rates of population change. There are only three general, mutually exclusive things a population can do: increase, stabilize, or decrease. In the past, such words as "maintain," "preserve," and "perpetuate" have been used in stating objectives for a population. Is a population maintained if it decreases by 20 percent? If only one male and one female are left? If it increases by two times? The population could be said to be maintained in all three situations. Only work with less clear objectives or a few court cases will convince the skeptical wildlife manager that it is a good idea to be very precise in stating objectives.

A manager's success in achieving the stated objectives is usually judged subjectively. An objective alternative is the *difference-squared criterion (D)*. This is a useful but demanding method for judging managerial performance. The equation is simply

$$D = \sum_{t=1}^{n} (\text{Desired population} - \text{Actual population})^2,$$

where t = years of managerial influence or concern, from year 1 to n. The manager's ultimate objective is to minimize D. The manager seeks to achieve the objective exactly—not too few, not too many. Those wildlifers working to increase game may observe that it is probably better to be over than under the objective, but this is *not* so. Crop damage, timber damage, overexpectations of hunters and dissatisfactions in later years, and even undesired hunter shifts between areas, are frequent results of overabundance.

Figure 3-2 illustrates the use of the difference-squared criterion. The computation of D for wildlife manager A is

$$
\begin{aligned}
D &= (400 - 400)^2 + (400 - 300)^2 + (400 - 450)^2 + (400 - 250)^2 \\
&\quad + (400 - 450)^2 \\
&= (0)^2 + (100)^2 + (-50)^2 + (150)^2 + (-50)^2 \\
&= 37{,}500.
\end{aligned}
$$

A perfect score is zero. Penalty scores for deviating from the objective may be considered to be awarded as the square of such deviation. Conversely, even slight moves toward the objective, when far from the objective, can be very rewarding. The closer one gets to an objective, the more difficult it is to achieve that precise objective. However, fine changes near the objective are not as important as the larger changes in most systems.

An alternative objective to minimizing D is to redefine D as D^*, a performance within some stated percentage, say 5 percent, of the objective. As before, the scores are computed annually or as data are available. Assume an objective is to stabilize a population at 400 ± 5 percent. If the population is within plus or minus 5 percent of 400 (380 and 420), the achieved value is assumed equal to the desired value. If the achieved value is less than 380, then 380 is established as the goal; if the achieved value is greater than 420, 420 is set as the goal. The computations thus are

$$
\begin{aligned}
D^* &= (400 - 400)^2 + (380 - 300)^2 + (420 - 450)^2 + (380 - 250)^2 \\
&\quad + (420 - 450)^2 \\
&= 25{,}100.
\end{aligned}
$$

For manager A in Figure 3-2, D is 37,500; D^* is 25,100. D^* for manager B, working under the 5-percent assumption, is 9100. Note the relative differences in scores between the modes of stating an objective.

Determining a measurable population objective is the least scientific and most human act of wildlife management. *Objectives are not discovered, they are decided.* Scientific techniques may be of assistance in eliciting, tabulating, and analyzing objectives, and even studying their consequences, but objectives themselves are choices. The decision maker is all-important. The wildlifer will take steps to clarify who the proper decision maker is (for example, the commissioners or the director, the supervisor or the public) but will often end up serving two masters—a difficult task at best.

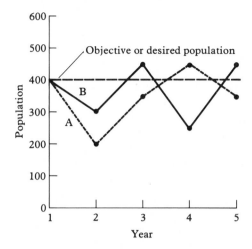

FIGURE 3-2

By comparing wildlife managers' minimizations of *D*, a statistical index of deviation from the objective, a relative measure of managerial performance can be obtained. In this example, manager *A* performs significantly better than manager *B* (A = 37,000 versus B = 47,500).

Other problems typically encountered by wildlife population manipulators are the following.

1. Undefined or broadly stated objectives, or objectives with a wide percentage bound (as in the example cited earlier), or changing objectives.

2. Large territories that are highly variable.

3. Projects involving multi-objective, multi-species, and multi-habitat complexes, simultaneously.

4. Slow start-up times both in public funding of projects (for example, 1 to 5 years) and in typical responses of the natural system (for example, 50 or more years for some forest and range species).

5. Relatively short periods (ecological seres) that are maximally productive of wildlife, with either long waits between or long waits for the end of an economic harvest period (for example, a forest rotation) before post-harvest seres can begin.

6. Fluctuating and catastrophic changes in habitats and thus in populations dependent on them (for example, results of fire, storms, and floods).

7. Limited control over bird watchers' and other resource users' attitudes or actions.

8. Limited (relative to agriculture) habitat manipulation techniques.
9. Typically increasing demands for human benefits from a shrinking land resource with decreasing potential to produce.

Whatever the demands on the wildlife manager, written objectives in a measurable form make the job easier. The simplest (and a very effective) objective is: We want the population to be at the same level as it was X years ago. This suggests that 6 years ago, for example, a complex set of objectives (not actually specified) was being satisfactorily achieved. It can be graphed as in Figure 3-2, where the first year is the base year. The problems with such an objective are that in that year the population may not have been the best possible; it may be that it was only the least bad for a series of years and so few complaints were heard. In a dynamic society, with changing human population density and values, what was good yesterday, in all probability, will not be today or tomorrow. Stable management systems in an environment of dynamic objectives are examples of planned failure.

Better objectives are developed by weighting species, using forage production and other biological and physical limits, observing levels at which injury changes to damage, and using indices to system performance. Examples of objectives include:

1. *To stabilize a harvest of at least one animal of species X per ten hunters per year.* Note that stabilizing a harvest when a hunter population is increasing or decreasing is very difficult.

2. *To maximize the squirrel population density on forested lands of age 40 and older.* Note that increasing populations on tracts within an area in which forests are being cleared results in lower mean densities. Maximizing mean densities *may* be the objective, but the wildlifer may have been handed the controls of a doomed ship.

3. *To minimize the reported wildlife-caused damage in the Rolf Watershed.* Note that the population may stay the same if the reports decrease. Note also that a change in crops might reduce damage and thus reports. It is also possible that the perception of the threshold between injury and damage can change (for example, as a result of inflation). The size of wildlife populations is all-important, but only within a specific context.

4. *To minimize the difference between the potential quality-weighted person-days of hunting opportunity each year and the days actually achieved.* Note that total days of species-specific hunting periods, adjusted by the weather and other conditions actually in effect and adjusted by the hunter densities that can be suitably tolerated, determine the potential. This level will change each year, as will the actual participation and the quality of that activity.

The method for obtaining an estimate of the achievement (for example, a mail questionnaire) is not included in the objective. Improved estimation methods may be found; the objective does not change. The difference-squared approach, described earlier, can be used with this objective.

5. *To harvest 268 deer of either sex.* Note that the scale of this objective is limited. It is probably for a management area. Some workers call the broader objectives "goals" and the lower-order objectives such as this, "objectives." Less time can be spent debating the meanings of the words and more time on actually articulating measurable objectives.

Some people will persist in arguing that *no* time should be spent on stating objectives and that the wildlife manager should get on with manipulating populations. In a sloppy system with few checks, no bases for evaluation, no threat of suits for ecological malpractice, or no danger of firings for mismanagement, they are right. When any of these feedback mechanisms come into the wildlife management system along with objectives (as they are presently beginning to do), those people with no practice in, and little concept of, measurable objectives will be ill-prepared. Their management units may be so ecologically out of phase that they will never, in their lifetimes, achieve high performance scores and the associated rewards.

Each species has its own unique characteristics that permit, and even require, highly specialized knowledge and application of unique mixes of tactics to produce desired change. There are some general principles that apply to most managed species. In this chapter an artificial division is made between populations, habitat, and people because by manipulating habitat or people, assistance may be gained in achieving wildlife objectives. These will be mentioned in this chapter and emphasized in later ones.

To achieve objectives, a manager can manipulate population structure, dynamics, or relations between factors affecting population. To manipulate is to implement a decision, to set in motion a system to achieve an objective. To select an objective and to create such a system is to design a population. The better the analysis, the better the design will be. The more that analysis and design interact, the better will be *both* analysis and design. Design can usefully follow the fundamental categories of analysis.

Manipulating Population Structure

Species Lists. Range maps for most wildlife species are deceptively complete. Local maps and species lists are lacking. In the twentieth century the most primitive sampling and range identification studies have yet to be done.

Authoritative lists for such gross units as counties are rarely available. The wildlife manager's first step is to discover species distributions and publish the findings.

Rarely will efforts be made to reduce a species list. However, an *ecoectomy*—the purposeful removal of a species from an ecological system—may sometimes be useful for studying ecological processes. In the past, far more was learned about the physiological action of an organ of the body by removing it than by studying the whole system. Analogously, studies of whole ecological systems, while essential, may not reveal as much about ecological processes as studies of systems that have undergone ecoectomies. Reductions or prevention of increases in species can be achieved by fencing, poisoning, and shooting or trapping. Reductions can be achieved by combinations of other techniques discussed later. Effective techniques for ecoectomies are yet to be developed.

To increase the number of species in an area, types not present can be transplanted. Often states have traded starter populations of wildlife. Snowshoe hares, wild turkey, and mountain goats are examples of species used in both primary and secondary stocking. Minimum necessary stocking populations are rarely known. The number is usually limited more by available stock and labor than by optimal considerations. Minimal thresholds have yet to be determined by collecting regional data on past successes.

Stocking should only occur after detailed habitat, parasite, and pathology studies, as suggested in Chapter 2. Subsequently, quarantine may be necessary. The stresses of quarantine should be reduced as much as possible to assure transplanting success. The shortest possible time from capture to release is desired. Reducing this time may involve (1) trapping so as to reduce time in the trap, (2) allowing immediate transportation in dark, well-protected devices with ample care (for example, beavers must be wet down), and (3) transporting animals by aircraft. Delivery must be made without delay to release sites. The projects must be planned with military rigor. Though the costs may be great, they tend to be lower than those associated with game farm activities for such purposes.

Waterfowl can be attracted to areas by means of decoys, wing-clipped or pinioned flocks, and even broadcasts of recordings of feeding calls of ducks and geese. Scent trails (laid down by dragging a carcass behind a vehicle) and planned feeding areas (typically garbage dumps) can attract mammals. Baits (food, scent, or tethered live animals) can be used to attract many animals. Very secretive species in an area may be discovered by using unusual baits and examining carnivore feces or owl pellets (disgorged hair and bones). Whether baiting is modified into a feeding program will depend on objectives. Establishing use patterns, for example, trails, may be the primary task. Where predators are to be increased, they may be attracted by high rodent populations, the planned secondary result of a feeding or planting program.

Encouraging, discouraging, introducing, or removing hybrids is a way to change a species list. Hybrid waterfowl (for example, mallard-domestic white crosses) are viewed by some as very undesirable and a species threat.

Preventing the extermination of species is a management problem for which few cases and few successes can be cited. All of the approaches in this chapter can be used, but most important are:

1. Special protection (laws, management, personnel, fines) from poachers, collectors, photographers, predators, and accidents, including laws against transportation and sale.

2. Rewards for information leading to convictions of violators of such laws.

3. Back-up efforts in zoos, use of incubators, use of surrogate mothers, and placental transfers.

4. Artificial insemination and hormonal induction of breeding.

5. Acquisition or creation of refuges of suitable location, size, and number.

6. Phased habitat management to assure stable or increasing areas of suitable food and life history requirements throughout the year.

7. Creation of buffer areas to protect critical areas from fires, catastrophe, or human intrusion.

8. Protection of the quality of associated watersheds, groundwater, and airsheds.

9. Area-specific educational efforts (for example, along migratory routes).

10. Hybridization as a last-resort preservation of a genetic residual.

11. Monitoring of population and related factors.

12. Stabilization of management funds, personnel, and programs.

13. Mass media and journalistic efforts to create national awareness and esteem for such species.

14. Continued work on improved international treaties.

15. Improved identification.

16. Reduced competitive livestock and wildlife.

17. Increased research to discover needs, causes of endangerment, and measures to be taken.

18. Search for new means for equitable allocation of limited budgets to such species.

Density. When hunters complain that all the game has been shot out of the area, they are expressing the law of diminishing returns (see Figure 3-3). The returns on hunting efforts increase to a point but then level off. Each extra day spent on

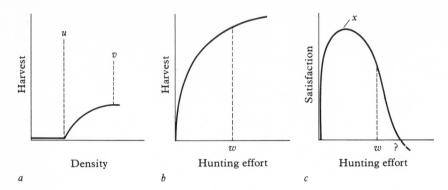

FIGURE 3-3

General relations found in hunting in an area by a given number of hunters employing normal hunting practices. The point w is the limit beyond which hunting effort will not be expended because of insufficient returns. Harvest opportunities remain (as shown in b), but satisfactions decrease and dissatisfactions (< 0) may increase.

the same area does not yield the same returns of harvested animals. Satisfactions increase, then decline. Assuming no other constraints, there is some point at which hunters will stop hunting. This varies among hunters but is a socioeconomic group statistic. There is a minimum density below which rational hunters will not hunt (u in Figure 3-3a). Chance harvests and hunting by nondiscriminating hunters keep the harvest from being zero.

To maximize the harvest, determine the density at which harvest will be greatest (v in Figure 3-3a). There is no need to invest in increasing population density beyond this point. Determine w (Figure 3-3b and c) from dropout rates on areas having different population densities. This is the point beyond which average hunting efforts should not be allowed (by seasons, education, permits, and so on). Observe the w harvest intercept in Figure 3-3c. This is the density that will maximize the harvest. But if the objective is to maximize hunter satisfactions (as measured by several indices), then the hunting effort should be regulated to achieve x, not w.

Techniques for manipulating density are:

1. Using chemical repellents (or attractants such as scent baits).
2. Using scare devices such as broadcast distress calls of birds.
3. Using attractant calls.
4. Using fences to move animals to the areas where higher densities are desired. Net change will be zero.
5. Harrying or hazing animals with helicopters or from horseback, moving them to other areas.
6. Manipulating natality and mortality (described later).

7. Releasing game (the closer to the open season, the greater will be opening-day densities).

8. Managing predator populations.

9. Managing buffer species populations.

10. Regulating disease and parasites.

11. Regulating the intermediate hosts of parasites, for instance, by using molluscicides.

12. Reducing populations by means of: (a) entanglement devices such as nets or adhesives on bird roosts, (b) soporifics or drugs, which increase predation potentials, (c) surfactants or detergent-like substances (in aerial sprays) that remove feather oil and thereby reduce insulation and cause energy loss, (d) poisons and poisonous gases (for example, for rabid bats in caves and crop-consuming woodchucks (*Marmota monax*) in their dens).

13. Implementing effective wildlife law enforcement systems (see Chapters 5 and 10).

14. Controlling accidents, as by regulating vehicle speeds, using warning signs along highways, fencing animals out of hazardous areas, removing habitat along road edges, and closing roads during critical periods.

15. Reducing pollutants of all types.

16. Controlling the type, amount, carriers, time, method, frequency, and cleanup of toxic substances in the environment.

Sex Ratios. Manipulation of sex ratios is one of the most effective controls a wildlifer can exert on a population. To increase the tendency of populations to grow, increase the productive component of the population. To decrease populations, reduce that component.

Hunting regulations or trapping policy can be used to regulate the sex of animals taken. Antlerless seasons will harvest female animals and fawns. A bearded-gobbler-only or bucks-only season will tend to increase the female segment of the cohort. The wildlifer who seeks a revision in a bucks-only season is usually doing so because the population has reached a limit of its food supply or is causing crop damage. The objective is a population decrease, or, if the manager has taken care to allow the population only to approach the margin between injury and damage, the objective at this point may be stability. A bucks-only season can have the results shown in Table 3-1.

Note that the crude natality of the population in Table 3-1 is increasing. The result is that increasingly larger numbers of males must be taken to keep the population in check. This does two things: (1) increases the productive portion of the population further and (2) leaves more food for the females, which may then increase their fecundity. The natality may increase from 1.2 to 1.5 or more. The result is great population increase, a natural dimension of population

TABLE 3-1

Changes in a particular cohort subjected to a constant annual removal of 20 percent of the adult males.

Year	Sex ratio	Portion of cohort		Total pre-hunt population		20 percent buck harvest	1.2 refined natality			Total population			Crude natality
		Male	Female	Male	Female		Male	Female	Total	Male	Female	Total	
1	100:100	500	500	500	500	100	300	300	600	700	800	1500	0.50
2	87.5:100	533	467	700	800	140	480	480	960	1040	1280	2320	0.54
3	81.3:100	552	448	1040	1280	208	768	768	1536	1600	2048	3648	0.57
4	78.1:100	561	439	1600	2048	320	1224	1224	2448	2504	3272	5776	0.58

survival over the ages. The control of these natural processes is the task of the wildlife manager.

Sex ratios can be manipulated by two means: (1) the fecundity of animals can be changed or (2) animals can be removed. For the population manager, sex ratios are typically indices to production. If animals are made sterile, the female is present but not productive. Indices to the productive component of the population other than sex ratios can be used, such as adult sex ratio or simply proportion of producers. Sex ratios may be changed by chemicals that increase the rate of maturation. The proportion of producers can be changed in males by castration or various modifications in the vas deferens, or by chemical means. It can be changed in females by chemosterilants (birth control pills in baits) and direct removal of ovaries or uterus.

Most practical is removal of males where they can be discriminated in the field by hunters by size, weight, color, or physical characteristics (for example, the beard, or unique group of breast feathers, of the wild turkey).

The limited evidence available suggests that the primary sex ratio, which is typically 100:100, may be modified by viruses, chemicals, and nutrition. For the wildlifer to use these means effectively, much more must be learned, particularly about nutrition. Perhaps when overpopulation occurs and food quantity and quality are low, the population has a built-in feedback mechanism that reduces the proportion of young females produced (for example, 110:100).

Age Ratios. Age ratios can be manipulated by setting size and weight limitations on animals that are hunted (for example, only bears over 100 pounds) or specifying other correlates of age such as antler and horn development. Such regulations select for certain ages and protect others, thus influencing the age ratios. Since age ratios strongly influence age-weighted natality in populations, this ability to change the age ratio is the ability to cause a population to do what the manager wants it to do—increase, stabilize, or decrease. Functional age ratios can be changed in the same ways as functional sex ratios. The age of puberty can be increased by chemicals and nutrition. Breeding age can similarly be extended.

Hunting permits that specify sex and age criteria for an animal to be taken can be issued. *Exact* control can be achieved if it is wanted badly enough. Usually such exact control is not desired; it may be too expensive or too difficult to apply (for example, a particular species may not have suitable field characteristics for hunters to determine age or sex).

Manipulating Population Dynamics

Whether a population rate is good or bad depends upon its relationship to other factors. When the rate reaches X, crop damage may occur; when it declines to Y, hunters may attempt to override regulatory control with legislative control. A population rate, for the wildlife manager, is an index to the performance of a system.

Natality. Natality can be changed upward or downward, depending on the objectives for a population, by (1) influencing sex ratios, as previously discussed, (2) influencing age ratios, also discussed, and (3) influencing fecundity. Fecundity can be enhanced or blocked by hormones, by nutrition, and by disease. Long weaning periods reduce fecundity.

Where social bonds are strong, the influence of a sterile male can significantly reduce natality. Crowding appears to reduce natality, not only through the nutritional effects of reduced per capita food, but also through physiological pathways—typically those of the adreno-pituitary axis. Pollutants may cause reduced ovulation, pre-natal mortality, and terratogenicity (birth defects), all of which are hidden in a single index to natality.

Reported natality can mean a number of different things, so the prudent wildlife manager will be explicit about the data being used. Reported natality taken at the opening of a hunting season, say, in September, will be much lower than that statistic determined for animals at the end of their first weeks of life, which is lower than that measured when the young first suckle, which is lower than "immediately post-partum," which is lower than *in utero.*

Every situation is different with respect to species, terrain, budgets, skilled labor, and a host of other factors. The intent here is to provide an extensive list of potential means for achieving population rate control. Usually techniques do exist to achieve the objectives, but whether the objectives *will be* achieved depends on funds, public sentiment, and legal and other constraints that are part of the manager's total system-control responsibility. The manager may, by skillful use of the numbers, achieve natality objectives without expending any funds or leaving the office. In some cases this is precisely what should be done; in others, it is a matter for ethical or judicial review.

Migration. Migration routes vary and, although much studied, are still poorly known. The origin (destination) of some birds has not yet been determined, and consequently management of such populations is possible within only one portion of their life history.

Animals can be moved into areas (stocked) or taken out by trapping or other means. Air and boat removals have been used with limited success on populations subjected to the rising waters of a new dam. Horseback herding has also been done. Elk are said to be herdable "anywhere they want to go." Helicopters have sometimes been used to move animals within large areas, but rarely can long-distance moves of the nature of migration be achieved by such means. Herds split up and one or more groups will stay within an area.

Fences retard migration and cause abnormal densities and great habitat and range abuse. Roadways and other human developments—for example, a town like Jackson, Wyoming, in an ancient pathway of elk migration—can produce barriers as effective as fences. Antelope will not go over fences. New fence designs have been created, including vertical baffles through which deer and antelope, but not cattle, will pass. Underground highway crossings have been used to allow migration in some areas. Cattle guards, the corrugated metal or wood crossings on roads that allow cars to cross a fenced area without dealing with a gate, are crossed by wildlife but not cattle. They are costly, but costs are only relative to how well important objectives are achieved.

Preventing large dams that cover migratory routes is a responsibility of active wildlife management in situations where an objective of population stability or increase has been set. Not only are animal movements blocked by dams, but when the animals do swim, at extreme energy cost, they may encounter shelf ice that prevents them from climbing out of the water. Crossing may be delayed until ice forms, but slipping injuries and associated mortality are high for deer and elk.

Radio, television, and other towers, especially lighted ones, when placed in migratory routes, can cause high mortality. Preventing their erection or getting them relocated may be important in the management of migration.

The course of migration can be influenced in a number of ways. Dogs have been used to stop or slow migration as well as to herd animals. Broadcasts of threat and danger calls may modify some migration. Drift fences, those without the ends closed, can be used to move a population from one area to another. Since animals tend to move downhill where possible (to use less energy), fences can be used to protect habitats and to achieve desired densities in other areas. Vegetation barriers such as hedgerows can be used to control wildlife as well as hunters. The movements of wildlife can be manipulated as the barriers are grown, as they are trimmed, and as entries or exits are cut in them and allowed to regrow.

Laws, and their enforcement, can reduce harassment of migratory populations, allow their regular movement, and reduce the energy drains in what is typically a very costly activity for migrating populations.

Supplying water in periods of drought can reduce movement tendencies. During such moves, mortality is typically very great.

Mortality and Survival. Mortality and survival are opposite sides of the same managerial coin. Whether mortality or survival is to be increased, held steady, or decreased is a decision dependent on objectives. The general concepts are presented here; how they are applied will determine how a population performs.

Accidents are a conspicuous, but proportionately inconsequential, mortality factor. Control must be studied and made cause- and species-specific. Manipulation may include reducing highway speeds by signs and "bumps" near wildlife crossings, fencing, closing roads, preventing towers and lines from being erected in bird flight paths, and removing cover along roadways.

The most conspicuous mortality factor is predation. Predation can be controlled by poisons, chemosterilants (see Linhart and Enders 1964, Balser 1964), traps, fencing and improved prey protection, shooting, scare devices, and removal of prey.

Bounties are a much discussed technique of predator control. The bounty system is designed to provide incentives for the public to kill predators. It is an ineffective technique, however, for a number of reasons:

1. The millions of dollars that have been paid have not had the desired effect and could have been better used elsewhere.

2. Fraud is rampant. Chicken heads are substituted for hawks, foot pads are substituted for noses, and different parts of the same animal are submitted for multiple bounties in areas where the laws differ (for example, ears to one county, tail to another). Bounty payers may also cheat the system by reselling pelts and fur, keeping inaccurate counts, or granting overliberal rewards.

3. Rather than increasing predator kills, bounties are frequently paid to opportunists who redirect their existing activities, for example, road kills (foxes) and train kills (wolves) are submitted for bounty, and trappers turn in parts of their normal take for additional income.

4. Evidence (for example, hides) for bounty payment is brought to bounty areas from adjacent areas in which the bounty is not paid.

5. Rarely does the amount offered for a bounty pay the costs of taking the predator; thus, the interest in bounty hunting, which may be high at first, rapidly wanes.

6. Hunting is stimulated in areas of the greatest density of animals—that is, where hunting is easiest and not necessarily where damage is being done. The objective is shifted from reducing damage to increasing income.

7. When bounties are high, the bounty hunter syndrome is created. The bounty hunter becomes a population manager, manipulating the predator population to sustain an income from bounties, for example, by releasing all females, or by going on vacation during the breeding season.

8. Bounties may encourage removal of animals that can provide benefits associated with other methods of removal (for example, hunting and regular trapping).

9. Bounties may discourage or negate other approaches that might preserve the animals, for example, through re-evaluation of the net benefits of the predator.

10. Where bounties are paid, the number of predators taken per year stabilizes, indicating that the predator population is still present and productive.

11. Population reductions tend to increase birth rates; bounties can effectively increase a problem in some species and areas.

12. A compensation principle operates in that as bounty hunters become more successful in their techniques, the density of predators declines. Thus, to stabilize or increase their income they must work harder, use more traps, travel farther, and, in general, pay more. They stop at the profit margin. Many reproducing predators remain in the wild at the bounty hunter's margin.

Gustavson et al. (1974) and Garcia et al. (1974) have employed bait shyness as a coyote control technique. After coyotes consume several meals of minced lamb flesh, skin, and wool infused with lithium chloride (a nonlethal poison) and then experience lithium illness, they refuse to attack lambs. They are even reported to have run away from lambs and retched. Recently, tethered lambs wearing collars with lithium crystals have been used near flocks. Although the results are inconclusive, after the coyotes attacked the lambs the same repulsion occurred. The technique is called *aversive conditioning*.

Unfortunately, predator control is usually synonymous with killing carnivores. The future emphasis must be on the design and continuous effective operation of a damage control system. The entire complex predator-prey system must be studied and manipulated at each of its parts. A harmonious, cost-effective, managed system can be created with enough feedbacks to show why what was effective control last year might not work this year. An optimum mix of evaluation, improved husbandry, and wildlife population manipulation can be achieved. Emphasis is needed on *individual* animals that are offenders and *localized* control programs. Where rewards are offered, they should be designed as system controls (for example, $100 for a pregnant female, nothing for males). No more penny-ante predator control research studies should be done—that is, studies on limited areas, with no control areas, variable techniques, inadequate hypotheses and incomplete ecosystem analysis. The results can only be inconclusive. The needs are for large, well-designed regional and national long-term studies. Until these can be carried out, management programs must be guided by the best large computer simulations that can be devised.

Predator control as now generally practiced (or allowed) by wildlife agencies is hardly the action of a sophisticated cadre of managers operating from a base of knowledge or respected theory. Predator populations have rarely been considered game, and therefore their control has been relegated to other agencies. The federal government has passed the issue from agency to agency. It has funded programs in some years, cut them drastically in others. Agencies have paid bounties and supplied control agents irregularly. Universities, with few exceptions, spend little more than a few lectures or seminars on predator control. There are opportunities for leadership in predator management at all levels.

Since predators are a type of faunal pest, the manager will typically want the population to decrease. But it is *damage,* not necessarily pests, that must decrease. It may be that by reducing the number of pests, damage will also be decreased. There are many other ways to reduce damage, however, than by increasing mortality. Most of these have been sketched as they apply to predators and discussed in detail for wildlife in general. An optimum mix of techniques is required. The mix can be judged on the basis of the objective stated in terms of damage reduction (not merely injury) per dollar spent plus the other social and ecological costs.

There are many techniques for reducing damage. Aircraft warning systems may divert or delay aircraft until flocks have moved from flight paths. Although these systems may not modify bird or animal behavior, they can reduce hazards and damage. Animals may be captured and either killed or relocated. If the animal cannot be removed, then the crop or item of value can be removed from the animal by changing the crop, fencing, netting (for example, protection of berry crops from birds), and repellents. Finally, chemicals can be used. There are stupefying substances (for example, alphachloralose) and other substances that cause bizarre behavior in animals that feed on it. Such behavior then repels other animals from the crop. Reproductive inhibitors (such as ornitrol and avitrol) have been used to reduce natality.

In the urban environment, major pest control can be achieved by reducing pest food supplies (for example, removing pet feces, litter, and garbage, and improving solid waste disposal) and by fencing or exclusion (for example, keeping bats out of attics). Architectural design can reduce nesting places and roosts. Where roosting places are essential they can be designed to be self-cleaning and located where droppings will not be unpleasant or create health hazards to city dwellers. When songbirds become disease carriers, they, like other wildlife, must be controlled, no matter how unpleasant the task may be. Rather than wait for a crisis situation, with its characteristic high costs, threats to human life, and precipitous, often suboptimal, action, the wildlife manager would be well advised to pursue a continuing, low-cost program of prevention.

Parasites and disease should be diligently studied to determine control methodologies. The journal *Wildlife Diseases* and the *Bulletin of Wildlife Diseases* both tend to be analytical, diagnostic, and rarely prescriptive. (See Anderson 1971, Davis et al. 1970, 1971). Disease and parasite control can be achieved by:

1. Reducing introductions of disease vectors and new animals as potential carriers.
2. Maintaining high energy and nutrient supplies in the habitat.
3. Reducing and dispersing feeding and watering areas.
4. Preventing high densities, contacts, or both.
5. Reducing vectors or intermediate hosts (for example, certain molluscs are intermediate hosts of lungworms).
6. Managing habitats for host and vector alike.
7. Monitoring disease.
8. Using oral vaccines.
9. Preventing human contacts.
10. Educating citizens in relevant areas to reduce human hazards and contacts.

Certain disease control measures may have the opposite results of those intended. Knowledge of the ecology of disease is imperative. For example, fox population reductions to prevent rabies outbreaks may allow vacancies in habitat and thus encourage immigration of infected animals into areas from which they were once excluded by defensive occupants.

Wildlife is a carrier of and a major factor in a host of diseases transmissible to humans. These include plague, rabies, tularemia, psittacosis or ornithosis, spotted fever, trichinosis, anthrax, brucellosis, and tuberculosis. There are many transferable parasites. Overzealous advocates of urban wildlife may find themselves in the midst of conflict if their wildlife successes bring with them human disease and death. To achieve a safe balance is difficult, but very important.

Wildlife managers and others have found that disease is usually not the *cause* of population declines, but a symptom of a more serious malady. It is easy to blame the deaths of many deer on a pathogen. It is far less easy, but more correct, to inform the public that the deer died *with* a pathogen but *from* a deteriorating food supply. The reduction was brought on by plant succession; even if the food supply had remained constant, the increasing population would have had less food per capita. The interactions inevitably have the same results—starved or stressed animals. Stressed animals have lower disease resistance. Disease runs rampant and may be judged the terminal cause of death. Such causes are almost irrelevant; what is important is the ecology of disease. To reduce mortality from disease in a system that will tolerate only a limited number of organisms, other forms of mortality must be substituted. The question of *appropriate mortality* is a question of human objectives and their associates, ethics and morality, neither of which is typically a question of science.

The disease rule, that pathogens are initially a function of animal stress and not the cause of it, has an apparent exception, which is that under certain combinations of ecological events parasite populations can explode (for example, ticks). Even the most healthy animals cannot survive such attacks. This condition is not really an exception to the rule, however; it is simply that the rule has been incompletely stated. A general biological principle is that pathogens that do not destroy their hosts have the greatest evolutionary success. An animal population may have evolved in symbiosis with an organic pathogen, which comes to serve as normal a function in its long-term survival as a spleen. Only since the advent of the agricultural age in human history has the pathogen been identified as something "bad." Therefore, the rule should be: The response of animal populations with average or less than average parasite and pathogen populations to those parasite and pathogen populations is more related to the quality of the total environment than to the parasites or pathogens themselves.

Although the evidence is, as yet, fragmentary, it appears that foxes and rabies are such an evolutionary ecological entity. Rabies is essential for the survival of the fox population. When fox populations become very dense, crowding occurs and animals are stressed. Resistance to the rabies pathogen, which is always present (like the common cold among humans), is lowered. Symptomatic rabies is manifested. Animals die; densities are reduced; the population lives on. Rabies is a desirable population feedback mechanism; it is a density-dependent survival force. The presence of humans changes the picture, for some rabid foxes, affected by the neurological disease, may lose all normal fears and attack humans and cattle. This situation is intolerable for humans, and thus rabies and its typical vector, the fox, must be controlled.

The wildlife manager, aware of the ecological complexities, can keep fox population densities at a subrabies level (by the various means indicated in this chapter), maintain the role of the fox in ecosystems, and preserve foxes for game and other reasons. Failing this, the manager can still predict when rabies outbreaks are likely to occur and see to it that appropriate immunization, advisory, and treatment services are available.

Hunting is a major cause of mortality in some populations, but very few populations are hunted enough to remove their annual production, an act which, in general, would stabilize a population. Because such removal is not achieved, most populations tend to increase, even when hunted. Populations of quail can increase by about 7 times in one year; rabbits, 12 times; and deer, 0.5 times. Thus, populations can easily become large enough either to cause direct monetary problems (for example, crop, forest, and range losses) or to impair their own habitat and perpetuate the erratic peaks and crashes of unmanaged wild populations.

Hunting is intrinsically neither good nor bad. It is many things to many people. Some populations can be managed with it, some cannot. For some populations, there is almost no other means of effective control. For some species, hunting is a surrogate form of predation. Humans replace the predators they have removed. We cannot effectively restore wolves nationwide, for obvious reasons. For other species, hunting is one means by which resources are used and benefits gained by some people. The managerial role relative to hunting is (1) to assure appropriate use of resources—in amount, time, location, distribution, means of use, and benefits experienced, and (2) to minimize costs, disproducts, displeasure, and safety hazards to segments of the public.

Hunting may be a cost-effective managerial approach to population manipulation. That does not make it appropriate for all citizens, all species, or all areas. The manager must study and articulate the opportunities, costs, and disproducts of hunting as well as those of not hunting. In most societies today a general goal exists of achieving maximum net returns from resources. Whether hunting maximizes returns or not is a decision that must be made in every situation. The manager may well improve the period of hunting and overcome major objections to it by stressing concern for young animals. The manager may seek only licensed hunters who can shoot well, have tested eyesight, and are able to prevent waste of the kill. Regulations may be sought that will allow hunting in some areas and not in others. The more specific the management, the greater are the managerial costs, but the more likely it is, too, that complaints and real displeasure will abate in large segments of the public. Maximizing benefits from the wildlife resource to society is the quest of the public wildlife manager. The articulation of full costs and full benefits for all segments of society will provide, increasingly, more enlightened and rational decision making about hunting throughout the society.

To regulate hunting, it is necessary to regulate the number of hunters. This can be done by:

1. Issuing permits, thus allowing only a fixed number of people to hunt. To harvest 260 animals where 10-percent hunting success is typical, issue 2600 permits (that is, $2600/0.10 = 2600$).

2. Allowing hunting only in certain areas. This limits hunters to the number of people willing to travel and to contend with the hunter densities and hazards of such hunting.

3. Setting license fees so as to increase or decrease the number of hunters. Studies of surrounding area fees or even market analyses can be performed to determine at what point hunters stop buying licenses.

4. Informing hunters about prospects and openly encouraging or discouraging hunters in general or in some particular period or area. Reports of success tend to increase hunters; low previous harvests discourage hunters.

5. Allowing only certain people to hunt—for example, only residents, only

those with certain schooling or demonstrated abilities, past success (or lack of success), age, sex, or accompaniment (for example, father-son hunts).

Hunting can also be regulated by regulating the weapons used. Each weapon has a measure of effectiveness. By observing the ratio of the animals harvested by weapon type X to the total hunter hours spent with weapon type X, the effectiveness can be measured. Effectiveness of weapon can be used interactively with the number of hunters so that q permits can be given to hunters with rifles, r permits to those with shotguns, s permits to those with bows and arrows, or t to those with smooth-bore weapons.

In focusing on mortality, it is easy to lose sight of the benefits being sought from the resource. If these are defined as hunter-hours, it may be appropriate for the manager to maximize the hunter-hours spent by emphasizing, or only issuing permits to, those with relatively ineffective weapons, so that more time will be spent per animal harvested. Other factors that must be considered include maintaining acceptable hunting success ratios by various groups, maintaining the desired harvest, and maintaining a diverse hunter clientele. In fishing, as in hunting, the emphasis is rarely on the fish, or the kill, but upon the many recreational, ritual, esthetic, and escape dimensions of the so-called fishing trip. See Table 3-2.

In addition to regulating the weapons used, other techniques can be employed to increase or decrease the harvest. These include regulating caliber or muzzle velocity; archery bow "pull" as well as arrow style, weight, and cast; types of bullet or pellets, by size and weight; the number of shots (or shells) that may be used per day or per trip. In the future, limits on hunters or increased opportunities on otherwise unavailable areas may even be obtained by specifying the use of primitive weapons like spears, slingshots, and snares and deadfalls.

How hunting is conducted may enhance or reduce the kill. The relative effectiveness of various approaches has not been quantified, but could readily be (as for weapon effectiveness) by hunter questionnaires and at checking stations. The objective is to be able to specify very precisely the kill in a season if a particular hunting strategy is used. The decision maker must choose, often a year in advance, what the strategy will be—that is, what complex set of time, permits, weapons, and other factors will be in effect to harvest exactly Z animals and produce W quality-weighted person-hours of hunting. The decision maker needs to be able to predict hunting success, not for the individual, but for the total population. The conduct of the hunt can be regulated in categories of drives, stalks, blinds, towers and shooting platforms, safety clothing and camouflage, use of calls or attractants, use of baits, and use of dogs, horses, or vehicles.

Time of day for hunting should be adjusted to the behavior of the animal. To kill more animals, the time should be set to maximize the take when animals are

TABLE **3-2**

Benefits from hunting and fishing activities. The actual kill is only one benefit and it is weighted low in most studies.

1. Enjoying natural surroundings.
2. Learning about nature.
3. Improving general health.
4. Obtaining recreation and rest.
5. Obtaining exercise.
6. Enjoying companionship with friends.
7. Enjoying companionship with family.
8. Experiencing environmental challenge (risk taking).
9. Experiencing hunting and fishing challenge.
10. Experiencing pioneering challenges and skills.
11. Escaping from daily routine (achieving diversity).
12. Finding solitude.
13. Enjoying camping.
14. Obtaining prestige from hunting or fishing trip.
15. Obtaining prestige from killing an animal or taking a limit or trophy.
16. Killing an animal or taking a limit or trophy.
17. Obtaining food.
18. Enjoying working with hunting dogs.
19. Collecting and using equipment.
20. Building character.
21. Providing business favors and trade incentives.
22. Teaching others hunting and fishing skills.
23. Exploring new territory.

moving or not wary. To take fewer animals, hunting should be allowed only when animals are resting, denned, or very wary. Time of hunting should also be adjusted to hunters' habits. To harvest less game, weekends and major holidays should be excluded; to take more, these periods would be included.

The problem of setting length of season and starting dates is extremely complex and beyond the scope of this book. The general need is to analyze the objectives of hunters (about 5 to 15 objectives), weight them, determine graphs or equations expressing the general ecological trends in the system that produce each, sum the curves to get the weighted potential for each day to achieve the hunters' and society's objectives, then select opening and closing dates that maximize 90 to 100 percent of the objectives, subject to whatever legal constraints there are. Giles and Lee (1975) have described a general methodology.

The opening day phenomenon is shown in Figure 3-4. This is largely a sociological phenomenon but somewhat related to removal rates. The more

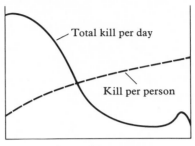

FIGURE **3-4**

Schematic diagram of general hunting
season phenomena. The addition of
extra days to most seasons does not
appreciably increase the total kill.

game that is removed, the lower is the probability of harvesting game later. The
logic is clear, the results not so clear. Harvest per person increases through the
season over broad areas. In select areas, harvests within a season may decline
due to the phenomenon of marginal returns. As shown in many studies, where
there is good cover small game populations cannot be overharvested by normal
shooting. When the population has been reduced to a low level, hunters cannot
see the game or will not hunt long enough to make further inroads on the
population. The natural productivity of small game is such that they can restore
their numbers to the pre-hunt density by the following hunting season.

In some areas, a special use of the opening day phenomenon has been made to
increase harvests. The season is opened, then closed, and then opened again
several days (about 10) later. The opening day phenomenon is thus repeated (see
Figure 3-5).

In some areas, species such as bear and coyotes, because they are listed as pest,
predator, *and* game, have been recommended for year-round seasons. It is likely
that such a decision would result in reduced total harvest because the opening
day phenomenon would be removed. Seasons have a way of increasing the value
of a resource, for it is then no longer common property; it has become regulated
and of only limited availability. Seasons thus influence the supply and demand
relationship.

Hunting mortality can be regulated by limits on daily take, season limits,
possession limits (for example, in the freezer) and even lifetime limits (for
example, certain bighorn sheep). Mortality can be regulated by limiting hunters
to only one species rather than allowing them to "shoot anything that moves."
Hunts can be specific for age, size, sex, antlers, or other physical characteristics.

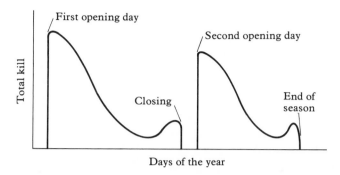

FIGURE **3-5**

By closing the season during a year and then reopening it, the opening day phenomenon can be used to increase harvests. Extending the season only has the result shown in Figure 3-4.

The hunter's behavior can be regulated by the presence of wildlife law enforcement personnel. In fact, such regulation seems to be essential. The hunter's actions can be guided—either encouraged or prohibited—by education, signs, markers, maps, and aids. A feeling of confidence about one's location seems to encourage hunting as well as the perceived quality of the hunt. Weapon sighting-in grounds can improve hunter confidence, increase kills, and reduce crippling loss. Firing lanes free of cover and other means can be used to increase the probability of game being in the hunter's vicinity. Of course, the opposite (for example, vegetative obstructions, pathways away from prime habitat) is possible, where the objective is to allow hunting but to reduce harvests.

A peculiar psychological phenomenon is said to operate among hunters. Unsuccessful hunters in an area evidently managed for game may conclude that the managers are doing what they can and that they themselves are just unlucky. They may have a pleasant experience without a harvest and still praise managerial efforts. The same hunters in an area of no evident management and having no success, may blame their lack of success on the manager. The two game populations may be of equal density, and the difference in the perceived hunter success and the quality of the experience may be determined by the conspicuousness of the management itself. At the population level, harvest, by definition, is essential to hunting. For the individual, successful hunting does not require a harvest, since many other benefits may be derived from the experience. Hunting harvest is the only cost-effective means of necessary removal of some species in a world modified by humans. Failure to allow hunting removal of these species (1) reduces recreational and hunting-related opportunities for a segment of the population and (2) increases costs to all segments of society to achieve the animal removal by alternate means.

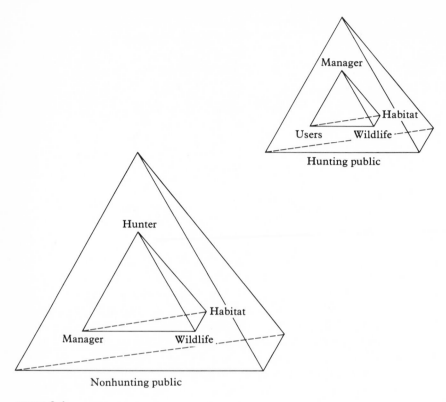

FIGURE 3-6

A diagram of the hunting subsystem. In the past, emphasis in analysis and design has been placed on the hunted game population. A total system must be dealt with and efforts made to balance allocations of time, research, and labor. Similar subsystems exist (see background).

Managerial precision is most needed in hunting regulations when monogamous species are being hunted, when animals are in an isolated area, when concentrations may occur (as on winter range), when animals have a high trophy value or endangered status, and when they have low natality.

Unfortunately, there have been few regional or national studies of harvest regulations. These are necessary if the wildlife manager is to develop a predictive theory of harvest. Each state, working independently, and changing some regulations each year, creates a situation of a unique event each year. There are, thus, no replications, no tests of whether, if a particular complex strategy were duplicated next year, harvest would be the same. A predictive theory is possible, but it will require regional or national cooperation, a common statistical data base, and more attention to hunters, time spent, area hunted, weapons used, and expressed success, than heretofore evident. Knowledge of the animal population

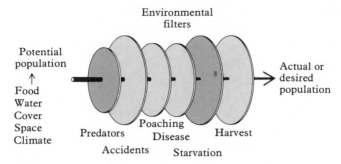

Potential population
↑
Food
Water
Cover
Space
Climate

Environmental filters

Predators
Accidents
Poaching
Disease
Starvation
Harvest

Actual or desired population

FIGURE 3-7

Population mortality factors can be conceived as environmental filters. Population components (sex, age, weight, appearance) are differentially affected by these filters.

is only a fourth of the manager, hunter, habitat, and hunted interaction. This system exists within the context of the nonhunting public (see Figure 3-6) and all parts of it are influenced by this context.

Mortality factors can be seen as population filters (Figure 3-7). By manipulating those filters, a desired result can be achieved. By manipulating the population itself, *density-dependent* mortality factors, as stated previously, can be regulated. *Density-proportional* mortality factors are related. If a constant percentage or proportion of a population is removed, the means is said to be density-proportional. Even though the total kill may vary, the proportion is constant. A 10-percent kill of 1000 animals results in a higher kill than the same factor operating among 750 animals. The kill is higher, the proportion the same. Even though a population may increase over time, a particular mortality factor may stay constant. Hunting permits and highway kills (a strip-removal) are examples of density-proportional mortality. Predation is density-proportional over a range, but best analyzed as density-dependent.

Density-independent mortality is that which has no relation to densities, such as mortality resulting from range fires and floods. The mortality *rate* (not the total kill) does not vary with population density, only with the severity of the factor. Most pollutants may be considered density-independent, but it has been demonstrated in humans that crowding increases respiratory diseases. It seems likely that the three categories are not as neat as once believed and that the responsible manager will analyze each mortality factor in the detail feasible and build the results into complex and interactive computer models of the population. The categories work well for teaching the initial phase of comprehension of what is involved in population manipulation, but the specific solutions now only seem feasible with assistance from computer models.

Manipulating Relations Among Population Factors

There are few direct ways to manipulate relations among the factors affecting populations. Populations that are cyclic are going to cycle whether hunted or not. The manager can sustain hunting opportunity by preventing seasons from being closed by well-intentioned laymen. The harvest in the trough years of the cycle will be low. The concept of marginal returns will reduce hunters and leave a residual population. All known cyclic game species are small game and thus cannot be overharvested by normal hunting means in dense cover. Public pressure has been notorious for closing seasons on cyclic species in bad years; this is a waste of recreational opportunity for those who like to hunt and also understand that success may be very low. Education with responsible season setting can reduce hunters' displeasure while allowing conditional use of the resource.

Stress, already discussed under density and disease, can be regulated by the means used to control those factors, as well as by manipulating habitat to reduce contacts.

Behavioral responses can be modified by such techniques as removing antlers and horns, using hormones, dyeing display hair and feathers, and using stupefying drugs. These techniques are not suitable for widespread use, however.

The wildlife manager works against heavy odds in attempting to manipulate populations. Some say those who are successful have mastered the art of wildlife management. Increasingly, however, a *science* of population manipulation will emerge as more knowledge is gained, interactions are better understood, improved decision aids are developed (for example, computer simulators), and more sensitive controls over chosen practices are applied *during* their implementation (for example, in some states hunting seasons can be stopped when the desired harvest is achieved).

There is a large arsenal of population manipulation techniques. Whether they will be used or not depends on many factors. Some wildlifers may claim that the techniques listed are not practical. There is no reply except to ask: Practical compared with what? Each situation is unique in respect to citizen emotion, wildlifer's knowledge, apparent funds available, actual funds available, skilled labor, and, of course, the natural dynamics or ability of animal species and habitat to respond to management acts. A positive attitude focused on objectives, not on limitations or past failures, will enable singificant improvements to be made in population manipulation.

Farmers, industrialists, and others who operate large systems to achieve objectives know there are no sure things. Risks are high. The wildlife manager plays a gigantic formal game against nature. Many of the moves of nature are known; more can be discovered. There are some apparently random moves that nature and society will play. By studying these with the aid of computers and game theory (Luce and Raiffa 1957), modern wildlife managers will surely improve their D scores and, though not win every year, substantially increase their wins over the long run.

Study Questions

1. Why should wildlife populations not be allowed, as a rule, to fluctuate naturally? Under what circumstances should they be allowed to do so?

2. Is population stability a universally desired condition? Why has it been emphasized?

3. Graph an objective of a 5-percent increase, plot various populations achieved around this objective for at least 5 years and compute a D score.

4. Why should a squared deviation be used in computing D? Why not a cube relationship? Why not an absolute value?

5. Why is a base-year approach to objective setting likely to be suboptimal?

6. What are the three major categories over which the population manipulator has control?

7. How can the number of species in an area be changed?

8. What is an ecoectomy?

9. How can density be changed?

10. How can sex ratios be changed?

11. Compute a table similar to Table 3-1, using hypothetical data or data from a publication.

12. How can natality be manipulated?

13. How can migration be changed? How can human-caused barriers to migration be reduced?

14. Dividing up the work with classmates, review the relevant literature on predation and develop an annotated bibliography. Exchange notes and discuss them. Continue to engage in such team exchanges after school.

15. Animal control measures (for example, trapping) are said to have driven some animals out of an area. Can you find any evidence of predators having come into adjacent areas following such an exodus? Discuss.

16. Snakes have been hunted avidly for years. How do you explain their survival in the face of such removal pressures?

17. What are the limitations of bounty systems?

18. What is aversive conditioning?

19. How can wildlife accidents be reduced? Should they be? What amount of limited budgets should be spent on control of accidents?

20. How can wildlife diseases be controlled?
21. What are the general relationships between disease and habitat quality?
22. What is the opening day phenomenon?
23. Do a survey in your class and on campus (if possible compare results with past studies) of the proportion of actual hunters, those willing to hunt, those not willing to hunt but willing to let others hunt, and anti-hunters.
24. How can the number of hunters be regulated? The time they spend? Their effectiveness in harvesting animals? The animals taken?
25. How can crippling loss be reduced?

Selected References

Balser, D. S. 1964. Management of predator populations with antifertility agents. *J. Wildlife Management* 28(2):352–358.

Davis, J. W. and R. C. Anderson (eds.). 1971. *Parasitic diseases of wild mammals.* Iowa State University Press, Ames. x + 364 p.

Davis, J. W., R. C. Anderson, L. Karstad, and D. O. Trainer. 1971. *Infections and parasitic diseases of wild birds.* Iowa State University Press, Ames. ix + 344 p.

Davis, J. W., L. H. Karstad, and D. O. Trainer (eds.). 1970. *Infectious diseases of wild mammals.* Iowa State University press, Ames. xi + 421 p.

Garcia, J., W. G. Hankins, and K. W. Rusiniak. 1974. Behavioral regulation of the milieu interne in man and rat. *Science* 185:824–831.

Giles, R. H., Jr. and J. M. Lee, Jr. 1975. When to hunt Eastern gray squirrels. In *Forest resource management: decision-making principles and cases* (Vol. 2, Chapt. 49), ed. W. A. Duerr, D. E. Teeguarden, S. Guttenberg, and N. B. Christiansen. O. S. U. Book Stores, Corvallis, OR.

Gustavson, C. R., J. Garcia, W. G. Hankins, and K. W. Rusiniak. 1974. Coyote predation control by aversive conditioning. *Science* 184:581–583.

Leopold, A. 1933. *Game management.* Charles Scribner's Sons, New York. 481 p.

Linhart, S. B. and R. K. Enders. 1964. Some effects of diethylstilbestrol on reproduction in captive red foxes. *J. Wildlife Management* 28(2):358–363.

Luce, R. D. and H. Raiffa. 1957. *Games and decisions: introduction and critical survey.* John Wiley and Sons, New York. 509 p.

Ricker, W. E. 1958. *Handbook of computations for biological statistics of fish populations.* Fisheries Research Board of Canada, Bul. 119, Queen's Printer and Controller of Stationery, Ottawa. 300 p.

Chapter 4

Habitat Analysis and Design

A habitat, or environment that supports an animal population, includes space, food, cover, and even the presence of other animals. To *evaluate* a habitat is to go beyond analysis to the comparison of that habitat with some standard or objective. "How good is this habitat?" can only be answered by "compared with what?" or "for what?" To say that a deer range is overbrowsed implies that there exists a standard of properly browsed or underbrowsed. To say that a range is understocked means that densities are lower than some criterion, or basis for deciding. Analysis is an effort to describe a system in the most objective way possible. Evaluation is analysis plus the act of valuation. Analysis results in *observations* of a system, its structure, dynamics, and relations. Evaluation results in *conclusions* about a system's relative state or performance. There is, of course, no purely objective analysis, for in the act of specifying the subsystem for study (the plot, the community, or the ecosystem) the analyst implies some concept of relevance, importance, or purpose to which the analysis may later be put.

Habitat may be either micro or macro (see Figure 1-3). Habitat analyses have typically been micro-analyses, but both tools and needs have changed and more macro-analyses are needed. A wildlifer can spend a lifetime analyzing a particular habitat and manipulating hundreds of acres of land. In a year, all of that work can be destroyed by a dam, a highway, or a nuclear power plant.

The wildlifer must keep both macro- and micro-perspectives. Some wildlifers will emphasize one or the other; some will achieve both; some will work in teams to achieve both.

To be able to describe, explain, or predict what any system will do is to understand that system. To understand it is to be able to control it to achieve objectives.

Space

Wildlife needs space. Space is an essential component of the resource tetrahedron of space, time, diversity, and energy (Figure 2-1). Space is multidimensional; it includes latitude, longitude, altitude, points, zones, layers, and edges. These are the primary analytical elements of habitat.

The search for areas to support wildlife has led to the creation of wildlife *refuges,* where some degree of management and protection is provided for wildlife. On such areas, protection can be lifted for periods such as for hunting or observation. Originally conceived as sources of excess populations that would "spill out" onto adjacent areas, refuges are no longer seen to serve this purpose, except for highly mobile animals such as waterfowl. Newer knowledge of the limited territory of most animals, and their specific habitat needs, has replaced the older hypothesis. The species for which refuges might appropriately be considered are those with high cruising radius (annual and daily), high tolerance to crowding, noncyclic population, high productivity (capability to withstand a high annual harvest), and ability to escape overharvesting.

Refuges may mean explicitly those areas owned by the U.S. Wildlife Refuge System, a division of the Department of Interior, Fish and Wildlife Service. These areas are extremely diverse in size and function. There are at least five major types of refuges. A single tract of land may contain several of the following: (1) production, (2) wintering, (3) migration or resting, (4) depredation (Lee Act), and (5) big game ranges.

The U.S. Wildlife Refuge System is the most underdeveloped public wildlife resource in the nation. With about 30 million acres, it is virtually unknown to the public. It is an administrative no-man's land—a prime example of how failure to consolidate a system and to provide consistent leadership can prevent a system from achieving its potential. Without sufficient legislative support or resources for management, it has been consistently mismanaged (as judged by numerous criteria, including ecological change, erosion, and range misuse). Except for the Bear River and Tule Refuges and portions of other refuges designated as wilderness areas, refuges have no congressional protection. Disposal of a wildlife refuge may be prevented only by a public outcry. The Fish and Wildlife Service has tended to treat the refuges as unwanted responsibilities rather than building them into a land management agency fully as productive of public benefits as the National Forests and National Parks. It will take leadership, modern managers, an objectives-oriented plan, several congressmen who can see the needs, and infusions of funds in a reorganized agency to enable the Refuge System to achieve its full potential (Giles and Scott 1969).

Sanctuaries are areas where total protection to wildlife is afforded. They are a major tool in rare and endangered species management. *Parks* are usually sanctuaries and, although they are dedicated to public or private recreation and education, physical utilization of wildlife resources is prohibited (with the usual exception of fish). *Preserves* typically are areas where resources are intensively managed to provide wildlife for hunting recreation. Shooting preserves are usually privately owned and require highly intensive management of facilities, habitats, game populations, and clients for such enterprises to be successful. They can relieve hunting pressures on public lands and wildlife populations. Typically higher-quality hunting experiences, as judged by the clients, are obtained on preserves than on other lands, and thus preserves are considered worth the costs.

Management areas vary widely in size and purpose. This is an omnibus term and must be clarified in each locale. Typically, these areas are administrative areas in which uniform regulations, fees, or permits apply, or are areas around equipment or management centers. The management area is a valuable concept. Even refuges can be divided into such areas to ease administration, provide improved record keeping, assure uniformity, and, in the final analysis, improve decision making. Designing an optimum area is difficult. If boundaries are suboptimally drawn, they can form the basis of conflict, territorial disputes, duplication, and waste. In the past, rough boundary lines, such as counties and parishes, were sufficient for management purposes. Errors tended to take care of themselves. Increasingly, the *watershed* has been recognized as a very meaningful unit of land management, but the problems of overlapping ownership and jurisdiction within such areas have not been resolved. Watershed authorities, entities that enable old territory to exist but enable new forms for negotiation, arbitration, referenda, and pooling of resources—both monetary and expertise—seem much more likely than in the past.

Dynamic management areas appear to be a viable approach to grouping areas for resource management. Natural resources—both their supply and public demands for them—are dynamic. Changing agricultural practices influence wildlife populations; industrial development and urbanization influence public health. Static regions, those adequate only for the present circumstances, are no longer appropriate. Suboptimization of regions is likely to occur at an increasing rate. The structure of regions must be checked periodically and changed when information shows significant change has occurred in the criteria defining the regions.

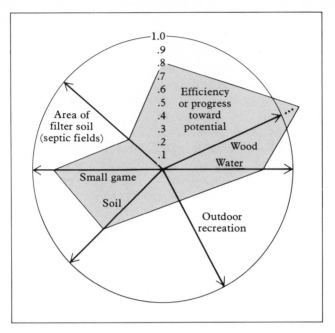

FIGURE **4-1**
Vector diagram for a management area with seven major criteria for
judging system effectiveness. Levels of achievement are marked as
proportions of a set radius.

A simple graphical approach to visualizing the activities on a wildlife management unit is the *vector diagram* shown in Figure 4-1. Each objective or each
resource associated with objectives is represented as a line radiating from the
center of a circle. The radius is scaled in all cases to 100 percent, to some predetermined objective, or to some upper constraint. The levels of achievement
are then plotted as proportions of the maximum. The approach has great
explanatory usefulness. By plotting several years on the same figure in different colors, progress can be readily seen. Excesses can also be plotted. By
using a dot grid or planimeter, the total area in the polygon can be compared
with the area of the circle. The ratio is suggestive of total system achievement,
effectiveness, or health.

The same diagram can be employed for an individual animal (expressing
physiological systems), for a species (expressing niche relations), or for populations. By attaching costs to each vector, rates of change along certain vectors
can be explained or predicted.

Access

The space available for wildlife is like a resource in that it has a *potential* utility. When only the sport recreation objective is assumed, then it can be argued that the only relevant space is huntable areas. Areas may be owned, but if they are not accessible because of legal or behavioral constraints, it is inappropriate to employ them in computing production and yield.

Increasingly, landowners are posting property. There are several reasons for this. The chief reason is simple self-interest. There is little more reason for a farmer to share game with the public than to share peaches, corn, or milk. Another reason is a new awareness of landowner liability. People injured on private land may bring suit against the landowner. No matter what the ruling, the litigation costs are intolerable for the average owner. Other reasons for posting are incidental destruction of property (damaging fences, driving off roads when ground is wet, destroying gates or leaving them open, hunting through crops, shooting farm animals, allowing fires to escape, using outbuildings for firewood, and littering) and the danger of hunters shooting too close to farm buildings. Land closure is easy to understand and to justify. However, wildlife damage to cropland and forests is well known. Hunting can help control such damage. It is difficult to strike the proper balance between the good that hunters can do in regulating populations and reducing damage, and the harm and nuisance that they cause on some areas.

Hunting opportunity can be acquired and retained in the following ways:

1. Purchasing land.
2. Leasing land.
3. Making cooperative arrangements between agency and landowners, including policing.
4. Posting "safety zones."
5. Educating owners as well as users.
6. Regulating hunter diversity by permits to zones.
7. Stepping up enforcement.
8. Holding permit hunts and requiring special licenses.
9. Charging fees for hunting.
10. Requiring all hunters to have liability and property damage insurance.

Studies suggest that over half of those owners who post land will permit hunting if permission is requested before the hunting season. Assisting with posting, maintaining trails, plowing, sponsoring children at conservation youth camps, improving game habitat, and even making fertilizer or seed payments have all been suggested. Assisting with post-season litter cleanup has also been suggested. Trading a landowner a hunting opportunity of a type not present on his land may provide additional hunting options.

Access to wildlife can be increased by means of foot and horse trails, jeep and wagon trails, bridges, fence crossings, aircraft landing strips or heliports, and maintained woods roads. Providing access is initially an expensive technique of wildlife management but certainly no more so than the practices of stocking or artificially feeding animals. Over the long run it may be most economical. Of course, the wildlife benefits must equal or exceed the costs. Secondary benefits are easy to recognize, but these should not be counted to justify acquiring access of marginal value with wildlife funds.

The access trail assumes increasing importance as a tool of wildlife management as it allows managers to keep animals in balance with their environment. It allows animals to be harvested where they are injuring forests and range. It provides increased recreational opportunities; provides opportunities for more intensive wildlife management practices such as seeding and cultivation; and, in itself, provides a new habitat that, if properly maintained, can supply food for wildlife.

Like other good management practices, trails must be planned. They must not violate other priority land use objectives such as wilderness values. They must be constructed for use, be located with objectives firmly fixed, be of possible benefit for secondary uses such as fire, insect, and disease suppression, and be easy to maintain. They must be maintained and protected from abuse in certain seasons and under certain conditions. These requirements mean that the good trail, whether it be for foot, horse, or jeep, must be planned and constructed by engineers, foresters, wildlifers, and land specialists. Wildlife benefits from trails can be enhanced by maps, signs, guide service, and motorized game-kill pickup services.

When access is available, hunters can be encouraged to hunt farther back off the roads by zone permits or differential license costs. Generally the lower preference area is farther from roads, particularly for nonresidents. James et al. (1964) found that in North Carolina roads were just as effective as trails in distributing successful hunting pressure. Their studies provide the data for demonstrating one of the most useful applications of the concept of the "zone of influence."

The *zone of influence* is a general concept that can be applied in many types of analyses. A road can have a zone of influence either in spreading toxic lead or in broadening park rangers' control. The zone on both sides of the road within which hunters or recreationists are active is a function of the road. Lakes have a zone of influence around their edges, whether supporting water animals, providing habitat for amphibians, or generating noise from recreational boats.

A simplistic zone, for example, the area hunted by a large proportion of the hunters, is easily drawn and becomes useful for such purposes as describing harvests, deciding where benefits can be received from investments, and doing stratified sampling for various range studies.

Accessible area, A^*, can be analyzed as:

A^* = Area in zone of influence of roads or trails
— Area in water, trails, facilities, or reservations
— Areas unavailable due to slope, thorns, and so on
— Areas unavailable due to rivers or other boundary conditions.

The proportion of the dividend to the total area provides a useful index for comparison over time or between areas. Access points can be counted and analyzed as the percentage of a total area that each point would open to specific wildlife management purposes. Posting of land against hunter or fisherman access can negate management efforts, for it prevents benefits from being experienced. Educational and other efforts to reduce posting can be planned and priorities set based on the areas involved. Contracts and easements may be needed if opportunities are to be retained for the public to benefit from wildlife management expenditures on, or behind, private lands. Relative opportunity space per unit cost may become a useful criterion for directing management investments. Linear miles of trail or roads have little meaning, as Figure 4-2 illustrates. Computer maps can aid in such analyses.

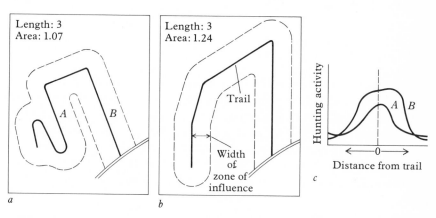

FIGURE **4-2**

Access trails with the same linear measurement, such as those as shown in (*a*) and (*b*), may not have the same spatial influence. Areal analyses are preferable to linear analyses of access. Diagram (*c*) shows a cross section of hunting activity as it is likely to vary with distance from a main artery as in (*a*).

Leasing and Hunting Cooperatives. The increasing pressure being placed on lands for hunting has resulted in a hunter density exceeding the density-tolerance levels of many landowners. As landowners become aware of the decreasing benefits-to-cost ratio of allowing hunting privileges on their lands, more private lands are closed. This situation has spawned a number of *leasing* or *fee-hunting enterprises,* which sell hunting rights for a specific period. The sales price depends on (1) length of the lease, (2) wildlife populations on the area, (3) number of users or leases, (4) convenience of the area to users, and (5) market demand.

Leases and fee-hunting programs can (1) provide monetary income, (2) maintain good public and community relations, (3) enable trading of hunting and fishing opportunities, and (4) reduce bird or animal damage by hunting removals. These are design objectives. There is evidence that typical farmer problems with gates, fences, and trespass are less on leased lands than on nonposted lands. These are reasons, however, why more fee-hunting is not practiced, and these provide insight into improved design of a leased-land system:

1. The tradition of free hunting is difficult to overcome.
2. Property damage and threats to family safety may occur.
3. Visitors require at least some care, supervision, or direction.
4. Violators and "extra" users of permits cause problems.
5. Privacy may be lost.
6. There is a risk of damage suits.
7. The tradition of private property makes many landowners unwilling to share the game on their lands.

Leasing is more economical than purchasing land for wildlife, but complete rights are needed for long-range planning and for species that require habitats in advanced ecological stages. (For example, it is more important to have fee simple ownership for managing wild turkey than for bobwhite quail.)

Land values and the number of marginal farms have increased. While consolidation of farms has occurred, shifting the distribution of farm size in one direction, there has been an increase in land investment and inheritance or estate building.

A minimum acreage is needed for hunting and other wildlife uses. Where existing areas are too small or landowners are unwilling to sell to enable larger tracts to be formed, *cooperatives* are a viable land use. A method of estimating the minimum acreage for a cooperative is shown in Box 4-1.

Box 4-1. How to Estimate the Minimum Acreage Required for a Hunting Cooperative

1. There is a maximum density, D, of deer (or other species) obtained per acre. The value of D should be obtained from the best sources available. A reasonable estimate with appropriate feedback to assure that it is checked and improved may suffice.

2. The land holding is the management unit. The acres in the unit are A. Even though a unit may receive benefits or advantages from adjacent units, these cannot be considered since mutual advantages occur and management decisions must be based on the resource under the control of the manager.

3. The area must sustain a probable harvest, Q, to maintain consumer interest, that is, to stabilize a market. This is desirable for several reasons, including sustaining a fee income or a level of user satisfactions (user-groups) and sustaining population control through hunting.

4. The allowable harvest is a proportion, H, of the total deer population.

5. The probability of hunting success, p, can be established for an area by collecting data at check stations or by interviews. It is the mean probability that one hunter will take a unit of game in some specified period, for example, 10 years.

6. The total herd, P, is the adult deer plus the new reproduction. Where S is proportion of females and R is reproduction per female:

$$P = AD + ADSR.$$

7. Then Q = Probable desired harvest = PH.

8. To approximate the number of acres that would sustain Q, a harvest of, for example, 10 per tract of land, set $Q = 1.0$ and solve for acres, A:

$$Q = PH = (AD + ADSR)H$$
$$A = Q/[H(D + DSR)]$$

Inserting representative values,

$$A = 10/\{0.3[0.02 + (0.02)(0.60)(0.5)]\}$$
$$= 1282 \text{ acres needed per hunter.}$$

The acres needed to sustain Q for hunters, h, with success p, is

$$A^* = Ah/p.$$

Where a clientele of 40 hunters exists and $p = 0.4$, then $A^* = 128,200$.

Gross return to landowners for hunting leases are sufficient in most cases to pay land taxes. The trend in hunting costs indicates that lease rates will go up. The fees charged should be reasonable and should at least cover taxes and costs of area development for wildlife and hunters. A development (such as food plots or road turnoffs) costing $200, amortized at 7 percent over a 10-year duration, would incur annual costs of about $14.50. With fixed annual maintenance of $25, the total annual operation costs will be at least $39.50. These should be met by the fees.

There are problems with wildlife or hunting cooperatives, but cooperatives are needed. They may be the only way to sustain highly productive big game herds (deer, bear, turkey) throughout much of the United States.

Land Purchase. Where leasing is infeasible, wildlife lands can be acquired by purchase with monies from license fees and general funds as well as accumulated donations. The U.S. Congress appropriated money for wildlife land acquisition as early as 1924. After the passage of the Migratory Bird Conservation Act in 1929, funds were appropriated for a refuge system. Later, in 1934, the waterfowl stamp became a requirement for hunting waterfowl, and the revenues, millions of dollars annually, were used to acquire wetlands. The so-called Pittman-Robertson and Dingell-Johnson funds (the Federal Aid to Fish and Wildlife Restoration Act) also provided and still provide substantial funds. Acquiring lands for wildlife production, feeding, and wintering; public hunting; and other wildlife-related recreation is included in the concept of restoration along with natural resource agency coordination, research game stocking, habitat development and maintenance, gaining access, and protecting sensitive habitats and species from disturbance. These funds are derived from an 11-percent manufacturer's excise tax on sporting arms ammunition and fishing tackle. After the federal government deducts up to 8 percent for administrative purposes, the remainder is allocated to the states, where it is available to pay up to 75 percent (3:1 matching) of costs on approved projects.

There are many problems associated with direct land acquisition. It is no wildlife management panacea. Suitable areas available for sale are limited. Funds are restricted. Only 25 percent of the annual Pittman-Robertson allocation can be spent on land acquisition. Land values are increasing. Available funds do not always exist when suitable areas go on the market. Once land is acquired, coordination and planning costs may be high. Maintenance, patrol, boundary marking, and so on are all extras that are part of a decision to buy land. Pursuant expenses may outweigh acquisition costs. An additional impediment to wildlife land acquisition is the reluctance of local governments to lose these lands from their tax rolls.

Keeping a balance of money available for use each year over and above the year's appropriation is financially expedient for the states. However, in reserving funds for uncertain acquisition opportunity (or as a buffer against unexpected expenses) a state risks not being able to obligate all Pittman-Robertson appropriations. Failure to obligate, with consequent reversion of lands, results in a higher proportion of the state's wildlife restoration being paid entirely with state funds or else not carried out at all. Therefore, state wildlife funds do not go as far as they might with federal aid.

No matter what the problems, outright purchase has been found to be a necessary tool for successful restoration and wildlife management in certain situations, particularly for water-related habitats.

The Animal's Environment

As a tree or bush is a part of an animal's environment, so is another animal. Herds and coveys are habitat. As Moen (1973) and others show, other animals may function as windbreaks, as in a herd, and may radiate useful energy. Herding and flocking may reduce exposed body surface and thus energy loss, as when coveys of quail squat in their rings, tail-to-tail. Response to other animals may also entail energy costs. As elements of the environment, animals are predators or prey, mates or challengers, antagonists or family members.

Animals do not distribute themselves randomly or regularly over the land. They usually tend to cluster. Nevertheless, when wildlife managers speak of populations, they speak of densities or animals per unit area. Computations of densities (see Box 4-2), raise a number of realistic questions for the manager. These include: (1) how evenly spaced are my animals, (2) can I reduce the tolerable distance apart to increase a population or increase the distance to reduce my density, (3) can I assure all of an animal's needs are met in each unit (or can I remove the critical element if I desire to reduce the population), and (4) what energy must be supplied to enable the animals to move freely over an area to partake of the life resources there? Similarly, a manager wants to know if the animals will move, how many animals will be influenced by a facility, and how many animals will become potential targets if access is increased.

Animal behavior in space has been interpreted in several ways. Typically, *territory* is defended space. Territoriality is an innate population characteristic, but all animals do not display it. It undoubtedly has survival value, for it reduces aggression (energy loss) over the long run and enables animals some control over the energy resources available to them in the field.

For birds, fish, and mammals, territory is three-dimensional. The extent to which birds will engage an intruder of the same species can be observed and marked on a map, as shown in Figure 4-3a. There is evidence that by moving boundary markers, animals can be made to shift their territories. Managers may wish to design environments with such markers at the corners

Box 4-2. Density and Relations of Animals to Habitats and to Each Other Computed in Terms of Hexagons

Animals' territories and home ranges may overlap. Double counting may occur (a). When territories are treated as tangential, areas may be omitted (shaded portion) (b) and thus undercounted. Regular hexagons or equilateral triangles (c) can be used effectively to compute area, theoretical distance between animals, and defended area.

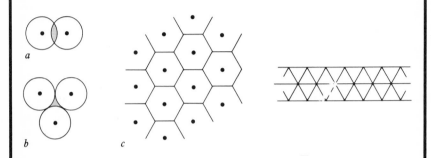

Equations for Regular Triangles and Regular Hexagons

Definitions: S = area; a = length of one side; R = radius of circumscribed circle (the distance to the vertices); r = radius of inscribed circle (the distance to the mid-point of the side). Where n = number of sides, $S = \frac{1}{2}(nar)$.

	Triangle ($n = 3$)	Hexagon ($n = 6$)
S/a^2	0.4330	2.5981
S/R^2	1.2990	2.5981
S/r^2	5.1962	3.4641
R/a	0.5774	1.0000
R/r	2.0000	1.1547
a/R	1.7321	1.0000
a/r	3.4641	1.1547
r/R	0.5000	0.8660
r/a	0.2887	0.8660

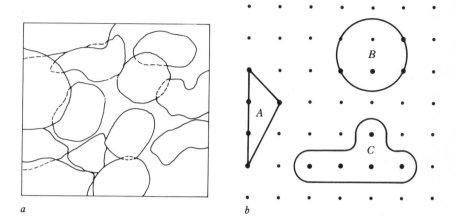

FIGURE **4-3**

Territories of birds and other animals can be plotted (*a*). Home range and cruising radii are variously computed, often from multiple field observations (e.g., live trapping and release) from points on a grid. In (*b*), A shows the minimum area approach, B the encompassing circle approach, and C the half-distance approach. Each set of points represents a different animal. Each small dot is a sample point; each large dot is an observed animal.

of triangles or hexagons constituting species support areas. Rocks, shrubs, and posts contain information. Animal "scenting" or urinating or defecating on prominent spots is thought to be a means by which some animals establish territory. Chasing behavior and displays at the edges are other means.

Home range has intuitive appeal as a phrase, but over the years it has been very difficult to quantify, much less to define satisfactorily. Basically, it is the area in which an animal spends most of its life or the area a wildlife manager might reasonably consider his working area for an average individual of a species. It does not include the migration areas of birds or big game, nor the seasonal junkets of young beaver or muskrats. It includes the territory and some additional areas of foraging and other activities, which will not be defended. It is a behavioral statistic useful in management, for the average home range is indicative of resources available to animals, as well as of animals' needs. How to compute one home range is shown in Figure 4-3. The best method for computing home range can only be decided based on available data and how precise the statistic must be to answer the questions being posed. Some see home range as a function of habitat, others behavior, and others both, with several other concepts (for example, energy balance) operating.

Cruising radius is another term with various meanings in the wildlife literature. Some recognize the extent of an animal's movement as the outer reaches of a circle and halve this distance, the diameter, to express a radius. The elongate ranges of wolves, cougar, and bear make this concept functionless. The distance between the limits of a range seems a clear enough expression, though it could be given a code like λ (lambda) for limits. The cruising radius for rabbits may have more meaning than that for wolves, but its determination is fully as subjective as how to draw the limits on home range (Figure 4-3b). It, too, typically involves fitting a circle within known points of occupancy. The limits of a habitat and the territoriality of adjacent animals influence such measures. They are useful to approximate, for they can be used to determine zones of influence around points and to help judge whether an area has within it all of the seasonal needs of an animal.

Layers and Occupied Space

Maps typically depict two-dimensional strata, or layers. *Cover maps,* or ecological community maps, provide a useful device for analyzing various strata. Boundaries around similar communities are drawn, sometimes directly on aerial photos. A map of each stratum can be developed. Cover maps can be used for a number of purposes:

1. To assess range quality.
2. To form strata for improved sampling schemes, including census route layout.
3. To improve evaluations for purchase.
4. To estimate needs and select sites for habitat manipulation.
5. To improve species-specific management.
6. To predict the future appearance and support potential of an area.
7. To establish a historical base or standard for future comparison.
8. To aid in hunter instruction and other educational work.

Maps of all types are essential for the wildlifer. Increasingly, computer-generated maps are being used. Table 4-1 presents useful conversions not readily available elsewhere.

Contour maps can show three dimensions in two-dimensional space. Animals rarely occupy area; they occupy three-dimensional *space* (one reason why linear statistical models poorly fit wildlife data), though undoubtedly latitudinal and longitudinal dimensions are more important than the altitudinal dimension for most. Birds can be seen to occupy particular layers of forests (see Figure 4-4). Some species have broad layers, others very narrow ones. The oven bird (*Seiurus aurocapillus*), for example, probably occupies a layer no higher than

TABLE 4-1
Map scales and conversions.

Representative fraction	Inches to miles	Miles to inches	Feet to inches	Acres per square inch	Centimeters to kilometers	Kilometers to centimeters	$\dfrac{km^2}{cm^2}$
1:600	105.6	0.0095	50.0	0.0574	166.66	0.006	0.000036
1:1200	52.8	0.0189	100.0	0.2296	83.33	0.012	0.000144
1:2400	26.4	0.0379	200.0	0.918	41.66	0.024	0.000576
1:2500	25.34	0.0394	208.3	0.0067	40.00	0.025	0.000625
1:3600	17.6	0.0568	300.0	2.066	27.77	0.36	0.001296
1:4800	13.2	0.0758	400.0	3.673	20.83	0.48	0.0023
1:6000	10.56	0.0947	500.0	5.739	16.66	0.060	0.0036
1:7200	8.8	0.1136	600.0	8.264	13.88	0.072	0.00518
1:7920	8.0	0.125	660.0	10.0	12.626	0.0792	0.00627
1:10000	6.34	0.1578	833.3	15.92	10.00	0.10	0.01000
1:10560	6.0	0.167	880.0	17.777	9.469	0.1056	0.01115
1:12000	5.28	0.1894	1000.0	22.936	8.33	0.12	0.0144
1:15840	4.0	0.250	1320.0	40.0	6.3131	0.1584	0.02509
1:20000	3.17	0.3156	1666.0	63.688	5.000	0.20	0.04000
1:21120	3.0	0.333	1760.0	71.111	4.735	0.2112	0.0446
1:24000	2.64	0.379	2001.0	91.82	4.166	0.24	0.0576
1:25000	2.53	0.3945	2083.0	99.6	4.00	0.25	0.0625
1:31680	2.0	0.5	2640.0	160.0	3.156	0.3168	0.10036
1:62500	1.01	0.986	5208.0	622.7	1.60	0.625	0.3906
1:63360	1.0	1.0	5280.0	640.0	1.578	0.6336	0.4014
1:100000	0.634	1.578	8333.0	1592.0	1.00	1.00	1.0000
1:125000	0.507	1.972	10416.0	2490.0	0.80	1.25	1.5625
1:126720	0.5	2.0	10560.0	2560.0	0.7891	1.2672	1.6057
1:250000	0.2535	3.944	20832.0	9910.0	0.400	2.50	6.250
1:316800	0.2	5.0	26400.0	16000.0	0.3156	3.168	10.036
1:500000	0.1267	7.891	41666.0	39900.0	0.200	5.00	25.00
1:1000000	0.063	15.783	83333.3	161000.0	0.100	10.00	100.00

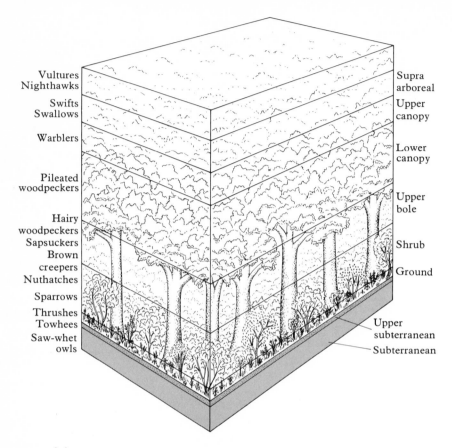

FIGURE **4-4**

Schematic of nine layers of an advanced forest, with the birds that typically inhabit each. Some layers may be lost as a result of fire or practices such as grazing. Rock or soil type may reduce the potential soil layers.

1 meter for 90 percent of the time. Different species of bats fly only in certain, probably insect-specific, layers. Altitude is computed as above-sea-level. While ground level may be 1000 meters, the layer from 999 to 1000.2 meters may be of significance for the marmots, shrews, and microtines. The layer from 1010 to 1020 meters may be specific habitat for treehole-mosquito vectors of a wildlife disease. Each layer can be analyzed as a habitat. Diversity at a point or site (typically specified by latitude and longitude) is a function of the layers present and their associated species. Perhaps increases or decreases in diversity are largely a function of gains or losses in layers. Animal density surely is such a function.

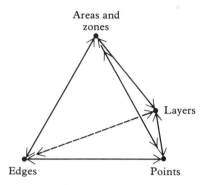

Areas and
zones

Layers

Edges

Points

FIGURE **4-5**
The components of the spatial subsystem
of wildlife habitat.

Edges

Another important component of the spatial subsystem of wildlife habitat, besides area and layers, is edge. See Figure 4-5. Wildlife managers may wish to explain why one area has more wildlife than another. Edge may be a factor for some animals. Basically, *edge* is the boundary where one kind of land use starts and another stops. Because of the complex associations of land use, this boundary is usually not a clear-cut line, but rather a transition zone, or *ecotone,* where plant and animal communities grade into one another. Ecotones have depth but are narrower than the adjoining community areas themselves. Just as each community has binding relationships within itself, so may an ecotone with sufficient depth have binding relationships—even to the point of forming a new community. It is this community of the edge that interests the wildlife manager.

Edge zones frequently have the ability to support larger and more varied wildlife populations than either adjoining community. This phenomenon is called the *edge effect.* Wildlife species have differing habitat requirements, but many of them at some time in their lives will become subject to edge effect. Even within forests, the association of conifers and hardwoods forms an edge that will evidence the phenomenon.

Sportsmen show an intuitive understanding of edge effect when they hunt the field borders rather than the field centers, the brush piles rather than the crop rows, the brush fence row rather than the wire fence, the broken forest rather than the park-like stand, the shrubby coverts near pines rather than pure pine stands, and when they fish near shore, next to the lily pads, and near the logs.

Aldo Leopold (1933:132) noted that game with mobility and requirements for several plant types is "a phenomenon of edges." The animals seek the edges because (1) they have simultaneous access to more than one environmental type, and (2) they have access to a greater richness of desirable border vegetation. Well-developed edge communities may contain organisms characteristic of each of the overlapping communities plus species living only in the ecotone.

The wildlife manager may wish to increase species that are a function of edge effect by developing cultural practices and patterns to maximize edge. Food patches or clearings for wildlife have been planted in forests for years. One major reason for doing so is to create edges. Or, to reduce certain species, for example, pest species, the manager may seek to reduce edge. The measurement of edge is value-free analysis; how good the edge is is a matter of evaluation; whether edge will be increased or decreased is a design decision.

Variety of Edges. The quality of a habitat is roughly proportional to the variety in the composition and arrangement of its component cover types. This is a principle applicable to many forms of wildlife, particularly farm game species having small home ranges. The different types and age classes of plants present where two or more plant communities join provide not only a selection of food and year-around cover, but a continuing supply of food that meets the varied nutritional requirements of the animal. Fruit failure of one or more species of plants at an edge does not affect wildlife as severely as such failure might in a single plant community. Alternate foods, perhaps secondarily preferred, are available. Wildlife food preference varies seasonally. A variety of plant types theoretically provides a year-around food supply because of overlapping periods of productivity of different plants.

Depth of Edges. Edge is a line value, but must be visualized as a condition of depth. Edge is a zone. Research is needed to determine desirable widths or depths for possible application in forest and land management. Deer pellet group counts occur densely in zones near edges. Track counts or occupancy may reveal edge width. Edge begins within the woodlot where the influences of the field stop, and it extends out into the corn field to where soil moisture, root competition, and shade influences no longer are evident. It is the brushy border between field and forest, the grass-shrub complex between fence and field, the emergent growth between field and water that establish small strips of new edge—new communities within themselves.

Length of Edges. A quantitative measure of edge, and the best measure of edge effect, is possible through a study of length—the distances around individual plant communities. Population densities are positively related to the number of feet of edge per unit area of community.

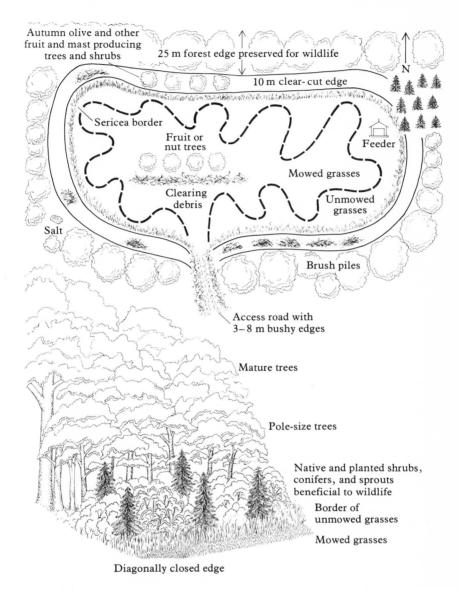

Autumn olive and other fruit and mast producing trees and shrubs

25 m forest edge preserved for wildlife

N

10 m clear-cut edge

Sericea border

Fruit or nut trees

Feeder

Mowed grasses

Clearing debris

Unmowed grasses

Salt

Brush piles

Access road with 3–8 m bushy edges

Mature trees

Pole-size trees

Native and planted shrubs, conifers, and sprouts beneficial to wildlife

Border of unmowed grasses

Mowed grasses

Diagonally closed edge

FIGURE **4-6**

Recommended features of forest wildlife clearing design and edge management.

Small woodland clearings of approximately one acre have long been recommended for their benefit to forest game. See Figures 4-6 and 4-7. The amount of edge provided is a major reason for this recommendation. It is interesting to

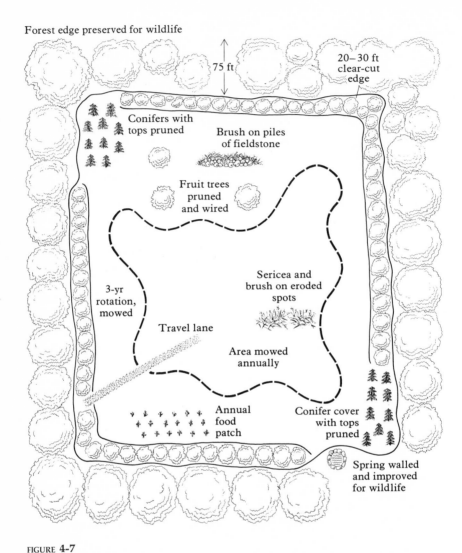

Forest edge preserved for wildlife

75 ft

20–30 ft
clear-cut
edge

Conifers with
tops pruned

Brush on piles
of fieldstone

Fruit trees
pruned
and wired

3-yr
rotation,
mowed

Sericea and
brush on eroded
spots

Travel lane

Area mowed
annually

Annual
food
patch

Conifer cover
with tops
pruned

Spring walled
and improved
for wildlife

FIGURE **4-7**

Old homesites in forest areas can be maintained as wildlife areas. They are much like other
clearings but may require special practices. If clearings are large, travel lanes that provide
animal cover can be extended toward the center. These may be living fences. These also
reduce hunter (or poacher) fields of view.

consider length of edge as related to the shape of such clearings, even as related
to other types of land use. Simple mathematical calculations allow the following
observations: Edge increases as an area is elongated from a circle to a narrow

rectangle; a circular acre has 11 percent less edge than a square acre. The more striplike these wildlife clearings, the greater will be their edge effect. See Box 4-3. Limitations to minimum width are established by tree height, shading, and competition.

Composition of Edges. "Composition" differs from "variety" in that it denotes the plant types and their associations with one another. "Interspersion" is the term frequently used to describe the edge characteristic that is vital to optimum wildlife populations. Though a variety of plants may be available, these plants and plant groups must have an arrangement conducive to wildlife production. Perhaps "corner effect" would better describe the characteristic. Wildlife is most abundant where many types (composed of a variety of plants) come together. Corners where a variety of plant types intersect are valuable to wildlife. The more such corners that can be provided—that can be interspersed throughout the land—the greater will be the wildlife habitat and, as a consequence, the larger will be the wildlife populations. Most game species require three or more environmental types on each unit of habitable range.

True linear values of edge existing as a result of past land use or wildlife management must be obtained from a map or from an aerial photograph. The difficulty involved and the time and costs required to make direct measurements often preclude the use of such values in any large-scale land management effort. Schuerholz (1974) has shown how edge can be estimated from aerial photos. Because of the importance of edge to wildlife, reasonably accurate measures of edge should be readily available to the manager in order to allow discriminating comparisons to be made between units, to reduce measures of variance among units, and to reduce errors of prediction.

Edge effect, then, is the sum of the influences of all the characteristics of edge. The main functional component is composition, with contributing dependent factors of variety, length, and depth.

There remains to be collected what a critical scientist would call proof of edge effect. It is a concept grown into a theorem by usage rather than by more scientific methods. In those situations in which edge effect occurs, no one has, apparently, described the causative theory except as in the preceding general way. What follows here is a hypothesis and it should be recognized as such. It appears, however, to be consistent with a pattern of ecosystem analysis described in this chapter, as well as with the concept of production functions (Chapter 2). It explains why some edges have greater density and more animal diversity than others. It is consistent with the community concept of the ecotone and with the characteristics of edge previously described. It denies a mystical synergism of factors at the edge and employs an additive principle. It includes a dynamic element, explaining why the same edge may not have the same effect in different years.

Box 4-3. Basic Geometric Relations for Wildlife Areas

Circle $A = \text{Area} = \pi r^2$ $(r = \text{radius})$

1 acre $= 43{,}560 \text{ ft}^2$	1 hectare $= 10{,}000 \text{ m}^2$
$43{,}560 \text{ ft}^2 = (3.14)r^2$	$10{,}000 \text{ m}^2 = (3.14)r^2$
$r = \sqrt{43{,}560 \text{ ft}^2/3.14}$	$r = \sqrt{10{,}000/3.14}$
$\quad = \sqrt{13{,}872.6 \text{ ft}^2}$	$\quad = \sqrt{3184.713}$
$\quad \cong 118 \text{ ft (approximate sq rt)}$	$\quad = 56.4 \text{ m}$

$C = \text{Circumference} = 2\pi r \text{ or } \pi \text{diameter}$

$C = (2)(3.14)(118)$	$C = (2)(3.14)(56.433)$
$\quad = 741.04 \text{ ft}$	$\quad = 354.40 \text{ m}$

Square $\text{Area} = (\text{side})^2$

$43{,}560 = (\text{side})^2$	$10{,}000 - (\text{side})^2$
$\text{side} = \sqrt{43{,}560}$	$\text{side} = \sqrt{10{,}000}$
$\quad = 208.71 \text{ ft}$	$\quad = 100 \text{ m}$

Perimeter of a square $= \text{side} \times 4$

Perimeter of one acre $= 208.71 \text{ ft} \times 4$	Perimeter of one hectare $= 100 \text{ m} \times 4$
$\quad = 834.84 \text{ ft}$	$\quad = 400 \text{ m}$

Rectangle $\text{Area} = \text{length} \times \text{width} = A = lw$

The distance around a rectangular-shaped acre would depend on the length of l and w, which are unknown. Edge increases as the rectangle is extended from a square to a line. A useful variable is the length-to-width ratio, z, where

$$l = zw \text{ (e.g., } l = 3w),$$
$$A = zw^2,$$
$$E = \text{Edge} = (2l + 2w) \text{ or } (2zw + 2w).$$

Ellipse $\text{Area} = \pi ab$, where a and b are axes shown in Diagram A. Since these are unknown, circumference cannot be computed. When a and b are known,

$$C = 2\pi \sqrt{\frac{(a^2 + b^2)}{2}}.$$

The same edge relations exist between an ellipse and a rectangle as between a circle and a square. A circular area has the minimum edge possible per unit area, 741 ft for an acre, 354 m for a hectare. An acre ellipse with the short axis, b, less than 163 ft will have an edge less than a square acre, which has an edge of 835 ft. An ellipse with b greater than 163 (or long axis equal to or greater than 340 ft) will have more edge than a square. A rectangular acre with a long axis equal to that of an ellipse will have more edge (Diagram B).

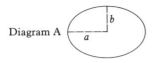

Diagram A

Wildlife areas are often elliptical. Diagram A shows how the major (a) and minor (b) axes are labeled. Diagram B shows how edge increases with change in shape even though the area remains constant.

Diagram B

To find the break point between the edge of an ellipse and a square of equal area, the following may be used. A 1-acre area is used for a demonstration. Since $A = \pi ab$, then $b = A/(\pi a)$ and

$$C = 2\pi \sqrt{\frac{a^2 + [A/(\pi a)]^2}{2}}.$$

The edge of the square acre is 834.8 ft or 835 ft, and the solution is in the values of a and b for an ellipse of this same edge:

$$835 = 2\pi \sqrt{\frac{a^2 + [A/\pi a)]^2}{2}}$$

$$2(17{,}663) = a^2 + [A/(\pi a)]^2.$$

Numbers for a and b must be picked such that the edge will be greater than 2(17,663) or 35,326.

$$A/\pi = 43{,}560/3.14 = 13{,}873,$$

therefore $b = 13{,}873/a$. By trial and error, pick a value for a; divide it into the value of b; then find $a^2 + b^2$, and test to see if it exceeds 35,326.

If a is set equal to 160, then $b = (A/\pi)/a = 13{,}873/160 = 86.7$:

$$a^2 + b^2 = (160)^2 + (86.7)^2 = 33{,}117$$

$$C = 33{,}117 < 35{,}326.$$

Choosing another value, $a = 166$: $C = 35{,}073 < 35{,}326$.

When $a = 167$: $C = 35{,}406 > 35{,}326$.

Therefore, any acre-size ellipse with major axis (a) ≥ 167 ft and a minor axis. (b) $= 86.7$ ft will have a greater edge than a circle or square of the same area.

We can use the identical calculations for a hectare. The edge of a hectare is 400 m. Therefore,

$$400 = 2\pi \sqrt{\frac{a^2 + [A/(\pi a)]^2}{2}}$$

$$2(4053.3) = a^2 + [A/(\pi a)]^2.$$

The critical value is 8107 m; a number for a and b must be picked such that $C \geq$ this value. $A/\pi = 3183.3$ and $b = 3183/a$. When $a = 81$, $C = 8105 \cong 8107$. Thus, $a \cong 81$; $b = 39.3$ m.

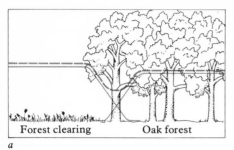

(*a*) Sharp, narrow edges of diverse communities rarely exhibit edge effect; in fact, they have less wildlife than either community.

The dashed line shows the sum of the wildlife population in both communities.

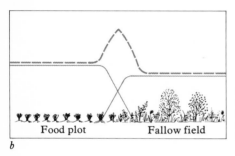

(*b*) The additive effect of two communities is shown in the dashed curve. The community curves show the animal densities specific to the two communities.

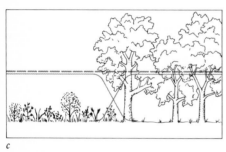

(*c*) As communities change (*a* or *b* could change to the conditions depicted in *c*), edge effect may be lost. Here there is no measurable difference between the edge and the communities.

FIGURE **4-8**

A hypothesis for the causation of edge effect. The sum of the areas under the density or species production curves for the two communities may be greatest (see *b*) at the edge.

The hypothesis is shown in Figure 4-8. It is simply that edge effect is caused by the aggregate population density curves and the species frequency curves for the two communities at the edge. These are production functions. The curves in Figure 4-8 represent wildlife densities; similar curves accommodate the increased number of species associated with edge. Has edge effect occurred when densities are greater but species the same? Vice versa? These questions and Figure 4-8 reflect the lack of precision in the concept. Perhaps edge effect can be discarded (except as convenient for public education) by the wildlifer who can do detailed analyses of points, edges, and communities and employ production functions that describe densities and frequencies of wildlife species. Where species have a different importance to people, these densities and frequencies can be weighted or multiplied by the benefits likely to be provided by an edge. Edge effect can than take on a concept of potential benefit production.

Design of Edges. What is the optimum design for a wildlife clearing or food plot, one that meets species needs at minimum costs? The lowest cost is for zero acres. Clearing, fertilizing, and so on increase the costs, usually linearly, with acreage. Trees shade wildlife patches, and their root systems reduce grain or grass production at the edges. Most wildlifers want more edge. Figure 4-9 shows the fundamental curvilinear spatial relations between different-shaped clearings and their edges. (See Table 4-2.) If the objective is edge area, then an equilateral triangle is the most productive shape for regularly-shaped areas, and a circle least productive. As total areas get larger, the area gains per linear feet of edge diminish (Figure 4-9b). Where animal density is related to such edges, the implications are clearly that the relative gains in edge effect decrease with the size of the clearing.

Rules of thumb are often employed by people in the field to decide on the most suitable width for a patch. Between the extremes of a 1-hectare patch 1 meter wide (which would maximize edge) and a circular hectare (which would produce the least edge) lie a variety of possibilities. The optimum configuration for edge production, even if it could be calculated, might not be attainable on the land. The cost of determining optimum widths for each clearing may exceed the benefits derived. The manager, using a decision rule based on tree height, usually makes a choice that is a compromise between policy and terrain. It may even involve pacing off the zone of influence of tree shadows and root competition on existing clearings to refine further and justify local practice. Setting the width of proposed clearings as a multiple of the height of trees already standing is a practical yardstick for the heavy-equipment operator working in the clearing.

What might the modern wildlife manager do with a rule of thumb? With a computer the manager creates a table (see Table 4-3) of all reasonable alternatives from the rules about clearing width, based on the equation:

$$E = 2l + 2w$$

when $l = A/CT$ and $w = CT$, or

$$E = 2(a/CT) + 2(CT)$$

where $CT \leq A/CT$(width $\leq$ length),
$\quad E$ = number of feet in edge,

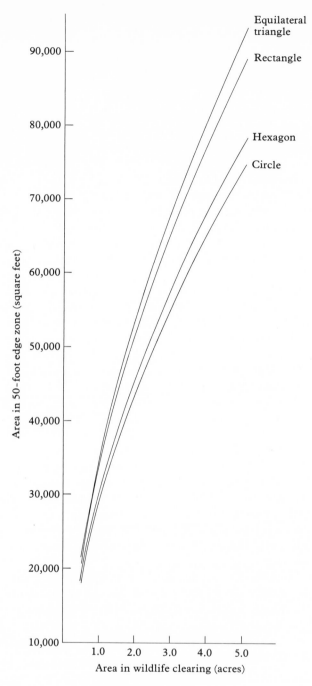

a

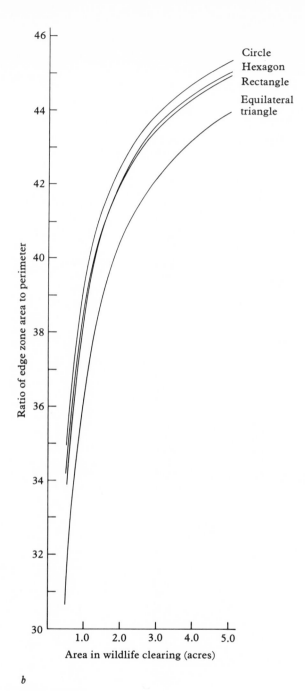

b

FIGURE **4-9**

The area of the edge zone increases as acreage increases, but shape is an important factor (*a*). The ratio of the area in an edge zone to the perimeter is a useful measure of the effectiveness of a manager's efforts to produce edge (*b*). Note that the curves in (*a*) and (*b*) are reversed.

TABLE 4-2

Characteristics of edge, edge zone of influence, and the area-to-perimeter ratio of four different shapes and sizes of wildlife clearings.

Acres in circle	Hectares in circle	Perimeter in feet	Sq ft in 50 ft edge zone	Ratio of area to perimeter
0.5	0.2	523.2	18304.0	35.0
1.0	0.4	739.9	29139.0	39.4
1.5	0.6	906.1	37452.9	41.3
2.0	0.8	1046.3	44462.0	42.5
2.5	1.0	1169.8	50637.0	43.3
3.0	1.2	1281.5	56219.7	43.9
3.5	1.4	1384.1	61353.5	44.3
4.0	1.6	1479.7	66131.9	44.7
4.5	1.8	1569.5	70619.9	45.0
5.0	2.0	1654.4	74865.0	45.3

Acres in hexagon	Hectares in hexagon	Perimeter in feet	Sq ft in 50 ft edge zone	Ratio of area to perimeter
0.5	0.2	549.4	18807.6	34.2
1.0	0.4	776.9	30185.1	38.9
1.5	0.6	951.5	38915.4	40.9
2.0	0.8	1098.7	46275.4	42.1
2.5	1.0	1228.4	52759.7	43.0
3.0	1.2	1345.6	58621.9	43.6
3.5	1.4	1453.5	64012.8	44.0
4.0	1.6	1553.8	69030.5	44.4
4.5	1.8	1648.1	73743.3	44.7
5.0	2.0	1737.2	78200.7	45.0

Acres in rectangle	Hectares in rectangle	Perimeter in feet	Sq ft in 50 ft edge zone	Ratio of area to perimeter
0.5	0.2	626.1	21306.6	34.0
1.0	0.4	885.5	34274.2	38.7
1.5	0.6	1084.5	44224.5	40.8
2.0	0.8	1252.3	52613.1	42.0
2.5	1.0	1400.1	60003.6	42.9
3.0	1.2	1533.7	66685.1	43.5
3.5	1.4	1656.6	72829.5	44.0
4.0	1.6	1771.0	78548.4	44.4
4.5	1.8	1878.4	83919.8	44.7
5.0	2.0	1980.0	89000.0	44.9

TABLE **4-2,** *continued*

Acres in equilateral triangle	Hectares in equilateral triangle	Perimeter in feet	Sq ft in 50 ft edge zone	Ratio of area to perimeter
0.5	0.2	672.8	20650.7	30.7
1.0	0.4	951.5	34585.4	36.3
1.5	0.6	1165.4	45277.8	38.9
2.0	0.8	1345.7	54292.0	40.3
2.5	1.0	1504.5	62233.6	41.4
3.0	1.2	1648.1	69413.3	42.1
3.5	1.4	1780.1	76015.9	42.7
4.0	1.6	1903.1	82161.3	43.2
4.5	1.8	2018.5	87933.3	43.6
5.0	2.0	2127.7	93392.4	43.9

C = multiple of tree height,
T = height of tallest tree in feet, and
A = area of patch in square feet (1 acre = 43,560 sq ft).

Thus, if a 2-acre (87,120 sq ft) clearing is to be cut in an area of 70-foot tall trees, the possible amounts of edge, based on differing widths (multiples of tree height), can be compared and a decision made taking into account the topography and known effects of alternative widths. For example, if the patch is made 35 feet wide (0.50 times 70; Table 4-3 Part I), a 2-acre clearing would yield 5048 feet of edge; a width the same as the tallest tree (Part II) would produce 2629 feet of edge; 1.50 times the tallest tree (Part III), 1869 feet; 2.00 times (Part IV), 1525 feet. The smaller the width, the greater the edge (see Figure 4-10). The selection of the width criterion should not be taken lightly since linear changes in the decision rule do not produce linear changes in edge.

The decision maker will notice in Figure 4-10a that in the vicinity of 80 feet ($\pm$ 10), edge does not change as rapidly as for smaller trees. It is more important to be correct at the left of the graph. Decision-making risks are greater there than toward the right. Observe in Table 4-3 that if, on a 2.5-acre plot, the tallest tree is 60 feet, then, with a rule of width being 0.5 times the height, it is possible to create 7320 feet of edge; simple application of a decision rule of twice the height of the tallest tree would produce only 2055 feet, a significant difference when the objective is to maximize the amount of edge. (To reduce some wildlife species, of course, the objective would be to reduce edge.)

Forest cutting in very large tracts has resulted in concerns by wildlifers about edge and wildlife use of such areas. Assuming that a given range of relations exists between area of clearing, tree height, and length of edge, a manager can

TABLE **4-3**

Length of edge (in feet) in forest clearings as a function of acreage and width
determined as a multiple of tree height at the clearing edge

I. C (multiple of tree height) = 0.50

Acres in clearing	Height of Tallest tree (feet)							
	30	40	50	60	70	80	90	100
0.25	1482	1129	921	786	692	624	574	536
0.50	2934	2218	1792	1512	1315	1169	1058	971
0.75	4386	3307	2664	2236	1937	1714	1542	1407
1.00	5838	4396	3535	2964	2559	2258	2026	1824
1.25	7290	5485	4406	3690	3181	2802	2510	2278
1.50	8742	6574	5277	4416	3804	3347	2994	2714
1.75	10193	7663	6148	5142	4426	3892	3478	3149
2.00	11646	8752	7020	5868	5048	4436	3962	3585
2.25	13098	9841	7891	6594	5671	4981	4446	4020
2.50	14550	10930	8762	7320	6293	5525	4930	4456
2.75	16002	12019	9633	8046	6915	6070	5414	4892
3.00	17454	13108	10504	8772	7537	6614	5898	5327

II. C = 1.00

Acres in clearing	Height of tallest tree (feet)							
	30	40	50	60	70	80	90	100
0.25	786	624	536	483	451	432	422	418
0.50	1512	1169	971	846	762	705	664	636
0.75	2238	1714	1407	1209	1073	977	906	853
1.00	2964	2258	1842	1572	1385	1249	1148	1071
1.25	3690	2802	2278	1935	1696	1521	1390	1289
1.50	4416	3347	2714	2298	2007	1794	1632	1507
1.75	5142	3892	3149	2661	2318	2066	1874	1725
2.00	5868	4436	3585	3024	2629	2338	2116	1942
2.25	6594	4981	4020	3387	2940	2610	2358	2160
2.50	7320	5525	4456	3750	3251	2883	2600	2378
2.75	8046	6070	4892	4113	3563	3155	2842	2596
3.00	8772	6614	5327	4476	3874	3427	3084	2814

TABLE **4-3,** *continued*

III. $C = 1.50$

Acres in clearing	Height of tallest treet (feet)							
	30	40	50	60	70	80	90	110
0.25	574	483	440	422	417	*	*	*
0.50	1058	846	731	664	625	603	593	590
0.75	1542	1209	1021	906	832	784	754	736
1.00	2026	1572	1312	1148	1040	966	915	881
1.25	2510	1935	1602	1390	1247	1148	1077	1026
1.50	2994	2298	1892	1632	1455	1329	1238	1171
1.75	3478	2661	2183	1874	1662	1511	1399	1316
2.00	3962	3024	2473	2116	1869	1692	1561	1462
2.25	4446	3387	2764	2358	2077	1874	1722	1607
2.50	4930	3750	3054	2600	2284	2055	1883	1752
2.75	5414	4113	3344	2842	2492	2236	2045	1897
3.00	5898	4476	3635	3084	2699	2418	2206	2042

*Width becomes greater than length ($CT > A/CT$).

IV. $C = 2.00$

Acres in clearing	Height of tallest tree (feet)							
	30	40	50	60	70	80	90	100
0.25	483	432	418	*	*	*	*	*
0.50	846	705	636	603	591	*	*	*
0.75	1209	977	853	784	747	728	723	*
1.00	1572	1249	1071	966	902	865	844	836
1.25	1935	1521	1289	1148	1058	1001	965	944
1.50	2298	1794	1507	1329	1213	1137	1086	1053
1.75	2261	2066	1725	1511	1369	1272	1207	1162
2.00	3024	2338	1942	1692	1525	1409	1328	1271
2.25	3387	2610	2160	1874	1680	1545	1449	1380
2.50	3750	2883	2378	2055	1836	1681	1570	1489
2.75	4113	3155	2596	2236	1991	1817	1691	1598
3.00	4476	3427	2814	2418	2147	1954	1812	1707

*Width becomes greater than length ($CT > A/CT$).

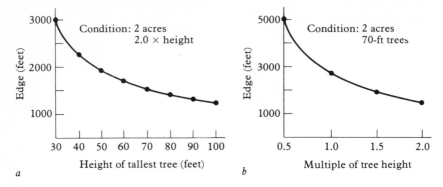

a *b*

FIGURE **4-10**

(*a*) Edge length changes in a 2-acre forest wildlife patch as related to tree height (given a decision rule that clearing width should not be more than 2 times the height of the tallest tree). (*b*) Changes in edge length in a 2-acre area can vary significantly as the decision rule is changed.

use computer-generated tables to estimate the amount of edge that will be available to wildlife.

The likely density of animals in the zone of influence of a clearing can be computed or estimated. The width of the zone will vary by species and micro-climate, and it too can be determined by research or estimated. The total number of animals in the zone of influence of the edge, typically greater than surrounding or interior populations, increases linearly as the length-to-width ratio increases. As the wildlife manager elongates the clearing, the zone of influence consumes more of the interior of the clearing. Eventually, the acreage in a meaningful zone of influence reaches a limit for any particular clearing. This limit should be approached but not passed. It represents a potential and, therefore, a standard for measuring managerial performance. It is obtained when the clearing width is the same as the width of the zone of influence ($W = ZI$).

It can be shown that hexagons leave no waste or unaccounted space between units, and enclose more space per unit edge than any other regular polygon. Thus, clustering hexagons represent the configuration of management units producing the *minimum* amount of edge for the number of units and for the total area involved. The minimum is emphasized since it is a theoretical limit that can be obtained as a basis for further computations. A maximum edge cannot be computed since units may be rectangular and approach an infinite length. There must be an interior for an edge to exist, by definition. A grouping of N hexagons (where N is the number of management units, grassland or forest stands or fields, within an area), each of average size and therefore equal, can be used to estimate *minimum* edge existing within an area. Shared sides are not counted twice.

Since stand or tract acreages are easily computed, used for many purposes, and available in most operational data bases, total edge in an area can be estimated from such acreages. The equation for minimum area edge is

$$E_{\min} = (6n - S_n)H,$$

where n = the number of stands in a forest compartment or tracts in a management unit,

S_n = number of shared sides in a group of n hexagons and is a correction factor to prevent double-counting of sides, and

H = mean unit area of a regular hexagon
= (mean unit area in sq ft/2.598)$^{1/2}$.

This relationship establishes the lowest possible edge and provides a theoretical base for explaining or comparing differences between areas. It can be used to predict future wildlife change if land patterns change.

Since edge is not uniformly important to all species, the edge in a unit is weighted as

$$E_j^* = \hat{E}W_j,$$

where E_j^* = the weighted importance of edge of the unit for the jth species,

$\hat{E}$ = the estimated edge length (read E-hat), and

W_j = the importance of edge to animal species j, as determined by the subjective estimates of experienced wildlifers or by research.

Subjective estimates are not in favor with wildlifers unfamiliar with Bayesian statistics and the variety of managerial techniques that effectively employ them. They may be used when a decision must be made and research results are not available. The decision maker must rely on the best information and problem-solving methods available. Where resistance is encountered, the risks of an improper decision should be reassessed and weighed against the costs and delays that further study would entail. When no progress can be made in overcoming objectives to subjective estimates, the decision maker should set them equal to 1.0 (for example, $W_j = 1.0$) and move on to more important questions. Subsequent feedback will improve these estimates.

Coverts and Point Habitats

Food patches planted for wildlife can be perceived as points on a map. The same is true for such wildlife, hunter, and manager entities as water holes, salt licks, hunting blinds, stake-outs for poachers, observation blinds, and campgrounds. A covert (Figure 4-11) is a special type of "point" or one-dimensional habitat

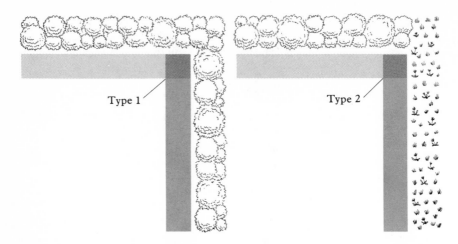

FIGURE 4-11

Two types of coverts: type 1, with only two adjacent cover types (field and woods) and type 2, with two or more adjacent cover types (two types of field and a woods).

formed where two or more vegetative types come together or where a corner of less than 120° occurs. A covert is a special place for wildlife during particular seasons, providing unusual amounts and diversity of food and cover.

Coverts are named by the number of adjacent cover types. Although it is theoretically possible to have a very large number of adjacent cover types (for example, where hedgerows and fences intersect), practically, no more than six types are likely to occur. Figure 4-12 shows the seasonal dynamics of coverts and emphasizes the need for time-specific analyses of these habitat units. Figure 4-13 shows an ideal cottontail rabbit covert. Coverts, like other wildlife habitats, tend to be species- or group-specific. Coverts are most valuable to species having low cruising radii. In general, a manager of these species will attempt to maximize the number of coverts. The increase in game density and diversity, sometimes said to be an example of synergism (a total effect greater than the sum of the individual effects), is probably caused by the aggregation phenomenon shown in Figure 4-12. This is a complex point-application of the aggregate production function concept previously described as the basis for edge effect (Figure 4-8). The concept needs research. There are undoubtedly optimum designs of coverts, or ways to maximize the area under all soil- and site-specific production curves per unit cost.

Each point habitat has a zone of influence—a distance over which wildlife is attracted, from which views are possible, or from which behavior may emanate. The manager will usually want to disperse point habitats throughout the wildlife area so that every part of it will lie within a zone of influence. A regular

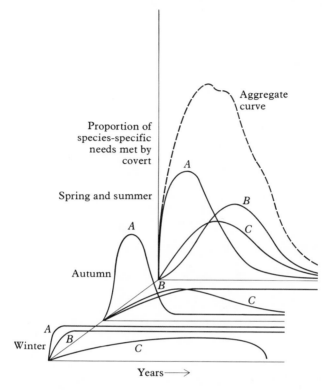

FIGURE **4-12**

The quality of coverts changes seasonally and over the years as communities change with succession. Rather than synergism, aggregation seems the main reason why such coverts produce abundant diverse wildlife. Summing the aggregate curves produces a picture of the annual support potential of each covert over time.

hexagon can be used to accomplish this. By placing points on a map, each at the center of a hexagon of appropriate size (zone of influence), it is possible to avoid overlaps, see gaps, plan future developments, and prevent budget misallocations.

The use of hexagons and equilateral triangles in calculating habitat areas is shown in Box 4-2. If it were estimated that some point habitat such as a covert or a water hole had a "drawing power" or zone of influence for about 90 percent of the individuals of an animal species for 900 meters, the area of the zone of influence (hexagon) could be computed by $S = \frac{1}{2}(nar)$, where $n = 6$ and r (the radius of the inscribed circle) $= 900$. The value of a could be determined by use of the a/r ratio from Box 4-2. Since $a/r = 1.1547$, then $a/900 = 1.1547$, and

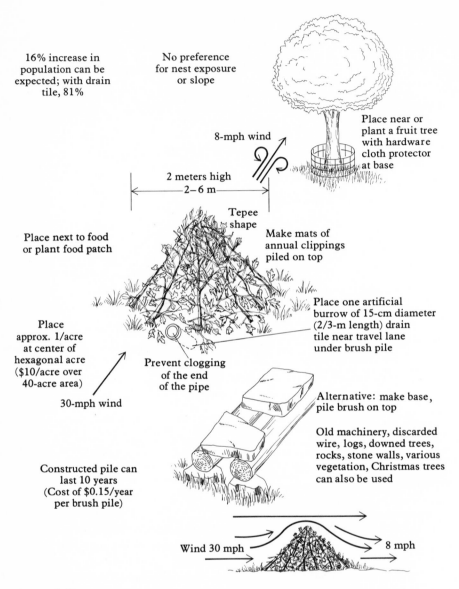

16% increase in population can be expected; with drain tile, 81%

No preference for nest exposure or slope

Place near or plant a fruit tree with hardware cloth protector at base

8-mph wind

2 meters high
2–6 m

Tepee shape

Make mats of annual clippings piled on top

Place next to food or plant food patch

Place approx. 1/acre at center of hexagonal acre ($10/acre over 40-acre area)

30-mph wind

Prevent clogging of the end of the pipe

Place one artificial burrow of 15-cm diameter (2/3-m length) drain tile near travel lane under brush pile

Alternative: make base, pile brush on top

Old machinery, discarded wire, logs, downed trees, rocks, stone walls, various vegetation, Christmas trees can also be used

Constructed pile can last 10 years (Cost of $0.15/year per brush pile)

Wind 30 mph

8 mph

FIGURE **4-13**
Optimum brush pile construction for cottontails and other wildlife.

$a = 1039$. Thus, the area of the zone of influence of this point habitat is 2,805,300 square meters (or 280.5 hectares, or about 693.2 acres). For management units, the computed area of a single zone of influence can be divided

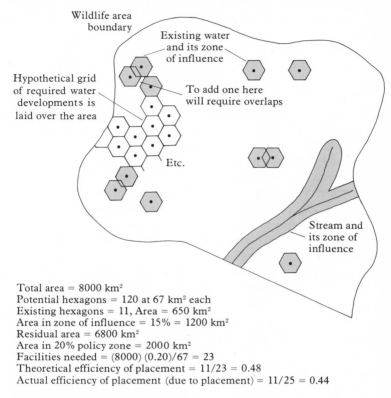

Total area = 8000 km²
Potential hexagons = 120 at 67 km² each
Existing hexagons = 11, Area = 650 km²
Area in zone of influence = 15% = 1200 km²
Residual area = 6800 km²
Area in 20% policy zone = 2000 km²
Facilities needed = (8000) (0.20)/67 = 23
Theoretical efficiency of placement = 11/23 = 0.48
Actual efficiency of placement (due to placement) = 11/25 = 0.44

FIGURE **4-14**

Eleven water developments and the stream put 15 percent of the area in a zone of water influence. If they were perfectly spaced, 23 facilities would have been needed in total to achieve the 20 percent coverage policy. Because of overlaps caused by previous suboptimal placement, or nature, two additional water holes are needed. Placement efficiencies are, thereby, computed as 0.48 or 0.44.

into the total unit area to calculate the number of similar facilities needed to cover the entire area.

A wildlife manager may be directed by policy to have at least 20 percent of all management units within Z meters of free water. Using a map and compass, the manager would compute the area within the required distance of existing free water, counting only once any overlapping areas. The area within the total of the zones of influence divided by the total area of the management unit will give the proportion of the area presently covered. How well the water is spaced is determined by dividing the total actual water holes by the number of water holes that would be needed following a hexagonal placement rule (see Figure 4-14). The number of water holes needed to achieve the policy goal is 20 percent of the unit area minus the percentage of the area covered, divided by the area in a single zone of influence using hexagonal placement. There are many reasons why a symmetrical placement will not always work. There are roads, rock, and ravines. The computations just described provide area-wide planning guides, criteria for comparing performance, standards to be achieved, and budget request justifications.

The problem for the wildlife manager is how to produce the greatest amount of edge per unit area simultaneously with the greatest number of coverts uniformly distributed and yet retain practical use of fields, for example, for cultivation and possibly for hunting or observing wildlife? As with most wild-life and ecosystem management problems, there are trade-offs to be made. Long strips of cover close together produce much edge per unit area. Very small patches of cover produce abundant coverts. Coverts are, thus, in conflict with edge. Among the geometric structures that nest together and can be fitted into a management area, equilateral triangles provide the most edge zone and the maximum corners per area enclosed.

Figure 4-15 (Conlin and Giles 1972) shows how a wildlifer can fit as many triangles into an area as possible given the local conditions. The lines shown can be any type of hedgerow, quickset, living fence, or cover strip. Great diversity can be achieved with three intersecting types of hedges. The interiors of the triangles should be regularly (or randomly) cultivated, grazed, flooded, or planted to wildlife food plots. Openings 4 meters wide are provided for hunters, dogs, and farm equipment.

Juxtaposition and Interspersion

Juxtaposition is a measure of the proximity of different habitat units. More specifically, it is a measure of the adjacency or proximity of year-around habitat requirements to a site being analyzed for a particular species. Adjacency of two or more habitats needed by a species is often desirable for the animals to minimize energy losses (Moen 1973). Where habitats are very similar, it appears unlikely that edge effect occurs. Dissimilar habitats, if arranged properly (for example, food adjacent to cover; nesting cover adjacent to brood feeding areas) tend to produce and support large numbers of wildlife. See Figure 4-16.

Interspersion is a measure of system *relations*. It is the intermixing of units of different habitat types. An area would have good interspersion if the habitat types were well distributed throughout the unit and not clumped into one area. Interspersion can be estimated by various diversity indices. Generally, the more coverts, the greater is the interspersion. Desirable juxtaposition is a function of interspersion. Interspersion indices are described in Box 4-4.

Table 4-4 shows how a detailed juxtaposition index can be developed for a tract. This can be species-specific or general, though the latter is not very

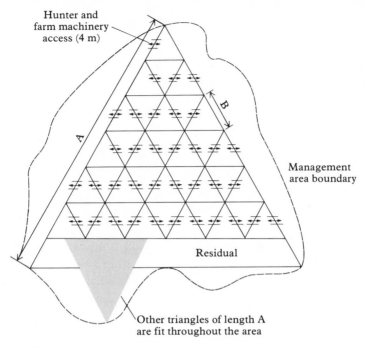

Hunter and farm machinery access (4 m)

A

B

Management area boundary

Residual

Other triangles of length A are fit throughout the area

FIGURE **4-15**

A computer-generated figure like this can accompany a report to a land-owner to show how to fit equilateral triangles into an area.

meaningful. Such field analysis is appropriate for intensively managed areas. Weights (column 2 in Table 4-4) can be assigned by an individual or by teams of local or visiting experts.

For rapid analyses of large areas, juxtaposition can be measured as the ratio of the number of adjoining units within a group of hexagons. It is a value that can be expressed as a percentage of the potential, as well as the average number of adjoining sides for each stand. This is best done by a computer program. The wildlifer set upon increasing wildlife will attempt to increase this percentage. The value is particularly revealing of potential wildlife production for an area.

The effectiveness of wildlife habitat management should be measured against a concept of potential rather than percentage changes in past populations. Potential production of an animal on an area is useful not only for evaluating effectiveness, but also for preventing investments to achieve increases in natural populations beyond the potential productive ability of the ecological community. Efforts to achieve production beyond potential (for example, by excessive fertilizing) can have harmful effects on ecosystems.

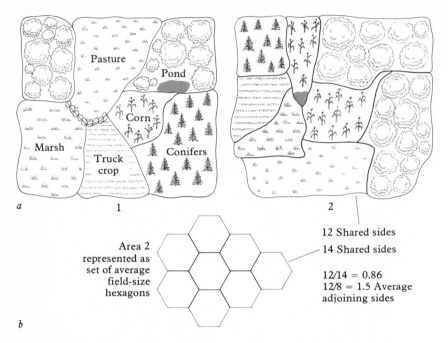

FIGURE **4-16**

Juxtaposition effectiveness can be compared as in part (*a*), where area 1 is shown to have better juxtaposition than area 2; computed as in Table 4-4; or computed as in part (*b*), as the ratio of actual shared sides to the shared sides within a group of hexagons, each one of which has a size of the average habitat type or "stand."

Migration

It is tempting to think of habitat in terms of fixed locations. However, an animal population inhabiting one area today may migrate to another area tomorrow. The habitat has not changed; the animals have selected an alternative. They migrate at great energy cost and risk but in doing so achieve long-term water and energy balance. By migration, animals achieve for themselves a relatively uniform environment over the year.

There are two general types of migration, but these may be only humanly perceived categories of the same phenomenon. First, there is *seasonal* migration of two kinds: altitudinal and continental. Altitudinal migration is common in the western states. Animals such as deer and elk move off summer ranges as the land becomes covered with snow. This migration seems to be a function of weather, but some herds will start at a stimulus undetected by human observers and travel 8 to 100 kilometers, crossing mountains to reach their destination. Movement of

Box 4-4. Ways of Computing an Interspersion Index

There is no agreed-upon method for computing interspersion. Various indices are used to compare areas, as measures of progress and as variables in regression analyses useful for explaining population densities. These include:

1. Total cover types in an area.

2. Total areas in different cover types with significantly different ages.

3. The variance of the areas in 1 and 2.

4. The number of relevant edges intercepted by a line drawn across a map or aerial photo of a wildlife management area. ("Relevant" implies the difference to a species between a forest-crop edge and an edge between corn and wheat fields.)

5. The total length of relevant edge per unit area (for example, meters/hectare).

6. The ratio of actual contiguity to the potential contiguity if all stands were of the average size and were hexagonal.

7. Elaborate computer techniques are also available.

TABLE **4-4**

A hypothetical juxtaposition analysis for a tract. A juxtaposition index is developed by comparing the multiple score total with the maximum potential score in all categories. Here the index is $490/(65 \times 10) \times 100 = 75$.

Wildlife needs	Weighted importance of factor	Achievement in adjacent or nearby tracts	Multiple
Winter foods	10	6	60
Spring foods	6	10	60
Summer foods	5	10	50
Autumn foods	9	5	45
Water	2	10	20
Nest site	10	9	90
Winter cover	10	10	100
Poacher cover	9	5	45
Escape cover	4	5	20
Total	65		490

deer herds to winter "yards" in the northeast is an alternative behavior for more limited habitat conditions. The continental migration of waterfowl and song-birds is clearly seasonal and quite well known, although some causes, routes, and terminal areas are poorly described.

The second type of migration, *continual* migration, is rare. Even caribou that migrate over very large areas return to an area for calving. These return areas, however, do shift slowly, probably as a result of changes in range quality. In these areas, one food staple, lichen, is so slow growing that very long periods of range rest-rotation are necessary. Tundra recovery time is directly proportional to the degree of animal disturbance. Trampling has greater detrimental effect on lichen than does grazing. The size of unmanaged caribou herds increases and decreases in response to the quality of the range. The natural shifts in populations and movements in response to range are generally unacceptable to wildlife managers who are bent upon stabilizing or increasing caribou benefits over time. Their efforts have been thwarted by human behavior that has blocked herd movement, restricted natural wandering, increased fires, and increased competition from reindeer, resulting in even greater population fluctuations because of greater range abuse.

The use of winter range—the lowlands and flat areas—for crops, industrial development, and settlement of all kinds has drastically reduced the acreage and quality of big game winter range throughout the western United States. Since verdant summer habitat, not the winter bleakness, is observed by summer recreationists, it is little wonder that they cannot understand that reduced wildlife is their own doing (or lack of doing), not the result of disease, poachers, dogs, or the dozen essentially insignificant causes usually cited for population reductions.

Migration has been the subject of intensive study. Significant advances have been made by marking animals with colorful collars, ear ribbons, and radio transmitters and following their progress. Banding of birds has been a mainstay in such studies. Recently, trapped bears have been given a low dose of radioactive phosphorus and tracked by excreted radiation. By examining feces found along trails, researchers have been able to record the travels of individual bears. However, the factors that trigger migration are incompletely identified, and the orientation mechanisms even less well known. How a young goose returns, after a long winter journey, to the same marsh in which it was hatched is still unexplained. Whether explanations will aid management decisions remains to be seen.

Time

Seasonal differences in habitats are well known. Animals have different seasonal needs owing to the seasonal nature of lactation, reproduction, and other processes. A habitat should be seen as a seasonal entity and evaluated by season for each species. The food-habits analyses of the past have not yielded the information they might have; although they showed what foods an animal was eating at the time of capture or kill, they rarely showed what was available on the site or the condition (good or bad) of the animal that might have produced a particular feeding behavior. A food availability-to-utilization ratio is needed in most such studies.

Time in ecological systems is important as both an instantaneous concept and a sequential concept, though greatest emphasis is placed on continuous and cumulative phenomena such as growth and succession. Instantaneous events include:

1. The season, day, or month in which wildlife forage on plants; whether they consume dormant or flowering parts.
2. Whether certain seeds freeze or not and thus achieve the condition for germination.
3. Whether frosts occur at a critical stage of flowering.
4. When plowing or disking is done in wildlife areas and thus what viable seeds or vegetative reproductive structures will be available.
5. When a wild animal contacts a teratogenic herbicide (one causing birth defects) and the period of pregnancy of that animal.
6. When a fire occurs and what insects, seeds, and soil conditions are affected.
7. How long after a fire, a freeze, or heavy rain that a rain occurs.

The list can easily be extended. The wildlifer will come to appreciate that the instant of convergence of several of these factors is one of the most pervasive and influential of all habitat factors. The nearly infinite variety in nature is largely a function of the sequence and simultaneity of events. These are observable, reportable, and explainable. They can be simulated, for the most part, by a computer. The computer will not tell the manager when, for example, a wildfire will occur, but it will tell what will result if the fire occurs at time t_1, t_2, or t_3. In so doing, it can prepare the manager to play a winning game in the future. A simulation can tell what the most likely outcomes will be, even if a variety of events occur. It may help the habitat analyst explain why a certain very special environment, perhaps unique, exists on a particular management area.

Phenology is the study of periodic biological events such as leaf fall and egg hatching. Phenological observations are essential for meaningful forage or cover density studies, unless total ecosystems are to be modeled and all factors observed and controlled. Phenological similarities or differences are required for integrating many site factors, for controlling variance, and for permitting useful analyses of differences among areas, treatments, and years.

Differences in habitat among years are usefully treated in regression analyses (recall Chapter 2). Figure 4-17 shows hypothetical points. An expression often used in discussing range is *trend:* "The trend has been downward in both range quantity and quality since the bucks-only season." If all that is wanted is trend, then whether b is equal to, less than, or greater than 1.0 is all that is needed; rate is not necessary. Sample sizes for making gross determinations of habitat trends can be much smaller than when rates of change are needed or when prediction is desired. Suppose that an equation, describing a declining habitat, was computed for Figure 4-17 as $y = 520.0 - 10.33x$, and the last year, x_t, was 1976. The analyst might wish to predict y in 1980. If the value of x is coded simply as 6 for the last year, then y in 1976 was $520 - 10.33(6)$ or 458. In 1980, when $x = 10$, then $y = 520 - 10.33(10) = 417$. The statistics are oversimplified to show clearly the relation of the concept of time to habitat, no matter how it is measured.

The more that data vary and the wider the band or variance about the computed regression, the less confidence a wildlifer can have in such numbers as 458 above. When making predictions (a risky but essential aspect of the job), a manager can quantify the risk in the so-called confidence bands extending outward on both sides of the regression (Figure 4-18). If the data are extended too far past the observed points, the results may be absurd. For example, if $x = 51$ (for the year AD 2027) is inserted into the equation, the result would be an area producing negative vegetation, a meaningless concept. Long before even zero production is reached, other factors would become operative. To project by using regression implies the assumption: If the same conditions operate as those for which the data were collected, then . . . .

If the wildlifer is going to all the trouble of collecting data on wildlife food or cover or habitat conditions, the data should be recorded on forms that can be read electronically and processed by the regression programs that are standard software with computers. Without data and computer aids, trend can usually be observed from photos consistently taken from permanent picture points. Society is poorly served when merely told, "The habitat is improving this year." The obvious responses to such a statement: How much? Significantly? How close to perfection are we? From what point is the improvement determined? Was the change due to natural or decision forces? What can we do to effect habitat change? There are powerful analytical tools readily available to help the wildlifer answer such questions. Elementary sampling procedures are reviewed in Box 4-5.

Food

Past failures to manage wildlife habitat successfully have, for the most part, been failures to analyze adequately the concept of food. Oversimplification has

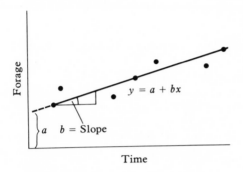

FIGURE **4-17**

Hypothetical relations of forage production (y) to time (x). Each point represents an annual mean from samples. A simple linear regression analysis is performed, and an equation is produced in the form $y = a + bx$. The independent variable, x, may be an environmental or a population factor.

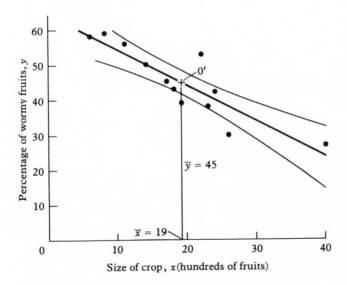

FIGURE **4-18**

A regression is useful for explaining (past) and predicting (future). When prediction is done, the further the values of x are from the known, the less predictable the system, the less confident the predictor, and the broader the confidence bands. (Reprinted by permission from *Statistical methods*, sixth edition, by George W. Snedecor and William G. Cochran, © 1967 by the Iowa State University Press, Ames, Iowa.)

Box 4-5. Elementary Sampling Considerations and Procedures

An application of statistics to habitat analysis can be seen in the question: How large a sample must I take? The question arises frequently and usually involves plot size and whether to use a line-intercept method or a belt transect.

There are four basic and interactive elements of the sampling question (Diagram A): sample size (n), variance (s^2), Student's t statistic, and tolerable error (d^2). The basic equation is

$$n = \frac{s^2 t^2}{d^2}.$$

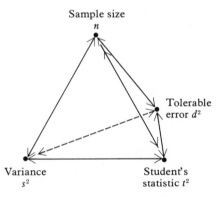

Diagram A. The four major components of the sample size question.

The tolerable error d^2 is a measure of accuracy. (The term d is the mean, multiplied by some desirable range of accuracy, z, for example, 10 percent.) The reader should appreciate that there are many sampling equations for different populations, different totals, and different ways of selecting a sample (for example, simple random, stratified, or systematic), but one can be sure that the four elements given above will be the fundamentals of conversations with statisticians.

The dependent variable, n (the proper sample size), is usually to be computed. The problem may be to find n when $s^2 = 30$, $t^2 = 5.5$, and $d^2 = 33$. The variance is estimated from a quick preliminary sample, prior studies, or the literature. The other two values are not facts to be discovered. They are based on decisions about an acceptable confidence level (the t selected from a table) and acceptable accuracy (the value of z). Performing the calculation, the value of n under these circumstances is 5.

Someone in another situation may have a sample of 16 and want to know how good it is. Starting with $n = 16$ and the variance and mean probably known, it is possible to discuss the trade-offs between confidence and accuracy that a decision maker must be willing to make in order to use information from the sample in a decision. You might see that, since $n = s^2 t^2 / d^2$, then, with the variance known to be 10, you would have $16 = 10 t^2 / d^2$. You could then simulate, saying: What if I observed a t value of 1.75 (0.95 confidence level at 15 degrees of freedom)? Then t^2 is 3.06 and d^2 must be 1.91 and d is 1.38. But $d = $ (mean)z and the mean is known to be 6.9. Solving for z in the equation $1.38 = 6.9z$, $z = 0.20$. However, a level of accuracy of only 20 percent is intolerable. What if I re-evaluate my desired confidence level? Perhaps I was trying too high a level (a 0.95 level means I can tolerate making a wrong conclusion from my sample no more than one time in 20). Using a 0.90 level of confidence, the t value is 1.34 and the equation becomes $16 = 10(1.34)^2 / d^2$. Then $d = 1.06$ and solving for z in the equation $1.06 = 6.9z$, the accuracy level becomes 0.15, or 15 percent.

The danger of this approach is that the numbers seem to have their own power; they can change a wildlife manager's mind. Some say the manager using this approach tends to "rationalize." However, if the analysis is done carefully, it can be useful and can bring into question how well the criteria of confidence and accuracy were set.

Sample size is dependent upon available personnel and skills, money, equipment, including vehicles, and time allotments (though time restrictions can often be overcome by more equipment and workers). All of these can be tied to the previous equation in either t^2 or d^2. The question is: How dangerous is it to draw a wrong conclusion? For the whooping crane it is very dangerous and a 0.99 level is necessary; for the cottontail rabbit, it is rarely dangerous and conclusions can be made at the 0.60 level. If, before the sampling begins, the wildlifer determines that n samples cannot be collected with the available resources, the effort should not be undertaken. No conclusions can be drawn from an inadequate sample and no decision made. It is easy to forget that wildlife management is a science of decision making. What are the alternatives when either reasonable accuracy or an acceptable confidence level is not possible with the available data? The alternatives are to seek additional support to allow for the precise, calculated, justifiable amount of resources needed to do the sampling, to wait until funds are collected, or to study something about which conclusions can be drawn.

been rampant. The dimensions of wildlife food use shown in Figure 4-19 provide a basis for studying this critical component of habitat.

Presence. Food presence is the structural statement—the species list or likely species list of all food items, both plant and animal. Often plants are a very subtle expression of the differences between areas and habitats. Why certain plants are *not* in an area is a very difficult question, one almost impossible to answer. Many factors interact to determine absence. Presence of a plant, however, is an indication (1) that it was introduced, and (2) that all of the factors necessary for its year-around survival are present. Wildlifers often collect data from plots laid out in the forest and fields to estimate the number of plants useful to wild animals. Results are used to evaluate the desirability of areas for animals, to predict success, and to account for changes due to fire, fertilizers or overbrowsing.

Table 4-5 shows the relationship between F, the proportion of all plots examined in which at least one specimen of the species in question was found, and M, the average number of individuals per plot. This table is based on the relationship $M = \ln(1 - F)$ established by Greig-Smith (1964:14). Plots can be of any size, for example, 1 meter $\times$ 1 meter or 0.01 acres (10.9 ft $\times$ 20.9 ft). Density is seen not to be related to frequency in a straight-line fashion. The relation is logarithmic. When plants (or any other items collected from plots, such as acorns, spent gun cartridges, or even animal tracks) are distributed randomly, density may be obtained from frequency counts. The relationship explains how statements such as "I saw a lot of . . ." may be misleading. It makes a difference whether the field observer is commenting on number of places (plots) in which items were sighted or on how dense they were, on the average, within the observation area.

Quality and Quantity. The biomass or standing crop of plants produced by the interaction of soil, moisture, and sun can be analyzed in terms of quality and quantity. (Prey, as carnivore food, can be analyzed by the same categories.)

Quantity should be measured as species-specific quantity, occurring in specific habitat layers. It is expressed both spatially and temporally as density per unit time. Typically, food quantity is measured by:

1. Clipping and weighing vegetation in plots or portions of plots. For manual computational ease, the following has been used: grams of browse in 100 sq ft plot $\times$ 0.96 = pounds per acre.
2. Counting and weighing seeds or nuts in plots or in collecting devices.
3. Counting twigs and twig length and converting to total weight or amounts removed.
4. Estimating weights visually after training and "eye-calibration."

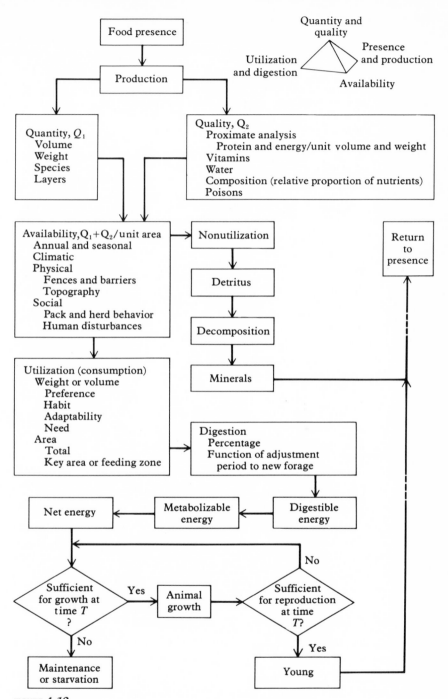

FIGURE **4-19**

Wildlife food use is a complex phenomenon. Its structure is analyzed here according to the four major categories of production, quality and quantity, availability, and utilization and digestion.

TABLE **4-5**

The average number of individuals per plot M as a function of the proportion of the plots in which at least one observation of an individual occurs.

Proportion of plots (F)	M	Proportion of plots (F)	M	Proportion of plots (F)	M
0.01	0.01005	0.34	0.41552	0.67	1.10866
0.02	0.02020	0.35	0.43078	0.68	1.13943
0.03	0.03046	0.36	0.44629	0.69	1.17118
0.04	0.04082	0.37	0.46204	0.70	1.20397
0.05	0.05129	0.38	0.47804	0.71	1.23787
0.06	0.06188	0.39	0.49430	0.72	1.27297
0.07	0.07257	0.40	0.51083	0.73	1.30933
0.08	0.08338	0.41	0.52763	0.74	1.34707
0.09	0.09431	0.42	0.54473	0.75	1.38629
0.10	0.10536	0.43	0.56212	0.76	1.42712
0.11	0.11653	0.44	0.57982	0.77	1.46968
0.12	0.12783	0.45	0.59784	0.78	1.51413
0.13	0.13926	0.46	0.61619	0.79	1.56065
0.14	0.15082	0.47	0.63488	0.80	1.60944
0.15	0.16252	0.48	0.65393	0.81	1.66073
0.16	0.17435	0.49	0.67334	0.82	1.71480
0.17	0.18633	0.50	0.69315	0.83	1.77196
0.18	0.19845	0.51	0.71335	0.84	1.83258
0.19	0.21072	0.52	0.73397	0.85	1.89712
0.20	0.22314	0.53	0.75502	0.86	1.96611
0.21	0.23572	0.54	0.77653	0.87	2.04022
0.22	0.24846	0.55	0.79851	0.88	2.12026
0.23	0.26136	0.56	0.82098	0.89	2.20727
0.24	0.27444	0.57	0.84397	0.90	2.30258
0.25	0.28768	0.58	0.86750	0.91	2.40794
0.26	0.30111	0.59	0.89160	0.92	2.52573
0.27	0.31471	0.60	0.91629	0.93	2.65926
0.28	0.32850	0.61	0.94161	0.94	2.81341
0.29	0.34249	0.62	0.96758	0.95	2.99573
0.30	0.35667	0.63	0.99425	0.96	3.21887
0.31	0.37106	0.64	1.02165	0.97	3.50656
0.32	0.38566	0.65	1.04982	0.98	3.91202
0.33	0.40048	0.66	1.07881	0.99	4.60516

5. Describing the site in general, often using photographs.

6. Weighing and determining the volume of bird crops and mammal stomachs.

7. Observing a semi-tame animal (for example, a deer) on a leash, tallying the bites taken and food eaten. With caged animals, food containers before and after feeding can be weighed.

Box 4-6. How to Relate Food Quantity and Availability in a Preference Index

There are two formulations of a solution. Where U_{ijk} is the amount of food species i utilized by wildlife species j in an area or zone at a particular time k (usually a few-day sampling period of t length, for example, during the opening days of a hunting season), and A_i is the amount of plants of species i available to wildlife, then a preference index R_{ij} can be computed:

$$R_{ij} = \sum_{i=1}^{r} \sum_{j=1}^{s} \sum_{k=1}^{t} (U_{ijk}/A_{ik}).$$

Where past studies have been made, then A_{ik} can be redefined as food species observed to be utilized by a wildlife species during normal conditions over a long period, A^*_{ijk}. This refinement will tend to take the "noise" out of food preference studies. What is done with knowledge of preference? Preference is a gross index of food quality. Habitats are designed to have food supplies that are likely to be consumed.

The interaction between quantity and availability becomes evident when a wildlifer observes 100 crop analyses and is unable to tell what they mean except that the 36 plants identified have been eaten. If it were known that plants were present in the areas from which the bird crops were taken at the time they were taken, the tedious sorting, weighing, volumetric determinations, and identification would have meaning. That meaning is symbolized as *preference*. By expressing preference, the information obtained per unit dollar spent on food analysis studies may be increased. See Box 4-6.

Analysis of food quantity has been a dominant interest in the wildlife literature. Important as quantity is in the overall food picture, it has been overemphasized. The importance of food *quality* is being recognized more and more. Quality of many foods is reported as a *proximate analysis*. A basic analysis is depicted in Figure 4-20. There are other aspects of food quality not identified by proximate analyses, and these have rarely been studied. Energy and protein will be of overriding importance in most instances. These provide the context of other nutritional elements such as vitamins. It is possible that there will be significant shortages in food elements, but the apparent shortages can usually be related at a fundamental level to inadequate energy. (Even protein is converted

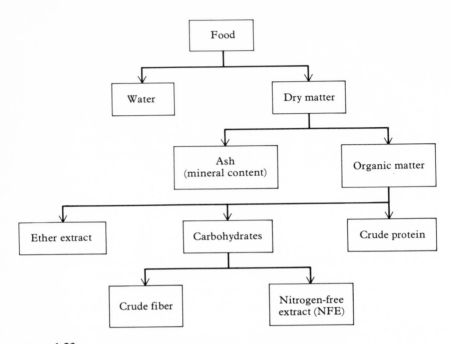

FIGURE **4-20**
The basic components of a proximate analysis, typically performed on wildlife and livestock foods. Such analyses provide insight into food and range quality and may provide correlates to changes in animal behavior, reproduction, or survival.

to energy during advanced starvation.) There is little need to argue over which is more important for wildlife, energy or protein. The answer is both.

Food quality is especially important to the wildlifer responsible for trophy production, but it is universally important as it relates to growth of young animals. Young animals require more protein than adults for growth. Young grouse and turkeys require 90 percent or greater protein diets. This is usually supplied by insects and other fauna. In the ungulates, the microbial activity of the young is not at maximum efficiency, and they cannot use nonprotein nitrogen sources as well as adults. They are provided milk protein and generally need at least 20 percent protein in their diet. Pregnant and lactating females have especially high protein requirements.

The source of this protein is forage. The amount of protein present in forage is a measure of its quality. Succulent spring browse usually has less protein per unit weight than dormant (drier) fall and winter forage. Bissell and Strong (1954), studying deer in California, found that a dried spring plant analyzing 15 percent protein may contain only 5 percent protein on a wet basis. Progressively lower amounts of protein are found in browse in flower buds, vegetative buds, terminal twig tips, and the remaining current twig growth. Crude protein content declines rapidly with the onset of flowering. Shrubs have higher protein than grasses but lower energy. Forbs are intermediate in energy and protein.

Food quality, however measured, is a function of soil, adjacent plants, aspects (the direction a slope faced relative to the sun), shadows on the photosynthetic surface, stage of growth and portion of a growing season, time since managerial treatment, time since fires, time since rain, and, of course, year-to-year weather. The abiotic (physical and climatic) environment is a very significant part of the habitat of wildlife. It, too, must be mastered by the wildlife manager. The two major components of the habitat subsystem that override all other managerial considerations are solar radiation and water.

Water is a major component of food quality. Many animals drink no free water; they receive all they need from their foods and employ highly efficient physiological systems and water conservation mechanisms to reduce water needs. In some areas, animals must consume very large amounts of vegetation to obtain needed nutrients because the plants are so succulent. Very large energy expenditures are required to gather, masticate, digest, and excrete waste water. For some animals, water abundance is a limiting factor. The larger animals, such as bear and deer, may need water during certain periods, for example, during lactation. Water is, of course, necessary for waterfowl and also for fur-bearing animals. Aquatic habitats are amenable to analysis and design by the approaches outlined in this chapter. Figure 4-21 presents an analytical pattern for reaching a decision about developing water resources for wildlife.

Food quality depends to some extent on its diversity. In feeding studies of wildlife, when single plant species rations have been fed to penned animals they usually lose weight or experience other problems. The addition of only one other plant to their diets will "bring them around" or enable them to gain weight. The ecology of the stomach (or stomachs) of animals is extremely complex. More studies are needed to understand and design optimum forage mixes for wildlife. Such mixes can be achieved through range and forest manipulation, planting, fertilizing, and a host of other habitat management methods. It is possible, once a food analysis is made, to create a habitat that will provide most of the species-specific needs. Of course, feeding is a possibility. There are some major problems with this practice, which will be discussed later, but optimum feed mixes may sometimes have more advantages and lower cost per animal benefited than other techniques.

Succession. Food production varies with succession—the orderly, largely predictable, sequence of changes in vegetation and associated animals through which a site progresses over time. A large part of the habitat manager's job is to manipulate succession, either holding it where it is, slowing it down or setting it back, or advancing it. All of these can be done, but all cost time, money, and energy. There are seven major ways to manipulate succession:

172

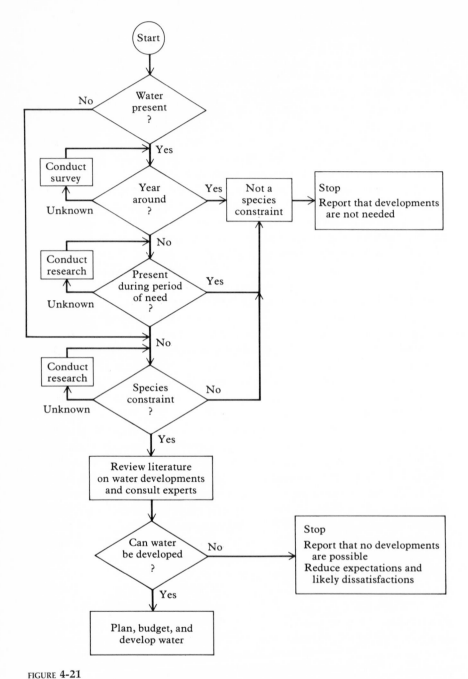

FIGURE **4-21**

An analysis of the decision to design and implement a water development such as a pond, water hole, or well for wildlife.

1. Farming (planting, pruning, and cultivating).
2. Fulminating, including burning and blasting.
3. Forestry (axing, planting, rolling, crushing, and herbicides).
4. Flooding and irrigation.
5. Fertilizing.
6. Feeding (direct, grazing).
7. Fencing (livestock or wildlife in or out).

These seven practices constitute the "f⁷" *action checklist*. The managerial costs per unit of time for reducing succession are generally less than for advancing it. Every successional step changes the benefits available from a habitat, and a manager must be aware of the potential conflicts between resource users, as well as the ecological consequences of manipulating succession.

Feeding is one way to beat succession, since it reduces the time and risks of growing forage. The purpose of feeding wildlife in the winter is to carry a larger number of the animals through the winter alive than would otherwise survive. In effect, it is an energy-intensive means of manipulating succession, both temporally and spatially. The purpose of feeding may also be to enhance reproductive success. Winter feeding is usually done only when increasing populations are desired. On big game ranges, if surplus animals are not being harvested by hunters, then seeking a greater surplus is not logical. However, if a properly managed herd is being harvested adequately, winter feeding can become a practical and economical method of increasing the population. Winter feeding is a problem because these *ifs* are rarely satisfied.

On most big game ranges in the United States, stable or decreasing populations are now desired because the ranges cannot support greater numbers. To produce surplus animals is mismanagement; yet no one wants to see or know of animals starving. The concerned public must be made aware of the risks involved in feeding and the counterstrategies that may have to be applied later if a feeding program is undertaken. Winter feeding is acknowledged to have a long history of past failures. Accounts of deer dying near feed stations with their stomachs full of hay are numerous. However, feeding programs have failed in the past primarily because feeding was begun far too late in the winter. Programs are generally not started until near starvation is noticed. An alarmed public or game department then initiates a feeding program. Artificial feeds may produce physiological shock, killing animals. A suddenly switched diet may either not be digestible by the unique floral and faunal mix of the animals' rumens, or the animals may be in such late starvation that they have digested the last of their rumen flora and fauna. Suitable supplies of bacteria take two to three weeks to multiply to a desired level in the rumen to allow digestion.

Feeding must be done gradually. The feeding must be such that no sudden change in diet occurs, and the animals must not be allowed to approach the starvation level where they cannot forage for themselves when favorable conditions return. Such long-term feeding is very rare because it is costly. In mild winters the animals are at high elevations or are not congregated. Feeding is expensive; some food put out will go uneaten. An entire winter may be so mild that virtually none of a feeding operation is utilized. Cries of "waste" arise. The alternative is to wait until conditions get rough. There is always the tendency to wait and see if there will be a long "bad spell." Then it is usually too late.

Winter feeding should be discouraged in most cases because (1) it concentrates predators, (2) it provides sites for disease transmission, (3) it turns large numbers of animals onto the spring range, thus increasing range problems, (4) it works against the natural selection process, (5) it damages the feeding site itself, and (6) since it is rarely sustained, it results in more conspicuous starvation than when feeding is not done. In most cases, the time and costs of feeding can be better spent in population regulation, habitat analysis and manipulation, and public education programs designed to reduce animals on winter ranges and to reduce the grief associated with reports and observations of starving animals.

Availability. No matter how much food is produced or of what quality, only a limited amount may be *available*. A plant may only have edible accessible portions at one season of the year. A wind storm may make lichen from trees available to the woodland caribou (*Rangifer caribou*) or the tops of fallen trees available to browsing animals. Wind-thrown trees, such as in a lodgepole pine stand, can make large areas inaccessible to elk. Forage, no matter how unlimited, becomes unavailable. Snow may cover abundant food supplies. Some species may be blocked from food supplies, while others, like the moose (*Alces americana*) may still high step with relative ease to the supplies. Snow may form a crust strong enough to support animals and thus allow them to reach food previously unavailable. In some areas, snows may raise the problem of *net* available food. What amount of food is made unavailable by snow (for example, lost animal-days of feeding) and what amount is subsequently made available by crusted snow?

For those who wish to understand and perhaps develop a computer model of the forage subsystem, each factor can be further described. Under availability, for example, snow has been discussed as a factor. This one element of the system may be detailed as date of fall, rate of fall, wind during snowfall, elevation, solar radiation of the surface, relation of areas of fall to proportions of forage present, actual snow depth, snow depth relative to vegetation height and density (wind effect), snow density, snow crust, relation of snow to water storage in soil and in snow pack, whether snows prevent freezing of seeds for which freezing is a prerequisite for germination, energy for an animal to move through various snow depths and densities, height of forage species relative to snow depth, density, and crusts, and the manipulation of snow depths in clearings and fields by managing wind. By detailed modeling of subsystems, holistic explanatory and predictive systems can be created.

Fences, highways, or human disturbance (a fear barrier) may prevent animals from obtaining food. For game, such barriers are a problem; for pests, the barriers are primary population control mechanisms. Topography can greatly influence availability. The concept of a zone of influence can be used to assess relative availability around trails or feeding areas.

The temporal aspects of availability include (1) the migratory behavior of animals, and (2) the simple behavioral and physiological realities that animals can glean only a certain amount of food from the wild in real-time, that they have behavioral needs other than feeding, and that there are physical and chemical rate limits on digestion.

Utilization. In a range with a low population density, the available forage supplies may not be completely utilized. The wildlife manager must distinguish between biological or potential productivity and effective productivity. Suppose a constant population of about 100 animals is needed on a range. It is not managerially appropriate to produce forage for 500 animals. In most cases, the manager will attempt to make forage yields equal forage needs based on previously decided objectives. This means minimizing the difference between the total amount produced (as a result of managerial action and investment *and* natural processes) and the amount needed (using the D score, as for populations in Chapter 3).

Utilization can be analyzed as weight or volume. Amounts utilized are a function of *preference* or palatability. A preference index is computed in Box 4-6. In the early literature of wildlife management, highly palatable or much sought after plants were called "ice cream" plants. If these desirable plants are missing from sites where they are expected the wildlife manager would surmise that there were many animals consuming them and that they are even overbrowsed. "Beef steak" plants are the staple plants, not highly preferred but eaten regularly and forming the major volume of food. "Spinach" plants are those rarely eaten or only eaten when the going is rough and when the first two types are depleted. This high, medium, low preference classification was and still is useful in field diagnoses of wildlife ranges. The classification is an excellent one for explaining range relations to the public.

Leopold (1933) used the wildlife food categories of preferred, staple, emergency, stuffing, pasttime, mineral or tonic, and poisonous. Self-explanatory, they are a useful analytical framework.

Palatability is thought to be a function of taste, size, appearance, feel, work required per mouthful, and ease of swallowing. Deer apparently prefer bitter, succulent, high-protein plants. Thorns do not seem to be a deterrent. Animals new to an area (as when stocked) may take years to achieve a stable food preference because of previous feeding *habit*. Much information is communicated from parent to offspring in feeding behavior in the wild. Similarly, new plants in an area, though highly nutritious and palatable elsewhere, may not be used. Both of these phenomena can be grouped under habit.

There is a type of displacement behavior familiar to any horseback rider: A well-fed horse will continue to nibble. It seems that some wildlife feeding signs along trails are of this type and do not reflect preference and certainly not utilization.

Utilization rates in ungulates vary over the years. There are undoubtedly species-specific patterns of intake regulation, but it now seems that utilization is also influenced by a critical relationship between the animals' physiological systems and their habitats. Consumption is a homeostatic activity, performed at varying rates to maintain a constant level of body warmth. Intake is related to digestible energy: The volume eaten is increased to a point as digestible calories decrease. Other stimulants of eating (energy needs such as lactation, pregnancy, rapid growth, and stress) cloud the phenomena. Geist (1971) observed that mountain sheep and goats reduced food intake of low-quality forage in mid- and late-winter to a point below that observed in fall or early winter. Silver et al. (1971:45) suggested that drops in fasting metabolic rate and thyroid activity may compensate for seasonal changes in temperature so that low temperatures result in little or no increase in energy requirements. The animal spends less time eating to maintain the new energy regimen and thus maintains energy balance by this seasonal efficiency. Such adaptation allows the animal to survive on lower-quality foods when foods are scarce. Activity pattern (and energy costs) are also reduced in winter. The end result is an entirely analyzable system of branching relations, a system both theoretically satisfying and managerially useful. The principle is: Feeding behavior is a function of energy demands constrained by total volume eaten and digested. As a managerial tool, the concept explains why ranges differ in productivity, suggests why identical populations can cause different range utilization indices, indicates the results of increasing forage quality, shows how increased animal activity caused by disturbances relates to food supplies, and highlights the needs for understanding the physiological and nutritional relations of wildlife food and the environment.

Food utilization is zone- or area-specific. Certain areas are blown clean of snow and animals congregate and bed there; others receive cooling winds or breezes that discourage flies or other ectoparasites of animals. Some areas have salt or water, and thus surrounding vegetation receives extreme utilization pressures. Because of the intensity of their use, these areas are called *key areas* and are often used as the basis of habitat analysis systems. They are most useful for studying trends (for example, whether a key area is more beaten down, compacted, and eroding this year than last), but they can be used to extrapolate various observations to management areas.

Two important aspects of utilization are *regeneration* and *vigor*. Utilization can progress so far as to prevent regeneration. The plant may be present, but a gap may exist in the age classes present. Such gaps, as might be produced at the close of a hunting season when foraging animals are left undisturbed, can set up profound forage system disturbances over time and reduce the long-term chances for a manager to balance production and utilization.

Some animals forage on woody twigs and leaves. This is called *browsing*. Like human pruning, this activity can, depending on season and amount, reduce plant vigor or ability to produce new biomass equivalent to that of unbrowsed plants in a similar area. Since most minerals are in the thick, unpalatable stems, no great mineral losses to the plants occur from browsing. Calcium supplies are usually adequate in shrubs, but phosphorus levels are often deficient during the dormant season. Heavy browsing can occur, retarding growth and possibly lowering the nutrient content of such growth. As expected, different plants respond in a variety of ways to browsing. Desert plants can be grazed up to 30 percent in late spring and winter without a loss in nutritive value and growth. Where food supply improvement or stability is an objective, then utilization greater than 30 percent can be judged "overgrazing."

Range shrubs grow tallest when unbrowsed but bear less foliage and twigs than browsed plants. Light and moderate browsing induces more twig and crown development and higher forage yields than heavy browsing. Lightly browsed plants grow taller and are more sparse underneath than heavily browsed ones. Heavy browsing prevents height growth and increases the amount of dead material in the crowns. Light browsing during an inactive period stimulates almost all species to greater productivity. Removal of a terminal bud results, usually, in two or more new twigs from lateral buds. However, twig removal can become a devitalizing process if carried too far (too much removal over too long a period). Signs of serious degeneration may not show for years, but the decline will be evident not only in yields but also in seed production.

Robinette (1971) estimated that 60-percent removal of the annual growth of clover is "complete utilization" and does not damage the plant. This distinction makes it imperative that utilization be modified to include a coefficient, such as 0.60, for the acceptable utilization limit for every species. Dasmann (1964) found that the vigor of some plants, such as willow (*Salix*), is unaffected by removal of 100 percent of the annual production, while others, such as white cedar (*Chamaecyparis*), suffer from 20-percent removal. Garrison (1948) proposed a rule of thumb that browse species may be safely utilized to 50 percent of current growth of twigs from fall to late winter.

Heavy grazing or browsing results in reduced litter fall and partially interrupts part of the nutrient cycle. Although urine and feces of foraging animals add plant growth-promoting substances to the soil, the amount removed exceeds the amounts returned and the concentrations vary significantly. It has been suggested that in some communities nitrogen may be limiting because of the large amounts tied up in large, long-lived biomass, as for example, in elephant herds. Since nitrogen (as protein) is critical in most animal diets, it is important to recall that nitrogen needed for growth the next year moves out of leaves into the plant before leaf fall. Heavy or untimely browsing can severely affect future food supplies. Ranges with depleted vigor are not simply restored; periods of 20 to 40 years rest or removal of grazing are required for depleted western grass ranges.

What is overutilization? It is an expression only relative to some objective. The objective may be so implicit that it is unrecognized. Overutilization typically is observed as (1) removal of more than 60 percent of the current growth, (2) erosion, silt, and sediment in streams, (3) trampling of seedlings and other plants, (4) formation of trails, (5) secondary drought damage (however, heavy clipping may reduce transpiration rates and allow plants to withstand drought), (6) failure to set seeds, (7) increases in rodent and certain insect populations, and (8) unusual distributions of plants.

Digestibility. The average habitat observation tells little about the real needs of a wildlife population being managed to achieve a set of objectives. A key part of such an analysis is *digestibility*. These relations are seen in Figure 4-22.

As the specialized ruminant system of ingestion and digestion is unfamiliar to many, this system is sketched in Box 4-7.

Wildlife researchers have developed equations relating the amount of food eaten by deer and similar animals to the weight of the animal. The average weight of the animals in a deer herd varies widely with soils, forage available, and the sex ratio, as well as proportion of young to old animals. Careful analyses of populations allow the average weight to be used to determine how many animals can be taken, and often must be taken, to keep a herd in balance with the available forage produced in an area. To compute the forage required per acre to meet the needs of a herd of a computed mean body weight:

$$F = \frac{(\text{animals/acre})(1.0 - \text{proportion harvest})(365 \times \text{daily kg forage/kg body wt})}{0.60(\text{i.e., a 60\% forage consumption constraint})}.$$

The mean daily forage requirement for a white-tailed deer in Virginia as a function of body weight (50 kilograms or 110 pounds) is about 0.8 kg (2 pounds), based on a gram of forage containing an average of 4.2 kilocalories of energy and

$$\text{Daily forage (kg)} = 0.045 \times (\text{Deer weight in kg})^{0.75}$$

As further research clarifies requirements per unit of body weight and as seasonal multipliers become available, more precise estimates can be made.

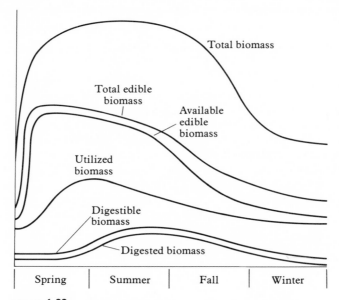

FIGURE **4-22**

Field analyses of biomass or forage supplies may have very little
correlation with the functional portion of the biomass, that portion
actually utilized for the support of wildlife populations in each
season.

Cover

Wildlife *cover* is hard to define. Today it has little meaning; tomorrow, except as
an educational phrase, it will be a mere symbol of imprecise thinking. The term
cover usually implies hiding places, shelter, and protection from the weather
and mortality factors. Surprisingly, it is usually used with reference to individual animals, rather than populations. Types of cover include *escape* (as
from predators and hunters), *nesting*, *resting* (loafing areas with infrequent
disturbances), *play*, *travel lanes*, and *climatic* (particularly wind, rain, snow, and
desert evaporation). *Visual* cover is concealment. One type is planted along road
edges of fields to reduce poaching from cars. Cover can be hedgerows, brush
piles, windbreaks (including ground depressions and living fences), and conifer
trees for roosts. *Distance* itself is a type of cover, separating predator and prey,
providing ample flight-response time, and preventing access, as across a cord-
grass marsh. Cover must be increasingly conceived as a population concept.
Cover has become the average space in which animals can probably achieve
energy balance within their environment within a suitable time.

Box 4-7. A Brief Review of Ruminant Ingestion and Digestion

During feeding, ruminants generally pull or cut browse between their lower incisors and upper (prehensile) gum. The large, rough tongue plays an important role. Feeding is usually only for short periods. See Diagrams A and B.

    Food is moved through the mouth and esophagus into the ventral sac of the rumen and some goes into the reticulum. In the ventral and dorsal sacs of the rumen the food is mixed with mucus and acted upon by the rumen flora (bacteria and protozoa). Some of the short-chain organic acids (acetic acid upward) produced from the attack on cellulose are absorbed into the circulation from the rumen (having papillae covering). The remaining pulp is regurgitated, chewed, and again swallowed. Finer particles pass to the reticulum (a network

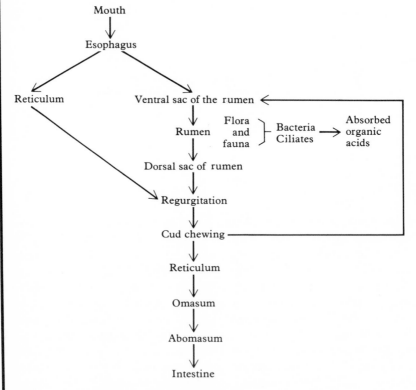

Diagram A.   Schematic of the ruminant four-stomach digestive system

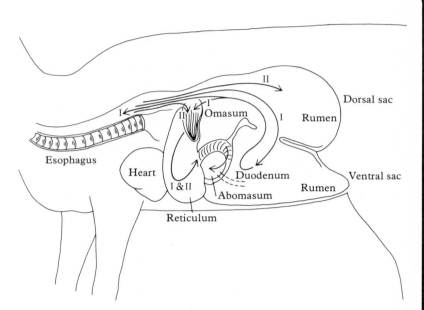

Diagram B. The ruminant feeding process

of ridges), coarser materials again go to the rumen. From the reticulum the food goes to the omasum (an organ with muscular folds) where it is further broken down by muscular action. Bacteria use nonprotein nitrogen of urea and amides to synthesize their own microbial protein (later absorbed in abomasum and intestine). Liquids are passed by the omasum into the abomasum, the "true" stomach with peptic glands. The nutrient broth is then absorbed through the walls of the stomach for use by the animal.

Energy from digestion is absorbed into the body from the stomach as glucose, or as propionate, in the case of the ruminant. The latter has an energy equivalent of half the glucose molecule. This energy is stored as body fat or glycogen or is processed at the cellular level in the Krebs cycle. The glucose is converted into the high-energy bonds of adenosine triphosphate (ATP) with energy losses at every step of the cycle. ATP is a critical component of many biochemical pathways, and it seems likely it can be limiting, for example, in the production of FSH, LH, or progesterone. Energy from food intake is thus transformed to cellular energy, where it is used in life-maintaining processes and behavior, production of young, lactation, and even antler production.

Cover may be analyzed by (1) using a radiometer, (2) measuring percent obstruction of vision, (3) making photographs, (4) measuring relative light transmission through overhead cover with a photographic light meter, (5) measuring relative wind velocity, (6) counting stems per acre, and (7) making subjective estimates (for example, light, moderate, or dense on a 0 to 10 scale).

Dens, runways, and trails provide information for wildlife (Margalef 1968:23). By patterning behavior, they reduce energy requirements. Dens are cover; runways for voles and shrews are cover. Trails for wildlife must also surely be cover.

The Unity of Food and Cover

Food and cover are relatively meaningless divisions of one phenomenon. An animal requires food energy in winter. It can consume and digest the requisite kilocalories of food energy (input) or it can move to a warm, wind-protected, south-facing slope and eliminate energy losses (output). The animal is a homeotherm, an energy balancer. Cover is an energy radiator in the night, a reflector (and animal cooler) in the day. It provides micro-climates where an animal can achieve a desirable energy balance. It may be needed for shade or for heat radiation. It may not be needed at all where there are forage energy surpluses.

The modern wildlife manager is an energy balancer, budgeting habitat analysis and plans and manipulating funds to achieve a space within which a population has ample opportunity for achieving its long-term energy-balance needs. Food must be interpreted relative to the energetics of cover. Cover must be interpreted relative to digestible (or stored) energy available to animals. Escape cover is a means for reducing the energy costs of prey (energy intake) to a predator. Such cover determines the likely predator density in that it determines the level of energy likely to be gained per acre per unit of energy expended. The relations between forage and distance as cover can be applied in locating feeding areas, as shown in Box 4-8.

For a better understanding of wildlife energetics, the reader is strongly encouraged to study Moen's (1973) book *Wildlife Ecology*. It seems likely that in the future wildlife management will largely be applied energetics. Following is a brief summary of the relevant energy concepts.

All animals tend to be homeotherms or energy balancers, the warm-blooded species more so than cold-blooded species. Only energy balance in warm-blooded creatures will be discussed here, but literature exists for fish and reptiles. Mammals regulate their temperatures between about 35° and 39°C, birds between 38° and 42°C.

The animal is a system. Inputs of food energy (Q_f) and atmospheric energy (Q_a) must equal outputs or losses (Figure 4-23), including metabolic energy

Box 4-8. How Energetics Can Be Used in Decisions to Acquire or Locate Deer Feeding Areas*

The ability of white-tailed deer, and other animals, to achieve a condition of thermal balance is a function of the physical state and activity of the animal and the energy regimen within which it lives. One of the major aspects of a herd's ability to achieve homeostasis is its proximity to alternative energy sources at the time of thermal imbalance. The wildlifer can attempt to minimize the cost (in kcal/kg/hour) to animals of moving vertically or horizontally to feeding areas to achieve homeostasis.

The placing of habitat developments is a decision with many variables. Such a decision can be improved by giving attention to the energy needs of a population. If the majority of animals in a population must expend as much or more energy to reach food as they derive from digesting the food consumed, then there is no net gain. To achieve more protection from wind, a deer might move to a conifer stand, expending energy in the movement. In the conifer stand, heat loss from the deer due to convection is reduced and heat is gained from the reradiated energy of the trees. However, due to possible large expenditures of energy required in moving to the favorable thermal micro-climate, there may be a net loss to the deer. Moen (1973) made it very clear that such energy concepts are needed in studying deer and other animal behavior. Where to place wildlife developments is perhaps best conceived as a problem of maximizing net available energy. What land to acquire specifically for deer is probably best thought of as a problem of acquiring lands on which the managerial costs are lowest for creating a favorable environment. This environment may be characterized as one in which the greatest number of animals with a particular characteristic can, over many years, achieve a state of homeostasis.

Tables A and B can aid in considering the above as well as in solving such mundane problems as: Where should I place a food planting, site 1 or site 2, so as to minimize the energy required for a deer (the mean of a population) to use that planting located a specific distance from the mean resting area of the population?

Calculations were made of the expected energy loss of deer in making various horizontal and vertical movements. Blaxter (1962:105,108) discussed the additional energy expense, observed in sheep, due to standing and to horizontal movement. We used Clapperton's (1961) values of 0.00645 kcal/kg/meter for vertical movement and 0.00059 kcal/kg/meter for horizontal movement, both at 1.5 mph (2.4 kilometers/hr). We judged them to be appropriate for the stated purpose because of similarities between the basal metabolism of deer and sheep. Some wildlifers are very reluctant to transfer knowledge in this manner. Of course, there are risks and it must be done with caution. But the alternative is inaction. We sought to advance, with feedback, from what was

---

*By E. B. Rayburn and R. H. Giles, Jr.

TABLE A

Total daily energy (*TDE*) required for a 50-kg deer (kcal/24 hours) making given horizontal and vertical movements.

Vertical displacement (meters)	Horizontal displacement (meters)									
	0	200	400	600	800	1000	1200	1400	1600	1800
0	1859	1865	1871	1877	1883	1889	1894	1900	1906	1912
100	1891	1897	1903	1909	1915	1921	1927	1933	1938	1944
200	1923	1929	1935	1941	1947	1953	1959	1965	1971	1977
300	1956	1962	1968	1973	1979	1985	1991	1997	2003	2009
400	1988	1994	2000	2006	2012	2017	2023	2029	2035	2041
500	2020	2026	2032	2038	2044	2050	2056	2062	2067	2073

TABLE B

Relative efficiency (*RE*) of movement to a habitat type or habitat development.

Vertical displacement (meters)	Horizontal displacement (meters)									
	0	200	400	600	800	1000	1200	1400	1600	1800
0	1.000	0.997	0.994	0.991	0.987	0.984	0.981	0.978	0.975	0.972
100	0.983	0.980	0.977	0.974	0.971	0.968	0.965	0.962	0.959	0.956
200	0.966	0.964	0.961	0.958	0.955	0.952	0.949	0.946	0.943	0.941
300	0.951	0.948	0.945	0.942	0.939	0.936	0.934	0.931	0.928	0.925
400	0.935	0.932	0.930	0.927	0.924	0.921	0.919	0.916	0.913	0.911
500	0.920	0.918	0.915	0.912	0.910	0.907	0.904	0.902	0.899	0.897

known. The species differences were not considered significant, since energy reported as being required for vertical movement is similar enough between species to suggest an interspecific value. Speed of animal movement is problematic, but average long-term behavior is needed, that is, over the life of the feeding area to be developed. Speed, of itself, is undoubtedly more influential than species differences in energy-cost relations.

Silver et al. (1969) established that the mean fasting metabolic rate (*FMR*) for deer is 33.8 kcal/kg/24 hours. We approximated the minimum energy requirement (*MR*) for a deer as (see Brockway 1965 and Crampton and Harris 1969:15):

$$MR = 1.1(FMR).$$

MR is an estimate of the energy required above FMR for standing in place. It is developed for a population that does not have to move about to satisfy requirements for food or cover. However, natural populations do not have this minimum energy requirement. There are other losses that occur in foraging, playing, and mating. The general, simplified energy relation is

$$TDE = MR + E_v + E_h,$$

where TDE = total daily energy,

$\quad\quad E_v$ = energy required in vertical movement, and

$\quad\quad E_h$ = energy required for horizontal movement.

We assumed constant environmental conditions as did Silver et al. (1969 and 1971).

We assumed that both up- and down-hill movements result in energy drains. The actual horizontal-vertical distance moved is the summation of these movements made on different trips during that day. Thus, if a deer were to make two trips on one day, one of 1000 meters horizontal, 200 meters vertical, and one of 600 meters horizontal, 200 meters vertical; the total distances moved would be 1600 meters horizontally and 400 meters vertically.

Table A presents estimated TDE for a 50-kg deer. For example, a deer of 50 kg moving once a day to a feeding site 200 meters away and at the same elevation requires 76 kcal less expenditure of energy than if moving to a site 600 meters away and 200 meters higher (1941 − 1865).

Table B shows the relative efficiency, RE, of such areas, computed as

$$RE = MR/TDE$$

for meeting the energy required by a population with such movement characteristics. The wildlifer will try hard to increase efficiency or decrease costs while retaining high area efficiency.

Since the data now available for MR and movement do not allow us to discriminate between linear and exponential functions for adult deer, estimates of TDE of different movements are approximately the same for animals of all sizes. Though the absolute values of RE of movements do not differ greatly from 1.0, we believe that a system such as outlined is useful in estimating the relative value of different locations for habitat acquisitions and development if other factors are equal. To account for effects of low temperature and snow impending deer movement on TDE and RE, increases can be made in FMR (Silver 1971) and in the values for horizontal movement, and the tables easily recomputed.

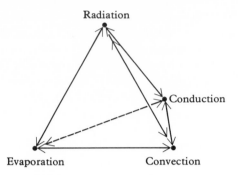

FIGURE **4-23**
The four basic modes of thermal energy exchange between an animal and its environment are radiation, conduction, convection, and evaporation.

(Q_m), energy of production (Q_p) such as milk and young, and energy of waste (Q_w) such as in urine and feces. Unless these two sides of the equation are balanced by the natural processes and feedbacks of the animal, death ensues:

$$Q_f + Q_a = Q_m + Q_p + Q_w.$$

The second law of thermodynamics, the entropy principle, favors the right-hand side of the equation, and, in fact, many animals have at least as much difficulty in dissipating these losses as in gaining energy. Each part of the energy equation will be described in turn.

Food is merely a carrier of energy, Q_f. The nitrogen-free extract component of food analyses is made up of starches and sugars. Crude fiber may be barely digestible by animals, but digestibility varies in nonruminants from 3 to 78 percent. In ruminants, the digestive biological broth of the stomach typically breaks down 50 to 90 percent of this fiber into volatile fatty acids. Only 50 percent of the large amounts of crude fiber in browse may be converted. Ether extracts are all the oils, fats, and other substances that dissolve in the ether used in the analysis. Their meaning differs for each species and time. There are 9 kcal of metabolizable energy per gram of ether extract (by convention) in the diet. In late starvation, protein may be converted to energy. The energy determinations are typically made by bomb calorimetry.

Energy from the atmosphere comes as 1.98 calories per square centimeter per minute (the solar constant). The amount may be reduced by clouds and dust. Once it reaches an object (animal or plant), absorption or reflection takes place. The immediately important parts of the electromagnetic spectrum for the wildlifer are the visible and infrared. Moen (1973:79) showed almost 92 percent absorptivity by black cattle when the sun is at right angles to the hair, 84 percent by brown cattle, and 60 percent by white cattle. Brownness of hair coat is a day-night, summer-winter evolutionary optimization—a fantastic series of trade-offs between blackness and whiteness over time to achieve best long-term species homeostasis. This is a fundamental replacement, by energetics, of a part of Gloger's Rule (see Kendeigh 1961:9): "In warm-blooded species, black pigments increase in warm and humid habitats, reds and yellow-browns prevail in arid climates, and pigments become generally reduced in cold regions."

Also the "camouflage hypothesis" for the cause of snowshoe hare (*Lepus canadensis*) pelage color change can be replaced with an energetic hypothesis. The hare in winter typically suffers food energy shortages. Throughout its range, grasses and forbs are covered by snow; forage is low in energy, high in crude fiber. The amount of energy received in the short daylight periods of winter on a white coat and reflected (perhaps 50 percent and thus foregone as an input) is insignificant relative to the failure of a white body to emit energy at night or in dark conditions. The hare over the eons has traded major internal energy conservation for a minor sun-to-hair surface energy input. Perhaps the whiteness reduces predator detection, but predators are not known to control prey populations; in fact, just the reverse holds. What of the zebra? The nearly equal black-white pattern is probably an alternative evolutionary tactic, generally equivalent, in the tropics, to brownness.

Animals receive energy from the sun and indirectly from clouds, vegetation, and other parts of the environment, including other nearby animals (see Figure 4-24). The radiation that an object such as dense conifer shrub emits is governed by the Stefan-Boltzmann law, which states that the amount of radiation emitted by a black body is directly proportional to the fourth power of the absolute temperature (Q_r) of the object. Thus

$$Q_r = \varepsilon\sigma T_s{}^4,$$

where Q_r = radiant energy emitted in kcal/m²/hr,
   ε = emissivity (in a range of from 1.0 to 0),
   σ = Stefan-Boltzmann constant = 4.93×10^{-8} kcal/m²/hr, and
   T_s = surface temperature of the object (°K).

The emissivity, ε, of the snowshoe hare or other animals in winter is likely to be about 1.0. Observe the difference in Q_r using $\varepsilon = 0.95$ and later 0.98 when T_s is 308°K. A small percentage of a very large (or small) number is still a very large (or small) number. Wildlife receives radiation from cover, the earth, and other animals, all of which can be computed from the above equation.

On the loss side of the equation, metabolic energy is high. It is composed of environmental losses, basal metabolic losses, and activity expenditures. Animals lose heat as a function of the environmental factors, according to the following relations (from Moen 1973). Where Y is the surface temperature of body (°C) and X is air temperature (°C), then

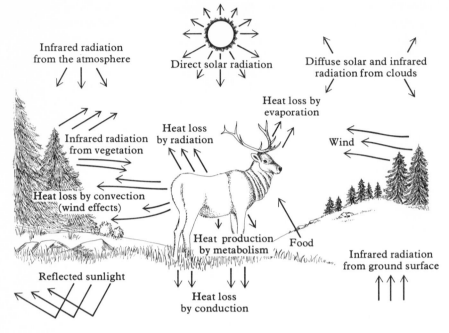

Thermal energy exchange between an animal and its environment. (From *Wildlife ecology* by
Aaron N. Moen. W. H. Freeman and Company. Copyright © 1973.)

$$Y_{deer} = 6.559 + 0.944X$$

$$Y_{grouse} = 5.25 + 0.870X.$$

Wind (U) influences the surface temperature relation in deer approximately
as follows:

$$Y = 9.5 - 0.54U + 0.15UX + 0.75X.$$

Wind velocity, U_z, at height z, is a function of cover management, quantified
by

$$U_z = (U_*/k)\ln(Z/Z_0),$$

where U_* = friction velocity,
$\quad k$ = von Karman's constant = 0.4,
$\quad Z$ = height in cm, and
$\quad Z_0$ = "roughness" of surface; the height at which velocity is zero.

Given a wind velocity of 13.9 miles/hr (622 cm/sec), the velocity at 2 meters over a stand of grass 60 to 70 cm high will be 433 cm/sec, while over snow it will be 572 cm/sec.

The wind and temperature are interrelated in convective heat loss, Q_c, in calories:

$$Q_c = h_c At(T_s - T_a),$$

where h_c = the cylinder convection coefficient, $6.17 \times 10^{-3}(U^{1/3}/D^{2/3})$,
   U = wind velocity in cm/sec,
   D = mean diameter of the animal (or some part, for example, the leg) if losses are to be partioned over the body,
   A = area,
   t = time,
   T_s = surface temperature of animal, and
   T_a = surface temperature of the air.

Moen (1973) pointed out that small "cylinders" (such as small animals or legs) are more efficient convectors than are large ones (such as large animal bodies). This energy conservation inefficiency for small mammals is probably matched by the efficiencies of lower wind velocities where they live.

Conductive heat losses, Q_k, occur as

$$Q_k = [kAt(T_1 - T_2)]/d,$$

where Q_k = calories of heat transferred,
   k = thermal conduction coefficient ($k = 2.066 + 0.00648T_a$ for air where T_a is air temperature in °C),
   A = area,
   t = time,
   T_1 = temperature of first surface °C,
   T_2 = temperature of second surface, and
   d = distance between surfaces.

This equation explains insulation, relates hair depth to insulation, relates the conductivity of hair or feather types (k), explains why animals "nest" thereby reducing conductivity, and quantifies the energetic basis of the spread-eagle prone position of canids and even deer on hot days as they increase their conductive area.

The effect of oil on waterfowl and shorebirds is largely based in this equation. Oil spots can both increase the thermal conductivity of the feather layer, accelerating energy loss, and decrease the depth of the feathers, that is, reduce d. In cold waters it is impossible for animals to replace energy as fast as it is lost.

Panting is an efficient cooling mechanism. There are 575 kcal of energy lost at average temperatures for every gram of water that evaporates. (The relation is: Heat of evaporation (kcal) $= 595.59 - 0.5376T_a$.)

Cover can protect animals from wetting and thus the associated energy losses of chilling. Wind, temperature, and moisture saturation of air all interact complexly.

The energy to be lost by convection or conductance comes from the energy of basal metabolism, Q_{mb}, which is computed by

$$Q_{mb} = CW^b,$$

where $C =$ a constant that is species-, sex-, and age-specific,
   $W =$ animal weight in kg, and
   $b = 0.75$ (see Watt 1973:66).

The average white-tailed deer in winter loses 75.6 kcal per $W^{0.75}$ every 24 hours. In summer the loss is 84.4. An average figure, $Q_{mb} = 70W^{0.75}$, applies for almost all birds and mammals. Many factors such as activity influence the measurements of Q_{mb}. To compute energy required for maintenance, use $93W^{0.75}$ as an operational managerial guide.

The energy of activity is about 1.33 times basal metabolism. Extra activity caused by human disturbance, TV camera men, researchers, and thoughtless pilots of hazing helicopters can cause excessive energy drains on animals at critical periods and cause death, abortions, or other population-energy balance problems. Animals on winter range with high energy drains and sparse forage will not willingly climb hills. The costs are too high. As the winter progresses, animals will have all moved to lowlands because of the physics of the situation, and there public outcries about starvation are the loudest—especially from the person standing in the roaded suburb near an industry with an airport. Both people and animals have sought habitats with the lowest possible energy requirements or the easiest access to energy sources.

Food digestion results in heat. Digestion itself is, thus, a heat source in winter, but it provides additional energy to be dissipated in summer. Shivering also produces heat.

Production as Energy Loss

Animal production is of tissue, fetus or fawn, and milk. The metabolizable energy is usually about 80 percent of digestible energy (Moen 1973:352).

The energy required for pregnancy and gestation of a deer, Q_{ep}, is

$$Q_{ep} = [e^{2.8935 + (0.0174t_d/0.71429)}]/f,$$

where Q_{ep} = energy required for pregnancy per kg of fetus,
  t_d = gestation time (in days), and
  f = fawn weight at birth (in kg).

At about 200-days term, this costs the deer about 50 kcal per kg of fetal weight (about 2.2 kg).

Moen (1973:355) reported deer milk contains 0.7 kcal/g. The amount produced is a function of the deer, habitat, and fawn. Even the rate of fawn rumen development influences the requirements. At a milk consumption of about 600 g/day per fawn, a doe with 18-kg twins must have very high forage consumption to meet these needs *and* achieve her maintenance energy requirements. Such computations provide new insight into the importance of the available energy on summer ranges. While typical habitat analyses may show thousands of pounds of available forage on such ranges, the real answer to how many animals a range will support lies in how much metabolizable energy is present per unit. It seems that re-analysis of most wildlife habitats will be appropriate. Many of the old mysteries of disparate production and of unexplained losses (probably due to poachers, wild dogs, or elves) will unfold for rational explanation. Maybe something can be done to improve the situation based on the explanation. Often nothing can be done; the situation will have gone too far—the war for wildlife habitat will have been lost. At least, with such knowledge, frustration and dissatisfaction can be reduced and efforts spent, as in the triage concept, on lands and populations yet responsive to management.

Alternative Methods of Habitat Evaluation

Organisms that occupy an area can be considered integrators of their environment. Billings (1952) listed over 100 factors that influenced plants and plant growth. Gaussen (1957) introduced the concept of plants as integrators. Plants "integrate" information on the topography, soil, and climate; these factors are all reflected in the "quality" of the plants on the area. The idea of integrators is an extension and elaboration of the older "plants as indicators" concept of Clements (1928) and others. Herbivores are one step higher than plants in energy flow models and acquire some environmental information from plants.

Several indirect methods of habitat evaluation are available or are undergoing research and development.* These methods usually involve measuring a particular characteristic of a wild animal and then inferring from this the condition

---

*The rest of this section was contributed by Roy L. Kirkpatrick, Ph.D., Professor of Wildlife Science, Virginia Polytechnic Institute and State University, Blacksburg, Virginia. Dr. Kirkpatrick is a wildlife physiologist specializing in endocrinology and pesticide ecology.

of the animal and of the habitat in which it lives. These characteristics have come to be known as "physiological indices" or "condition indices."

There is much variability in the form and accuracy of indices presently in use. Some can only be obtained from the animal after death (femur fat, kidney fat, and so on), whereas others must be obtained from living animals (blood characteristics). Still others (antler and skeletal measurements, body weight, and so on) can be gathered from both live and dead animals.

Riney (1955) and LeResche et al. (1974) have suggested desirable features of a good *condition index*. Such an index should:

1. Be sensitive to subclinical changes in nutritional status.
2. Be specific in its indications, that is, capable of indicating energy, mineral, protein, and other kinds of balance.
3. Be easily obtained from tissues or measurements from both live and dead animals by relatively unskilled personnel.
4. Measure conditions of different age groups and sexes at different times of the year and be little affected by the stress of collection.
5. Be objective and reproducible.

Each of the most widely used indices and those showing the most potential for future use will now be discussed briefly.

Probably the most widely known index of habitat conditions is that of *bone marrow fat* in deer (Cheatum 1949). This index is used primarily to determine if dead deer found in the spring died of starvation or some other cause. The middle third of the femur marrow is used and the percent fat can be determined chemically or estimated visually. Since marrow fat is believed to be the least fat source depleted in a poorly nourished animal, a low bone marrow fat is indicative of extremely poor nutrition and hence poor habitat conditions.

Recently, the use of *fat in the mandibular cavity* of deer has been proposed as an index of condition (Baker and Lueth 1966; Nichols and Pelton 1972, 1974). This is also a marrow fat and the technique is similar to that used for femur marrow fat. However, the mandible is much easier to collect from hunter-killed deer than the femur and in fact is often routinely collected for aging purposes. Nichols and Pelton (1974:540) reported that mandibular cavity fat "was found to separate into more distinguishable condition classes than was fat from the femur marrow tissue. . . ." Further research is needed to evaluate this relatively new index under controlled conditions.

Riney (1955) studied several condition indices in red deer in New Zealand and concluded that the *kidney fat index* was the most accurate and useful in measuring the condition of the animal and its habitat. The kidney fat index is obtained by removing the kidney and its surrounding fat from the abdominal cavity of a dead animal and then cutting the fat at both ends of the kidney, perpendicular to the main kidney axis, and discarding that not remaining affixed to the kidney. The ratio of the remaining total weight to the weight of the kidney is the kidney fat index.

Ransom (1965) combined the kidney fat and bone marrow fat indices in white-tailed deer and proposed that animal or range condition could be measured accurately over a wide range by the two indices combined.

As stated previously, these indices are usually used to indicate the quality of winter range. They probably reflect nutritional intake (primarily digestible energy) over the two to three months prior to sampling.

Antler beam diameters are also often used as indices to habitat conditions (Severinghaus et al. 1950). Since antlers are growing primarily from April through August, this index is most useful in evaluating spring and summer range conditions. Antler beam diameters can be affected by many nutritional factors, and thus differences between areas can be difficult to interpret. Minerals such as calcium and phosphorus have a marked effect on antler growth, as do both energy and protein intake (Magruder et al. 1957). Thus, antler measurements are not a very satisfactory index because they can be influenced by so many different factors.

Skeletal ratios as an index of habitat conditions are based on differential growth of certain bones after birth (Klein 1964). Femur/hind foot ratios have been used by Klein to compare and contrast habitat conditions on two islands. The growth of the metatarsals, which comprise most of the length of the hind foot, is relatively more complete at birth than is that of the femur. Thus, the ratio of the two in an adult deer can indicate the amount of skeletal growth occurring over the lifetime of the animal and hence the past nutritional regime of the animal. A low femur/hind foot ratio would be indicative of poor nutrition (and poor range), whereas a high ratio would be expected in deer on better diets.

Chemical composition of rumen contents of ungulates is another method of habitat assessment. Proximate analysis of rumen contents has been used to evaluate range conditions by Klein (1962), Kirkpatrick et al. (1969) and Skeen (1974). Although foodstuffs do undergo changes in the rumen and protein content of rumen material is higher than that of the forages consumed (due to microbial synthesis of protein and nitrogen recycling), these workers showed that proximate analysis could reflect changes in habitat between areas, seasons, and years.

The Southeastern Cooperative Wildlife Disease study at the University of Georgia has developed an index relating deer populations to carrying capacity by use of abomasal parasite counts. The basis for this index is that abomasal parasite counts go up as deer populations approach the limits of their forage supply.

Whole body fat has been used as an indicator of animal and habitat condition in small rodents. However, interpretation of fat levels must be done with care since fat levels may increase as habitat conditions deteriorate on account of cessation of reproductive activity in these mammals (Batzli and Pitelka 1971; Estep 1975).

Numerous blood characteristics have been investigated as indicators of animal and habitat condition for wild species. Included in these are packed cell volume, hemoglobin, differential cell counts, total serum protein, various enzymes, thyroxine, cholesterol, and blood urea nitrogen. These have been reviewed by LeResche et al. (1974) for the cervidae (deer), the family in which most of the work has been done. Although many blood characteristics do change when diets are severely deficient, it appears that most are relatively stable over a wide range of habitat conditions. An exception to this is blood urea nitrogen levels, which have been shown to correlate well with protein content of ingested foods (Franzman 1972, Seal 1972, Skeen 1974, and Kirkpatrick et al. 1975).

Several other measurements have been used or suggested as indicators of habitat condition in wild animals. These include *whole body weight, heart girth, sulfur content of hair, ovulation rate,* and *fawning rate.* Heart girth and body weight of an animal of given age are indices of overall body growth and fatness. Although these are among the least accurate of indices, they are widely used because of their ease of collection.

Sulfur content of hair has been cursorily investigated by Sanders (1971) as an index of habitat quality, but results were inconclusive. The use of reproductive rates to evaluate habitat, like whole body weight, is relatively insensitive and also requires a large sample size. Added to this is the unknown influence of early nutritional history on reproduction in later life.

The use of physiological indices in habitat evaluation will undoubtedly increase as wild animals become managed more intensively in selected areas. Emphasis thus far has centered on use of only one characteristic at a time as an indicator. Sets of characteristics are likely to delineate habitat conditions accurately. More research on how to take such measures of habitat conditions and integrate them is warranted.

Carrying Capacity

The concept of *carrying capacity,* designed to integrate concepts of habitat and populations, is rife with subtleties. The term is so variously used that the majority of wildlifers will always be misusing it (see Edwards and Fowle 1955, Barker 1974). It is a term that any barbershop biologist can use in confident ignorance. Just as pH has logarithmic units difficult for the average person to understand, so does a proper concept of the managed population. Carrying capacity is a land parameter measured in animal units. (Some range managers speak of carrying capacity for plants, meaning the maximum number of plants a range can sustain through the most critical time in a 100-year period.) Carrying capacity is a whole, broad band concept, not an exact idea. All definitions of it have major theoretical problems, lack of precision, or lack of a conceivable means for measuring the expressed concept. The concept is so complex it should be used only in the most superficial way with the public. Wildlifers, however, should be very aware of the numerous components and articulate each very carefully.

There are two types of carrying capacity: *species-specific* and *composite-species*. The user should state the type being used as well as whether *actual* or *potential* capacity is meant. Whether the public's or manager's benefits are sought should be explicit. *Carrying capacity is the user-specified quality biomass of a particular species, under the influence of social or behavioral constraints, for which a particular area, having user-specified objectives, will supply all energetic and physiological requirements over a long* (but specified) *period.* This definition of species-specific, actual capacity need be only slightly revised for composite species.

Definitions are the basis of theory. It is very important that they meet appropriate criteria. A suitable definition of carrying capacity must accommodate herbivores and carnivores, include land and animal parameters, allow animals with equivalent forage consumption rates (for example, many fawns and does versus few bucks), specify a time, be a dynamic expression (actual carrying capacity can differ between years), include social limits to population densities, enable managerial influence to increase or decrease the capacity, and imply lack of range "harm" or continuance. It is expressive of human desires and the uncertainty associated with the environment. The above definition meets these criteria. The definition is long and difficult to understand, but that is the nature of a complex concept.

A rancher may turn 100 head of cattle onto a pasture that will support, as a result of seasonal forage production, only 95. The rancher estimates 100, turns out the animals, and then discovers too late that the correct number was 95. The game that the rancher, and similarly the wildlifer, must play is one of how to avoid some range damage yet not waste (that is, underutilize) the forage produced on the land at high costs. Typically, the rancher will bet against the weather, overgraze 3 out of 4 years, and suffer gradual range quality declines. The wildlifer, by personal choice or public pressure, will typically allow too many animals to return from a hunting season onto wildlife ranges. The ability of the land to produce desired types of animals (for example, k percent of the biomass in bucks with greater than 4-point each year) declines. Management objectives for an area may be for stable pine production. The carrying capacity for deer under this objective, acting as a constraint, will be less than on an identical area without such a management objective. This difference is between *actual* (or current) and *potential* capacity. The first is expressive of the local and temporal factors in operation, the second a theoretical maximum given the natural conditions in each year. These different measures make the carrying capacity problem one of the most difficult of ideas to communicate to sportsmen and legislators. The more that is known, the harder becomes the decisions.

Potential capacity differs from *saturation point* in that the latter is the theoretical maximum number of social units (for example, coveys of quail) of a species that can occur in an area. Intensive management cannot cause the saturation point to be exceeded.

There are several important management principles hidden in the words of the definition of carrying capacity:

1. The wildlifer knows that more "poor" deer than healthy deer can be supported on an area. Quality biomass implies there will be a user decision to specify at least minimum levels of quality.

2. Management is for a population with a specific sex and age structure, not just animals. Quality biomass implies health, vigor, meat production, and perhaps palatability for humans.

3. Animals can exceed their carrying capacity, a condition that denies the denotation of the phrase. (How does one carry more than 40 liters in a 40-liter capacity pail?) Animals will eat the "interest" of forage production for years, but will also eat the "principal." When this occurs, most managers for typical wildlife areas will agree that excesses have occurred.

4. Any food consumed above that required for maintenance will be used for growth, but later this can be damaging (via forage demands for maintenance of the larger biomass) to the resource base and thus the animal population.

5. Habitats have a "vacuum effect," that is, they quickly fill to their limit—and then some. Few populations have ample feedback mechanisms to prevent their "overshooting" the limit (Figures 4-25 and 4-26). Animal populations typically recover faster than plant communities.

6. Interspersion and juxtaposition bring together population essentials, increase production from the same area, reduce the area needed, and increase the capacity.

7. All forage consumed by a game animal after it reaches a harvestable condition is wasted. All forage consumed by a harvestable animal that will die unharvested (for example, by starvation) is wasted.

8. Some wildlifers have used carrying capacity and "limiting factors" almost synonymously. The model is much like that of a barrel with several bungs at different levels. Whichever one, no matter how small, is knocked out will determine the real capacity of the barrel, although the potential remains the same. The analogy suggests, too, the difference between a potential limiting factor and an actual one. Interactions are omitted in the barrel and bung analogy, but it is intended only as a simple, didactic analogy. An alternative

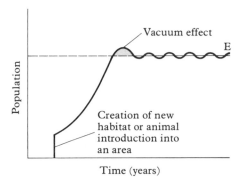

FIGURE **4-25**

The change in a population over time is shown. Equilibrium, E, sometimes conceived as carrying capacity, is reached and exceeded before feedback mechanisms can bring the population under control.

analogy (all analogies are merely models, representative of a part of reality) is that of the same barrel on a wave-tossed boat. The analogy expresses the dynamics of capacity. See Figure 4-27. Students may wish to unify an analogy of carrying capacity as a barrel with bungs on a boat.

Carrying capacity, for some purposes, can be replaced by:

1. Maximum potential biomass of species i per unit area.
2. Maximum potential biomass production of species i per unit area.
3. Current biomass of species i per unit area.
4. Current biomass production of species i per unit area.
5. Maximum animals or biomass per unit area of species i to achieve a particular objective.
6. Ecological homeostasis (kcal/m^2/unit time) using least squares as a measure of fit to a zero rate of change.

Most wildlifers will resist these substitutes, for they are simplistic. They contribute little to the quest for a constantly improving estimate of the potential.

A good way to compute potential production is to use the concept of production functions (Chapter 2). These curves have a variety of related uses including expression of erosion over time, utility of cars in a motor pool, agency personnel performance over time, and research team effectiveness. When used for computing food or net available energy to a species, the resulting pictures provide a number of special insights:

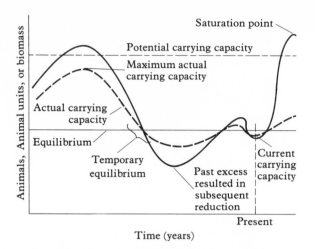

FIGURE **4-26**

The relations, over time, of animal population to the habitat's carrying capacities. Changes represent responses of the animals both to the habitat and to the wildlife manager's treatment of the habitat.

1. "Bunched" decisions have unusual, long-lasting effects. (After a spate of forest clearcutting, how can browse equivalent to the years after the cut be matched by management over the next 50 years?)

2. Most biological phenomena are skewed. When the tails are all added, cyclic or oscillating aggregate curves result. It is infeasible to obtain a straight line.

3. The assumption that wildlife will tend to expand to the energetic or other limits of their habitat is essential.

4. The production function approach assumes potential yields and long-term strategies. It is impossible to predict whether a poacher will be operating in 1994. Therefore, wildlife curves can be treated similarly to forest curves. They are the basis of long-term management and planning. There are other management acts such as predator control, feeding, and law enforcement that can be applied annually within an area. All production curves can be scaled so that maximum likely yields (the highest point on the curve) are 1.0. This provides a common scale and will usually result in the wildlifer's talking about relative efficiency or effectiveness of various years to meet user needs.

5. Such scaling enables relative weights of resource importance to be assigned to each curve (for example, pines 80, quail 16). The breaking point of the

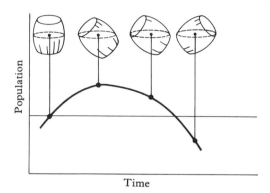

FIGURE **4-27**

Carrying capacity is sometimes likened to a barrel of
water on a boat at sea. The maximum amount of
animals that an area will support indefinitely without
impairing future capacities is like the amount of water
the barrel will hold under all storms, waves, and winds
moving the boat. But then capacity is as much a
function of the boat as the barrel.

weighted curves is sought for managerial guidance. It provides the basis
for multiple species management on the same areas.

6.   Where data on curves are lacking it is appropriate to use expert opinion and
to employ subjective estimates as first approximations and best available
information. Computer simulations can be employed to examine how
decisions might change if the estimates were off by various amounts. The
method enables the experience of old-timers to be "captured" and meaningfully employed.

Figure 4-28 shows how a habitat objective can be set. The level may be at
carrying capacity. By initiating habitat production curves (by forest cutting,
plowing, or fires) the deficit can be met by the aggregate curves. Proper size of
units and time of starting production on areas in a management unit enable a
best fit to be achieved to the objective function.

Funding Habitat Management

What solar energy is to plant systems, money is to habitat management systems.
Changing demands and priorities, budgetary limitations, land use changes,
increasing management alternatives, and better articulated risks call for greatly
increased sophistication in spending limited wildlife funds on habitat management and other practices.

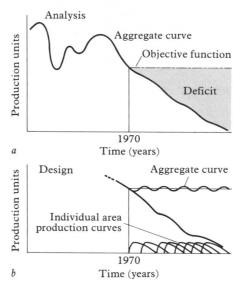

FIGURE **4-28**

(*a*) The aggregate curve for wildlife benefits produced by coverts throughout a management area declines over time. An objective of stabilizing production at the 1970 level is set. A deficit is realized. (*b*) The exact number of coverts (for example, brush piles), each having a production function of rabbit benefits over time, can be computed or graphed to achieve an optimum fit to the objective line.

There are two major types of wildlife management decisions. One type involves decisions not requiring primary allocation of money. These, in the final analysis, are very few. From one point of view, if a professional wildlifer makes a decision, it costs money; thus, all decisions require allocation. However, some decisions having profound effects, such as the setting of hunting seasons, may involve costs so small as to be inconsequential. Even adding the total costs for data collection to those for the final decision-making process, the costs are inconsequential relative to other activities. Such decisions are best improved by using existing statistical techniques, regression estimates, and computer simulation.

The other type of management decision involves all activities for which money from a budget is allocated. These decisions can be divided into (1) research allocation and (2) allocation for land purchase and population manipulation, various efforts to change user pressures and success, and habitat manipulation. The decisions are vastly complex, but can be analyzed as in Figure 4-29. Much information is needed for such decision making, but by screening data the amount required can be minimized.

Advanced management sciences can be employed in wildlife management to accommodate risk and include supply levels, use levels, public values, and political considerations. Budgeting alternatives must be studied, appropriate levels of funding determined, and time schedules developed for activities that meet agency requirements and that produce the highest valued production per unit costs.

An objective function for the agency is to maximize the production of wildlife resource benefits for a given budget (such as annual Federal Aid budgets to states, which are determined by a formula) and to minimize the cost of achieving the desired benefits from the resource. The general approach within both is to determine the user needs from the wildlife resource; determine what is available and what will become available largely due to ecological succession; determine what would be produced naturally and what as a result of expenditures; compare the differences; estimate the costs of reducing the differences by possible combinations of management techniques that actually produce change; and report a best solution—a mix of activities (and the ranges of expenditures over which the solution remains "right"). Computer technology (linear programming) can be used to obtain the solution that is an optimum mix for all species, in all regions of the state, over all years of the planning horizon, while satisfying scheduling, resource and manpower availability, rules of thumb, program continuity, and other judgmental aspects of the problem.

There are few well-documented studies of costs of producing wildlife. Population estimates are of themselves a difficult problem, but they are made more complex by the need for associating user-days or other benefit units to the animal produced or present. Purchase, operation, and maintenance cost data are variable and expensive to obtain and keep current. They vary as a function of the local mechanics as well as the equipment manufacturers. They are almost meaningless for the public wildlife agency that operates with variable manpower, over harsh terrain, and frequently with undependable "surplus" equipment.

The following is a tested framework for integrating available knowledge and experience in the area of habitat management. The answers to four general questions are used for estimating *costs, production, production requirements,* and *budgets.*

1. What is the peak?
2. What is the lowest possible?
3. What is the most likely?

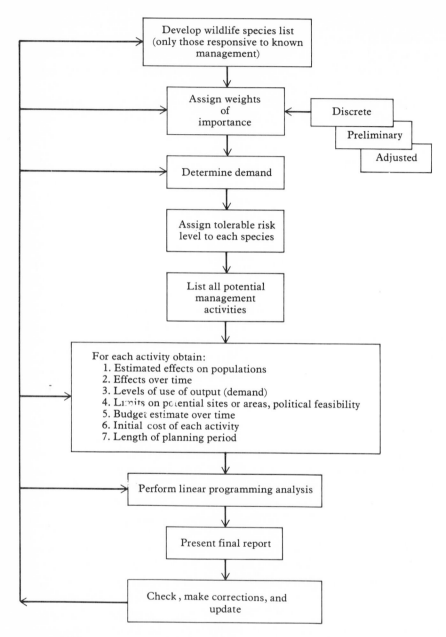

A flow diagram of a system for optimum allocation of wildlife management monies. (Based on MAST system by Lobdell 1972.)

4. What is the level of risk that the decision maker is willing to assume in making a decision based on an estimate? (For example, for endangered species one must be very sure; for others, perhaps rabbits, one can take more risk since being wrong is not as serious a problem.)

These are answered by research or subjective probability estimates by experts. "Estimate" is used here in the formal sense of being the best information available. With periodic usage and dynamic feedback to verify or improve estimates, continuing improvement can be assured. Where data are lacking or questionable, allocation of funds for survey and research may be indicated.

Site factors, extraneous disturbance (such as poachers or dogs), and past use (such as grazing) have heretofore been the complexities not amenable to any solution system. The use of estimates to establish site-specific production curves incorporates such factors.

Production is an environmental response to an expenditure. There are four general types of production:

Option 1. The effect of the activity may last only one year. Examples of such activities are an annual lease of right-of-way, stocking of fish or wildlife on a put-and-take basis, and maintenance of annual food patches.

Option 2. The effect of the activity on a use opportunity is prolonged and is expected to affect supplies up to t years. Production is expected to reach a peak in p years. Activities whose effect over time could be described in such a manner would be the realm of habitat manipulation practices such as clearcutting, clearing, or other activities to alter the successional stage of the area. The effect of the activity would change supplies of various opportunities for wildlife use in different ways. For example, a 160-acre clearcut in a mature hardwood forest might have a measurable effect on supplies of deer hunter-days for 100 years, whereas the peak production might occur in about 25 years. However, this same activity could affect supplies of turkey and turkey hunter-days for the next 250 years (until a mature forest was re-established). The peak year for outputs derived from turkeys might be about 80 years. On the other hand, a forest clearcut could stimulate small game (quail) production for about 20 years, the peak year occurring around the fifth year. Trout may be adversely affected for about 5 years, the first year after timber harvest being when the most damage occurs. For each activity, the duration of the effect and the year that the production peaks differ for each wildlife species.

Option 3. The effect on the activity is prolonged and is expected to last at least as long as the planning horizon. Such effects can be described best in terms of a constant rate of change based on present production. In other words, production is expected to change by a constant percentage yearly. Activities that would fall into this category would be land acquisition and development of access. The result is that on a particular area known production is changed, since the area available for utilization is increased without significantly changing the succession on the area.

Option 4. The effect on the activity is essentially constant throughout the planning period. The activity may be feasible every year or feasible in only one particular year of the horizon. This option might be used to describe acquisition of land that, for one reason or another, is available only in a specific year.

After the production option is determined, wildlife species are listed. Comparisons of importance or value are then made between all species. A numerical scale from 1 to 100 is assigned each. These are the relative weights of importance assigned by the *responsible decision maker*, the voting of a commission, or other means including, perhaps later, citizen voting.

Next, the estimated needs are assessed. This is the demand for species-specific benefit units over time. These are trend extrapolations or estimates and derived the best way feasible. A number of methods are available.

Then, the present production is assessed. Subtracting present production from the demand determines the deficit. How that deficit will be met is the question. First, the amount that will be filled by the natural progression of the existing habitats is determined. The allocation of funds is made to make up the difference. Since funds are usually limited, how they will be allocated is the problem. They typically will be used to make up the differences in proportion to the species importance and what each habitat management practice contributes to making up the difference for the lowest cost. The methodology, as stated, is complex, but has been computerized by Lobdell (1972) in a system called Management Activity Selection Technique (MAST). The system is used to aid state wildlife agencies in allocating available funds. The pattern is all-important and should be used by all wildlifers, whether they rely on a computer or not.

In this chapter, the habitat has been analyzed and ways suggested for manipulating it to achieve human objectives. The biological and physical problems are complex enough; to these must be added the problems of human influence on habitat and human determination of wildlife values and management funding. The next chapter is about the third major dimension of the wildlife management system—people.

Study Questions

1. What are the four fundamental structural properties of habitat?
2. Define and compare *refuge, sanctuary, preserve.*
3. What are dynamic management areas? Why are they recommended?
4. Name four major reasons for posting.

5. List ten ways of retaining and acquiring hunting opportunity.

6. Roads provide access. What are other ways of creating access to wildlife areas?

7. Conduct a local study to determine the zone of influence of roads or trails. How far off the road do people in your area hunt? What percentage of the total area is hunted by 50 percent of the people? 80 percent? 95 percent?

8. What factors retard fee hunting?

9. Discriminate between territory and home range.

10. Make a vector diagram of a study area, or any system with measurable criteria of effectiveness.

11. Calculate the area (in sq ft, in acres, in hectares) of a circular food patch with radius of 208 ft.

12. Compare the area obtained in question 11 with a square measuring 208 on one side. What is the total edge in a 1-acre plot when it is circular, square, elliptical ($l/w = 2$), and rectangular ($l/w = 2$)?

13. Calculate the total wildlife food produced (at 80 lb/hectare) on an area that is 10 meters wide and 500 meters long; one that is 20 meters wide and 250 meters long.

14. Design how you would put in two types of shrub hedges (all are 10 ft wide) throughout a square area of 100 acres:
    A. To maximize edge.
    B. To provide hunter access and access to birds.
    C. To maximize coverts or points where hedge types intersect.
    Present your final results on graph paper using a scale of 208 ft = 1 inch.

15. Students may wish to perform a simple sampling experiment. The following technique (Dulley 1958) can be used to study, for example, wildlife food available in grain fields, crop damage studies, forest acorn production, forest leaf litter, effects of crop residue on erosion control and soil improvement, and food availability.
    A. Make a sampler frame 2.95 ft square (1/5000 acre).
    B. Take five samples (for example, food) at random.
    C. Combine them (that is, a 1/1000-acre sample).
    D. Air dry the sample.
    E. Weigh to nearest 1/10 pound.
    F. Divide weight by 2.
    G. Result is number of tons of food per acre.

16. Laser beams are used in surveying and in air pollution monitoring. Is it likely laser technology can be used in cover density analyses?

17. What are the major characteristics of edge?

18. What is the major difference between a type 1 and type 2 corner?

19. Define juxtaposition.

20. Define covert.

21. As you increase equilateral triangles in an area, what happens to edge? As you increase the length of the leg of the triangle? What happens to the number of coverts as you increase the length of the leg of the triangle?

22. What happens to the area in the zone of influence in a triangle as the length of the leg increases? Can you determine the break point between edge (and edge zone) and coverts if 50 units of edge area are equal to 1 covert?

23. In an area the weed seeds per acre were expressed as $Y = 6.02 + 0.2X$, where X was years up to about 10. What was the amount at year 0, that is, a bare field? Is this possible? Why? What are the pounds per acre in year 9? If we overextended the equation to year 20? Sketch the likely curve.

24. Conduct a class debate on whether few results from a wildlife study are better than none.

25. If the variance doubles, what happens to the needed sample size? If you double your requirements for accuracy, what happens to the requisite sample size?

26. Sketch from memory the major categories of wildlife food use diagramed in Figure 4-19.

27. If a key forage plant occurs in 36 out of 40 plots, what is likely to be the average number of individuals per plot?

28. Define proximate analysis.

29. Discriminate between food *availability* and *utilization*.

30. What is a safe percentage of browse utilization before plant vigor is impaired?

31. If an animal stays on the same contour, but must move a certain distance daily, how much more energy is required by an animal that must move 1600 meters than by one that must move only 600 meters?

32. What is the primary animal energy input mechanism? What are the four primary loss mechanisms?

33. How much energy is lost by an animal "panting" away 1 gram of moisture?

34. List at least 10 ways the animal itself can be used to analyze the habitat.

35. Define species-specific carrying capacity.

36. Why is it said: "All forage consumed by harvestable animals that will die unharvested is wasted"?

37. How does the wildlifer fill in the deficit on an aggregate curve?

Selected References

Baker, M. F. and F. X. Lueth. 1966. Mandibular cavity tissue as a possible indicator of condition in deer. *Proc. S.E. Assn. Game and Fish Commissioners* **20**:69–74.

Barker, P. A. 1974. Carrying capacity in resource-based recreation and some related research needs. *Proc. Utah Acad. Sciences, Arts, and Letters* **51**(Part 1):123–128.

Batzli, G. O. and F. A. Pitelka. 1971. Condition and diet of cycling populations of the California vole, *Microtus californicus*. J. Mammal. **52**(1):141–163.

Billings, W. D. 1952. The environmental complex in relation to plant growth and distribution. *Quarterly Rev. Biology* 27(3):251-265.

Bissell, H. D. and H. Strong. 1954. Crude protein variation in the browse diet of California deer. *California Fish and Game* 41:145-155.

Blaxter, K. L. 1962. *The energy metabolism of ruminants.* Hutchinson and Company, London, 329 p.

Brockway, J. M. 1965. Posturally associated changes in the heat control of sheep, p. 395-404, in *Energy metabolism,* ed. K. L. Blaxter. Proc. 3rd Symposium held at Troon, Scotland, May, 1964. Academic Press, London. xiv + 950 p.

Cheatum, E. L. 1949. Bone marrow as an index of malnutrition in deer. *New York State Conservationist* 3(5):19-22.

Clapperton, J. L. 1961. The energy expenditure of sheep in walking on the level and on gradients. *Proc. Nutr. Soc.* 20:xxxi

Clements, F. E. 1928. *Plant succession and indicators.* H. W. Wilson Company, New York. 453 p.

Conlin, W. M. and R. H. Giles, Jr. 1973. Maximizing edge and coverts for quail and small game. *Proc. First National Bobwhite Quail Symposium,* Oklahoma State University, Stillwater, p. 302.

Crampton, E. W. and L. E. Harris. 1969. *Applied animal nutrition,* 2nd ed. W. H. Freeman and Company, San Francisco. xxiv + 753 p.

Dasmann, R. F. 1964. *Wildlife biology.* John Wiley and Sons, New York. 231 p.

Dulley, F. L. 1958. *Estimating the amount of crop residue on a field.* USDA Agric. Handbook 136. 31 p.

Edwards, R. Y. and C. D. Fowle. 1955. The concept of carrying capacity. *Trans. N. Am. Wildlife Conf.* 20:589-598.

Estep, J. E. 1975. *Seasonal variations in body fat and food habits of pine voles from two Virginia orchards.* Unpub. M.S. Thesis, Virginia Polytechnic Institute, Blacksburg. 71 p.

Franzman, A. W. 1972. Environmental sources of variation of bighorn sheep physiological values. *J. Wildlife Management* 36(3):924-932.

Garrison, G. A. 1948. Effects of clipping on some range shrubs. *J. Range Management* 6(5):309-317.

Gaussen, H. 1957. Integration of data by means of vegetation maps. *9th Pacific Sci. Congress Proc.* 20:67-74.

Geist, V. 1971. *Mountain sheep: a study in behavior and evolution.* University of Chicago Press, Chicago. 383 p.

Giles, R. H., Jr. (Ed.). 1971. *Wildlife management techniques,* 3rd ed., revised. The Wildlife Society, Washington, DC. vii + 633 p.

Giles, R. H., Jr. and R. F. Scott. 1969. A systems approach to refuge management. *Trans. N. Am. Wildlife Conf.* 34:103-117.

Greig-Smith, P. 1964. *Quantitative plant ecology,* 2nd ed. Butterworths, London. xii + 256 p.

James, G. A., F. M. Johnson, and F. B. Barick. 1964. Relations between hunter access and deer kill in North Carolina. *Trans. N. Am. Wildlife Conf.* 29:454-462.

Kendeigh, S. C. 1961. *Animal ecology.* Prentice-Hall, Englewood Cliffs, NJ. 468 p.

Kershaw, K. A. 1974. *Quantitative and dynamic plant ecology*, 2nd ed. Elsevier, New York. x + 308 p.

Kirkpatrick, R. L., D. E. Buckland, W. A. Abler, P. F. Scanlon, J. B. Whelan, and H. E. Burkhart. 1975. Energy and protein influences on blood urea nitrogen of white-tailed deer fawns. *J. Wildlife Management* 39(4):692-698.

Kirkpatrick, R. L., J. P. Fontenot, and R. F. Harlow. 1969. Seasonal changes in rumen chemical components as related to forages consumed by white-tailed deer in the southeast. *Trans. N. Am. Wildlife Conf.* 34:229-238.

Klein, D. R. 1962. Rumen contents analysis is an index to range quality. *Trans. N. Am. Wildlife and Nat. Resour. Conf.* 27:150-164.

Klein, D. R. 1964. Range related differences in growth of deer reflected in skeletal ratios. *J. Mammal.* 45:226-235.

Leopold, A. 1933. *Game management.* Charles Scribner's Sons, New York. 481 p.

LeResche, R. E., U. S. Seal, P. D. Karns, and A. W. Franzmann. 1974. A review of blood chemistry of moose and other cervidae with emphasis on nutritional assessment. *Naturaliste Can.* 101:263-290.

Lobdell, C. H. 1972. *MAST: A budget allocation system for wildlife management.* Unpub. Ph.D. Dissertation, Virginia Polytechnic Institute, Blacksburg. 227 p.

Magruder, N. D., C. E. French, L. C. McEwen, and R. W. Swift. 1957. Nutritional requirements of white-tailed deer for growth and antler development II. *Penna. Agric. Expt. Stat. Bull.* No. 628. 21 p.

Margalef, R. 1968. *Perspectives in ecological theory.* University of Chicago Press, Chicago. viii + 112 p.

Moen, A. N. 1973. *Wildlife ecology: an analytical approach.* W. H. Freeman and Company, San Francisco. xviii + 458 p.

Nichols, R. G. and M. R. Pelton. 1972. Variations in fat levels of mandibular cavity tissue in white-tailed deer (*Odocoileus virginianus*) in Tennessee. *Proc. S.E. Assn. Game and Fish Commissioners* 26:57-68.

Nichols, R. G. and M. R. Pelton. 1974. Fat in the mandibular cavity as an indicator of condition in deer. *Proc. S.E. Assn. Game and Fish Commissioners* 28:540-545.

Ransom, A. B. 1965. Kidney and marrow fat as indicators of white-tailed deer condition. *J. Wildlife Management* 29(2):397.

Rayburn, E. B. 1972. *A measure of land for supporting deer populations.* Unpub. M.S. Thesis, Virginia Polytechnic Institute, Blacksburg. ix + 195 p.

Rayburn, S. B. 1972. *Analysis of factors influencing decisions to acquire public lands for wildlife.* Unpub. M.S. Thesis, Virginia Polytechnic Institute, Blacksburg. viii + 122 p.

Riney, T. 1955. Evaluating condition of free-ranging red deer (*Cervus elaphus*), with special reference to New Zealand. *New Zealand J. Sci. Tech.* 36, sec. B (5):429-463.

Robinette, W. L. 1971. *Browse and cover for wildlife.* USDA Forest Ser., Gen. Tech. Rpt. INT-1. p. 69-76.

Sanders, O. T., Jr. 1971. *Sulfur content of deer hair.* Unpub. M.S. Thesis, Virginia Polytechnic Institute, Blacksburg. 42 p.

Schuerholz, G. 1974. Quantitative evaluation of edge from aerial photographs. *J. Wildlife Management* 38(4):913-920.

Seal, U. S. 1972. Nutritional effects on thyroid activity and blood of white-tailed deer. *J. Wildlife Management* **36**(4):1041–1052.

Severinghaus, C. W., H. F. Maguire, R. A. Cookingham, and J. E. Tanck. 1950. Variations by age class in the antler beam diameters of white-tailed deer related to range conditions. *Trans. N. Am. Wildlife Conf.* **15**:551–570.

Silver, H., N. F. Colovas, J. B. Holter, and H. H. Hayes. 1969. Fasting metabolism of white-tailed deer. *J. Wildlife Management* **33**(3):490–498.

Silver, H., N. F. Colovas, J. B. Holter, and H. H. Hayes. 1971. Effect of falling temperature on heat production in fasting white-tailed deer. *J. Wildlife Management* **35**(1):37–46.

Skeen, J. E. 1974. *The relationships of certain rumino-reticular and blood variables to the nutritional status of white-tailed deer.* Unpub. Ph.D. Dissertation, Virginia Polytechnic Institute, Blacksburg. 98 p.

Snedecor, G. W. and W. G. Cochran. 1967. *Statistical methods,* 6th ed. Iowa State University Press, Ames. xiv + 593 p.

U.S. Department of Interior. *Annual report. Federal aid in fish and wildlife restoration: annual report on Dingell-Johnson and Pittman-Robertson programs.* Wildlife Management Inst., Washington, DC.

Watt, K. E. F. 1973. *Principles of environmental science.* McGraw-Hill, New York. xiv + 319 p.

Chapter 5

Management of People

People are an integral part of the population-habitat-people triad of wildlife management (see Figure 1-1). To make changes in the system as a whole, to improve its functioning, necessarily means manipulating its parts. The idea of manipulating people's attitudes and behavior may sound like a threat to individual freedom. Yet, realistically, people are being manipulated already—by advertisement from manufacturers, by industrial public relations campaigns, by politicians and political image makers, by religious institutions, by community customs and beliefs, and by the educational process. Human behavior is constantly under pressure to change. There is abundant evidence that behavior can and does change and that changes can be controlled and guided toward objectives.

It is a strange logic that allows people to manipulate their environment at will and yet condemns the manipulation of people themselves. People and the environment are inseparable. People are manipulated subtly by environmental change. This chapter is about overtly manipulating people to enhance the achievement of society's wildlife objectives.

Management of people (in their relationship to wildlife) can be viewed as a subsystem of wildlife management. The subsystem can be manipulated separately or as part of a total system designed and managed to achieve a set of objectives. Wildlife agencies are primarily game and fish agencies. Although they have been exhorted, for 20 years, to change to a broader-based management concept and to become integrated resource agencies, they have not done so. Consequently, they do not now operate at peak efficiency; they could do more, and do it better, with the resources they now have. The massive environmental problems that have recently become evident demand sophisticated solutions. Whether or not existing agencies choose to lead change or to be drawn along, change from a narrow faunal focus to a resource system view seems inevitable. Management of people is an essential part of that view.

In the past, wildlife managers have been poorly educated (if at all) to deal with the human dimensions of the developing science of wildlife management. They have been disinclined, for many reasons, to work with the human subsystem. Many still harbor the false notion that little factual information is known about people-management processes. Others have adopted single-minded approaches to specific age groups or narrow agency approaches that divorce the educational agency from the "real" wildlife agency. The lack of national or regional approaches in programs, media, or methods has further retarded development in this area. Then, too, there is the persistence in wildlife, as well as in educational, circles of an ethic that research should not be conducted on humans to test the effects of alternative practices.

Abundant psychological, educational, political, managerial, and operations research knowledge is now available to solve human-management problems. However, the literature is largely unsynthesized and unused by wildlifers. Few even know it exists. Wildlifers can start with *Educational Index* and search for relevant ideas and equations for application among the *Journal of Abnormal and Social Psychology, Psychological Monographs, Journal of Personality, Human Relations, Psychological Review, Public Opinion Quarterly, Journal of Personality and Social Psychology, Psychological Bulletin, Journal of Experimental and Social Psychology, American Psychologist, British Journal of Psychology, Psychology Today, Recreation, Journal of Leisure Research, Journal of Environmental Education, Canadian Journal of Psychology, American Psychologist, Child Development, Developmental Psychology, Merrill-Palmer Quarterly, American Sociological Review, Social Forces, Journal of Psychology, Journal of Social Psychology, Journal of Conflict Resolution, Journal of Social Issues, Sociometry, Psychonomic Science, Journal of Applied Behavioral Science, Social Problems, Behavioral Science, Social Science, Law and Society Review, Social Science Information, Human Factors, Adult Education, Continuing Education, Convergence, Management Review,* and *Public Administration Review.* Readers of journals such as these will quickly move beyond Gilbert's (1971) *Natural Resources and Public Relations* to relevant questions of how to modify individual or group behavior to achieve agency, employer, or public needs.

Wildlife management, when done well, is a sensitive balancing of populations, habitats, and people. These three elements must coexist in the minds of managers and those involved in the management agency. In all cases, if this triad is out of balance, the user will be poorly served, or even hurt.

Consider an example of the influence of balance on allocating wildlife funds. Assume there is a demand (*people*) for doubling the number of animals of a particular game species (*population*). The cost of doing so is estimated to be $1000 (*habitat*). There is field research evidence to indicate that a more acceptable alternative would be to increase the population, not by a factor of 2, but by a factor of only 0.5 (*population*). The total cost of doing the latter is estimated to be $300 (*habitat*). It is also known that an expenditure of $300 for education plus $300 for habitat management, a $400 savings results from the original cost estimate of $1000. By combining the three management alternatives of population, habitat, and people, significant savings, or significantly increased production per dollar, can be achieved.

For another example, consider the osprey or fish hawk (*Pandion haliaetus carolinensis*), believed by many to be endangered in some areas. Managers can manipulate the population, with great difficulty (*population*). They can also manipulate the food supply and the number of suitable nesting sites, at great expense (*habitat*); but with $25 worth of leaflets, wildlife managers can cause 200 refuge users to appreciate this bird's value and behavior and to invest hundreds of hours in observations without disturbing the population or habitat (*people*). It seems irrational to engage only in efforts to influence supply.

A program designed to manage human behavior can be considered a success only if a *measurable* change in behavior occurs as a direct result of managerial effort. This sort of evaluation shifts the emphasis *away* from money spent, animals fed, acres planted, pages produced, people employed, and movies shown *toward* the measured effects produced by these means. If the objectives of a management effort have been carefully stated in behavioral terms—that is, in terms of the ways a population of people is expected *to act* as a result of a specific program—then the effectiveness of the techniques used in relation to the objectives can be more precisely evaluated. The wildlife manager's monthly report will include not only numbers of activities performed, but also indices of the progress of these activities toward a predetermined goal.

Some measures of changes in behavior that might be used include:

1. A reduction in the number of gripe letters.
2. Fewer negative congressional inquiries.
3. Increased positive votes in commissions or on public issues.
4. Increased use of facts, as opposed to opinions, in public hearings.
5. An increase in the number of requests for a particular educational item.
6. Increased funding for meritorious projects.
7. A reduction in the number of law violations of a particular type.

8. Reduced soil erosion or runoff in an area of special concern.

9. An increase in the weights of deer on an overused range (where the cause of overuse was public insistence on a particular type of season).

10. A reduction in the number of requests or applications for introduction of exotics.

11. Reduced pollution at a monitoring station.

12. Reduced vandalism in a specific management area.

13. Higher scores by the public on tests or opinion polls.

When objectives are couched in measurable terms—when, for example, "public acceptance" becomes very specifically "greater than 40 percent affirmative votes on wildlife issue Number 16"—then programs can be designed to cause the desired behavior change. Through feedback, maximally efficient programs can be developed and alternative programs can be compared on a rational basis.

Analysis and Design

People can be analyzed for wildlife management purposes by the same general method used to analyze animal populations in Chapter 2. The major structural subgroups for people are sex, age, and economic status (or educational achievement, which is correlated with economic status). These subgroups vary in how they (1) value wildlife, (2) participate in wildlife activities, (3) drop out or enter user groups, and (4) obtain secondary benefits from such acts as hunting. Human populations can be analyzed to determine the total number of hunters or license buyers; the dynamics of annual satisfactions that are an aggregate of the satisfactions of each sex-age-economic group; the wildlife educational needs in a population that is changing over time; and the relative susceptibility of each subgroup to a management strategy or tactic.

Production curves can be used to aggregate individual enjoyment of complex outdoor experiences as a function of age (see Figure 5-1). They can also be used to observe and evaluate wildlife agent production as a function of the agent's years of experience (see Figure 5-2).

The parallels between the earlier chapters and this one on the management of people are evident and should be creatively studied. In this chapter, design concepts and fundamental system processes equivalent to those of the ecosystem (such as succession) are emphasized.

Only general systems theory can bring order to the chaos variously called environmental education, conservation education, public relations, information and education, and wildlife law enforcement. A systems approach to wildlife management, and to its people management subsystem, includes: (1) context, (2)

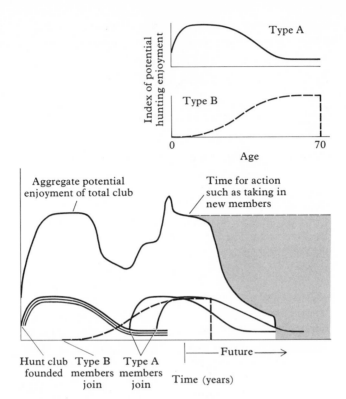

FIGURE **5-1**

Several types of hunters exist. The type A hunter experiences teen-age enjoyment that lasts for many years but diminishes with age. The type B person is introduced to hunting later in life and gains increasing skill and enjoyment throughout life. A club is formed, and the types of hunters join the club at different times. The aggregate potential enjoyment of the club decreases unless new members join the club.

objectives, (3) inputs, (4) processes, (5) feedback, and (6) feedforward. (Recall Figure 1-2.)

Objectives

Objectives for human behavior relative to the wildlife resource are decided by the person responsible for the resource. This is often the landowner or the general public (for public lands). The source of objectives is discussed in Chapter 1. The wildlife manager may unilaterally decide on objectives, of course, but only as the representative of the landowner or citizens. The appro-

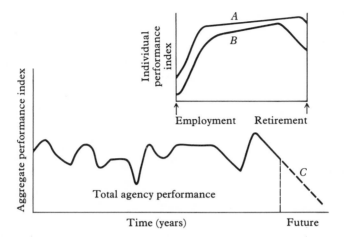

FIGURE **5-2**

The superior wildlife enforcement agent (*A*) may be very effective
initially, improve rapidly, continue to learn throughout his career, and
only slack off when ordered to and when clearing up retirement
arrangements and training a replacement. Others (*B*) learn more slowly
and start slacking off when they see retirement on the horizon. The
sum of such performance curves explains perceived agency effectiveness, shows the folly of mass hiring or firing, and indicates (*C*) when
action should be taken to stabilize agency performance.

priate source of objectives should be under continual debate. Whatever the
source, the wildlife manager must see that they are properly stated so that they
can be used and so that it is possible to decide whether they have been achieved.

Objectives for the management of people in the wildlife management system
should specify:

1. Who is responsible for changing the behavior.
2. Whose behavior will be changed.
3. Precisely what act a person should be able to perform after the contacts or
   stimuli.
4. The expected level of performance of such acts or behaviors.

Two examples of objectives might be (1) to have boy scouts or girl scouts
identify 90 percent of the songbirds seen in a particular area with at least
80-percent accuracy, and (2) to get the citizens of Hilltown to write at least 100
letters supporting chukar hunting in the surrounding county.

Target Groups. All objectives for the management of people must specify the
prime target group. There are sportsmen, nature lovers, protectionists, indus-

trialists, youth. Each has a different size, voice, political power, and per capita resource consumption. Analysis is needed to identify the group or groups which, if appropriate actions are taken, will produce the best control of the system per dollar invested. "Who is the public?" and "Who are the relevant publics?" remain questions to be decided, based on legislative mandate and the social, moral, and ethical dimensions of each wildlifer's view of the democratic process. Once the targets are identified, then specialized media and methods can be designed for hitting each target.

A problem with the target strategy, called "sitting ducks," is that the targets may be too numerous for any action to be effective or the guns may be too few or too light (or too inefficient) to reach the targets. A tactical decision within the target strategy is whether to use a shotgun or a rifle—whether, for example, to rifle into a group of game and fish commissioners with a dozen copies of *Wildlife Management* or spend thousands of dollars "shotgunning" sportsmen groups, trying to get them to sell a point or principle to commissioners. Presently educational programs are overweighted with the shotgun approach.

The preceding analysis may be more formally stated as an analysis of group amplitude or diversity. Management of people becomes more difficult with increased federation and mixing of people with different backgrounds. Insistence on regional or local educational programs may increase educational efficiency, inasmuch as people's value systems are shaped by their environments. In heterogeneous group meetings, value schemes must be resolved in addition to the usual problems in any public group meetings of belief in the data, acceptance of assumptions, and confidence in projected outcomes of various alternatives. Other aspects of group amplitude that should be considered, reduced where possible, or accommodated in program development are the habitat, custom, and culture dimensions of the target audience—for example, as articulated for a specific geographic subgroup in *Yesterday's People* (Weller 1966.) Other aspects are employment and socioeconomic amplitudes.

The leadership tactic is a primary aspect of the target strategy. Leaders must be cultivated, raised from the group, supported, informed, and taught group dynamics. Groups are often pooled ignorance; leaders can take them almost anywhere. The wildlifer should work with those from whom the objective-oriented payoffs will be greatest—the officers of the groups. It should be noted that very often secretaries or vice presidents have more group-manipulation power than presidents.

Closely related to the target strategy is the strategy called *preach-to-the-parade.* This approach is an expression of the dynamics of the target strategy. Educators often tend to feel, after many repetitions of the same message, that a change is needed. But after the "pitch" has been given to the first row of the parade, and even after it has been acted upon, it must be given all over again to the next platoon coming by. No platoons must miss the message. The one platoon that is missed may become the guerilla band that will defeat the program next year. Sustained inputs are necessary. People seldom learn from the mistakes of others—not because they deny the value of the past—but because they are faced with new problems. The scenery changes as well as the parade.

Objective-Weighting. All objectives are not of equal weight, value, or importance. They can be weighted in various ways. People will talk about relative importance; they will list objectives in order; they will assign a "most important" objective a value of 100 and consistently weight other objectives relative to it. How these weights are used, how objectives are selected, and how questions of legitimacy, social good, and justice are decided are all ethical questions. Most natural resource decisions have a high ethical load. Facts are not all that are needed. Facts must be viewed within the proper sociological and ethical contexts.

Every wildlife decision is value-laden, expressive of the ethical orientations of those who define the problem and those who elaborate the alternatives. The definition of the problem will determine how the ethical issues are posed. A "bad situation" can lead to coercive proposals. Desperate problems seem to require desperate solutions. Minor problems (those with light ethical loads) can be ignored or treated later. The value establishes the priority to be given to a problem, the funds to be allocated, the worker-hours to be spent, and the political risks to be taken.

There is a very valuable method, useful for decision making throughout wildlife management, called *objective-weighting*. In this chapter it is applied to the selection of an educational medium.

The first step in this method is to list objectives—for example, (1) to minimize costs, (2) to change the most people, (3) to cause the most change, and (4) to be easily operated and maintained. Although there are only four objectives for this example, in a realistic situation there may be 20 to 100 objectives and a computer may be necessary. The relative importance of the objectives is determined—for example, objective 4 is certainly not as important as objective 2. Weights are assigned by the decision maker or group who must take the risks of being wrong. Weights may come from group discussion, voting, or dictatorial edict.

Next, all feasible ways in which the objectives may be achieved are listed. Without reference to the importance weights assigned above, experts assign a real or estimated measure of how effective such alternative is likely to be in achieving each objective. These data can be secured from manufacturers, from research, or from expert opinion. Mean or modal values from a group in which the estimates differ can be used. The resulting matrix appears as in Table 5-1. The weight of each objective is multiplied by each of the efficiency scores for that column. Then, the products are added across the row to get a score for each alternative method, as in Table 5-2. The closer the scores to each other, the

TABLE **5-1**

An example of an objective-weighting matrix. Importance weights are assigned to each objective. Efficiency estimates are assigned to each feasible alternative for each objective.

Alternative methods	Weights of each objective	Objectives 1	2	3	4
		3	10	9	5
1. Movie		1	10	8	5
2. Leaflet		9	6	4	9
3. Speech		10	7	9	10
4. Radio		4	8	5	4

TABLE **5-2**

The objective-weights in Table 5-1 are multiplied to get importance-weighted effectiveness in each column; then scores are added by rows. The alternative with the highest score (*) is the best choice.

Alternative methods	Objectives 1	2	3	4	Score
1. Movie	6	100	72	25	203
2. Leaflet	54	60	36	45	195
3. Speech	60	70	81	50	261*
4. Radio	24	80	45	16	165

more difficult is the decision; however, the rational decision is the alternative method with the highest score, in this case method 3, speeches. It should be noted that the method works best when all relevant objectives are listed and when the weights of importance and efficiency are reasonably accurate. The more inclusive the model is, in terms of objectives and methods, the more likely it is the hierarchy of final scores will represent the real ranking of alternatives. The method does not work for combinations of techniques unless they are evaluated as set I, set II, and so on.

Further refinements in this method are (1) to multiply each efficiency score by a risk factor or probability of the estimate being correct, (2) to sum over the years (a third dimension to the matrix) using the production function concept to reflect changing efficiencies over time, (3) to test the numbers to see which combinations would have produced past decisions, and (4) to see over what range of values the answer stays the same.

This method of objective-weighting has been used for selecting equipment, agents, university courses, books, and policies. It can be used as a general decision-making model. It can show how two rational people can arrive at different solutions to a problem because of different (1) objectives listed, (2) weights, (3) risks, (4) perceived efficiency (over time), and even (5) errors in the mathematical computations.

The methodology is important because it puts scientific objectivity in its place, as only one of the factors involved in human decision making. More information may not be of help in some decisions, since the value scheme employed may overpower the importance of the data. The method also demonstrates that values other than monetary ones can be quantified and can be used in a practical decision-aiding methodology. It demonstrates how subjective probability indices can be used to describe the subtle and allegedly "indescribable" dimensions of a wildlife project.

Inputs

The management of people is sometimes called *social engineering.* To effect changes in people's actions, the wildlife manager must understand how their systems of decision making work and how they can be modified. The strategies to be employed, based on such understanding, are directed at *inputs* and *processes.*

Game and fish management problems have been said to be 90 percent people problems. This assertion is refuted by the *icebox principle,* which asserts that some people can sell iceboxes in the Arctic. Few wildlifers can sell an elk management program, much less an icebox. An icebox salesman approaching a customer knows what the customer wants; knows the product; and is motivated by having something at stake in the sale. The average wildlifer has only a sketchy idea of what sportsmen want. There are virtually no market analyses and few sophisticated demand studies. The wildlifer usually makes a sales pitch equivalent to saying about an icebox: "It's good. It's white. It's rectangular." Such an unimaginative presentation has never sold an icebox or an elk management program. A salesman must have information.

The wildlife agency working for the acceptance of a program must know population, habitat, and demand relations to achieve a "sale." The agency also needs committed salesmen. Many wildlifers have adopted a "take it or leave it" attitude in presenting programs. They feel that they have the facts and that there is not much point in debating them. In addition, they have little incentive for more intensive selling (they have few problems with job security or continuing salaries), and they often have been made ineffective as salesmen by laws and policies that directly contradict scientific findings. Wildlife agencies must realize that it does no good to curse the buying public; they must still approach the people—as advertisers and others approach them—with knowledge to change their behavior.

The inputs to decisions are inseparable from their source: "To believe the message is to trust the messenger." To "know" anything is to attach a relatively high level of confidence to it—sufficient confidence to act on it. The slick salesman, the unconvinced teacher, and the uninformed lecturer are all unconvincing messengers. The wildlife manager who is trying to produce positive results does not send the best movie on deer management with a person the viewers will not trust or respect. A good messenger is needed, whose presence will enhance the possibility for success.

The good messenger, in addition to being personally acceptable to the group, will also choose words carefully. Certain words have lost their meanings, and certain audiences need special interpretations or forms of the message. These efforts should not be interpreted as trying to make all of wildlife management intelligible to the village idiot. Sophisticated management of herd bioenergetics can hardly be explained to any general audience in the time it is willing to spend listening. A balance must be struck between citizen knowledge and confidence in professionals.

Studies reviewed by Watson and Johnson (1972:233) suggest the following about communicator credibility:

1. The more credible the source of information, the greater the attitude change that will occur immediately after an attempt to influence an audience.
2. The longer the contact (say, contacts over several weeks), the less important becomes the credibility of the communicator.
3. Highly credible communicators will cause greater change in audience attitudes the greater the difference is between the communicator and the audience.
4. A communicator with low credibility and great distance from the audience's views probably should not waste time attempting to change attitudes.
5. Characteristics of a communicator that are irrelevant to the topic (for example, clothing, gestures, profanity) can influence acceptance of conclusions (Zimbardo and Ebbensen 1969).

Many wildlifers appear to feel that the public is against them. However, few act as if nature were against them, although, from one point of view it is. The point of view is important. People can be looked upon as a challenge or as a target. Public agents, embittered, battered, and eventually calloused by the public, become ineffective and insensitive to the needs of people. They lose sight of the fact that resources, by definition, exist for people. If people are viewed, not as the antagonist, but as the objective of wildlife management, much of the distrust can be removed. People become intelligible to each other as holders of different values, and thus the reasons others "will not listen to reason" become obvious. Each person is applying different value multipliers and risk levels to the wildlife data. Perhaps more importantly, society has reached the point where the more information it receives, the less able it is to understand it—or to act upon it. There is a great need for new assistance.

There are several tactics that can be applied to reduce the distance between professionals and the public. One is the *go-and-get* tactic. This tactic recognizes the inadequacy of shouting from the hilltop that the agency is right and therefore others should support its efforts. There is abundant evidence that the hilltop position often taken in the past has been ineffective. The go-and-get tactic requires going however far is necessary to reach those whom the wildlife manager seeks to manage to achieve an agency's objectives.

A peculiar tactic that has emerged in wildlife management circles is the *united front* tactic. "Let's get together and present a united front" is the motif. Although concerted action may be theoretically desirable, it is not realistic at the present time, and there may be real questions about its ultimate value. Good wildlife management is not the uniform application of a set of general techniques, but a sensitive response to the specific needs of an individual area and its inhabitants. How a wildlifer prescribes a deer herd management strategy for a specific area with its traditional user clientele is not determined by other wildlifers (exclusive, of course, of hearings or boards of inquiry resulting from flagrant excesses). Sophisticated wildlife management cannot be done by committees; average answers are almost always suboptimal solutions for specific situations. There will be little agreement about management practices until (1) higher education is more unified and minimum standards of competence for wildlife managers are set, (2) citizen values are sampled, reported, and used as a basis for decision, (3) consequences of managerial acts are simulated, in all of their complexity, and presented to decision makers, and (4) citizens are made aware of the full consequences of decisions based on limited, personal, or self-interest concepts of utility. "United fronts" are established by technicians. The professional wildlifer will articulate the uniqueness of each decision, justify the decision before peers as necessary, and, as committees cannot do, take full responsibility for decisions. It is essential that *agreement* on basic ecosystem, population, and sociological phenomena be separated from united positions on policy and the application of the techniques in vogue.

Another tactic is called *roughing it*. In some public groups, procedures and discussions have sometimes deviated from the highest standards of courtesy and fair play. Efficiency dictates that the wildlifer be capable of providing vigorous, aggressive leadership, if necessary; otherwise, the Earth that the meek are due to inherit may soon become an impoverished mud ball. Roughing it (including vulgar challenges, embarrassment, and even physical threats) has been used successfully, and with humor, by more than one professional in the field. It is a tactical option when the situation demands it.

Another strategy for improving the credibility of the wildlifer is the *professional investment* strategy. Responsible resource management requires the use of men and women appropriate for the task. To hire a journalist to do the management described in this chapter is analogous to hiring a draftsman to do the work of an engineer. Those presently in agency administrative positions will object, "Where will I hire such people?" Unfortunately, the answer can only be vague because there is no employment pool. The necessary personnel must be obtained through the steps of (1) stating the need, (2) providing a guarantee for employment, (3) seeking out people from industry and the universities who have the needed skills, (4) demanding educational programs to produce such people, and (5) employing them.

The confidence the public feels in a wildlife manager is, in part, a function of the image of his or her agency. *Public relations* (PR) is the total subsystem that contributes to or influences agency *image* (Figure 5-3). It is designed primarily to increase confidence in an agency, both to encourage acceptance of inputs that may cause certain desired acts to occur and to prevent actions adverse to the wildlife agency. Not only the content of the materials that reach the public, but also the quality (for example, paper, design, layout, readability), influence image.

Very good educational programs may be bad PR in the short view but good PR in the long view. Few people like to hear bad news, but hiding such news may have far worse results than presenting it openly. The purpose of education is not good PR. Rather, good PR creates the environment in which wise natural resource use can be taught. The root of most agency educational problems is that personnel are forced (or are not brave enough to do otherwise) to sell agency policies, rather than explain wildlife principles. Having learned not to make political waves, not to be antagonistic to another agency policy, or not to oppose their own agency policy, most educational staffs resort to teaching nature study. Nature study challenges no one's position; it is safe and secure, but relatively functionless when it comes to achieving agency objectives.

The specific educational or informational inputs needed to change decisions vary in each situation. The wildlife manager is responsible for identifying the information needed, assessing what is already known, and trying to make up the deficit. The manager will do extensive data review, retrieving the information from personal or agency data banks and library, and will seek help from universities and readily available library searching services. Expert help will be sought to translate the data to the appropriate educational levels and language

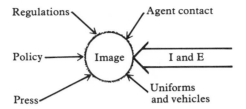

FIGURE **5-3**
Every public or private group casts an image.
Information and educational activities (I & E)
contribute significantly to the image, whether
good or bad.

for the target audiences. A guiding rule is: Never underestimate the intelligence of the public; always underestimate their information.

Processes

When people learn, they change their behavior; changed behavior or response is the only acceptable evidence that learning has occurred (See Figure 5-4). If there is no statistically significant difference measurable in a group before and after a management effort, whatever slight differences occur could be due to chance. *Significant* differences are the manager's criteria.

One way to cause behavior to change is to *teach*. Other ways of changing behavior include public relations, propaganda, threats, and rewards. The educational techniques of how to make effective slide lectures, show movies, or conduct field trips are well described in many places and are outside the scope of this book. Here we are concerned with the broader strategies of social engineering.

One strategy of social engineering is called *neutralization*. This strategy is usually played after a positive statement or move has been made by an opponent. A bill threatening widespread harm to the wildlife resource comes to Congress; the bill is neutralized by lobbying, letter-writing campaigns, news releases, visitations, and a host of other techniques, all of which are costly and take time away from work toward agency objectives. The results are that the bill is blocked, but at great expense and with no agency gains. Many agencies play this strategy, but it is no longer appropriate to the environmental tasks and problems ahead.

The neutralization strategy must be replaced with a preventative strategy that builds needed defenses. Offensive action is easier and less expensive than

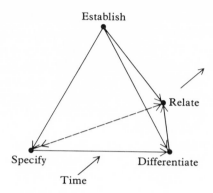

FIGURE **5-4**

Learning is the modification of measurable responses in organisms by sets of stimuli. The direct stimulus of any type is part of a set that may have antecedents (single-headed arrow) as well as concurrent components (double-headed arrow). The four major but not mutually exclusive responses are (1) To *establish* a new response tendency. (The organism does not have the tendency to perform an act, but through learning acquires the tendency.) (2) To *specify*. (This is a simple stimulus-response, in which the response is stimulus or stimulus-situation specific.) (3) To *differentiate*. (Selective or trial-and-error learning occurs from among a set of responses in a stimulus situation. Choice is significant.) (4) To *relate*. (This largely includes changing and sequencing complex language habits.) As a homeostatic process, a great deal of learning excludes or eliminates competing responses. (Based on Denny 1967: 32, 34.)

neutralization or defensive action. Defensive action frequently produces very bad public relations consequences, whether the agency is right or wrong, whereas offensive education builds on the capital value in public relations associated with past successes.

No amount of offensive or preventative action can eliminate the panic situation. All agencies know crises will arise. Why should they continue to be surprised by them? Agencies with imagination can develop crisis committees to simulate various types of crises and prepare contingency plans for programs. This is called the *prepare-for-panic* strategy. Crises can effect more personal behavioral change than can very large amounts of the most skillful propaganda. Panic situations are potent resources for initiating desirable changes; they should be studied and used effectively. Under panic conditions, motivational costs are lowest. In addition, certain situations can be cultivated, perhaps made to seem worse than they are for a purpose or perhaps made to seem less severe to avoid confrontations. Of course, there are hazards in such situations, and I shall not argue that the ends justify the means in all cases. Such situations arise infrequently, and it would be foolish and exhausting to attempt to overplay each of them. It is a tactic, among many, that should be considered in deciding how to manipulate a wildlife-human interaction.

For example, potential disease relations for humans and livestock in heavily populated areas may be emphasized to achieve the more difficult to communicate but more important restoration of quality food sources over the long run. Range trend predictions may enable wildlifers to prepare the public for the bad years ahead (resulting from past fires or cutting practices) and ward off confrontations by presenting the increases likely from natural succession. One useful tactic under this strategy is to take advantage of a panic situation to promote wildlife interests. In situations involving powerline location, airport extensions, interbasin transfer of water, or fossil fuel shortages, for example, wildlife may not be a major issue unless a wildlife manager makes it one.

A number of people management strategies and tactics have been presented for the wildlife manager. As with most systems, the more that is known about each strategy, the better it can be applied. The typical wildlife agency or group that will be applying these concepts and tactics is called the information and education section (I & E). Such departmentalization is unfortunate for it seems to segregate the people management function and imply that it is a narrow responsibility. In reality, all wildlifers must participate. As ecologists know, any single action in a system is usually ineffective, unbalacing, and inappropriately simplistic. Because of present resource consumption rates, there is no longer time for leisurely, step-by-step testing of ways to solve problems, either organizational or strategic. Entire sets of tactics must be initiated, and full recognition that there may be inefficiencies. With ongoing research and other feedback, the set can be improved while in operation. A traditional I & E effort may not be effective unless it is combined with other efforts. A simple *either/or* question of which methodology to select must be rejected out of hand. It seems imperative to accept the challenge of the *both/and* decision about process mixes and simultaneous assaults.

Psychological Mechanisms

To manage human behavior effectively, a wildlife manager must understand and have a functional model of the important psychological processes that govern behavior and decision making.

Before any decision can be made, the wildlife manager can help identify species—for example, make people aware of a bird song that they have long heard but never before noticed. To specify is to determine the structural "list" of resources.

All people have *needs* for specified quantities of specified resources. These exist along a continuum from "deficit" to "need," through "want" to "surplus." Needs and wants seem easily separated but become interchangeable in various societies. An automobile, once a want, has for many people become a near necessity.

Where a resource exists on the continuum is a function of the *values* assigned by an individual to a named resource. Indices to these values are the weights previously discussed. Values can be manipulated by wildlifers. They are a function of ethnic tradition, past and present socioeconomic status, future life prospects, and peer group pressures or support. To change a particular value, the wildlifer must present the image of a highly regarded peer holding the same general values as the others. When the speaker's values do not coincide with those of the audience, the speaker will be ineffective. To influence an audience's values, a communicator may visit, eat a meal, and learn about the local situation to establish some congruence of attitudes. Jointly held values on some things may be used to transfer value to others. A communicator will avoid making explicit any intent to influence values or risk taking (Walster and Festinger 1962).

Each person can be perceived to assess *risks* in making a decision. Risks are sometimes related to attitudes (see Watson and Johnson 1972:223) in that they are predispositions for response. A new theory will be eagerly engaged, played with, and tested by the person disposed to risk taking. Risk taking is a function of the resources (real or imagined, including religious) that a person has. The more extra energy a person has, the more likely he or she is to take risks. Risk taking is learned behavior and is not innate. It can be modified.

In assessing risks, a person assesses (1) the probability of a loss and (2) the magnitude of the loss. The decisions are so complex that much risk taking is pre-formed, a near automatic response to situations, handed down by parents, peer groups, communities, and custom. These pre-formed actions are highly energy-efficient, in terms of information transfer, as long as the system in which they were created stays constant. Under changing circumstances the old patterns of response may no longer be appropriate.

How are risks assessed? For most people, alternatives are dealt with in pairs. One alternative is compared with another, the worse one rejected, and the remaining one compared with the next alternative. There are far more sophisticated solution patterns available. The objective-weighting method demonstrates the weakness of a paired comparison. Poor or suboptimal decision processes can result in poor decisions.

form of a *team,* with common objectives, or of a *foundation,* with members having different objectives but operating under an agreed upon rule (such as the majority rule) as a means for making a decision. Generally, groups make decisions, including the decision not to decide. Individuals participate at various levels (voting versus elaborating on alternatives). Optimal participation occurs when each member contributes at least one alternative for choice. Too many people, or too many alternatives suggested by a few people, imply improper group design or management.

Group productivity is a *net* concept and requires subtracting the costs of motivation, coordination, and group leadership from the potential group production. As group size increases, so, in general, does the competence of the group's most competent member, and thus the potential productivity of the group. The quality of search and analysis typically increases in groups with some interpersonal conflicts. Some highly agreeable groups merely nod over the conventional wisdom. Conflict generates some search; too much can increase the costs of coordination and related activity and thus reduce net production.

Like the wise parent who will instruct, reinforce, warn, and, if necessary, physically ensure that a child will obey survival instructions, the wildlife and natural resource agency must at some point *control the public.* If instruction, warnings, and the like go unheeded, wildlife agents must exercise controls. Undesirable as they may be, legal controls now appear the only valid means to assure a high-quality environment. Education is a slow process. Sometimes, as in a disease epidemic, there is no time to educate people. Vaccination, quarantine, and medication are employed. It is proper to educate, but past a point, controls are imperative.

Wildlife law enforcement agents (wardens, rangers, conservation officers, wildlife protectors, and others) are a control force. Better law enforcement, control, and education would be achieved by separating these functions. The agents should retain certain instructional duties based on clear behavioral objectives, but the main emphasis of the agents and their staffs would be on modifying specific behaviors as denoted by the law. The parental connotations of the officer and the doctrinaire aspects of law, in the majority of cases, produce suboptimal learning environments. The educational psychologist would surely agree that the wildlife law enforcement agent is a good person to teach wildlife laws and regulations; but modifying land uses, changing voting behavior, and explaining the rationale for imaginative ecosystem design and management are best done by the manager with a less aversive image.

To *communicate* is to transfer information. The diagram of the communication problem in Figure 5-5 shows the large number and variety of parts in the process. It is no wonder that clear, unmistakable communication is so difficult and so unlikely. In the long run, wildlifers cannot effectively teach a person (1) what is not true, (2) what they do not believe themselves or have not mastered, (3) what is contrary to the observed experience of the audience, or (4) what the

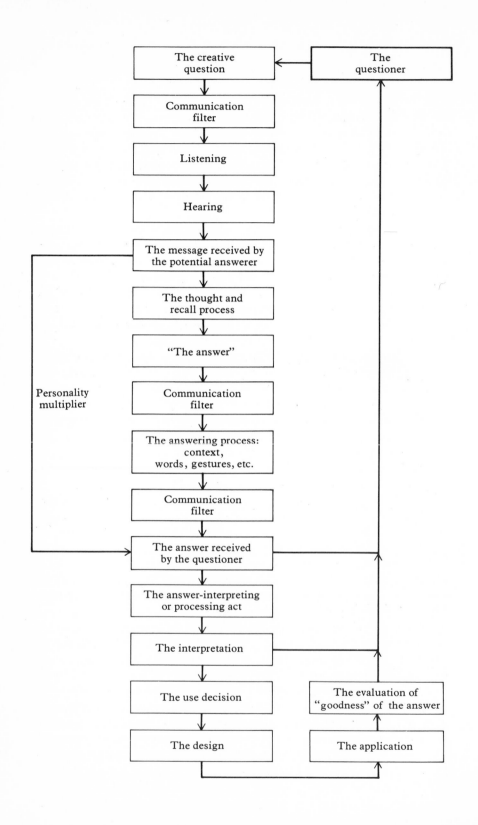

audience does not want to learn. Reigning over the short run will be lies, faulty logic, advertising pitches, and the implicit authority of wildlife regulations justified by poorly conceived principles.

Changing the ability of an audience to differentiate between alternative responses and to relate others is strongly influenced by the following processes (reviewed by Watson and Johnson 1972:233).

1. There is no simple solution to whether one- or two-way communication is more effective. In general, if the audience is opposed to an idea, a two-sided argument is more effective. If the audience is not opposed, a two-sided argument is more effective only if the audience is divided in educational background and some members are highly educated. Otherwise, a one-sided argument is sufficient (see Figure 5-6).

2. When the audience is opposed to an idea, the communicator must:
    a. Unfreeze the initial decision.
    b. Put the audience in a position in which choice can be made.
    c. Convince the audience that the proposed view is the one it should prefer.
    d. Establish a firm attitude that resists attempts by other communicators to change it.
    e. Deal effectively with counter-arguments:
        (1) If the arguments are salient
            (a) Simply acknowledge them, make an implicit refutation, and then present the pro argument,
            (b) Make a complete specific rebuttal, for an insufficient refutation strengthens the counter-argument, or
            (c) Use a delaying tactic and return to (a) or (b).
        (2) If they are not salient
            (a) Do not even mention them, or
            (b) Refute them in *reverse* of the order presented.

3. When the audience is not opposed, the communicator must give support to attitudes and engage in two-sided arguments to equip the members of the audience to deal with counter-propaganda.

4. The sequence in which arguments are presented is important, both for planning and for explaining failures. When a person becomes committed to the first communication received, the second communication does not have much effect. First arguments have no greater probability of being

FIGURE **5-5**

The question and answer process is the major form of communication. It has all of the characteristics of a general system. Words, like other stimuli, are only meaningful within a context. Identical words in an answer can be interpreted differently, depending on the personality of the answerer (where the multiplier is ψ, $0 \leq \psi \leq 1.0$), the situation, the "noise" present, and the personality or condition of the receiver.

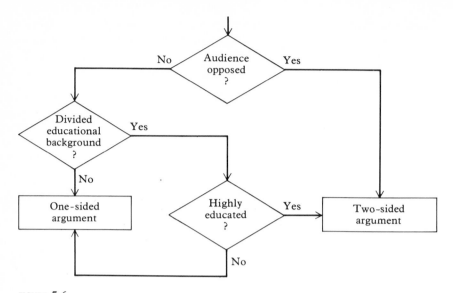

FIGURE **5-6**
A flow diagram of the decision for optimally employing one- or two-way communication.

remembered than later ones, but do have greater probability of being believed.

5. Emotional appeals that stimulate *too much* fear will result in messages being rejected and little or no attitude change occurring. The greater the fear aroused, the greater the attitude change, *provided* explicit possible actions are presented that will reduce the fear.

6. Moderate levels of emotional arousal will facilitate the changing of an audience's attitudes.

7. The communication should generally state explicitly the conclusion the speaker wants the audience to reach. When audiences are intelligent, implicit conclusions may be more effective.

8. The speaker should avoid forewarning an audience about an intent to convert their point of view.

9. An audience initially opposed to the communicator's point of view will be more influenced by the communicator's message if it is distracted during the presentation than if it is not distracted. Distractions prevent the continuous counter-argument typical during a presentation to an opposed group.

10. Individuals with low self-esteem are more easily influenced than those with high self-esteem. They are also easily swayed by subsequent counter-argument.

11. If an audience actively role-plays a previously unacceptable position, increases in acceptability are much greater than in situations of passive exposure to the same material. There are several reasons for this, one of which may be a type of simulated operant conditioning.

12. Audiences can be "inoculated" against undesirable arguments (McGuire and Papageorgis 1961). By providing small doses of arguments that an audience would have to overcome in order to maintain a belief, more stability is gained than would result from protecting them from the argument. Aiding them to *refute* an argument is superior to trying to help *support* their argument or position.

Cognitive theory holds that people tend, naturally, to be consistent and that apparent inconsistencies can be explained. According to Watson and Johnson (1972:244), "In order to change a person's attitudes you must create a state of imbalance among his present attitudes or between his attitudes and his behavior and then offer him a way to reduce this imbalance by changing his attitudes in the direction desired by the communicator. The wildlifer can employ cognitive theory concepts as follows:

1. By emphasizing inconsistencies, the manager can exploit the natural tendency of individuals toward consistency. The danger, of course, is that individuals may reject the preferred alternative and develop a stronger structure around the undesirable alternative.

2. By forcing a person into an alternative social role—for example, from a griper into a leadership role, from a group member into an officer—inconsistency is produced and behavioral changes will occur.

3. Changing the actual or perceived environment can cause behaviors to change. This is clearly evident in recent changes among industrialists, pesticide proponents, and the public toward environmental problems.

4. Causing one behavioral response to change may force others to change with it. Hardin's law, "You can never do just one thing," applies to the ecology of attitudes as well as the environment.

5. By highlighting the difference between the attitude of a respected individual and that of the audience, a state of imbalance can be created. The imbalance may be resolved by the audience changing its behavior *or* by disliking the formerly respected person. The strategy can only be played with some risk.

Because the environment is so large and complex, it is very difficult (probably impossible) to perceive in its totality. This often produces anxiety. Primitive religions, dogma, and tales were means to reduce this anxiety. Individuals are dependent upon other individuals for information to establish the validity of their attitudes. The attitudes of peers and reference groups are very important in forming and maintaining attitudes. "The support of even one person weakens the powerful effect upon an individual of a majority opinion. . . . a minority of two people who are consistent in their deviant responses can influence the majority of a group. . . . one's resistance to a communication which presents attitudes counter to group norms increases with the salience of one's group identification" (Watson and Johnson 1972:249). When attitudes have been changed, continuing social support is needed for the attitude to be maintained. This implies the need for organizations, magazines, newsletters, and other supportive measures.

Feedback

Biologists understand feedback very well. Feedback distinguishes biological systems from most physical systems. It is a regulating and controlling function, which checks the results of processes and the quantity and quality of inputs against objectives of the system. Feedback can only operate if there are objectives. Appetite, a classic example of biological feedback, cannot operate unless a criterion of "fullness" has been evolved. Until objectives are set for the management of people in wildlife systems, system effectiveness cannot be judged. In part, a fear of precise evaluation is the reason objectives are not better articulated. Until a destination is identified, any road will suffice.

Feedback must be applied to people management objectives, whatever their stage of development. Objectives can be improved by de-emphasizing methodology and emphasizing desired changes in behavior, including desired levels of competency. Objectives should exist for the agency or department in charge of people management. These too must be evaluated, tested, and revised in dynamic response to the total agency as well as to wildlife resource users. These objectives are the very basis for optimal organization, for testing policy, and for exercising leadership or shaping forces within the larger agency. Methods for applying feedback to objectives include the following:

1. Publish objectives in an evidently nonfinal form with requests for public comment.

2. Arrange for outside reviewers to advise on appropriateness of objectives and their formulation. (For example, reviewers seeing the objective "to have the people appreciate. . . ," might inquire "what do you want those who gain the appreciation *to do* as a result of this new state?")

3. Have annual internal review with opportunity for special meetings to consider review.

4. Give a person or group responsibility for assuring that such feedback occurs and is operational.

5. Develop regional and national teams or task forces to share ideas and coordinate the regional and national dynamics of objectives.

Feedback to inputs is the exercise of the question: Is this particular input (an idea, an article, a piece of information) essential for achieving the stated objectives? More than what is needed? Inadequate? In the right sequence? Answering these questions is very difficult, but it must be done.

Feedback can be improved by the following procedures:

1. Analyze, with the aid of educators if necessary, the behavior desired. Then list the inputs needed and sequence them. Delete all facts or items that are not essential. Omit the extras in releases, radio and TV tapes, speeches, and so on.

2. Develop the procedure just described for multiple objectives. Reward yourself or others when one input can be used to achieve multiple behavioral objectives. Screen your objectives (note that this is feedback to objectives), deleting those of low priority that require one-time use inputs. Retain those that can be achieved with inputs needed to achieve several objectives. The idea is to reduce inputs and encourage several uses of each.

3. Compare the cost of obtaining and communicating each input. With 1 and 2 above develop a cost per unit. Attempt to reduce this cost. Display the changes for all to observe.

4. Develop a time-of-retrieval score. Information is not information unless it can be obtained and used. Efficient libraries, computer searching systems, and filing systems are essential. How efficient is the criterion? Efficiency of retrieval should be tied to cost over time. How to do so is beyond the scope of this chapter.

Feedback to processes requires shifts in emphasis from people contacted, movies shown, papers printed, or miles traveled to objectives expressed as behaviorial change. The major industrial question is not how "busy" is a machine, but how many units of output are achieved per dollar? This is a responsible question for managers of people as well. The feedback methods include:

1. Do research on each type of influencing method. Devise research, at least to begin with, that answers the questions of the equation:

$$y_3 = a + bx_{12}.$$

That is, if I do some amount of work in activity Number 12, what change can I expect in desired behavior y_3?

2. Do research in combinations of activities. For example, give a questionnaire in three similar communities, provide different radio or TV tapes to each

community, only varying in content, and study the *change* in what citizens say they would do (as an index to what they might do) in a problem situation. Compare the effects of the methods. Report the results (so others can apply feedback to the study) and move ahead to other methods or combinations.

3. Compare costs of methods in terms of units of behavioral change. Select the lower-cost methods, but be sure the right mix of methods is available. There may be a small, articulate, powerful group that can only be reached by a high-cost methodology. Cost efficiency in such a case is not likely to be cost effectiveness.

4. Compare effectiveness of processes as a function of target group, messenger, location, time of day, time of year, and media used. Allocation of limited people management resources in such a complex system suggests that computer optimization (for example, at first by linear programming) may be very desirable, probably necessary.

5. Ask the fundamental feedback question: How far are we from the objective? This is a question that must, in general, replace the question: How far have we come? When a program is only 0.5 percent effective and a new program doubles effectiveness, there is little to brag about. In management of human behavior, the ultimate objectives are rarely achieved. Therefore, it behooves the manager to ask: What would happen if I do *not* apply this management strategy? The question can provide a new perspective on selecting managerial alternatives.

6. Evaluation specialists may be needed to work in agencies (or, cooperatively, in regions) to assist with feedback. Some feedback, however, must be done by all wildlifers. At the simplest level, wildlifers can at least use a simple, informal oral quiz at the end of a field trip conducted for the Chamber of Commerce.

No diagram of a general system shows a feedback arrow to *feedback*. But the feedback system, itself, must be kept under scrutiny and repair. Government agencies are a peculiar mix of excessive feedback (millions of dollars spent on auditing to prevent thousands of dollars of expense account problems) and almost no feedback (rarely are people fired for incompetence or mismanagement, since competence or management objectives are poorly defined).

In the same way that auditing is a feedback subsystem, so is wildlife law enforcement. Laws are an essential part of wildlife management. *Control*, as previously discussed, is an important strategy in the management of people. Laws, without enforcement, are functionless. The enforcement act is a feedback function in the control strategy of people management. Wildlife agents have various roles in education, management, and other areas, and distinguishing purely law enforcement action is difficult. Overlaps with other agency activities cloud the identity of the agent. Wildlife law enforcement can be creatively analyzed and tomorrow's enforcement designed as a feedback subsystem. This will be discussed in Chapter 10.

Feedforward

The prospect that population increases could mask the increases in wildlife law enforcement effectiveness is an example of feedforward. The wildlife manager must stay abreast of the dynamics of the human population fully as much as of wild populations. The resources for doing so are abundant. The idea is to see the future clearly enough so that budgets, agents, staff, and physical resources will be adequate to meet the future when it arrives. Educational programs are like ocean tankers; they do not start or stop instantly. From the time the signal is given, it takes a tanker 25 minutes to stop! It takes years for certain educational and behavioral modification programs to get started. Without an active feedforward function in agencies, there is the persistent feeling of running a catch-up race. To ignore feedforward is to jeopardize public relations, for those public behaviors that are earnestly desired today may be inappropriate tomorrow.

There are several means of achieving feedforward:

1. Develop scenarios.
2. Develop computer simulations.
3. Attend conferences and seminars on future trends.
4. Do statistical analyses and projections of changes over time.
5. Read widely in the "future" literature (for example, Toffler 1970).

There is no simple conclusion to this chapter. Management of people in the wildlife system must begin anew, with new money, new concepts and principles, new strategies, new applications of old tactics, and new research to meet the future pressures. If wildlife management is to be well practiced, it must establish the preeminence of a sophisticated system of people management. There are strategies, tactics, and techniques now available for doing so. What is lacking seems to be a willingness to put away ineffective techniques and programs and to focus on the objective of maximizing benefits to people from the wildlife resource.

Study Questions

1. Is it ethical to manipulate people's behavior?

2. Examine at least ten issues of the different journals listed and abstract four potentially useful in wildlife management.

3. Develop a local example of how people management, interacting with habitat and wildlife population management, can result in a more efficient or effective system.

4. List at least five measures of change that may result from people management.

5. Describe the icebox principle.

6. Why is it that more biological "facts" may not help to make some decisions?

7. Why is the use of the control strategy more likely than in the past?

8. Have an agent of an I & E staff visit your class or organization or take a field trip to an I & E office.

9. Sketch the learning tetrahedron, indicating at the vertices the mutually exclusive responses people can make to a stimulus.

10. Discuss: "Roughing it" is never an acceptable tactic for a professional to employ.

11. Give an example of classical conditioning that might be employed with people by a wildlife manager.

12. Give a relevant example of operant conditioning.

13. Sketch from memory the communications flow diagram.

14. Which is best to employ, one- or two-way communication in a sportsmen's club in a university community?

15. Outline the tactics to be employed when you must appear before a group opposed to stopping importation of exotics.

16. Give an example of applying the "prepare-for-panic" strategy.

17. The author argues that man is rational. Discuss this concept, being careful to define "rational" and to deal with the concept of potential rationality.

18. Compare public participation in wildlife management and in forest (or other) management. Which is greater? Why?

19. What are the major criteria for wildlife laws?

20. What are ten major first-order objects of wildlife law enforcement agencies as now practiced? Discuss which should be objectives.

21. Evaluate arrest rate as a criterion of agent effectiveness.

22. If the dread Agents' Virus (hypothetical, of course) epidemic struck within your state and all agents were hospitalized for a year, what would be the consequences for game populations? For hunter benefits? What if the Violators' Disease struck?

Selected References

Allen, D. L. 1962 *Our wildlife legacy*, Rev. ed. Funk and Wagnalls, New York. x + 422 p.

Bandura, A. 1969. *Principles of behavioral modification*. Holt, Rinehart, and Winston, New York. 677 p.

Denny, M. R. 1967. A learning model. In *Chemistry of learning: invertebrate research*, ed. W. C. Corning and S. C. Ratner. Plenum Press, New York. pp. 32–42.

Gilbert, D. C. 1971. *Natural resources and public relations*. The Wildlife Society, Washington, DC. xxiv + 320 p.

Kennedy, J. J. 1970. *A consumer analysis approach to recreational decisions: deer hunters as a case study*. Unpub. Ph.D. Dissertation, Virginia Polytechnic Institute, Blacksburg. 182 p.

Leopold, A. 1933. *Game management*. Charles Scribner's Sons, New York. 481 p.

McCormick, J. B. 1968. A procedure for evaluating the effectiveness of wildlife law enforcement. *Proc. Western Assn. of State Game and Fish Commissioners*. 12 p.

McGuire, W. J. and D. Papageorgis. 1961. The relative efficacy of various types of prior belief-defense in producing immunity against persuasion. *J. Abnormal Social Psychology* **62**:338–345.

Ritter, A. F. 1975. *Objectives and performance criteria for state wildlife law enforcement agencies*. Unpub. M.S. Thesis, Virginia Polytechnic Institute, Blacksburg. xii + 199 p.

Toffler, A. 1970. *Future shock*. Random House, New York. xii + 505 p.

Walster, E. and L. Festinger. 1962. The effectiveness of "overheard" persuasive communications. *J. Abnormal Social Psychology* **65**:395–402.

Watson, G. and D. Johnson. 1972. *Social psychology—issues and insights*. J. B. Lippincott, Philadelphia, 499 p.

Weller, J. E. 1966. *Yesterday's people: life in contemporary Appalachia*. University of Kentucky Press, Lexington. xviii + 163 p.

Zimbardo, P. and E. B. Ebbensen. 1969. *Influencing attitudes and changing behaviors*. Addison-Wesley, Reading, MA. 148 p.

PART II

EXAMPLES AND APPLICATIONS: THE RESOURCE

Chapter 6

Muskrat Management

To some, wildlife management seems a contradiction in terms. To manage is to reduce wildness. Once a population is managed it is no longer wildlife, but rather another form of agriculture or animal husbandry, perhaps more like forestry than lettuce growing. Wildlife is never really managed 100 percent. As in the concept of efficiency, the 1.0 level is never reached, it is a theoretical base or standard. A wild mink population can be managed to a degree, but when completely managed it passes into the realm of agriculture and the fur farm. The mink population is then housed on a mink ranch, where its genetics, food, shelter, natality, and mortality are carefully controlled for the objective of maximizing monetary profit.

The muskrat (*Ondatra zibethicus*), Figure 6-1, is not likely ever to be completely managed. It will forever present a challenge to wildlife management. One wildlife manager, who has worked with muskrats and marshes much of his professional life, said to me that when the last holocaust comes, there will still be muskrats and bullfrogs. His pessimistic remark was a testimony to the biological productivity, the savagery, the omnivorous habits, the wide range occupied, and the adaptability of the muskrat. These traits can be termed the animal's *ecological amplitude*—that is, the range of conditions in which an animal can survive. Endangered species have a narrow ecological amplitude; the muskrat has a broad one (see Figure 6-2).

FIGURE **6-1**

The muskrat (*Ondatra zibethicus*) varies by subspecies and races (about 15 of them) but is about 53 cm long (2.54 cm/inch) and weighs from 794 to 1588 grams (453.6 grams/pound). It typically lives in lodges, which it assembles, but also lives in dug bank burrows. It typically is herbivorous but also eats crayfish, mollusks, and sluggish fish.

How does anyone manage muskrats? Who even wants to, in environments undergoing increasing urbanization? Both questions will become more and more difficult to answer. Most muskrats are not managed—they are just out here. If there is no access to them or interest in them, then they do not exist as a resource. Like deep, thin coal or oceanic manganese nodules, muskrats can exist as a potential resource, unused for various reasons. Benefits must be perceived—whether monetary, ecological, or esthetic—before a resource is recognized as such and investments of money or energy made in it.

The muskrat manager faces fewer risks than other wildlife managers. The risk of making a wrong decision for a muskrat population is not as great, for example, as the risk for a musk-ox (*Ovibos moschatus*) population. The manager of muskrats, like the manager of cottontail rabbits (*Sylvilagus floridanus*), can be very wrong one year and yet natural population productivity will generally wipe the managerial slate clean within a year or two. How wrong the manager can be depends on who needs these muskrats. Twenty trappers, otherwise unemployed, who work the marshes when the pelts are prime, are dependent upon a stable or increasing population from which they can harvest a fur crop. Well-managed populations are essential to them, their families, and their fur buyers.

There is another, human factor that reduces the muskrat manager's risks. (By risk I rarely mean physical threat, though this has happened, but the professional threats, lateral moves or "promotions," and raises denied to those who

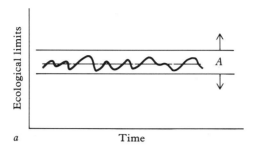

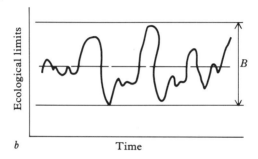

FIGURE **6-2**

Ecological amplitude is the range of conditions in
which an animal can survive. The species in (*a*) has
a very narrow ecological amplitude (*A*), the species
in (*b*), a broad amplitude (*B*). For most objectives,
the amplitude is inversely related to the need for
highly precise management.

raise the public ire.) Trappers are quite used to working in an unstable environment—both in the marsh and in the market. Just as a disease can wipe out an annual crop, a change in garment fur style can wipe out profits. Synthetic furs have drastically reduced some parts of the fur market. Styles fluctuate from long hair (for example, foxes) to short hair (for example, beaver). The muskrat trapper, used to fluctuations, is more able than many others to handle fluctuations resulting from managerial incompetence. However, that fact does not authorize or encourage incompetence. It is highlighted to emphasize the dynamic nature of the resource, the interaction of value and population dynamics, and the interaction of a dynamic value system with managerial needs.

The trapper is not only a major resource user but also a means by which the population can be regulated. The trapper population itself must be stabilized (or regulated) so that benefits as well as population regulation can be achieved.

How are muskrats managed? Like any other wildlife. The manager focuses on the three major subsystems—habitat, population, and people.

Habitat

Muskrats tend to be marsh dwellers, but they are found almost everywhere. They live in irrigation ditches, road culverts, stream and river banks, and in their conspicuous lodges in the marshes. The marsh is never stable; an animal that survives well there cannot be intolerant to change, rigid in habit, or fussy about what it eats. The muskrat is none of these. Its habitat is both the fresh-water and coastal marsh. Both types of marshes experience pulses or charges of water and nutrients, from the daily tides of the coast and from occasional devastating storms. The storms destroy some habitats but create new shallow water, stir the nutrients, and provide new interspersion and unique juxtaposition of sites. In the Northeast, muskrats climb into trees to wait the passing of the high waters released from dams for the pulp log drives. The waters scour some areas but deposit seed and fertile soils for new feeding areas.

In stable river backwashes, filled oxbows, and potholes of the glaciated areas, muskrats enjoy some of the benefits of a relatively stable environment but are subject to the juggernaut of succession, which brings a marsh into maximum production but just as surely continues the replacement of plants and conditions until such marshes will support few, if any, muskrats. Muskrat populations, though adaptable, perform best in an optimum habitat. The habitat predictable at a particular age in the succession of the marsh is called a *sere*. Unfortunately for those looking for quick solutions to increasing muskrat populations, the best successional stage or sere varies widely by region. Marshes are highly variable. Their dynamics can be discovered and generalized models developed that will go far in computing when such seres will occur in a particular area (or when they were passed). The skeptic who queries, "Well, what about an unpredicted storm? Won't it throw off any estimates and calculations?" must be answered with: "Yes." The hurt note in the manager's reply is from the pain of asking himself rapidly a host of managerial questions such as:

1. Why was the information sought or question about the optimal asked in the first place? Was there no real need to know?
2. Will an answer make any difference in managerial performance?
3. Isn't muskrat management recognized to be more uncertain than most management?
4. Aren't all managerial decisions made under conditions of uncertainty? No one expects complete knowledge or certainty, but at least the basic physical or biological laws (for example, gravity, photosynthesis) are unlikely to change.
5. Aren't all estimates and projections made with an implicit "given the conditions and phenomena operating as observed in the past"?

6. Is any storm unpredicted? All are predictable; time of occurrence is the problem.
7. Can't equations and the relations be put into a computer simulator and the fate of the marsh observed under randomly applied storms over 500 years? If a computer is not used, cannot a team of experts discuss the likely futures?
8. Couldn't we better stabilize the population (or at least social benefits from whatever population existed) if we had examined all of these possibilities?

It is one thing to observe a marsh and know that in 3 years it will reach peak muskrat production, and quite another to know how to stabilize it at that level. It is important to be able to set back succession in a marsh 10 years past its peak. It can be done using the principles of habitat design outlined in Chapter 4.

First, in each area of the country a typical marsh climax can be identified. (*Climax* is an ecological term whose definition is much debated. Here it means the expected final sere of a marsh, which is usually long-lasting.) Marshes tend to have their highest muskrat potential (density) when the marsh succession is arrested just short of climax (Penfound and Schneidau 1945). This can be done in a number of ways depending on local situations, available manpower, lay of the land, size of the marsh, and land-marsh-water juxtaposition. The techniques include (1) burning, (2) grazing, (3) mowing, (4) creating impoundments (dams and dikes), (5) manipulating water level (by dikes, culverts, dams, diversions, and irrigation), (6) ditching, (7) farming or tilling (after dry periods or drainage), (8) using herbicides, (9) clearing land mechanically or by hand, (10) disking, and (11) combining various of these practices. See Box 6-1.

The number of ways (3.6 million) these practices can be applied is impressively large; but there is also an infinitely large number of times and sequences in which they can be applied, and there are at least as many levels of effort and areas to which they can be applied. The result is a very, very large number of alternative pathways among which the manager may choose. The probability of choosing the right one, given a set of clear objectives, is very, very small. Given a hazy set of objectives, the chances for proper selection are little better. The manager's challenge is not to increase the haziness of objectives but to search for a nearly optimum pathway. Increasingly, as that selection becomes more critical, the manager must seek computer assistance. The computer works much like the human mind, so it is instructive to understand the managerial mind as it might work on a muskrat problem.

Space. A basic input for the decision maker is space. What is the area I must manage? The answer can be obtained from U.S. Geological Survey topographic maps, especially the 7.5-minute quadrangle maps for large marshes that would

Box 6-1. Combinations of Managerial Practices

The reader will recall from basic mathematics that combinations are sets of k elements taken from a given n elements without repetitions. The number of combinations of n different elements into groups of k elements is

$$C = \frac{n!}{k!(n - k)!}$$

where ! is the symbol for factorial.

Where there are ten major habitat management techniques for muskrat marshes and the manager wants to look at how many ways three approaches could be combined, the answer is

$$C = \frac{10 \cdot 9 \cdot 8 \cdot 7 \cdot 6 \cdot 5 \cdot 4 \cdot 3 \cdot 2 \cdot 1}{3 \cdot 2 \cdot 1(10 - 3)!}$$

$$= 120.$$

The combination of three approaches was arbitrarily chosen. Suppose for a particular marsh there could be 1, 2, 6, etc. approaches used. The permutations (P) are $n!$ Where there are 10 elements, $P = 3,628,800$. There are at least a few ways muskrat habitat can be managed!

typically be managed. Small areas will require field mapping (sketch maps or plane-table maps are usually adequate). Most areas in the United States have been flown for aerial photographs. Increasingly, satellite photography will be used to study marsh and wetland space, particularly dynamics. Aerial photos may show vegetation borders and muskrat lodges. Present high-elevation photos cannot make such fine resolution. For large muskrat areas (say over 5 square miles), the high-elevation photos now provide a resource previously unavailable to managers. They enable almost monthly changes in habitats to be observed and then muskrat populations related to them, through the concept of aggregate production curves (see Chapters 2 and 4).

It is essential to know area sizes because they are such a dominant influence on the manager's output. The manager may estimate 2.6 litters per lodge one year and 2.8 several years later. (That may be expressed as a change of only 0.2 of a litter (2.8 − 2.6), of 7 percent (0.2/2.8 × 100), or of more than 7.6 percent (0.2/2.6 × 100)—all of which are correct but one of which may better make the manager's point.) If the areas in which lodges can be built are changing by a factor of 10 to 50 percent, the litters-per-lodge factor is clearly overpowered. The lodging habitat may change, a not uncommon phenomenon due to storms, flooding from headwaters, gully-washers, tidal action, fires, grazing, dredging, and construction of barriers and inlets that modify sediment dynamics. Given 2000 hectares (about 4940 acres) of marsh suitable for muskrats, about 2.5 lodges per hectare, and 4 young per litter, a marsh can produce 52,000 muskrats at 2.6 litters per year or 56,000 at 2.8 litters per year. Assuming a fur price of $2.00 per pelt (it ranges from $0.25 to $4.50) the potential gross monetary yield from a harvest of two-thirds, is $73,920.

Time. The potential can only be realized if the habitat is worked. The habitat cannot be preserved in a desirable state by structural or mechanical means. To attempt to achieve structural stability in a dynamic environment is a display of ecological and physical ignorance. The marshland must be recognized as dynamic. The lodge area this year will not be the lodge area in a few years. The acreage may be the same, the locations will not be. Muskrats are nomads, but their habitat is also shifting. Wave action eats at their banks and lodges, upland storms sluice them away. Dams dry their areas at the tailwaters but provide new sites in the backwaters.

The manager may observe the habitat changes and announce to those who use muskrat populations the likely short-term (2 to 3 years) population trends. This is a valuable service and prevents overinvestments, overdependency, and over-expectations (with resulting dissatisfactions).

The manager may also work at the macro-level, assisting and encouraging watershed management and regulated flood control structures, managing stream flow, halting adverse channelization practices, improving water quality management, and in general reducing runoff and peak flows. For the muskrat manager to assume that management is confined to a particular marsh is a denial of every concept of ecological interaction.

The muskrat lives in the land sump. Everything that happens on the land has a direct, though often delayed, effect on the home of this creature. Erosion, acid rain from air pollution, herbicides from crops, insecticides, water quality plant overflows, increased runoff from areas of urbanization, increased peak flows from grazing or forest legislation—all converge on the marsh. Threats of oil, organohalides, and radiation pollution encroach from the ocean. The manager must deal with all of these personally and enlist the continuing support of specialists and agency task forces.

Management Methods. On the marsh, poling a boat, ignoring the mosquitoes for the redwings and the jet contrail invasion for the humorous paddling escape of a hen and her brood, the manager can get down to business—and enjoy it. The manager picks up a muskrat skull on a lodge and sees the teeth have the upper and lower, one-side, formula 1003/1003 and wonders why such biological "nice-to-knows" get converted into managerial "need-to-knows." It is evident that the skull is that of a muskrat, even before the incisors, the missing canines and premolars, and the molars are counted.

The manager has used aerial photos to locate the potholes in the marsh. Some were caused by oxbowlike cutoffs of the invisible streams that flow under marsh surfaces. Sediment dams typically make the cutoffs and they dry. Plant stabilization and water diversion complete the process. Others were formed by fires that burned deeply into peat. Others were blasted out by the preceding manager. The new manager visits a sample of them to make observations correlating age and vegetative development in and around them to muskrat population signs and potential. These correlations can be used to estimate the status of the hundreds of such holes mapped in this marsh. Each pothole (as any habitat type) has a production function for muskrats.

Permanent water was created, providing conditions for submerged vegetation like the pondweeds and waterlilies. These deepwater areas also protected against freeze-outs. In some wetlands, pumping water into these holes is not out of the question in drought years. Each pothole provides edge, diversity of foods, deepwater escape, and banks, as well as lodge sites. They obviously have waterfowl benefits. They produce floating, high-protein foods. Each has a zone of influence for muskrats around its edges. They can be blasted into marshes. Depending on management objectives, available money and manpower, and the size of the management unit, the manager can set about dispersing holes throughout the marsh in a planned fashion so that as each goes out of production due to sedimentation and the natural succession of bogs and marshes, new ones will be created and will be coming into production. Potholes are not "the" solution to muskrat habitat, but they provide a dominant diversifying element in the environment.

Burning of marshes can be done in some areas, but air pollution control laws must be observed. Where it can be achieved, the time of burning is all important. The intent is usually to set back succession in order to enhance muskrat habitat. It must be done when the water levels are at or above the root level. Such a burn adds nutrients to the soil and promotes short-term, succulent growth. That growth is only short term. Subsequent growth is likely to be reduced compared to unburned adjacent areas. Where muskrats are causing problems, or where areas must be set far back to achieve desired plant diversity, a root burn may be required. Root burns are made during a dry spell or drawdown of water. They cause root damage by drying or heat. Peat burns may be needed, and when they burn deeply (3 to 4 meters) the resulting potholes may be beneficial. They are, however, very difficult to control and should rarely be used.

The salinity of marsh water strongly influences the quality of muskrat habitat. In general, the less saline the better. Habitat improves inland. The coastal marshes can be made less saline by dikes, dune protection, pumping, irrigation, vegetative barriers, and fenced paths to keep cattle from destroying dikes.

Ditching of marshes is done to dry them out for agriculture, forestry, and mosquito control. The water level is lowered and the water permitted to flow off. Mathiak and Linde (1956) found that ditching without gradients increased muskrat production sufficiently to justify the costs, and they observed that benefits to waterfowl may have been greater than for muskrats. Gradient ditching, on the other hand, can be harmful to muskrat habitats.

The ecological adage "you can never do just one thing" applies well to the marsh habitat. In this chapter the assumption is made that many marsh wildlife species are of interest and that trade-offs will be required. However, muskrats have been treated as being of determinant management interest.

One problem to which the marsh manager is wed, one of immense dimensions, is that of insect control. Marsh flies or mosquitoes are potential pests and disease vectors. As urbanization and recreation encroach on marshes, pressures build for control. These have resulted in massive applications of chlorinated hydrocarbons. Alternative substances must be sought, land zoning encouraged based on realistic long-term pest-disease-costs relations, and integrated pest management systems encouraged. Water levels can be regulated for both insect and muskrat benefits. Control structures, of a semi-temporary nature, for doing so are expensive. Expense is always relative. Relative to keeping people out of the area during the peak insect period? Relative to zoning to prevent habitation? Relative to a perpetual spray program with its direct and indirect costs? Wildlifers can cooperate with health agencies and pest control operators to secure mutual ends. For example, dikes and dams can be used for mosquito control (deep, active water versus shallow water), but they are one-third more expensive than ditches, which can be used in the salt marshes. The benefits of ditches are great for muskrats but also provide fire breaks and water management potentials.

Strangely enough, wildlifers are often at odds among themselves—the waterfowl biologists versus the muskrat biologists. When objectives differ, conflicts are not surprising. Cartwright (1946) observed that marsh management is good for both waterfowl and muskrat populations. Waterfowl eat much of the same vegetation that muskrats eat. Snow and blue geese can "eat out" a section of a marsh. But so can muskrats. A drop in fur prices will stop trappers from going "back in." The muskrat population grows without the normal removal rate. The vegetation eventually is completely removed and geese fly over and do not produce "goose days of use," hunter opportunities, or goose-sighting opportunities.

Muskrat lodges are desirable waterfowl resting and nesting sites. Waterfowl managers release water through dikes to dry out areas so that natural seeds can germinate or so that some cultivation and seeding can be done. They will then close the dikes and flood the areas on which grains (for example, millet) are grown to provide prime feeding areas for waterfowl. Muskrats also will build burrows in these water control dikes, and when the dikes fail, the waterfowl objectives cannot be obtained.

Water stability, not drawdown, is what muskrats in a particular unit of a marsh need. While muskrats may benefit from a planted food source, the type and timing are not likely to be the same for muskrat and duck. The manager's decision-making task is one of weighting the importance of these two species (and others) and then, rather than trying to achieve mixed habitat benefits from every tract of the marsh, to diversify the arrangement of units so they produce desired relatively stable cumulative amounts of potential forage and spaces over time. To do so requires application of knowledge of local plant community dynamics, spatial analyses, and direct applications of the concept of the aggregates and the zone of influence.

It is undesirable to be specific about muskrat management in light of the dozens of local variables and diverse objectives. The general directions to be taken to increase muskrats (the converse is evident) are:

1. Maximize sedges and grasses and high protein food stuffs.
2. Stabilize water levels.
3. Reduce water flows.
4. Maximize species diversity (patchiness).
5. Minimize salinity.
6. Maximize trapping season lengths.
7. Minimize nutria.
8. Maximize water and soil control.
9. Maximize quality of water.
10. Maximize grazing and fire control.
11. Maximize access.
12. Minimize trap loss.
13. Maximize fur value and trapper profit.

Population

Muskrats cannot be stockpiled. To stop trapping for a few years will not allow them to build up. There are several reasons. A very old muskrat is three years old. The survival curve (Chapter 3) is much like type 5. Fecundity is related to the severity and dynamic state of the habitat.

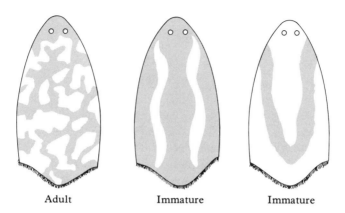

Adult   Immature   Immature

FIGURE **6-3**

Muskrat pelts are stripped off from a cut at the tail and hind legs, turned hair-side in, and dried on a metal frame. Adult hides are mottled. Immature pelts show various patterns. The whiter areas are prime sections of the hide; darker areas are unprime (Taber 1971:375).

In a 1-hectare marsh there may be from 1 to 7 lodges. The latter can be called overpopulation by almost any criterion, but it has been observed. In each lodge there may be 3 to 6 young per litter. Depending on regional temperatures and breeding season length, there may be 3 to 5 litters per year (the gestation period is 28 days). On a hectare of a mid-Atlantic marsh there may be an annual production of 168 young per year. The females breed in their first year (except in northern areas), adding further to the population reproductive potential. The muskrats may be monogamous during brief periods, but are largely promiscuous.

One way to determine the number to harvest so as to stabilize the population is to observe the age distribution in the fur take (see Figure 6-3). In this measure, early mortality of the young has already been integrated. Assuming young and old are equally trappable (or adjusting based on a coefficient determined from detailed research for that purpose), then the young-per-adult age ratio is also an expression of production. Observations of lodges made along a transect or from the air can indicate trends in adult populations. For population stability, the exact annual increment (to some point in the year) must equal all of the harvest plus the mortality. Mortality can be determined by tagging studies. Then the calculation, with example, is

$$\text{Harvest} = \text{Adults} + \text{Increment} - (\text{Adults} \times \text{Mortality})$$
$$- (\text{Increment} \times \text{Mortality})$$
$$= (100 \text{ Adults of } 100{:}100 \text{ Sex ratio})$$

$$+ (50 \text{ Females} \times 4 \text{ Young/Litter} \times 4 \text{ Litters/Year})$$
$$- (100 \times 0.90 \text{ Mortality}) - (\text{Increment} \times 0.65)$$
$$= 100 + 800 - 90 - 520 = 290.$$

Such calculations have given rise to a rule of thumb that two-thirds of a muskrat population can be removed with no change in the next year's population. In the example, a harvest three times the initial population is possible. Even the grossest estimates, based on local observations and published studies of populations in the region, will allow better harvest estimates than the two-thirds rule or "leave two pair per acre." Both rules are likely to underutilize the fur resource unless there are unusual mortality phenomena at work. In most wildlife populations, if a population is *slightly* overharvested, natality will increase (largely as a result of increased per capita energy). The catch-up is very rapid. In muskrats, fur is not prime in the very young, so once again there are trade-offs to make in maximizing profits from furs (not animals, not trapped animals, not numbers of high-value pelts, but mean 3-year trapper profits). Public costs on managed areas create a special problem in accounting and deciding what an appropriate management objective should be.

In an unmanaged marsh, populations rise and fall erratically. The populations "eat out" areas with the same effect as a storm or bank erosion. Cover is reduced, accessible per capita food supplies are cut, and predation from mink, great horned owls, and free-ranging domestic dogs increases. Weak animals become prey. Animals without stored food move during the winter and suffer high mortality. Fighting increases as both real and perceived density increases (the visual barriers are lost). Scars reduce pelt quality. Disease increases. Movements out of the marsh increase. In unfamiliar areas with irregular cover, mortality is very high. The density is effectively reduced.

There is much contradictory opinion, observation, and theory on natural muskrat population regulation. It is an exciting literature and one the student will want to study carefully. The needs are to "control" or understand very well the habitat and energetic phenomena in select areas, then investigate simultaneously endocrine mechanisms associated with dispersal, disease, and metabolism. (See Bronson and Eliftheriou 1965, Calhoun 1952, Christian and Davis 1964, Christian 1970, Wynne-Edwards 1962, and McLaren 1971.)

The exotic nutria *Myocaster coypus,* a beaver-size marsh animal, has confounded the muskrat management problem. These beasts are very similar in feeding habits to muskrats and therefore require joint utilization of a limited resource. The muskrat-nutria-waterfowl complex is now established in many areas, and it will be almost impossible to return to former conditions. Decision making now tends to be dominated, not so much by objectives, as by what may be feasibly obtained from the new resource mix.

Muskrats in the wrong place, or in too abundant supply, can cause major problems. The muskrats eat corn and other crops when they live in riverbank burrows. They become urban pests on their occasional meanderings (some think this phenomenon occurs at 9-year intervals). They burrow into farm pond dams. Because they are potential carriers of several human diseases (called *zoonoses*) control seems essential. Muskrat populations can be controlled by minimizing habitat, using alternative crops, using various wire barriers, trapping, and in some cases poisoning. The latter is done using zinc phosphide on vegetable baits of carrots and apples. The treated baits are put in burrows, in lodges, or on floating rafts.

People

Muskrat carcasses have been sold as "swamp rabbits." Although there is quite a difference in palatability between a rat and a rabbit, muskrats have a good taste and there are many good recipes for them. How a carcass is marketed strongly influences its importance and use. Habitat or population management may be counteracted by people's customary practices or aversions.

Management of people's behavior for the benefit of muskrats includes stringent protection, by law, of wetlands, the development of refuges and managed areas, and trapping regulations including seasons, quotas, trapping methods, and transportation. Other managerial acts will influence fire protection, decisions about zoning, insect control activities, use of muskrat marshes for solid waste and dredge fill disposal, and marsh conversion for urban, airport, and other uses.

Like a cloud over the micro-methodology of the marsh system manager, many almost uncontrollable factors affect the destiny of the marshes and their denizens. Energy shortages will reduce power for intensive marsh manipulation. Air pollution will probably increase, modifying light penetration of the atmosphere and therefore modifying photosynthesis. Similarly, rainfall will change and shifts of tenths of a centimeter over watersheds of hundreds of square kilometers will cause major changes in marsh dynamics. The muskrat manager is not typically geared to management at such a scale. Nevertheless, it must be attempted.

At the local level, the people management tasks may include:

1. Stabilizing or developing alternative fur or flesh markets.
2. Developing fur storage and transportation facilities.
3. Developing a stable trapper force with appropriate facilities, subsidies, and incentives as needed.
4. Developing optional employment opportunities in low market years.
5. Educating trappers to improve trapping efficiency, humaneness, and law obedience.

6. Passing laws and effectively enforcing them.

7. Marking boundaries and erecting signs.

8. Developing observation platforms (underground and underwater, as well as above the marsh) and viewing sites off roads and dikes.

9. Conducting field trips, demonstrations, and observations.

10. Securing funds to protect or manage muskrat areas.

11. Providing damage replacement rather than muskrat removal or control.

The manager can have little or great control over the muskrat management system depending on knowledge, leadership ability, and willingness to expend energy on the tasks. A manager's self-management, continued learning, and participation in securing educational opportunities for re-learning and updating will be reflected in marshland outputs over the long run. Use of increasingly more sophisticated decision aids such as automated data bases, computer simulators, and optimization programs will also become evident in the achievements of the system.

The Future

A major question for the future will be how society and managers communicate and resolve the question of trapping. There is a yet unmeasured anti-trapping sentiment. Rooted in love-of-life and neo-pacifist philosophies and with organized support from humane societies, groups are now working to stop trapping.

Trapping, like hunting, is one way by which resource benefits can be experienced. It is a management tool, but there are others. If it is stopped, then the others must be used. The costs will be different, as will the benefits. The successes will be measured in the rationality of the decision, in the consistency of the decision with other social decisions, and in whether the foregone benefits for segments of the public will be tallied as long-term costs or benefits.

The muskrat may become a very important monitor of the human environment. It already is an expression of the health of the marsh. Observing muskrat populations over time or their tissue content of pollutants may be as important to people in the future as regular readings of rain gauges or periodic medical examinations.

Research is badly needed on the aspects of the muskrat to which the management system is highly sensitive. The massive literature is unbalanced, more reflecting researcher interest than needs for knowledge. With all the past work, there is little real value in designing a highly precise and predictable system. The needs exist for computer models of marshland dynamics, vegetation succession, marsh production functions, muskrat energetics and endocrinology, and the seasonal protein and dynamics of energy in food plants. Extremely important is research into value systems and the total economics of public and private wetland systems for wildlife. All of the above must be conceived as a module, a subsystem of a guidance system for the large, increasingly urbanized watershed.

Study Questions

1. When a population of animals is managed, is it any longer wild?
2. Is an unavailable and inaccessible muskrat population a resource?
3. Define ecological amplitude.
4. Can good predictions be made about an unstable environment?
5. How many combinations of plantings of 15 grains can you make in 30 fields in your muskrat and waterfowl refuge?
6. Can remote sensing be used in muskrat management? How?
7. Sketch the likely shape of the production function of a marsh pothole for muskrats in your part of the country.
8. Draw 20 such curves and observe the aggregate production curve for a marsh. Report your hypotheses or findings.
9. Visit a muskrat trapper, a marsh, a bank burrow, a marsh manager, an agronomist working in such areas, a coastal zone planner.
10. How does controlling muskrats differ from increasing muskrats?
11. What is a nutria? Write a brief paper based on library work comparing the nutria and the muskrat. With someone else, compare the two with the beaver.
12. Is high or low salinity a more desirable condition for muskrat habitat?
13. Are insects a problem for the muskrat manager? How?
14. A group of trappers is willing to stop trapping for several years to build up the muskrat population. Prepare an argument against this.
15. What is an average muskrat density? High?
16. For a population with unbalanced sex ratio (110:100), 60 lodges, 3.5 litters per year, 4 young per litter, and 0.85 mortality, compute an appropriate harvest.
17. Study the literature on population regulation. Why do you think muskrats do not achieve densities of one per square meter?
18. Why is the muskrat a likely candidate for minotoring the health of watersheds?
19. How can people be managed in the muskrat management system?
20. How has technology influenced muskrat management?
21. What anti-trapping sentiment exists in your class? Among people in a sidewalk survey? Ask your teacher to record your findings and report them to future classes. What are the trends? Will they continue? What will be the consequences?

Selected References

Allen, P. F. 1950. Ecological basis for land use planning in Gulf Coast marshlands. *J. Soil and Water Cons.* 5(2):56–62, 85.

Arata, A. A. 1959. A quick method of gross analysis of muskrat stomach contents. *J. Wildlife Management* 23:116–117.

Bronson, F. H. and B. E. Eliftheriou. 1965. Adrenal response to fighting in mice: separation of physical and psychological causes. *Science* 147:627–628.

Calhoun, J. B. 1952. The social aspect of population dynamics. *J. Mammal.* 33(1):139–159.

Cartwright, B. W. 1946. Muskrats, duck production and marsh management. *Trans. N. Am. Wildlife Conf.* 11:454–457.

Christian, J. J. 1970. Social subordination, density, and mammalian evolution. *Science* 168:84–90.

Christian, J. J. and D. E. Davis. 1964. Endocrines, behavior, and population. *Science* 146:1550–1560.

Emerson, F. B. 1961. Experimental establishment of food and cover plants in marshes created for wildlife in New York State. *N.Y. Fish and Game. J.* 8(2):130–144.

Errington, P. L. 1957. Of population cycles and unknowns. In *Population studies: animal ecology and demography.* Cold Spring Harbor Symposia on Quantitative Biology. 22:287–300.

Errington, P. L. 1961. *Muskrats and marsh management.* Stackpole Co., Harrisburg, PA. 183 p.

Florschutz, O. 1967. Multiple use of salt marsh impoundments. *Wildlife in N. Carolina* 31(11):12–14.

Hammack, J. and G. M. Brown. 1974. *Waterfowl and wetland: a bioeconomic analysis.* The Johns Hopkins University Press, Baltimore. 128 p.

Hanson, W. R. 1952. Effects of some herbicides and insecticides on biota of North Dakota marshes. *J. Wildlife Management* 16(3):299–308.

Hensley, A. L. and H. Twining. 1946. Some early summer observations on muskrats in a northeastern California marsh. *Calif. Fish and Game* 32:171–181.

Krummes, W. T. 1940. The muskrat: a factor in waterfowl habitat management. *Trans. N. Am. Wildlife Conf.* 5:395–404.

Mathiak, H. A. and A. F. Linde. 1956. *Studies on level ditching for marsh management.* Wisc. Cons. Dept. Tech. Wildl. Bull. No. 12, 48 p.

McLaren, I. A. 1971. *Natural regulation of animal populations.* Atherton Press, New York. 195 p.

Metzgar, R. G. and D. A. Wharton. 1968. Planning the management of Maryland wetlands. *Proc. Ann. Conf. S. E. Assn. Game and Fish Commissioners* 22:68–82.

Penfound, W. T. and J. Schneidau. 1945. The relation of land reclamation to aquatic wildlife resources in southeastern Louisiana. *Trans. N. Am. Wildlife Conf.* 10:308–318.

Taber, R. D. 1971. Criteria of sex and age. In R. H. Giles, Jr., *Wildlife management techniques,* 3rd ed., revised. The Wildlife Society, Washington, DC, pp. 325–402.

Takos, M. J. 1947. A semi-quantitative study of muskrat food habits. *J. Wildlife Management* 11:331–339.

Wynne-Edwards, V. C. 1962. *Animal dispersion in relation to social behavior.* Hafner, New York. 653 p.

Chapter 7
Waterfowl

Waterfowl may be managed by all of the approaches and for all of the benefits expressed in Chapter 1. Waterfowl are the object of an elaborate annual recreational and cultural hunt. They provide the economic base for several communities, as well as the raw material for the occupation of professional guide. Honking geese, in seasonal flights, provide untold pleasures to observers across the country. Some waterfowl are threatened, and hence every managerial act is preservationist in nature; others are destructive to crops, such as winter wheat, and population reductions are much sought. In each area of the country and for almost every person there exist different objectives and thus different problems. Consequently, many different managerial strategies and tactics are employed. What is good waterfowl management may not be the optimum overall management for wildlife. This is to be sought among multi-objectives, multi-species, highly variable habitats, various laws, and a wide range of managerial expertise.

Waterfowl are ducks, geese, and swans. There are, according to Johnsgard (1968), 3 subfamilies, 11 tribes, 43 genera, and 146 recent species. (See Table 7-1.) Waterfowl are wildlife, but they are a very special kind of wildlife. Just what they are is a matter of definition by humans. Often the definition includes a concept of hunted birds, but there is no particular biological reason for leaving out of the group the three species of loons (Family Gaviidae), five species of grebes (Family Colymbidae), or a host of other water birds like the shearwaters,

260

TABLE 7-1

The nomenclature of natural waterfowl of the continental United States.

Family Anatidae
  Subfamily Anserinae
    Tribe Dendrocygnini: Whistling or Tree Ducks
      Black-bellied tree duck, *Dendrocygna autumnalis*
      Fulvous tree duck, *D. bicolor helva*
    Tribe Anserini—Swans and True Geese
      Trumpeter swan, *Cygnus cygnus*
      Whistling swan, *C. columbianus*
      White-fronted goose, *Anser albifrons*
      Snow goose, *Anser caerulescens* (Blue goose a color phase)
      Ross's goose, *Anser rossi*
      Emperor goose, *Anser canagica*
      Canada goose, *Branta canadensis* (perhaps 20 races)
      Brant goose, *B. bernicla*
  Subfamily Anatinae
    Tribe Cairinini: Perching Ducks
      Wood duck, *Aix sponsa*
    Tribe Anatini: Dabbling Ducks
      European widgeon, *Anas penelope*
      American widgeon or Baldpate, *A. americana*
      Gadwal, *A. strepera*
      Northern green-winged teal or European teal, *A. crecca*
      Mallard, *A. platyrhynchos*
      American black duck, *A. rubripes*
      Pintail, *A. acuta*
      Blue-winged teal, *A. discors*
      Cinnamon teal, *A. cyanoptera*
      Common shoveler, *A. clypeata*
    Tribe Aythyini: Pochards
      Canvasback, *Aythya valisineria*
      Redhead, *A. americana*
      Ring-necked duck, *A. collaris*
      Greater scaup, *A. marila*
      Lesser scaup, *A. affinis*
    Tribe Mergini: Sea Ducks
      Common eider, *Somateria mollissima*
      King eider, *S. spectabilis*
      Harlequin duck, *Histrionicus histrionicus*
      Oldsquaw, *Clangula hyemalis*
      Black scoter, *Melanitta nigra*

TABLE **7-1,** *continued*

       Surf scoter, *M. perspicillata*
       White-winged scoter, *M. fusca*
       Bufflehead, *Bucephala albeola*
       Barrow's goldeneye, *B. islandica*
       Common goldeneye, *B. clangula*
       Hooded merganser, *Mergus cucullatus*
       Red-breasted merganser, *M. serrator*
       Common merganser, *M. merganser*
    Tribe Oxyurini: Stiff-tailed Ducks
       Masked duck, *Oxyura dominica*
       Ruddy duck, *O. jamaicensis*

Source: Johnsgard 1968 and Linduska 1964.

fulmars, petrels, pelicans, cormorants, skimmers, auks, murres, and puffins. The coot (Family Rallidae), *Fulica americana,* is very duck-like. Surely the gulls and terns are waterfowl. But just because birds may look somewhat alike or live in or near water does not mean they are similar species, have the same behavior or habitat requirements, or should be managed similarly. Waterfowl, like wildlife in general, have been somewhat mismanaged due to a quirk of nomenclature. "Waterfowl" is an overgeneralized group; to continue to manage the large group called waterfowl is to invite failure in managing optimally any of its species or species groups. The same is true for wildlife in general. There must be increasingly specific management decisions for species-specific resources, for time-specific users, in specific locations. There are good reasons why this has not been done in the past—for example, available knowledge, pressures from users and on habitats, limited technology, computer assistance, and funds—but most of those have changed. There are now possibilities for species management and species-cluster management formerly undreamed and impossible.

Migration

Many waterfowl are migratory. Waterfowl are often dominant members of a migratory classification for wildlife. Such classification is as useless as the waterfowl classification. Terns, woodcock (*Philohela minor*), and many shorebirds (for example, the rails) are also migratory, as is the mourning dove (*Zenaidura macroura*). The migratory phenomenon is one of the dimensions of the appeal of waterfowl to humans. It is a behavioral classification criterion, another such behavioral class being predation. Other popular classification criteria are size (for example, big game) and habitat (for example, upland game).

These classifications influence how research is done, classes are taught, and manpower and resources allocated.

There were believed to be four north–south "flyways," or major migratory flight lanes. This concept has held sway over waterfowl management since 1935. It persists in the face of evidence (for example, Lowery 1951 and Bellrose 1968) that the lanes are not distinct, and vary in patterns and distance by years. Hunting seasons are still debated and guidelines provided for the flyway, a nonexistent phenomenon. See Figure 7-1.

Research on waterfowl is ongoing. One managerial problem is deciding how many studies must be conducted, or over how many years data must be examined, before conclusions can be reached or old conclusions changed. Another problem is getting a waterfowl management concept revised that was sold so well in the first place that it resists change when new studies indicate the need for change. To sell the flyway concept was a monumental job; it resulted, undoubtedly, in improved management. Now there are new concepts, new data on migration, and new means for waterfowl harvest management. These newer concepts are more difficult to sell than the former ones. The old ones must be un-sold, without agencies and wildlife managers losing credibility.

The migratory behavior of many waterfowl is a perplexing behavioral and biological problem. It is not likley to be solved by one unifying theory of migration. Species and their behavior are diverse, and in diversity is survival power. If there is any unifying theory, it is probably that birds will use, over the long run, the easiest, least energy-consuming, and least risky means for migration possible. Orientation remains a major question. There is evidence (Emlen et al. 1976) that birds can detect magnetic fields approximating strengths of those of the Earth and that these are involved in their flight direction finding, after flights are initiated by changes in photoperiod.

Whatever the causative and guiding mechanisms, migration is the managerial root of a massive human behavior management problem. It is known from banding studies that some waterfowl, like the blue-winged teal (*Anas discors*), make a trip of 11,000 kilometers (7000 miles) from northern Canada to mid-South America. (Or perhaps the teal flies from South America to Canada and is not the Canadians' bird after all.) These birds, like many waterfowl, are everyone's and yet no one's. They are a *common resource* and an example of one of the few common resources under intensive management.

On July 13, 1918, the Migratory Bird Treaty was signed with Great Britain. Later, a treaty was negotiated with Mexico. These treaties continue to afford protection to migratory birds. They have also been a basis for later laws, such as the Migratory Bird Conservation Act of 1929 and the Duck Stamp Act of 1934, that promoted acquisition of habitat for the migratory birds. These laws and treaties are examples of macro-management. They are not the solution to waterfowl problems but are one very important element among the tactics and strategies the wildlife manager must use in various mixes.

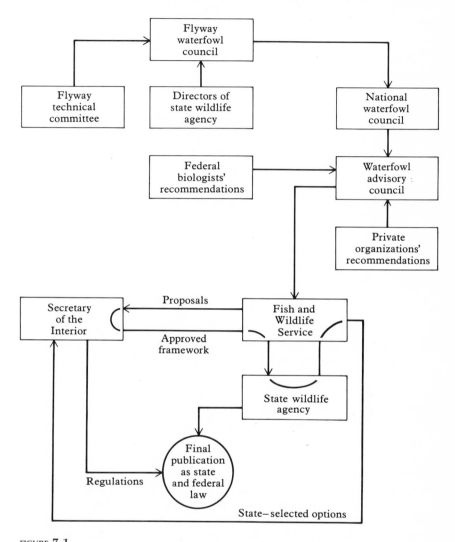

FIGURE **7-1**

The pathways to final passage of state and federal laws and regulations governing waterfowl hunting.

Waterfowl Habitats

Waterfowl, like all wildlife, are intimately dependent on their habitat. They are created from it, molded by it, sustained with it, and perish as it diminishes. The awesome reality of the difference between waterfowl and resident game is that this is true at every period along their entire migratory route. Waterfowl are a resource dynamically existing in time over very diverse space that must be arranged in just the right pattern—no gaps, no inverted sequences, no improper juxtapositions. If the pattern is broken and behavioral adaptations not made rapidly, the birds cannot survive.

There have been private waterfowl preserves for centuries. State and federal refuges were created, and the Duck Stamp Act of 1934 provided additional funds for land acquisition in the United States for waterfowl. All of this has been done in the face of nationwide waterfowl habitat destruction. As early as 1850, the Swamp Land Act permitted land drainage that caused loss of waterfowl habitat. Various agricultural laws, subsidies, and other policies also encouraged wetland drainage. Private landowners followed the publicly subsidized demonstrations. Over a half-million hectares a year were being drained from 1940 to 1953 (Madson 1960). Land drainage continues. The waterfowl manager, with an eye on the larger context, must wonder what the *net* national gains are of doubling waterfowl food production in his 500-hectare marsh. Perhaps this is just sweeping at the tides with a broom.

Waterfowl managers in North America must focus their attention on the breeding grounds of Canada (particularly Alberta, Saskatchewan, and Manitoba), the Dakotas, and western Minnesota. Here the prairie potholes, the shallow glacial depressions rich in food and nesting sites, reach 1 per 2 hectares (125 per square mile). They are the "duck factory" which is continuously dismantled by agricultural technology (for example, more efficient drainage and larger crop harvesting machinery), ravaged by the periodic droughts, such as those of the 1930's and late 1950's, and stirred by international politics and dealings in grain futures. Permanent aircraft flight lines (transects) are flown periodically by federal, provincial, and state wildlifers to determine the rate of habitat loss.

Outright land purchase has been attempted. Hundreds of units are now owned and managed by the U.S. Fish and Wildlife Service and other federal, state, and private groups. The federal lands were largely acquired by Duck Stamp monies, predominantly bought by waterfowl hunters. Ducks Unlimited acquires waterfowl lands in Canada. Inflation, escalating land prices, and relative stability of hunter populations have created a no-win situation. Land acquisition is still a viable waterfowl management practice. It must not, however, hide the fact from manager and public alike that the situation is not under control, but is growing worse.

Waterfowl managers, like other wildlife managers, must examine their entire system and identify those factors or changes to which the system is most sensitive. By controlling or changing these parts, usually more output per unit of investment is gained than by working with other parts. (The entire system must be managed; how to allocate managerial time and resources is the emphasis here.) For many waterfowl species, the prairie potholes are that critical factor. It will be managerially wasteful to create southern waterfowl feeding areas, refuges, and so on that are in excess of the future capability of the pothole region to produce waterfowl. To build larger warehouse, retail, and sales facilities in the face of declining factory production does not appear rational. It is likely that resource users in the future will be asking such questions, and the wildlife manager will want to be accountable.

Waterfowl production does not *have* to decline. To prevent it will require vigorous macro-management, large investments, sophisticated use of funds to obtain productive areas, and a complex mix of alternative land use policies and methods. These include:

1. Instituting computer-regulated watersheds on which cropping, flooding, damming, and other practices are conducted.
2. Providing feedback mechanisms that show the public and decision makers the ecological and hydrological consequences of drainage.
3. Obtaining easements.
4. Implementing use–value taxation.
5. Conducting on-site management, including fencing from livestock, fire lanes, nesting site improvement or construction, sedimentation and pollution control, minimizing human and feral animal disturbance, and vegetative enhancement.

Too much emphasis on the prairie regions is not wise, but it is very difficult to manage an international resource. It is typical to limit the problem by working on an easy part—like the pothole region. There are other massive habitat problems that are similar. One of these is associated with the American black duck (*Anas rubripes*). This 2.5-pound duck breeds mainly in Quebec and Labrador (but also Ontario south to North Carolina) and flies southward, stopping off all along its route, with many ending in Arkansas. There the flooded-forest habitat is being drained and bulldozed for soybean production. A conflict exists in that the citizen, through one agency (for example, the USDA or U.S. Corps of Engineers, both directed by Congress), subsidizes land drainage and forest removal and construction of dams that inundate marshlands and waterfowl-supportive stream systems, and through another agency buys and manages lands to offset these losses. The black duck manager is distressed by dams; the canvasback manager is delighted by the pools provided in the Mississippi by Corps' dams. Evidently it is not possible to achieve all desired resources from the same area. Benefits must be debated and weighted. Additionally, long-term costs and consequences need to be articulated better for decision makers by ecologists (for example, by using computer simulations and the concept of the production functions). The coordination and balancing of such a complex system has not been done, but it can be. In such a system waterfowl will not win, but neither will they lose. Without such operating systems, they seem likely to lose.

Johnsgard (1968:89) observed:

With the world's constantly increasing human population, and the resulting economic pressures to turn the remaining wild lands into croplands, one cannot look to the future with optimism. Only through continued efforts to educate the public regarding their moral responsibilities of sharing this world with other animals, to teach people that it is possible to derive as much or more pleasure from watching and studying wild animals as from shooting them, and to preserve natural areas for the preservation and propagation of endangered species, will it be possible to show our descendants the extraordinary beauty and incalculable value of waterfowl. Let us act so that the legacy provided by the sight of wild ducks slanting into a prairie marsh against a flame-red sunset, the vernal recrudescence of life expressed in a skein of migrating geese darkly projected against an April-blue sky, or the ethereal majesty of distant swans' voices softly penetrating the morning mists of October will not be relinquished willingly by our own generation or by those that inherit these riches from us.

Diverse Requirements of Waterfowl

There are puddle ducks that largely feed on the water surface. Mallards, pintails, black ducks, and teals are examples. Their feeding habitat requirements are for shallow waters. The muskrat marsh (Chapter 6) is ideal. The birds filter the duckweed (*Lemna*) from the top of the water and, tail-up, eat and pull up submerged vegetation as well as seeds, molluscs, and various invertebrates (Martin, Zimm, and Nelson 1951). There are diving or sea ducks that feed deep under water on fish, invertebrates, and plants.

Puddle ducks and geese are most readily managed. The waterfowl manager will construct a dike, flood it until late spring to prevent weed growth, drain it, seed the area with grains such as millet, and grow a crop. Later the dike is closed, reflooding the area, and the grains are available for feeding waterfowl. It is natural feed and usually attracts large numbers of birds. It can be used to attract birds to areas for public viewing (such as from raised blinds), to attract them away from croplands and thereby reduce crop damage, and merely to provide them food on their journeys. Migrating flocks can clean out such areas, or they can stay a day or two and, because of climatic or other variables, fly over, leaving a high-cost food supply almost untouched.

Some areas are not amenable to such practices. Managers have engaged in grain production or sharecropping specifically for direct feeding of waterfowl. In sharecropping, a local farmer will use the wildlife management area land, grow a crop of wheat or corn or other cash crop, and in lieu of land rent or other payment, will provide the area manager with half or some proportion of the crop or will leave part of the crop unharvested in the field. Stored grains can then be fed during the appropriate period to waterfowl. They can then be scattered in protected fields or in shallow feeding areas. Although not as "natural," such food production is more sure and controlled. The results are storable, can be distributed in response to bird flights, or even can be used on other areas where needs are high.

Protection of Waterfowl

Waterfowl need water, food, and protection. One thing from which they must be protected is hunting over baited areas. There are subtle, and to some people meaningless, distinctions about whether grain thrown in front of a hunting blind is significantly different from grain grown there. Hunting over baited blinds is illegal (except in special areas where crop depredation has resulted in law changes), but the question of what constitutes baiting continues to be debated.

Waterfowl are subject to harvest all along their annual migration routes. Natural mortality is high and hunting mortality may be added to it. In order to provide protection and also to achieve an equitable harvest among hunters in the states, elaborate procedures and sets of rules have been devised. Decisions about opening dates, season length, and bag limits are made with much past information, but *no* information about the season forthcoming. Only sketchy information is available about hunter or public perceptions of quality waterfowl-related experiences. Decisions must be made far in advance, rules printed, licenses sold, work leave arranged, and permits issued. A manager's success or failure for any season depends, first on the total production of waterfowl (not known until July) and then on how well the decisions that were made match the food, climate, crop harvesting, movement, ice, and wind patterns up and down the migration routes. It is a serious guessing game: Millions of dollars are involved, and thousands of hunters are influenced, many of them politically powerful. In most, though not all, regions waterfowl hunting is a sport of the well-to-do. Travel, blinds, decoys, memberships, and services add up to large expenditures for very little material gain (due to restrictions). Complete mastery of the habitat and population by the wildlife manager will not guarantee success in such a situation. In the aftermath, the manager will be blamed, for there is no satisfaction in blaming the weather.

More knowledge of all the factors involved can improve the fit between desires and outcomes. Skillful use of any managerial leeway will further improve the manager's record. More timely and better controlled processes such as a local manager's ability to advance or delay a season by a day to accommodate bird behavior, or the ability to close a local season when a quota has been reached, or more responsive data analysis that could allow southern states to harvest more (or less) as a function of northern harvest rates are all means of gaining more precise control. Whether such control is truly needed or can be afforded depends on value judgments. Objectives and criteria will change over time, and it is likely that ever more precise control will be needed.

The migration route is looked upon by some as a conveyor belt. From the duck factory, after the annual migration switch is thrown, the birds come south. Southerners claim northerners get all the birds. Others complain that refuges in the mid-United States "short-stop" birds flying south. Refuges are said to delay birds on their flight as they rest and feed (and make local flights off the refuge). On these local flights major hunting mortality is said to occur, progressively reducing the size of the migrating flock. Everyone complains about "sky-busters," people who shoot too early or those who shoot when birds are out of range, and thus scare birds, causing them to fly high over a hunting or feeding area. For winter wheat farmers, the birds (especially geese and swans) are pests that return annually to walk on their fields, trample plants into the mud, and eat large amounts of the succulent green.

Provisions for the protection of waterfowl include:

1. Federal, state, and private enforcement personnel.
2. Flights made to observe hunters and to look for baiting (corn is readily seen from the air; wheat and milo cannot be seen).
3. Outside hunting dates and options stated by the Fish and Wildlife Service.
4. State laws and regulations that provide modifications within these limits.

The waterfowl regulations are some of the most complicated of all game regulations (for example, see Kirby et al. 1976). These may include, for a state:

1. Season length, for example 25 to 105 days.
2. Single season or split.
3. Starting date.
4. Starting time of day on first day.
5. Starting time (relative to feeding and hunter's ability to identify species).
6. Closing time (same).
7. Ducks that can be bagged per day.
8. Number of birds that can be kept in possession at one time.
9. Number of various species permitted in bag including low abundance species such as canvasback, redhead, and woodduck.
10. County or area exceptions (for example, closed to hunting).

A point system has been used. A bird of each species is worth a designated number of points. The bag limit is reached when the point value of the last bird taken, added to the point value of the other birds taken, reaches or exceeds the allowed point value (usually 100). The system also assumes that the hunter can identify birds in the hand. This system allows the manager to adjust hunting pressure on species in accord with the breeding success and relative abundance of the birds.

Point systems are also valuable in bird watching, a so-called nonconsumptive use of waterfowl. Club members or individuals can vie for daily or seasonal point totals, with bonuses for certain species, as well as diversity of the observed birds (number and species).

Alternative protection systems include closely regulated blinds, hunting permit systems, agency distribution of hunters to blinds with specified ranges, numbers of shells to be fired, and official check-outs. Such highly regulated hunts are prized by some, disdained by others, and are only feasible on intensively managed areas.

Current management efforts are geared to assuring species protection by (1) improving habitats and (2) making laws more stringent in subsequent years (extirpation in one year is unheard of; recovery from overhunting alone is possible). However, the overriding concern is distributing the harvest as equitably as possible. This can be improved by:

1. Assuring every licensed person an option to hunt.
2. Assuring unlicensed persons, including those opposed to hunting, an option to experience local waterfowl flights and flocks year around without hunting (area management).
3. Requiring reasonably good or corrected eyesight, demonstrated shooting competence, ability to estimate distances appropriate to waterfowl hunting, and ability to identify harvestable waterfowl and to discriminate among protected species in a particular year.
4. Providing incentives (for example, reduced license fees in the future or license rebates for improvements in point 3 above and appropriate hunting behavior).
5. Providing deterrence (for example, threat of fine, license revocation, escalating license fees or fines).

Elaborate banding, recovery, and reporting systems now exist. Data are collected and processed by the U.S. Fish and Wildlife Service in Laurel, Maryland. There is now some reluctance to close completely any season, for to do so eliminates an invaluable data source. In addition, over 125,000 miles of flight- and highway-census lines are run annually.

General computer methodologies now exist for allocating a scarce resource progressively throughout a network. They can be applied to allocating waterfowl fairly to citizens on the basis of waterfowl abundance, available hunting areas, licensed hunters, and expressed desires and past success of these hunters. Such a system will not be easily formulated. It will be a dynamically evolving system, but it is possible. Such a computer system would exemplify sophisticated wildlife management that is appropriately responsive to the complexity, dynamics, and importance of a major resource problem.

Agency Cooperation and Conflict

Waterfowl hunters in the United States make up only about 10 percent of the hunters. Hunters are only 10 percent of the total population. Whether a waterfowl hunter is a person who only hunts waterfowl, hunts geese and also big game, or some other combination is a difficult problem, but one the agencies must solve in order to achieve sophisticated allocation of budgets, weight project priorities, and provide rational justifications for efforts.

Every agency has a clientele which it serves and from which it receives support. The strength of this support determines agency size, operation, and occasionally effectiveness. Waterfowl hunters are few but politically and economically powerful. The Fish and Wildlife Service (U.S. Department of the Interior) has in the past made great investments of public funds in waterfowl management—investments far out of proportion to the number of hunters or hunter-days. This illustrates, not only that agency performance is influenced by political demands, but also (1) that wildlife has not, and need not, be managed on a one-person, one-vote basis, (2) that certain types of hunting opportunity, such as waterfowl, cost substantially more than others; (3) that crises, such as duck poisoning, must be met with special allocations of funds; and, when crises subside, for example, when reasonable amounts of waterfowl habitat are acquired, then programs can be discontinued; (4) that participation rates are almost meaningless for allocating agency money, since hunting days (either real or opportunity-days) differ significantly in quality, as assigned by weights to different types of hunting days; (5) that agency officers, those responsible for making decisions (or reporting what committees seem to have decided), will tend to allocate agency resources to those things with which they personally are the most familiar. Hunting statistics are meaningless if they cannot be convincing in the oral debates and justification sessions that are part of the procedure of every agency, no matter how large or small.

The agencies working with waterfowl include privately funded ones like Ducks Unlimited, Inc. and The National Audubon Society. The Soil Conservation Service (SCS) of the U.S. Department of Agriculture employs wildlife biologists and works with agricultural landowners, providing advice on dams and other waterfowl management activities. The SCS, the Corps of Engineers (U.S. Department of Defense), the Bureau of Reclamation (U.S. Department of the Interior), and the Tennessee Valley Authority (TVA) are all so large and have such diverse interests, objectives, and clients that the same agency may cause or allow destruction of vital waterfowl habitat in the same year that it creates or increases production on other areas. Some of these activities are purposeful *mitigation*, that is, the replacement of losses. Some losses cannot be avoided if the objectives of the primary project are to be achieved. In such cases, mitigation should be one of the costs. In other cases, losses cannot be mitigated (for example, replacement of unique feeding areas or endangered species). Society, with the assistance of its agencies, must decide whether the long-term wildlife benefits of a proposed project (for example, a dam) will exceed the likely losses and lost opportunities associated with that project.

Another agency concerned with waterfowl is the National Wildlife Refuge System, a division of the U.S. Fish and Wildlife Service that contains 30 million acres in about 300 refuges. Much of the Refuge land was purchased, donated, and variously acquired with waterfowl primarily in mind. Subsequently, the lands' many other resources have been recognized, and these holdings now represent an important nationwide wildlife resource base. Because they have a dominant wildlife resource objective, in contrast to the parkland objectives of the U.S. Park Service, or the multiple use objectives of the Bureau of Land Management and the U.S. Forest Service, they have the potential for providing managerial diversity, ecosystem design competition for other agencies, experimental and demonstration areas, and knowledge about maximum production as bases for comparing how well less intensively managed areas are doing (Giles and Scott 1969).

At the time of this writing, however, the Wildlife Refuge System is poorly funded, mismanaged, and therefore a wasted national resource. It has focused so intensively on waterfowl that it has lost its perspective. The refuges contain national spectacles equal to those of the National Parks, cellulose production potentials equivalent to those of the national forests, grazing range equivalent to that of the Bureau of Land Management. They contain wildlife resources from Alaska musk-oxen to Florida key deer. They dot the national migration pattern and represent significant resting and feeding areas for waterfowl. But they are lost in a bureaucratic maze. They are without leadership, for they are partitioned among regions of the U.S. Fish and Wildlife Service. They are without a congressional spokesman, without enough identity, except locally, to justify a congressman making a national effort for their development. A presidential committee reported on the sorry situation of the refuges in 1968 (Leopold et al. 1968), and since then it has grown worse. Some refuges have been "mothballed." Perhaps new alternatives and leadership for this vast national wildlife and wildland resource will emerge.

Other agencies involved in waterfowl management include offices of all the states and provinces, various regional groups like the Southeastern Association of Game and Fish Commissioners, and of course the national agencies of Canada, the United States, and Mexico. This makes the waterfowl management problem, at one level of analysis, an institutional rather than an ecological problem. The agencies all have different objectives, resources, expertise, clientele numbers and intensities of interest, and ability to cause change. Canadians ask why they should bear the cost of producing ducks and experience so few of the rewards of hunting them. (Most hunting occurs south of the border.) Some groups are federated (for example, the National Wildlife Federation), and one wildlife expert may advise many groups. There are flyway councils with state, federal, and private organizational configuration, largely involved in season settling. Some individuals try to work within agencies, other individuals and groups try to influence agencies, sometimes through the courts (for example, the Environmental Defense Fund). Some people want more waterfowl (for example, Ducks Unlimited). Others band together to eliminate refuges as the source of crop-depredating birds.

Classical Conflicts

Waterfowl protection connotes controlling predators. It is true that predators kill ducks; however, studies suggest that the number is not great and that control efforts are uneconomical unless the predator populations' other, primary food supplies have been suddenly removed. Efforts to control waterfowl predators can result in secondary losses greater than those controlled. Skunk predation on duck eggs is known, but removal of skunks also removes predation on snapping turtle eggs, and these turtles are known predators on ducklings. A highly managed waterfowl area cannot, by any stretch of the ecological imagination, be considered natural or believed to be stable. There is no reason to expect waterfowl and predators to achieve a harmonious balance. The sensitive wildlife manager will keep tabs on both populations and, depending on objectives and available resources, decide whether predator control efforts are a cost-effective tactic. The morality of predator control must be continually debated. Ecological education—an improved understanding of the structure, dynamics, and relations of waterfowl habitat—can be influential in determining public attitudes.

The waterfowl manager (and naturalist) must be careful in studying waterfowl nesting not to create paths to nests. The occasional trips made to observe a typical nest during its 21 to 30 days of existence may wear pathways, which predators can follow. One technique is to carry a long pole and observe nests from the path, using the pole to part the grass obscuring a view. The pole can also be used to scoop up eggs for candling them (holding them up to the light) to determine the fertility or stage of embryo development. The predators that follow the path may be unaware of the adjacent nests. The researcher must always be on guard against his or her presence being a significant factor in the system under study. See Figure 7-2.

Efforts have been made to reduce lead in shotgun pellets, since it has been determined that the lead pollutes the waters and may cause lead poisoning in waterfowl (Cook and Trainer 1966). These pellets have been used for many years by waterfowl hunters. In front of an old blind, thousands of rounds of

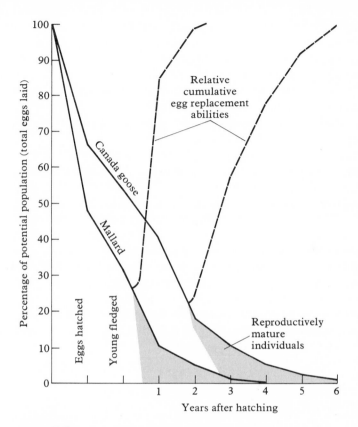

FIGURE **7-2**

Survival of the Canada goose and mallard based on banding data and
field studies. Mortality rates and expected egg replacement are related.
(Reprinted from *Waterfowl: their biology and natural history* by P. A.
Johnsgard by permission of University of Nebraska Press. Copyright
© 1968 by the University of Nebraska Press.) Anderson (1975) reported
75 percent of mallard mortality occurs *before* the birds are banded,
implying the above curve may be slightly biased. The mean life span
of a mallard is 1.6 to 1.8 years.

ammunition will have been fired. The range is not great (20–60 m) and the shot
falls into the water. Waterfowl feed off the bottom, straining invertebrates and
tubers from the mud, and pick up lead shot as well. Some efforts to remove
heavy lead concentrations have been made, but though removal may be feasible
in a few areas, most present great problems. Covering the blind with dredge
spoil has been done, but that usually destroys the site and the quality of the
blind. Rotating use of blinds allows sediment to cover the shot or the shot to
settle to lower layers. Reducing shots fired, using lead-free pellets, and attempting lead recovery are all possible measures to be taken.

Waterfowl, particularly the diving ducks like the canvasback and scaup, feed largely on invertebrates. They are carnivores, high in the food chain. At this trophic, or feeding, level they are subject to accumulated pollutants. Pollutants tend to be bio-accumulated. The higher the trophic levels, the greater is the amount received per unit volume of biomass consumed. The redhead and dabbling ducks, tending to eat vegetation, receive less lead, for they get it from surface contamination of plants and only small amounts from that taken into plants.

Protection for waterfowl is protection for humans—not only with respect to the quality of the meat a society eats, but also with respect to the total levels of environmental contamination it tolerates. The migratory birds, perhaps better than any imaginable device, unify human populations. No human community, however clean or how pure its environmental concerns, is assured that the geese on its water courses are pollution-free or are not contaminating the land with products gathered either north or south or east or west.

Protection of waterfowl from pollutants requires work with various watershed authorities, the Environmental Protection Agency, Coastal Zone Management agencies, various water pollution control groups, solid waste disposal and health agencies (to reduce pollution from improperly developed landfills and sewage), and of course with specific industries, targeting in on substances or practices particularly hazardous to waterfowl.

Environmental Impact Statements

With the passage of the National Environmental Policy Act in 1969, environmental impact statements (EIS) became required of all major federally funded projects. The potential impacts of a project on waterfowl, as well as on other environmental factors, must be assessed in an EIS before the President's Council on Environmental Quality authorizes the project to proceed. A Corps of Engineers' EIS for a proposed dam would typically contain sections on waterfowl impacts, including habitat loss as well as resting and feeding areas produced by the completed project. The EIS may be a valuable instrument for wildlife protection. The waterfowl manager can employ it by:

1. Requiring a waterfowl section.
2. Providing useful inputs to such sections, including species-specific, time-specific waterfowl requirements and likely benefits ("the dam will be good for ducks because ducks like water" is the level of some earlier inputs).
3. Relating the project to waterfowl migration patterns.
4. Relating the project to adjacent areas. A common fallacy is to claim days of waterfowl hunting *produced* when all that is done is to take hunters away

from adjacent existing spots. No *net* increase in hunter days has occurred, although the quality may be argued to have improved due to dispersion of hunters.

5. Relating the project to past habitat loss and all potential habitat remaining. When statistics are thrown around in an EIS it is easy to lose sight of the meaning of a proportion. The argument "only 1 percent loss will occur," must be considered in context. Is that pound of flesh from the heart or from the hindquarters? In some systems, a small loss may be insignificant; but in waterfowl systems, thresholds are being approached. Each creeping increment endangers the ducks, geese, and swans of North America. The waterfowl manager must halt these encroachments, often by proposing acceptable alternatives. To do so may require not only a thorough knowledge of waterfowl, but also mastery of the area in which the problem lies (for example, industrial technology, engineering structures, pollution control, agribusiness, watershed management). Occasionally, identity as a classical wildlife manager cannot be retained because of this changed role. For wildlife management, the ends probably justify the means.

In society's rush to exploit the last drop of oil as quickly as possible, there are likely to be an increasing number of tanker break-ups, pipeline breaks, offshore well leaks, and processing plant spills. All of these are extremely harmful to waterfowl habitat and to the birds as well. Environmental impact statements, of themselves, have no regulatory or injunctive power. A statement of untold impacts does not prevent an oil rig from being built offshore or a nuclear power plant from being built in a waterfowl marsh. The statements are informational. The will of society will be worked and, progressively, energy values will escalate. Relatively, wildlife values may decline. Energy and waterfowl are on a collision course. Neither legislation, policy, nor organization has been created to reduce conflicts or resolve the coming problem. Great safeguards must be taken, not only to consume and efficiently use every drop of precious fossil fuel, but to protect the birds. At present there is no effective way to rehabilitate populations of oiled birds. When society recognizes how precious are the energy reserves, then oil will be carefully handled and conserved, and then the birds will be naturally cared for—as a by-product. Until then, they will suffer the madness of the black gold rush.

Management Options

How does one manage waterfowl? There is no universal answer. Any answer must be tentative, dependent on changing conditions and competing needs for limited wildlife management funds. One thing is clear: Waterfowl must be managed internationally, for all the people of all the continents. In each area there are tactics that can be employed to produce ducks or reduce them, but these are useless if they are not geared to the strategies being adopted nationally and internationally. Communication, if not cooperation, can tend to improve local managerial decisions for waterfowl. Waterfowl must be managed holistically, and the only possible way to approach this is with computer assistance for climate modeling, water supply predictions, harvest allocations, and budgeting.

Aside from these general concepts, the major techniques and strategies available for utilization in a waterfowl management system include the following.

The *inputs* to the system include ideas, money, and energy. They can be regulated through:

1. Ongoing research.
2. Census and inventory of (a) clientele and hunter values and expectations; (b) habitats; (c) populations and their subunits, particularly mallards produced in Alaska, northern Canada, British Columbia, and part of Alberta (Anderson 1975); (d) mortality factors and threats.
3. Funding levels from Congress, hunters, and other sources.
4. Local energy for photosynthesis as modified by air pollution and climatic changes.
5. Information storage and retrieval systems.

How these inputs are *processed* is often a matter of management but also includes manipulating natural ecosystem processes. The process-type of actions available to the manager include:

1. Passing laws and regulations.
2. Enforcing such laws.
3. Acquiring diverse, abundant land, water, and shoreline and protecting them.
4. Preventing drainage and flooding.
5. Planting foods and making improvements in food quantity and quality.
6. Manipulating water levels to provide feeding, resting, and nesting areas.
7. Replacing lead with nontoxic shot.
8. Reducing pollution.
9. Instituting land use controls to prevent erosion and high runoff.
10. Promoting or altering agricultural practices to make them compatible with waterfowl.

11. Engaging in sharecropping.
12. Feeding (direct).
13. Using electronically broadcast calls to attract (or repel) waterfowl.
14. Using mechanical and live decoys (for example, wing-clipped birds) to attract waterfowl.
15. Building or protecting nesting sites (Doty et al. 1975).
16. Building loafing or resting sites, platforms, or log rafts.
17. Conducting cleanups of oil-soaked birds.
18. Reducing pressure on native birds by encouraging shooting preserves.
19. Seeking public funding.
20. Requiring hunter skills.
21. Requiring use of retrievers to reduce waste of shot birds.
22. Reducing disturbance or harassment of birds.
23. Introducing flocks of wing-clipped birds (for example, geese) to obtain returning wild young.
24. Increasing band returns by education and incentives.
25. Protecting tidal marshes.
26. Reducing ocean pollution.
27. Paying waterfowl damage to crops (after careful analysis). For example, at one-half pound of food per day a goose flock can consume tons of food in a month.
28. Reducing hybridization with domestic ducks.
29. Increasing public viewing sites.
30. Constructing and managing blinds (distribution, quality, intensity of use, lead, and so on).
31. Improving distribution of sanctuary and feeding areas.
32. Reducing migration route hazards (for example, towers).
33. Reducing mortality on wintering grounds.
34. Educating people to (a) encourage or discourage hunters in a particular year; (b) improve the general environment for waterfowl; (c) obey laws; (d) contribute to management programs.
35. Improving the quality of the hunter's experience.
36. Preventing introduction of exotics.
37. Controlling predators in select situations.
38. Reducing crippling losses through education (for example, Davenport et al. 1973) regulation, weapons, blinds, and retrievers.

39. Reducing contact between domestic and wild flocks to reduce disease.

40. Rotating feeding areas to reduce disease or eliminating feeding areas.

41. Controlling insects to reduce specific disease vectors of waterfowl (for example, black fly (*Simulium* sp. as a *Leucocytozoon* vector to geese).

42. Encourage agricultural, drainage, and stream management practices conducive to waterfowl.

43. Preventing marsh and prairie fires.

The *objectives* of waterfowl management can be improved as well as the analysis of the *outputs* of systems managed for them. The actions that may be taken include:

1. Making more abundant, more precise statements of waterfowl that are likely to be available for hunting or other uses.

2. Expressing objectives in terms of quality-weighted person-days of resource use.

3. Quantifying secondary as well as primary outputs of systems designed exclusively for waterfowl management.

4. Developing professional and public awareness of the concept of maximum potential production as a criterion to prevent overinvestments by managers and overexpectations by resource users.

5. Adding waterfowl objectives to other sets of land use objectives.

6. Clarifying species relations, making management as species-specific as possible.

7. Measuring output in appropriate genetic groups, clarifying hybrids and subspecific units and varieties (Heusmann 1974).

Feedback must be formally incorporated in management. The means for doing so in waterfowl management are:

1. Evaluating user satisfactions relative to expectations.

2. Improving equations and computer systems for predicting management action effects on populations, habitat, and people.

3. Improving cost-effectiveness studies.

4. Improving inspections, relating performance to objectives.

5. Increasing use of allocation models for improving budget controls.

6. Monitoring pollution, land use changes, and health of waterfowl.

Overshooting the present and undershooting the distant future so as to be most right over the planning period is the *feedforward* job of the waterfowl manager. Techniques available are:

1. Developing scenarios and computer models of future resources and use and adjusting present land acquisition, employment, and management systems responsibly to accommodate both present and future needs.

2. Developing a dynamically self-correcting system as the feedforward questions are asked and answered every few years.

Study Questions

1. What are waterfowl?

2. What is the scientific name of the mallard, the redhead, the Canada goose, the wood duck?

3. Laws are means of wildlife management. How long have migratory birds been managed by laws? Did wildlife management begin prior to that year? Explain and discuss.

4. Can you think of any way to reconcile one federal agency draining wetlands and another one preserving and creating them?

5. Where is the "duck factory"?

6. What is the point system for regulating harvests?

7. Waterfowl management is complicated by the number of agencies potentially involved. Name some.

8. What problem has been caused by lead shot?

9. What recommendations would you make as a waterfowl manager to a person about to prepare an EIS for a water development?

10. Give examples of important management practices for your area of the country, categorized as inputs, processes, objectives, feedback, and feedforward.

Selected References

Anderson, D. R. 1975. *Population ecology of the mallard: V. Temporal and geographic estimates of survival, recovery, and harvest rates.* Resource Pub. 125, Fish and Wildlife Service, USDI, Washington, DC. 110 p.

Bailey, R. O. and R. E. Jones. 1976. Mallard mortality in Manitoba's extended spring muskrat-trapping season. *Wildlife Soc. Bull.* 4(1):26-28.

Bellrose, F. 1968. *Waterfowl migration corridors.* Illinois Nat. Hist. Surv. Biol. Notes No. 61, Urbana.

Carney, S. M. 1964. *Preliminary keys to waterfowl age and sex identification by means of wing plumage.* U.S. Fish and Wildlife Serv. Spec. Sci. Rep. Wildl. (82). 47 p.

Cook, R. S. and D. O. Trainer. 1966. Experimental lead poisoning of Canada geese. *J. Wildlife Management* 30:1-8.

Davenport, D. A., G. A. Sherwood, and H. W. Murdy. A method to determine waterfowl shooting distances. *Wildlife Soc. Bull.* 1(2):101-105.

Day, A. M. 1949. *North American waterfowl.* Stackpole and Heck, New York. 329 p.

Doty, H. A., F. B. Lee, and A. D. Kruse. 1975. Use of elevated nest baskets by ducks. *Wildlife Soc. Bull.* 3(2):68-73.

Emlen, S. T., W. Wiltschko, N. J. Demong, R. Wiltschko, and S. Bergman. 1976. Magnetic direction finding: evidence for its use in migratory indigo buntings. *Science* 193:505-508.

Giles, R. H., Jr. and R. F. Scott. 1969. A systems approach to refuge management. *Trans. N. Am. Wildlife Conf.* 34:103-117.

Heusmann, H. W. 1974. Mallard-black duck relationships in the Northeast. *Wildlife Soc. Bull.* 2(4):171-177.

Hine, R. L. and C. Schoenfeld (Eds.). 1968. *Canada goose management: current continental problems and programs, a symposium.* Dembar Ed. Res. Services Inc., Box 1148, Madison, WI 53701. 195 p.

Hochbaum, H. A. 1942. Sex and age determination of waterfowl by cloacal examination. *Trans. N. Am. Wildlife Nat. Resource Conf.* 7:299-307.

Johnsgard, P. A. 1968. *Waterfowl: their biology and natural history.* University of Nebraska Press, Lincoln. xviii + 138 p.

Jordan, J. S. and F. C. Bellrose. 1951 *Lead poisoning in wild waterfowl.* Illinois Nat. Hist. Surv. Biol. Notes 26, Urbana.

Keith, L. B. 1961. *A study of waterfowl ecology on small impoundments in Southeastern Alberta.* Wildlife Mono. 6. 88 p.

Kirby, R. E., J. H. Riechmann, and M. E. Shough. 1976. A preliminary report on Minnesota's innovative 1973 waterfowl season. *Wildlife Soc. Bull.* 4(2):55-63.

Kortright, F. H. 1942 *Ducks, geese, and swans of North America.* Stackpole Books, Harrisburg, PA. 544 p. (See 1976 revision by Bellrose.)

Leopold, A. S., C. Cottam, I. McT. Cowan, I. N. Gabrielson, and T. L. Kimball. 1968. The national Wildlife Refuge System. *Trans. N. Am. Wildlife Conf.* 33:30-53.

Linduska, J. P. (Ed.). 1964. *Waterfowl tomorrow.* Fish and Wildlife Service, USDI, Washington, DC. xii + 770 p.

Lowery, G, H., Jr. 1951. A quantitative study of the nocturnal migration of birds. *University of Kansas Pub., Museum of Nat. Hist.* 3(2):361-472.

Madson, T. 1960. *The mallard.* Olin Mathieson Chem. Corp., East Alton, IL.

Martin, A. C., H. S. Zim, and A. L. Nelson. 1951. *American wildlife and plants: a guide to wildlife food habits.* McGraw-Hill, New York. (See Dover Editions.)

Mendall, H. L. 1958. *The ring-necked duck in the northeast.* University of Maine Studies, 2nd Ser. 73, Orono, ME. 317 p.

Rogers, J. P. 1964. Effect of drought on reproduction of the lesser scaup. *J. Wildlife Management* 28(2):213-222.

Salyer, J. W. 1962. Effects of drought and land use on prairie nesting ducks. *Trans. N. Am. Wildlife and Natural Resource Conf.* 27:69-79.

Vaught, R. W. and L. M. Kirsch. 1966. *Canada geese of the eastern prairie population, with special reference to the Swan Lake flock.* Tech. Pub. 3, Missouri Dept. Cons., Columbia. 91 p.

Wright, B. S. 1954. *High tide and an east wind—the story of the black duck.* Stackpole, Harrisburg, PA and Wildlife Management Institute, Washington, DC. 162 p.

Chapter 8

The Inland Fishery

At the beginning of this textbook it was pointed out that a close relation exists between fish management and the management of other wildlife. I hope that the reader will be able to extend the principles discussed in the previous chapter to fish and to find many parallels.

There are reasons for separating fisheries from wildlife management, chief among which is that there is more knowledge to master about *either* than can be achieved by any individual in a lifetime. It is as naive to think that one person can master both fields as it is to think that a medical doctor and a veterinarian should receive identical educations. As long as "wildlifer" implies synonymy between the fisheries manager and managers of the other wildlife resources, suboptimum resource management is likely. However, there are arguments for combining the two studies: (1) many of the relevant ecological and economic concepts are identical, (2) agencies now employ and are likely to continue to employ generalists who know much about both and must perform in both areas, at least seasonally, (3) even specialists receive general questions from the public, who tend to expect answers to questions even outside of the specialist's field, and (4) there are increasing needs for people who can provide the bridges between these two fields as they evolve from art to science.

The "inland fishery" taxon is used largely as a way to avoid the managerial complexities of marine resources, including mammals (for example, seals, porpoises, and sea otters), sea birds (for example, eiders), fish, and other sea creatures (for example, molluscs, shrimp, and crabs). In this chapter inland fish are grouped as still-water species and current dwellers, which are typically warm and cold water species, respectively.

Every effort to develop rational management principles and practices convinces me that only user-, species-, or site-specific management is reasonable. Feeding or behavioral groupings, as well as ecological community groupings, overgeneralize. Habitat classes do not work well because some inland or freshwater fish are *anadromous;* that is, they live part of their lives in the ocean and spawn in fresh water. (*Catadromous* fish live in freshwater but spawn in the sea.) Other categorizations may be useful for teaching, general conversation, and organizing conferences.

Fishery Benefits

The manager's chief concern is the *yield* from the fishery resource. Yield of what? is the modern manager's continuing question. The answer was formerly: pounds or numbers of fish of designated species. Now, however, studies, such as those summarized and extended by Hampton (1975), suggest that it is the *potential* physical yield of fish that justifies a fishery; if that potential exists, catches are not necessary for people to enjoy fishing. There is a complex set of objectives or "yields" desired by fish resource users: These yields include (1) escape from the everyday routine or from an urban environment (with family or friends, or away from them), (2) the outdoor experience, including its stimulating influence on thinking and conversation, (3) esthetic enjoyment of the natural environment, (4) the sporting challenge, including both the physical challenge and the challenge to skills and knowledge, (5) health benefits, such as increased muscle tone and reduced stress, (6) fish trophies (size, number, or limit), and (7) food.

The order of importance is approximately the order in which the benefits are listed, but of course it varies among user groups and types of fishery. The weights attached to each desired yield, or objective, will vary by region and clientele based on experience, tradition, education, and socioeconomic characteristics of the *potential* user population. In management, fishery as well as wildlife management, it is the potential user population that counts, not the *present* number of users. The present user may have little relation to the potential user. To survey licensed *fishermen* is to survey only those who, under present rules, regulations, and conditions, desire to buy and can afford an option to fish. Such surveys have little bearing on those who would fish if one or more conditions were changed. Since *long-term management* of resources is the professional's byword, such changes seem highly probable.

What people say they want or will do may be quite different from the way they behave. In surveys of expressed desires or weighing of objectives the assumption is made that there is a reasonable correspondence between the two, on the average. Developing coefficients and other means for adjusting expressed-to-actual performance by wildland resource users is a fruitful area for creative research.

Many fisheries managers continue to claim that there is a close relation between fish taken and all of the other benefits of the fishing experience. The fish in the creel is the index to the performance of the system. Such claims require the manager to assert either "We must develop a scientific, highly rational system for irrational fishermen," or "We must deny or refute a set of consistent weightings by fishermen." I suspect neither is appropriate and that managerial efforts to achieve the objectives of users will gain increasing acceptability and attention.

There are many factors that influence the achievement of fishing benefits, including the attitude of management or supervisory personnel (see Chapter 11); water quality; cleanliness of sites; size, number, and species of fish caught; facilities available; ease of access; weather; and amount of privacy.

How can these factors be manipulated? The following are suggestions presented to demonstrate how action can be taken.

1. Educate the public to change objectives or increase knowledge of resources available.
2. Put out signs, maps, and instructional leaflets.
3. Improve access, parking areas, road turn-outs.
4. Make trails around lakes and beside streams one-way to reduce contacts or increase privacy.
5. Require minimum distance between fishermen.
6. Provide sanitation containers, clean areas frequently, reduce litter carried onto areas, and educate the public on proper sanitation practices.
7. Improve facilities.
8. Limit people on an area by permits, licenses, fees, or counts through a gate.
9. Provide family and children's play areas away from fishing areas.
10. Make available to the public stocking records about time and amounts stocked and catch records.
11. Restrict seasons to the most suitable weather periods.
12. Create more water bodies.
13. Provide boats and ramps to reduce shoreline fisherman density.
14. Educate managerial and other staff in improved public relations.

15.   Emphasize natural beauty by providing trails to select spots, restricting fishing or boats from scenic areas, and planting or trimming vegetation to enhance beauty.

Each lake, each stream, each region, does not need all of the above. Searching for an optimum mix that balances achievement against costs and risks is the manager's job.

No matter how important the socioeconomic aspects of fishing, it is, of course, essential that the fishery manager master the ecological principles of fish yield. Managers of inland fisheries have been trapped by the history, logic, and numerical beauty of the commercial fishery and hatchery literature, with its emphasis on biology and aquatic ecology. The whole fishery management profession has assumed a strong biological orientation. In many states fishery (and wildlife) managers are called biologists. I contend that biology has been overemphasized, and that, from a narrow point of view, a fish is to the fishery of little more importance than a ball is to the football industry. It is essential, of course, but the managerial and research emphasis has been misplaced. One reason for this is that research that produces operational conclusions is easier for biological than for sociological topics. Another is that the profession is in the biological rut of the typical university fishery curriculum. The new managerial task is to achieve a reasonable balance between the socioeconomic and ecological aspects of decision making for the fishery.

Warm Water Fisheries

The warm water environment is typically the pond, lake, or reservoir. The majority of freshwater surface is in lakes and reservoirs, but ponds are emphasized here to simplify the discussion and to highlight principles. Complexities can be found ranging from the special problems of the Great Lakes fisheries to those of warm water rivers. The warm water environment is influenced by a thousand macro-environmental factors such as radiation and thermal pollution, point-pollution (for example, industries and municipalities), nonpoint surface pollution (for example, roads, crop fields, feedlots), and agricultural subsidy. Bodies of water are built, or not, as a function of state and national agricultural or watershed policy, local needs, and hydropower needs. They are opened or closed to fishing as a function of ownership, pollution threats, propaganda, and fee-fishing potentials. They are made accessible or not as a function of ownership, roads and trails, and airspace policy over wilderness areas.

These phenomena have more influence over the pounds of fish available or produced (actually harvested for food or trophy) than all of the microenvironmental changes the manager can make. There are many macro-environmental factors over which the manager has little or no control, such as precipitation, watershed size and configuration, and basic soil-water chemistry. These have been discussed in earlier chapters. Each macro-factor and approach is treated by many volumes. Here, the micro-approach is outlined. This knowledge can help isolate the sensitive parts of the managerial system and thus allow managers to make rational decisions about managerial commitments.

Fish can be managed to produce food for wildlife, to stabilize an aquatic ecosystem, to produce pounds of marketable fish (aquaculture), as well as to meet sport, recreational, or ecological objectives. Each requires a different orientation and actions, but all depend on the following fundamentals.

The Pond or Lake Habitat. Fish, like birds and mammals, live in three-dimensional space. (See Figure 4-4.) All of that space is not equally good at all seasons of the year. Figure 8-1 shows a cross section of a pond. That three-dimensional volume is a complex, dynamic system. Its temperature is constantly changing. The sun-heated surface waters are therefore lighter (less dense) than the cool (more dense) underlying waters. Water in its liquid state is most dense at 39.2°F (4°C), just a few degrees above the freezing point. For example, the difference in density between water at 10°C and 11°C is 12 times greater than between water at 4°C and 5°C. Water either warmer or colder than water at 4°C, maximum density, is lighter than that water and rises.

The warm water temperature zone is called the *epilimnion*. Winds that churn the lake or reservoir surface mix the water, causing such lakes to have thicker epilimnia. Such winds are more prevalent over larger lakes. The epilimnion is home for many fish, for it is where an energy balance can be achieved, where oxygen supplies can be obtained, and where food (also dependent on light, warmth, and oxygen) is relatively abundant. Fish may live here exclusively or forage into other layers. Under the epilimnion is the thermocline, a relatively thin layer of water. There is a rapidly dropping temperature in this layer, at least 1°C per meter.

Water holes, ponds, and lakes or reservoirs are not clearly defined; they exist along a continuum. The same principles operate for them all, but some principles are never meaningful because the conditions never exist in which they may be seen. Very shallow lakes do not stratify except for such short periods that the concept is managerially (and perhaps biologically) irrelevant. In large ponds (or small lakes) only two strata exist.

In deep, large bodies of water, the *hypolimnion* exists. It is a layer of dense cold water, usually quite stable. The hypolimnion may contain almost no dissolved oxygen and be almost uninhabitable by fish.

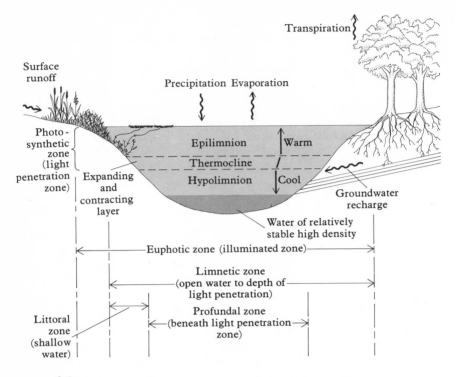

FIGURE **8-1**
Cross section of a pond or lake showing (1) thermal stratification, (2) succession, at the left, influenced by muskrat and other faunal activity, (3) input-output relations of the basic water cycle, and (4) a photosynthetic zone of variable depth depending on water turbidity and solar angle. Note nomenclature overlaps by depth, light, and temperature criteria.

The thermal strata of a lake are critical, for they determine its potential productive volume. Lake or pond *volume* is not all-important because it interacts with another major factor, *sunlight*. All fish, sooner or later, depend on green vegetation for food energy. This food only grows in the *photic zone* of the lake—the depth to which enough light, of the appropriate segments of the spectra, penetrates to allow efficient photosynthesis. Agricultural silting, boating, and bottom-rooting fish, for example, can so cloud the water that light intensity and spectral qualities can be reduced and photosynthesis inhibited. This water cloudiness is called physical turbidity and may be measured by a device called a Secci disc. Maximizing light penetration by limiting such turbidity will tend to increase fish food and consequently potential fish yields. "Tend to" means that other requirements for plant growth must be met. Extremely transparent waters that are infertile will not produce fish. Light can retard photosynthesis of the surface of lakes, but this is rarely a problem and the condition is needed to achieve desirable light levels in the epilimnion.

A manager's efforts to achieve large amounts of light, a thick epilimnion, and a highly nutritious water body for maximum fish food production may be self-defeating. The managerial task is to find an optimum balance. If the conditions just listed are achieved, a dense growth of algae may form in the zone. The situation typically arises under the influence of nitrate and phosphate runoff from croplands. The plants may consume all of the oxygen in the water at night, during periods of cloudy weather, or when the lake is under snow-covered ice. Of course, other respiration associated with decomposing plant and animal parts consumes more oxygen. Fish kills can result.

The layers are not permanent but change seasonally. Such changes have also produced fish kills. Remember that the hypolimnion is devoid of oxygen. When a lake is covered by ice and snow, light penetration is greatly reduced. Oxygenation by surface winds is eliminated. When all of the dissolved oxygen in the water below the ice is used up by fish respiration and the other respiratory action going on in the lake, then *winterkills* occur. In lakes where there is sufficient oxygen for a fish population to survive through a winter, the population may still be threatened by a *springkill.* The first warm, high sunlight-intense days may melt the snow cover on top of the ice, penetrate the lake deeply, and trigger photosynthetic activity, using up the last oxygen. In spring the surface water will warm uniformly to about 4°C. Warm water is then passed downward, gravity and wind driven, across the lake to the upwind side. Almost all lakes have this turnover. The spring lake turnover can bring oxygen-deficient waters from the bottom of moderate-climate lakes to the surface and suffocate fish already suffering oxygen shortages. Stratification once again occurs. Winds will continue to mix the surface layer, but "no ordinary wind will cause the light surface waters to invade the heavier deeper layers" (Bennett 1970:45).

In polluted ponds (or ponds overfertilized by a manager with the best intentions) a large algae growth, called a *bloom,* may occur. When these plants die and decompose, a large amount of oxygen is taken up in the process. The biological oxygen demand (BOD) of the pond is high and a fish kill can result. BOD, determined by chemical analysis, is one measure of the health of a pond. BOD can be reduced by preventing algae blooms and preventing organic pollution. Some chemicals and rock strata bind oxygen as oxides, sulfates, or carbonates, further decreasing the dissolved oxygen in water. BOD has come to be understood as biochemical oxygen demand.

Fish kills are observed frequently. They are believed by laymen to be caused by pollution or disease. Most often they are caused by suffocation resulting from the phenomena of the water density-temperature-light interaction.

What can the manager do about fish kills? First, predict them. By watching ice depths, snow cover, oxygen levels, and seasonal winds, and relating them to lake depth and fish densities, the manager can predict fish kills. Second, the manager can explain them to the public. In most situations there is nothing that can be done. The manager's job is to reduce dissatisfaction, to prevent inappropriate action being taken against "polluters," and to prevent exorbitant expenditures for diagnostic tests. Third, it seems possible to design the floor and banks of new lakes and ponds to minimize this occurrence. Earth can be moved and the lake oriented relative to winds, water depths, and circulation, to minimize fish kills. Fourth, compressed air has been used to form air bubbles deep in lakes. Strategically used, these can break up the thermal stratification and oxygenate the water. The costs are high, but then costs are always relative to objectives. In a high-intensity fishery, in a heavily populated area, where rare species may be involved, or where disposal costs of fish kills are high, the costs of such mixing may be quite appropriate.

The reader will not be surprised if the plot becomes more complicated. Even shape and size of lakes are dynamic. All lakes are continually filling. The dynamics are called *aquatic succession* (Figure 8-2). Aquatic succession is much like terrestrial succession, already described. The latter starts where the former ends (in Figure, 8-2, between *d* and *e*). The aquatic pattern is dominated by sedimentation due to erosion from the watershed and lake or pond edges and a gradual stabilization of the lake surface. The second dominant influence is organic matter added to the lake. In warm climates and shallow lakes, decomposition (respiration) occurs rapidly. However, in cold climates, decomposition is slow. Leaves and branches falling to the bottom of the small northern pond are nearly in an anaerobic (without oxygen) environment. They are "preserved." An acidic environment results, further reducing decomposition. Layers of organic matter build, often intermixed with silt. The process is like that of coal formation. Eventually, over many years, the lake or pond fills in. Vegetation grows where fish once swam. A stream meanders across the flat expanse of silt covered by willows where waves once tossed. These old lakes can now be seen on aerial photographs as circular pockets of spruce, in the age-steps of the vegetation of beaver-pond valleys, and in the *Juncus* covered meadows where stream, oxbow lake, and soil slump-created pond once existed.

The same processes continue unabated in farm ponds and lakes, which cover about a half of one percent of the continental United States. Each state now has thousands of farm ponds—all undergoing succession. Because so many were built in such a short time (see the concept of the aggregates), many will be in trouble at the same time. The "trouble" will be that they will reach a low-production stage of succession. Most ponds have been created for livestock watering and fishing recreation (though other reasons are thrown in to justify the costs—for example, fire protection, picnicking, land value improvement, and so on). Farm ponds are also a means of catching runoff from the land and taking a final crop from its dissolved fertility before it is lost, finally, to the ocean.

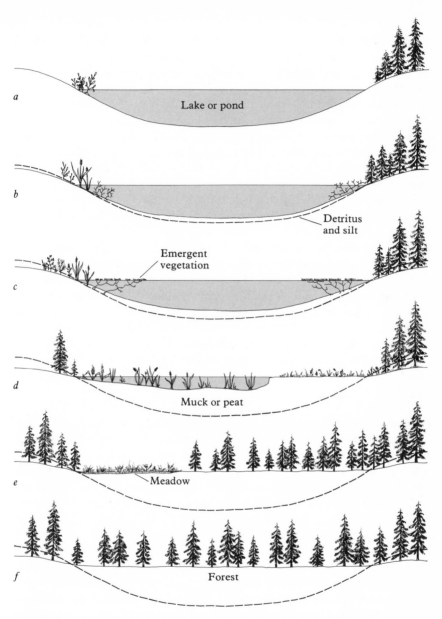

FIGURE **8-2**

Generalized pond evaluation or aquatic succession. Uplands erode into the water and organic matter adds to the silt (*a–c*). As the pond fills in, it becomes a bog (*d*). Eventually a meadow forms (*e*), and with increased evapotranspiration, as well as filling, an area dry enough to grow trees is created (*f*). Further evapotranspiration and soil building hasten the succession into the terrestrial seres typical to each biome. The successional pattern is consistent, although species and rates vary. Aquatic fauna (fish as well as food organisms) change with each sere.

Many ponds were built for swimming *and* fishing. When a beach is required, the objectives are usually mutually exclusive. A swimming beach with slope like that to the left of Figure 8-1 will undergo rapid succession. It will rapidly vegetate, usually with cattails (*Typhus*) or various rushes. These require hard work (or herbicides) to keep them out. Any relaxation of effort will produce discouraging results. Steep slopes (right of Figure 8-1) produce the best fishing conditions and fewer water weed problems. Notice also that a pond with surface area of one hectare (2.47 acres) has much greater volume if the sides are vertical than if gradually inclining. A great water volume in the photosynthetic zone is desired. If cattle graze the pond edges, swimming and motorboating are permitted, and silt is not abated, water turbidity increases. Turbidity influences light penetration and thus photosynthesis. The higher the turbidity, the lower the productive zone.

On and among the vegetation of the pond littoral, or shallow water, zone (Figure 8-1) there is another world of creatures. Aquatic insects live in the bottom and on plants. *Phyto*plankton, or minute freely floating plants, and *zoo*plankton coexist. Zooplankton eat phytoplankton. Most small pond and lake fish eat plankton of both types as well as insects. The larger fish feed on insects, invertebrates, and the smaller fish, all of which have concentrated and reassembled the amino acids into useful proteins.

Among the rooted vegetation, the small fish and larval or fingerling stages of the larger fish may hide. The vegetation provides escape cover from fish predators.

Stocking. The most significant managerial difference between fish and terrestrial wildlife is that terrestrial forms must grow to a particular size to survive. Fish have an indeterminate growth size. A fish population will respond to the support capacity of a body of water in a nearly infinite variety of ways; a wildlife population responds in only one way over the long run. Land capacity is often measured in individuals; water capacity is measured in fish weight. A pond may contain a food supply that will support 500 pounds of fish. That population may occur as 250 two-pound adults or 1000 one-half pounders or as 16,000 one-half ounce fingerlings. Once the capacity is reached, the populations tend to stabilize there. A pond is said to be out of balance when the ratio of large to small fish becomes very low. The desirable condition in a recreational pond is to have a large number of big fish for sport and food and to have an abundant food supply for these fish. Since large fish are typically predatory, a prey resource is managed for them. If they are overharvested by fishermen, the prey may get the upper hand. All fish will be of the same small size (stunted); all will grow gradually but none reach a harvestable or desirable size; they will age but not grow. (Fish age is determined by observing through a microscope the rings or annuli on their scales.)

An often-used combination of fish to stock into new ponds has been large-mouth bass (*Micropterus salmoides*) and bluegill (*Lepomis macrochirus*) in the ratio of 1:10. The bluegill multiply rapidly, are food for the bass, and they themselves are a catchable, tasty "pan" fish. Each area of the country will have a different optimum stocking ratio, depending on temperatures, water productivity (a function of soil), season length, and likely succession. A uniform 1:10 has been applied widely, with unfortunate results. It seems likely that a computer analysis that is pond-specific can provide a prescription for optimum species and rates.

Such an analysis will only be appropriate for a set of assumptions and for a particular fishing rate. Fishing rates stay high after ponds are built, but interest wanes, children leave home, and new pressures are brought by neighbors or retirement status. The dynamics of such pressures makes imbalance very likely. Pond balance and a recreational fishery can be regulated by keeping records and, when underharvest occurs, seining or even poisoning the pond to remove population segments.

Management Methods. "Fishing is no good" usually does not mean there are no fish. It means that all of the resources of the pond are captured in small or nongame fish. It will stay "no good" until managerial action is taken or until a winterkill sets conditions back to a new starting point. Either is costly, unpleasant, or requires a wait. Management—the regulation of benefits for people over time—can reduce the peaks of superb fishing and the troughs of the winterkill and achieve annually desirable yields.

The action principles of pond and lake fishery management include the following:

1. Maximize lake edge. Lake size has little to do with per area production.
2. Control aquatic weeds by dredging, cutting, pulling, dragging, winter drawdown, and, if necessary, application of herbicides by a licensed contractor.
3. Minimize introductions of bait fish (even ban their use). These forage fish add to the problems of population imbalance.
4. Use fertilizers to increase fish food production. Water chemistry analyses and continued fishing pressure are essential.
5. Fence out livestock. Water them from a trough at an outlet below the dam.
6. Provide for draining ponds. A standpipe with gate can allow a pond to be drained, fish removed, siltation recovered, and weeds controlled.
7. Drain ponds when they become imbalanced.
8. Seine or poison when ponds become imbalanced.

9. Keep records of production to avoid overexpectations or overinvestments. Ponds produce about 370 pounds per hectare per year (150 lb/acre/year). Peak pond production is about 2900 lb/ha/year.

10. Provide limited predator cover and fishing spots (for example, car bodies, artificial reefs) to concentrate fish and increase fishing success. (Such structures can obstruct harvesting operations.)

11. Use chemical precipitants to reduce severe temporary turbidity problems.

12. Encourage fishing pressure. Ponds and warm water lakes are almost impossible to overharvest. Cold water lakes and streams (discussed later) are low in productivity and can be overharvested or "fished out."

13. Control water levels to increase productivity.

14. Increase ledges.

15. Feed fish, when appropriate, with commercial fish foods or by natural means—for example, by using a light trap for insects or a wire cage in which carrion is placed to decompose and attract insects.

16. Introduce sterile hybrid fish.

17. Stock predatory fish as needed after careful study, by size or number, to achieve desired balance.

18. Require removal of all small fish caught.

19. Require barbless hook fishing and artificial lures, and require that predatory fish be returned.

20. Encourage fishing "fairs" and prizes for tagged fish to keep fishing pressure high. (Care must be taken to keep sporting quality high in such situations.)

21. Minimize snags and other obstacles to efficient fishing. Fish cover can be provided (see recommendation Number 10 above) without it "eating" all fishing tackle used near it.

22. Eliminate closed seasons on lake fisheries. Fish have high mortality; unless taken, they do not contribute to the fishery.

23. Promote fish edibility by service, recipes, education, and improved care, storage, and transportation.

24. Discourage muskrats in dams, stabilize spillways and tailwater areas, prevent grazing on dams, and prevent trees on dams, all to stabilize these structures and thus their fishery.

Pond management, as now practiced, is clouded by the problem of scale. There are over a million farm ponds in the United States. A team of 100 fisheries experts, each visiting one pond a day, would require 27 years to deal with the problem of making *one* management plan or recommendation. The numbers suggest the massive problem that exists—one in which needs for expert advice, service, and education are likely to expand. To accommodate the scale, complexity, and dynamics of this situation, entirely new programs and approaches are likely to be required, many with computer-generated prescriptions for each pond.

It is quite a feat to know and understand reasonably well the management of ponds. It takes years of study of research reported in such journals as *California Fish and Game, Limnology and Oceanography, Progressive Fish Culturist, Transactions of the American Fisheries Society, Commercial Fisheries Review, Bulletin of the Japanese Society of Scientific Fisheries, Hydrobiologica, Journal of Soil and Water Conservation, Animal Behavior, Ecology, Journal of Wildlife Management,* and various publications of state and provincial agencies as well as the Fisheries Research Board of Canada and the U.S. Fish and Wildlife Service. It is quite another feat to master a lake. Each lake or reservoir is large and has its own character, a unique bottom topography, a unique set of currents, turnover phenomena, input mix, outflow rate and character (some have a hypolimnion outflow), and species mix. Some fish have home ranges; what is present in an inlet cannot be generalized for a lake. The lake is an exciting challenge, one not mastered quickly, and one not mastered in the usual period given to agency personnel as they are moved up a career ladder or moved around for experience. Knowledge of the ecosystem for the long-term benefit of people must one day be the criterion for expert staffing of a lake or system of lakes—not the personal, short-term interest of the individual employee. There must be developed ways for fisheries scientists and managers to advance economically and professionally without being moved around too often.

The sophisticated micro-management of a lake or pond fishery requires knowledge of *yield.* Yield is measurable as fish length, for with such knowledge weight can be estimated. Weight in grams (W) is about the cube of the length in millimeters (L), that is,

$$W = aL^h.$$

The value of h is about 3.0 (2.0 to 3.5). When h is 3, then a can be used as a *condition factor* (K), an expression of fish plumpness: $K = 100,000 \ W/L^3$. K is one index of the health of the aquatic system. Each fish harvested (or a sample of fish) can be measured for length and a yield per hectare calculated. Better indices can be obtained as yield per cubic hectare of productive volume. See Table 8-1 for coefficients relating lake volume, area, and sources of inflow and outflow.

The weight actually harvested may not be the amount available for harvest. Commercial fishermen tend to want to take the total annual available production; recreational fisheries rarely approach such harvest. It is essential that

TABLE **8-1**

Water relations important in fisheries management.

1 acre	43,560 ft^2
	0.4047 hectares
1 hectare	2.471 acres
	107,638.7 ft^2
Water (or rain) 1 inch deep on	27,154 gal
1 acre (an acre-inch)	3630 ft^3
	102,788 liters
	1.027,901 hectare-centimeters
Water 1 cm deep on 1 hectare	26,417 gal
	0.972856 acre-inches
Rainfall of 1 acre-inch per day	71.380 liters/min
Velocity of 1 liter/min	0.2642 gal/min
1 gal/min	3.785 liters/min
1.467 ft/sec	1 mile/hour
1 ft/sec	0.682 miles/hour
1 ft^3/sec(cfs)	448.8 gal/min
	28.3 liters/sec
	1698.9 liters/min
	6.46 × 10^5 gal/day
	2450 m^3/day
	1.98 acre-ft/day
1 acre-foot/day	0.504 cfs
1 m^3 (1000 liters)	264 gal
1 gal	3.78 liters
1 liter	61 in^3

annual production be known, however, as a basis for rational investments in improving the fishery. If the surplus production is not harvested, how can investments in increased production be justified? This question is not always asked and therefore not answered. Funds from the Division of Federal Aid, Fish and Wildlife Service, are used by states in fisheries management, land acquisition, dam building, and research. These funds come from excise taxes on fishing gear levied according to the Dingell-Johnson Bill of 1950. The funds have come to be known as D-J funds. The bill provides for matching each dollar invested by the states with three federal dollars. There is room for improvement in how these funds are allocated.

As with wildlife, desired production is the fundamental criterion. It requires the computation of what a lake will produce in desired benefits, unaided by humans, and then a computation of *extra* benefits likely to be gained per dollar of D-J (or other) investment. Yield equations are essential. The concepts build as follows.

Figure 8-3 shows a *recruitment curve.* Maximum recruitment, or increases to

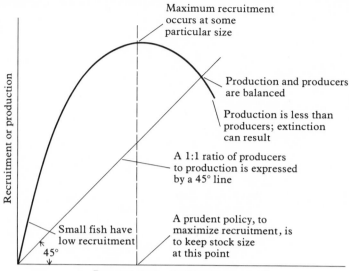

Maximum recruitment occurs at some particular size

Production and producers are balanced

Production is less than producers; extinction can result

A 1:1 ratio of producers to production is expressed by a 45° line

A prudent policy, to maximize recruitment, is to keep stock size at this point

Small fish have low recruitment

45°

Recruitment or production

Parental stock size (length or weight)

FIGURE **8-3**

A recruitment curve can be plotted for a pond or lake fishery. Observations are made over time and recruitment is adjusted to variable conditions or the conditions are assumed to be constant. A 45° line is plotted as a population in equilibrium and thus provides a basis for comparing population trends.

the population, implies a biologically satisfactory state of affairs, but for the fisheries manager all is not biology. It will be evident that the maximum physical yield may not necessarily provide the greatest revenue to the commercial fisherman (simple supply-demand relations), the greatest satisfactions to the sportsman, the greatest "profit" to commercial fisherman or pond manager (due to costs), or the greatest employment (technology flourishes best with mass production).

The manager needs to convert the vertical axis of Figure 8-3 to profit (fully accounted net returns on investment), or production (recruitment plus growth minus mortality), or employment, or revenue, or fleet stability, or community stability, or actual human food production, or a weighted set of all of the above, symbolized as Q, and *then* adjust the parent stock to that optimum size. That is easier said than done, but the concept is a goal to be sought and reduces wasteful, directionless searching.

Figure 8-4 shows that a recruitment curve is closely related to a cost curve. A rational investor will attempt to keep costs, not at the maximum production, but at the maximum return per unit of effort (that is, at A in Figure 8-4). A typical fishing effort curve appears in Figure 8-5.

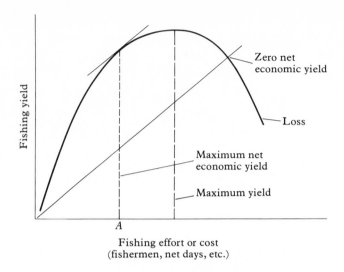

FIGURE **8-4**

A cost curve is closely related to a recruitment curve (Figure 8-3). The yield/cost or catch per unit effort ratio is highest at the asymptote of the curve (the tangent to the point is shown), not the maximum.

How can a fisheries manager resolve the conflicts between Figure 8-3 and Figure 8-5? If an assumption is made that all recruitment will be taken, then the vertical axes are identical. A three-dimensional "mountain" can result (Figure 8-6). The manager's task is to position the system on the surface as close to the optimum point (*) as possible. The manager either becomes involved in an empirical search by trial and error over the years, or, armed with research and computer technology, is able to discover the optimum position and the mix of means for achieving it. Fisheries research and computer applications are expensive. Over the long run, one basis for assessing whether research dollars are well spent is the question: Did the costs of research exceed the profits and other benefits that would have been reaped if the research had *not* been done? Every year of trial-and-error searching can be compared with the optimum. If the difference exceeded the cost of research and computer solutions, then a research investment would have been appropriate.

A simplistic model of yield is shown in Figure 8-7. How the manager achieves a "maximum sustained yield" was once the quest of students of fisheries science. It is no longer. The quest is now for maximum net yield from the resource, subject to the provisions (constraints) that these (a) be accounted as the sum over some period, or (b) be within some limits (reasonably stable) over time. The difference between (a) and (b) may seem to be a question of semantics or just too detailed a concept for a principles text. The difference, however, can be substantial. Consider Table 8-2. I would argue that fisheries manager A was the more successful by criterion (a), manager B better by criterion (b). Both "sustained" their populations.

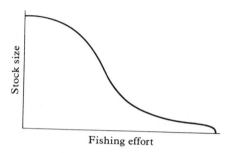

FIGURE **8-5**

A catch curve. As fishing effort increases, population size generally decreases. The last fish are more difficult to take, but, eventually, all can be taken or the population exterminated.

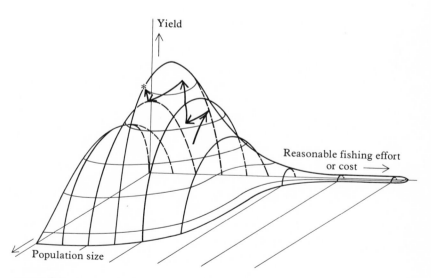

FIGURE **8-6**

Recruitment, cost, and catch curves can be integrated into a three-dimensional form. The fishery manager's task is to manipulate the three factors interactively, searching for the optimum relation of the three. This can be conceived as a spot (*) on the surface of the mountain. The pathways taken may be random, trial and error, or computed.

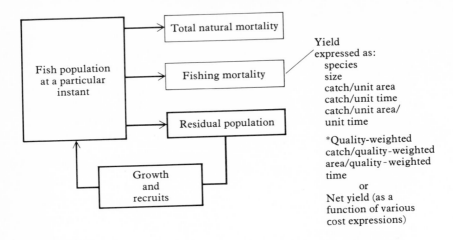

FIGURE 8-7
Yield is the harvested portion of a fish population; it can be expressed in many ways. Recreational fishery yield will increasingly be expressed as the complex statistic Y^*.

TABLE 8-2

Hypothetical yields (in unspecified units, see Figure 8-6) from an inland fishery achieved by two fisheries managers.

	Yields in benefit units	
Year	Manager A	Manager B
1	100	1000
2	350	900
3	7000	1000
4	3000	1100
5	50	1200
6	100	1000
7	100	1000
8	250	800
9	50	1000
10	1000	1000
Total	12,000	10,000

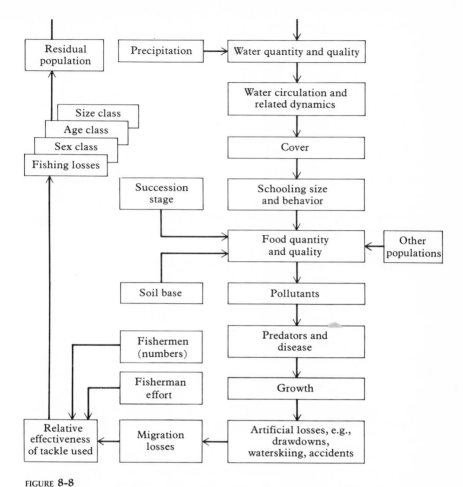

FIGURE **8-8**

A flow diagram of moderate complexity showing the factors for which data are needed and the relations that must be known in order to compute (or to simulate) the likely yields from a fishery.

By now the reader should be convinced that the computation of the appropriate removal from a lake or pond is extremely complex. A simplified elaboration of Figure 8-7 is shown in Figure 8-8. There are simple yield equations that assume the yield next year will be like that last year. There are others that require assumptions of stable environmental conditions. Still others require peculiar assumptions about age structures of the population. These were all needed prior to computers and programmable calculators. The computations for a dozen lakes in a state would take a year, and the system would have changed before the computations were complete. The simple equations were useful for teaching and first approximations. With computer models now available and with ready access to computers by all states, little more than the comprehension of the factors and their interplay (Figure 8-8) are needed at the beginning level.

All the preceding emphasis on physical yield may be misleading. Physical yield, while an essential ingredient in managing a recreational fishery, has very little to do with the desired or experienced benefits derived from such a fishery.

Cold Water or Stream Fisheries

Warm water and cold water fisheries managers are responsible for two quite different groups of organisms. The fish are managed under quite different economic, use, and habitat conditions.

The cold water sport fish principally include members of the family Salmonidae—the trout, salmon, and whitefish. Pike and perch are sometimes considered cold water species but can tolerate both cold and warm waters. The habitat of stream fish is rapidly being lost. Dams, highways, and stream channelization all take their toll on a limited resource of pure, fast-flowing water. What is left is being destroyed by land use that increases silt and destroys spawning beds, by barriers that either prevent migration or cause water fluctuations harmful to the fish, and by pollution. There are streams in public ownership (for example, U.S. Forest Service, state agencies, U.S. Fish and Wildlife Service, U.S. Park Service, U.S. Bureau of Land Management) as well as streams privately owned, some open and others closed to the public.

Trout Streams. Trout waters are special. They cascade from the mountains, the sums of a thousand springs. They are swift, cool, and oxygenated.

Trout streams can be drastically reduced in productivity and suitability for trout by (1) fires, (2) deforestation, (3) ill-advised agriculture, (4) overgrazing, (5) pollutants, (6) mining, (7) floods, (8) human-caused or natural drought, (9) dams and barriers that allow water to warm, silt-in, and lose oxygen (particularly in spawning areas), and (10) channelization. Oxygen levels following fire decrease because of increased silt, slower and sporadic flows, and washing of organic matter and detritus into the stream. Changes in pH also occur. Stream phosphorus and nitrogen levels increase dramatically. Other stream fish, such as carp and suckers, are likely to take over because of their greater tolerance of silt and lower pH, temperature, and oxygen supplies.

Trout streams are unstable systems; their existence is probabilistic. Such streams, if they are to be the habitat of self-sustaining trout populations, must be (1) cool, a maximum of 65°F, (2) oxygenated, greater than 6 ppm, (3) sufficiently large in volume, (4) possessed of ample cover, (5) supplied with adequate invertebrate food, (6) free of pollutants, and (7) underlaid with a gravel substrate suitable for spawning. The chances for one or more of the seven being missing is so great that trout streams must be viewed as critical, sensitive parts of the environment. They are indicators of how humans are managing their uplands; how they regard their water supply capital; and how perceptive they are of society's long-term water needs.

Trout streams, and all other running streams, are called *lotic* environments. Streams have longitudinal strata. The older successional stages are closer to the mouth. Many such streams are intermittent; they dry up during certain seasons. They may be invaded temporarily by trout, or stocked when running full. Many trout waters are also intermittent in production of the life-support system for an abundant, reproductive, harvestable population. Most trout waters are not very productive; that is, they produce little energy photosynthetically as the base of the food chain. There are algae on rocks and lesser amounts of plankton in water, but the mass is not sufficient to produce many pounds of fish. Basic stream productivity is a function of soil nutrients and the aquatic plants produced, but depends largely upon organic matter that falls into the stream. Insects, crustaceans, and small fish feed on the plant matter, and these in turn feed the trout, along with terrestrial insects, frogs, salamanders, and even small mammals. The selective forces in most streams favor small fish. The "lunker" is the exception—a creature hatched or migrated into a favorable environment in which there is cover, stable water, stable vegetation, and a productive stretch of water above its resting place assuring regular feeding. These large, wary fish, the basis for recreational anticipation, the catch, and tales and reflections, cannot be produced in the wild on demand. Management can encourage trophy production, but fishing demands are now so great (and have been for over a half-century) that wild production will not satisfy user demands.

Management Methods. There are options for designating wild streams and severely regulating trout fishermen by special license, random draw from among applicants, and imposition of a quota. These streams can provide diversity in recreational opportunities. They retain a fisherman option, one that few fishermen will be able to experience, but that does provide a base datum for quality fishing and relative human population satisfaction from recreational experiences.

Trout fishermen are a political power. Whatever the cause or base of power, trout can be and have been produced in abundance in hatcheries (more than three-fourths of all stocked fish). In most states, the annual hatchery production is about a half-million pounds of fish. Hatchery management and aquaculture constitute a very large and complex topic and will not be discussed in detail here. Trout are mass produced in state, federal, and private hatcheries. Hatchery scientists have reduced mortality, increased nutrition, increased growth, developed hybrids and selected for high producers, and reduced costs. The apparent demands cannot be met, but the production has now reached a point in most states where fishermen are reasonably satisfied and suspect any future increases in production will substantially increase their license costs. It appears that trout anglers have an insatiable demand for numbers of fish and large fish. "Enough" will never be produced. Increased production of trout seems to produce more anglers.

Given a hatchery production, distribution of the fish remains a problem. Hatcheries are located based on water quality, volume, and related conditions, not proximity to fishing streams. Fish are put into trucks of water, iced to reduce metabolic activity, aerated, and sped to the streams. Some are air-lifted to their destinations. Others are placed into plastic bags of water and "bombed" from low-flying light aircraft into high-mountain wilderness lakes. The logistics of annually dispersing one-half million pounds of a perishable live product to the most remote and inaccessible areas of a state are immense. Further research can improve the efficiency of the transportation system.

There are many stocking strategies, each with its own rationale and supporters. All, however, give special weight to the opening-day phenomenon in fishing, particularly trout fishing, which is more spectacular than the game-season phenomenon. Fishermen line up along stream sides, literally shoulder to shoulder, and await the legal time they can "wet a line."

The time and amount of stocking have evolved from the application of logic to the application of research. What was logical was not consistent (except after the fact) with the research findings. Trout streams, by nature, are unproductive. Stocking fingerlings or fry and expecting them to grow to big fish was counter to the conditions existing in the stream. The smaller the fish that is stocked from a hatchery, the cheaper is its production, but the lower is its survival. A few fingerlings might grow and survive but at the expense of the wild stock. The others would move, seeking more productive feeding grounds, or would starve or become victims of predation or disease.

Larger fish were then stocked. They were stocked early so they could become wild and lose the alleged taste imparted by hatchery food. The fish do not become wild. They become stressed. They rarely overwinter. A stream with a carrying capacity of one 10-centimeter brook trout per 50 meters suddenly has 50 rainbow trout, 35 centimeters each, gliding through pool and around rubble. There was little food before. The entire population begins to lose weight rapidly. Losses are high. Alternative strategies have been tried, but the situation has become known as a put-and-take fishery. Any delay from the time fish are put into a stream reduces the number of fish that will be recovered. Maximum recovery is desired. If it costs a million dollars to put out a million fish, then if all are taken, the fisherman achieves a fish at a cost of one dollar. If only half are recovered, the cost per harvested fish is two dollars. The cost per harvested fish increases rapidly as the time between stocking and opening day increases. A harvest of 50 percent is high.

Fishermen and the general public complain bitterly when fishermen follow the stocking trucks. When they fish at the stocked area, the results are the lowest possible cost per fish, but it does not seem to give the fish a fair chance (a dimension of the sport fishing and hunting ethic, of which there are many), nor does it give other fishermen a fair chance. Stocking fish has some characteristics of entering a card into a raffle. The cards must be well shuffled before it seems reasonable for all to participate. Alternate strategies have been employed, including closed pools or closed stretches of streams. This allows stocking throughout the season in such areas and depends on fish dispersal above and below such areas into areas where they can be harvested.

Once stocking decisions are made, the next decisions that arise are those related to the harvest. These depend upon local conditions. Generally a large proportion take is desirable. Where fishing pressure is low, large creel limits are possible, and the most effective bait and tackle can be permitted.

Recognize that once a fisheries manager has set a lower limit on bait and tackle, what restrictions fishermen set for themselves to increase the challenge, competition, feeling of success, or quality of the experience for them are their own business. If the manager provides the situation in which an optimum harvest can be taken, then whether or not it is taken may be a function of weather, some recent noteworthy event, or changing public behavior.

Figure 8-9 shows the general pattern of trout fishing harvest over a season. Subpeaks are local and related to actual or rumored stocking. Season length is much debated but seems to have little effect since such a low percentage of the harvest is taken after the first week of the season. Variations in fishing effort and pressure have obscured most population dynamics and structure phenomena in stocked trout streams. In local situations an analysis is needed to optimize the relations of fishing regulations shown in Figure 8-10. This figure is very simplistic. A more realistic and therefore complex criterion of managerial success is needed.

There exists some objective function for the fishery, an index perhaps called Q, which is the benefit-to-cost expression. The benefits are quality-weighted yield expressed as a function of fish stocked, location of the stream relative to the hatchery and to the fishermen, the time the fishery has been known to fishermen, the creel limit, size limits, and tackle and baits permitted. The costs must also be accounted in Q, including total aggregated costs such as administration and management, and then the sum of local stream costs of fish, transportation, and enforcement. Because the trout fishery has been costly, many states require a special trout license. These revenues should be subtracted from the total cost (they rarely exceed the total). The agency's objective is thus to maximize the

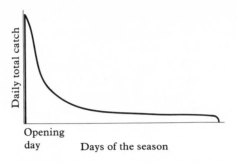

FIGURE **8-9**

Generalized relations of fish taken on the opening day and throughout the season.

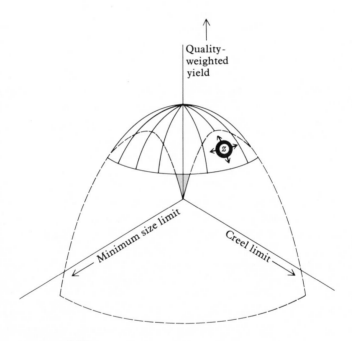

FIGURE **8-10**

A diagram of the relations of yield to creel limit and size limits. An optimum point, z, on the surface, relating the three factors, is an objective of the fisheries manager.

value of Q. Improvements over the years in either yield increases, cost reductions, or revenues will inflate Q as a measure of managerial performance.

The management of trout habitat to obtain increased natural stream production, given the concept of the fishing public, is unreasonable. Only a regulated put-and-take fishery seems reasonable. Some fishing pools or holding areas may be created to reduce stocked-fish dispersal. It may be that conspicuous fishery structures may enhance the quality of the fisherman's experience, much as game management "developments" do. Low success in such environments is reasoned to be the fisherman's problem; the manager has evidently done everything possible. In restricted or private streams, habitat improvement is possible and can result in increased production or increased yields. The practices utilized in trout management include the following:

1. Watershed protection, largely vegetation.
2. Stream bank protection (no cutting of forests on all sides for 50 meters, encouraging grasses and vegetative protection).
3. Stream-side vegetation protection.
4. Stream-side vegetation planting as needed.
5. Stream-side stabilization along areas of erosion.
6. Encouragement of bank undercutting by placing rock, log, or other structures.
7. Building log dams or barriers to encourage pool development.
8. Placing large limestone rocks to fertilize the water.
9. Placing unbroken bags of fertilizer into the stream or fertilizing stream sides likely to add slowly to the stream. (Numbers 8 and 9 must be closely supervised by a fisheries biologist.)
10. Removing excessive competing fish by use of rotenone or other poisons.
11. Law enforcement.
12. Stocking (put-and-take) when wild stocks are low.
13. Increasing oxygen by maximizing large, rough surfaces over which the water flows.
14. Placing light traps or other food-attractants near or over water to increase in-fall.
15. Requiring use of small, single, barbless hooks.
16. Requiring use of artificial flies for fishing.
17. Encouraging photography and requiring that fish be returned to the stream.
18. Setting very large minimum size and encouraging trophy fishing only.
19. Educating the public to minimize opening day phenomena (or eliminating opening day by having a year-around fishery) on such streams.
20. Managing and creating spawning areas (each species has specific gravel-rubble requirements relative to stream flow and oxygen in which eggs hatch).

21. Providing optimum mix of riffles and pools.

22. Increasing stream meander with partial barriers.

23. Making analyses of and limiting work to most productive streams (soil-geology base).

24. Removing beaver dams on trout streams if water tends to be warmed (not typically needed in high areas).

25. Regulating timber harvests to minimize the area cut at any one time near a stream, or in short cutting rotation, one above the other. Encouraging stream shelterbelts.

Most of the above tend to be labor-intensive. The costs are great. "Production" must be evaluated in terms of *extra* fish carried by the stream or yield after the investment. That investment or cost must be properly accounted over its expected life.

After the opening day, trout fishing takes on characteristics of an elitist activity. It is done by a few, in relative solitude. There are thus two types of trout fishing, and in fact two resources—the opening-day resource and the rest of the season. Each can and must be managed separately, as if "species-specific," if optimum resource management is to occur. The users are different; to assume that they are alike and that they experience identical or some "mean" set of benefits is to suboptimize.

Study Questions

1. Do you think fisheries and wildlife management should be a unified field of study? Explain your answer.

2. What is a fishery?

3. How is physical yield related to other yields of a recreational fishery?

4. What are macro-influences on warm water fisheries? Give examples.

5. Name the layers of a pond or lake.

6. Sketch a typical aquatic succession.

7. What are causes of winterkill and springkill?

8. Define BOD.

9. Describe a balanced pond fishery.

10. How many gallons of water fall in a 1.1-inch rain in a 600-acre watershed?

11. How many gallons of water are in a hectare-size pond with average depth of 6 feet?

12. Given the equation for K, if a fish from lake inlet A has a length (L) of 11 inches (279.4 millimeters) and weight (W) of 1.3 pounds (590 grams) and one from lake

inlet B has length 9 inches (228.6 millimeters) and weight 0.9 pounds (408 grams), which lake inlet has the better habitat-population balance?

13. List some ways by which pond fisheries can be improved.

14. What is the relation of fish length to weight?

15. Sketch a recruitment curve, a cost curve, and a catch curve.

16. Have a fisheries manager or biologist visit your class. Find out this professional's definition and concept of annual sustained yield.

17. Describe likely influences of a forest fire or other massive land use disturbance on a trout stream.

18. What are the seven basic characteristics or requirements for streams to support trout year-around?

19. Select an actual or hypothetical trout stream and debate with some one the optimum mix of regulation, stocking, creel limit, size limit, opening date, season length, tackle permitted, and bait permitted. Compute the number of decision alternatives combinations available to you (see the method in Chapter 6).

20. Recite quickly at least 15 means by which trout habitat may be improved.

Selected References

Ackermann, W. C., G. F. White, and E. B. Worthington (Eds.). 1973. *Man-made lakes: their problems and environmental effects.* Geophysical Monograph 17, Am. Geophysical Union, Washington, DC. xi + 847 p.

Allen, K. R. 1951. *The Horokiwi stream: a study of a trout population.* New Zealand Mar. Dept. Fish Bull. No. 10. 238 p.

Bennett, G. W. 1970. *Management of lakes and ponds,* 2nd ed. Van Nostrand Reinhold, New York. xx + 375 p.

Cristy, F. T. and A. Scott. 1965. *The common wealth in ocean fisheries.* Johns Hopkins Press, Baltimore.

Gerking, S. C. 1962. Production and food utilization in a population of bluegill sunfish. *Ecol. Monogr.* **32**:31–78.

Gulland, J. A. 1969. *Manual of methods for fish stock assessment. Part 1. Fish population analysis.* FAO Manual of Fishery Science. No. 4. 154 p.

Hampton, E. L. 1975. *Managerial implications of angler preferences and fisheries management objectives.* M.S. Thesis, Virginia Polytechnic Institute, Blacksburg. vii + 91 p.

Horton, P. A. 1961. The bionomics of brown trout in a Dartmor stream. *J. Animal Ecol.* **30**:331–338.

Lagler, K. F., J. E. Bardach, and R. R. Miller. 1962. *Icthyology, and study of fishes.* John Wiley and Sons, New York.

Lauff, G. H. (Ed.). 1967. *Estuaries.* Pub. 83, Am. Assn. Adv. Sci., Washington, DC.

Nikolsky, G. V. 1963. *The ecology of fishes.* (Trans. from Rus. by L. Birkett). Academic Press, New York. xv + 352 p.

Paulik, G. J. and W. H. Bayliff. 1967. A generalized computer program for the Ricker model of equilibrium yield per recruitment. *J. Fish. Res. Bd. Canada* **24**:249–259.

Ricker, W. E. 1958. *Handbook of computations for biological statistics of fish populations.* Queen's Printer and Cont. of Sta., Bull. 119, Ottawa, Canada. 30 p.

Royce, W. F. 1972. *Introduction to fishery science.* Academic Press, New York. x + 351 p.

Chapter 9

Forest Game Management

Every forest is different. Each varies widely in its productivity for wildlife, particularly game. The mature loblolly pine forest is a desert for game. The dense Douglas fir-red cedar forests of the western states are almost as barren. The mature deciduous forests of the eastern United States, with interspersed home sites and small clearcuts, have abundant and varied game species. In the early stages of almost all forests there are deer and rabbits. In the advanced stages of many forests other game species can be found—elk, moose, bear, squirrel, deer, turkey, and grouse.

Forests have been preserved by the public for watershed protection as well as other benefits. Consequently, there are millions of acres of public forest, many of which produce game and other wildlife, and most of which provide potential hunting opportunities. Forest land decreases generally as land use intensifies, nationwide. As private lands are closed off by posting, public forests will supply more and more wildlife use opportunities—if forest managers are *willing* and if they are *able* to do so in the face of intensified forest practices.

Forest practices are intensified to gain greater wood yields, to reduce waste and defect, and to utilize more wood. Increased management entails increased fire control, prevention of timber poaching, and increased technology. The price per unit of wood goes up, and foresters become less willing to forego any wood production for wildlife. Conflicts are inevitable between the forester, who is educated to maximize timber output, and the wildlife manager, who is educated to maximize quality wildlife resource use opportunities. The conflict is perpetuated by the various multiple-use laws for public lands. A few schools attempt to produce multiple-use experts, but their faculties disagree on what that means.

The forest-wildlife conflict is real but not very intense on private lands. Private forests must produce both wood and wildlife, not only because of public relations, but also because of a genuine desire on the owners' part to produce as much wildlife as possible—as long as it does not reduce timber production, or reduce it more than, say, 5 percent. On some private lands, wildlife hunting permit sales exceed potential long-term wood sales, but such a system can hardly be called a "forest"—it is an acreage of trees on which people hunt. It is as appropriate to subdivide "forests" for management as it is to subdivide wildlife for species management. There are many forests that are not and should not be considered wood producers.

The forest wildlife management problem is very real on public forests, both state and federal. Improved forest wildlife management is needed and can be achieved by attention to the principles outlined in this book. Many have been presented in earlier chapters, but it is useful to collect, integrate, and expand them for a particular set of problems—how to manage forest game.

The Context

There are six scales of forest wildlife management: (1) national, (2) regional, (3) state or industrial, (4) county or parish, (5) intra-state region, management unit, or watershed, and (6) forest. Each is different. At the national and regional levels, management includes decisions on timber harvest quotas, grazing policy in forested lands, official stance on forest taxation bills, cutting policy relative to threatened and endangered species, management coordination of migratory species, and research fund allocation. At the state or industrial level, decision types include land acquisition, sale, or trade; season setting; and permit systems and fees. At the county level, plans are made, seasons set, and special fees levied. At the intra-state level, decisions include what seasons *to recommend,* what stances to take on bills not affecting local conditions, the sequence in which to attempt land acquisition, and the placement of facilities. At the forest level, decisions may include some of those of the larger management unit but typically are those of maintenance schedules, planting stock, cutting rotations, personnel employment and supervision, road closures, equipment use, practices to be attempted or used, and boundaries to be marked.

All levels are important and interdependent. There is no *upper* level, no *lower* level of work; there are different *types* of work. Assignments should be made to improve efficiency and to divide the work load, not to recognize superior performance. Unfortunately, this principle has not always been followed, and resource abuses have resulted. The most competent managers (most creative, knowledgeable, and active) are moved *up,* and the forest level suffers; field incompetents are moved *up* because of the difficulty in government agencies of removing them, and the upper levels suffer. Adjusted pay scales (rather than promotion) based on competency and performance standards could reduce this problem.

Keeping in mind that the upper levels set the legal and other conditions within which managers at the unit and forest levels work, we shall turn our attention to the unit and forest levels—partially for brevity, partially because that is where many forest wildlifers will begin. It might be noted here that the Fish and Wildlife Service brings field managers to national and regional offices for work assignments, largely to allow them to comprehend all levels of the system within which they must function. All wildlife agencies might improve system performance by such exchanges—among all levels. It may not be *efficient* to have a highly paid national executive running a grouse census, but it might be very effective.

There are significant differences between public and private forest wildlife management. Such management differs according to scale (national or state), agency control (Park Service versus Forest Service), industry ownership (big or small), and forest managers. No matter what the law says about how land *should* be managed, no matter how many plans are inspected and authorized, the forest manager determines how it *is* managed. Given present criteria for judging management skill or objectives and the criteria of forest wildlife management laws, no forest manager would lose a legal battle in which he was accused of *not* managing for wildlife. There is much professional judgment involved—one reason why some wildlifers claim wildlife management is an art, not a science, and never will be a science. That remains to be seen.

The ownership and policy of management determine whether wildlife must be valued explicitly or not (see Chapter 1). The basic decision options are presented in Figure 9-1.

The purpose of management is to produce benefits, so analyses start with benefits in Figure 9-1. If there is to be no management (the left side of the figure), then money would be wasted in making detailed wildlife valuations. In the cases where a law or policy has been set and a decision has been reached to manage wildlife, the wildlife manager's task is only to determine relative values between species and other resources, such as pulp wood. An actual monetary value is not needed. When there is indecision about management (the right-hand side of Figure 9-1), for example, whether to staff a management unit or whether active wildlife management is possible in a seed-tree orchard or in an expansive cove forest stand, then explicit value estimates are needed. These are often used in a benefit-to-cost (B/C) analysis.

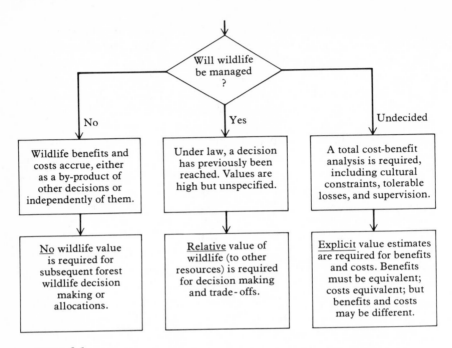

FIGURE **9-1**
Flow diagram of the preliminary forest wildlife management decision. Precise, explicit, monetary wildlife valuation is rarely needed.

The general rule is that B/C must be significantly greater than 1.0. When decisions are being made *between* managing several areas—both how much to spend and whether to manage or not—then the benefits and costs do not have to be expressed in the same units. For example, area A is estimated to produce 100 animals at a managerial cost of $1000 and area B produces 200 animals for the same amount. The B/C of area A is 0.1. The B/C of area B is 0.2. Decisions may be made rationally to allocate one-third of the budget to A $[0.1/(0.1 + 0.2)]$, or, in an all-or-nothing situation, area B will get the funds. The B/C ratios in the example are only good for making relative comparisons in an area. When the go, no-go decision is to be reached, using the rule that B/C must be greater than 1.0, then benefits and costs must be expressed in the same units. Dollars are not the only units available, as explained in Chapter 1.

Multi-Species Management

Detailed cost-benefit analyses are rarely needed in multi-species management. Where they are, the opportunity cost approach to a minimum monetary value of wildlife is very powerful. Translating kilocalories of energy required to produce an animal into monetary-energy values (dollars per kilowatt-hour or barrel of oil) is another method likely to become increasingly powerful. Either of these will enable dollars per deer or dollars per cord of wood to be assessed. Neither energy nor opportunity cost will provide accurate values, but they will be no worse than monetary values. They will be less familiar, of course, but there are such vagaries in the present monetary and market systems that overreliance upon monetary concepts seems unwarranted. Much more work is needed on wildlife economics, particularly on improved criteria for rational trade-offs between quite dissimilar resources—for example, plywood and panthers, dogwood and deer. For most public and private wildlife management, *relative values* are sufficient and, in some situations, far more useful than dollar-valuation efforts. These will be discussed.

First, however, after the need for relative value is seen, the wildlife species to be managed must be listed. This does not mean listing *all* species. Only those species should be listed that the wildlife manager can presently influence in some way—increase, stabilize, or decrease—or can expect to influence within the planning period. A bullfrog may be wildlife in a forest, but unless the manager intends to cause frog populations to change and is fairly confident that investment of money, time, or other resources will bring about that change, frogs should not be listed. A practical rule is: *List the manageable resources.* If no change occurs as a direct result of managerial action, no management has occurred.

For illustration, five species will be listed here: black bear (*Ursus americanus*), white-tailed deer (*Odocoileus virginianus*), cottontail rabbit (*Sylvilagus floridanus*), ruffed grouse (*Bonasa umbellus*), and eastern wild turkey (*Meleagris gallopavo*). The mix will differ by forest biome and managerial emphasis. These species have been chosen partially to illustrate certain principles. (See Figure 4-29).

Next, a unit of measure for each resource is chosen. This can be a hunter-day of hunting species *X*, a sighting, a day on which a kill is made, a prime pelt, or some other measure.

The game species (or all species, whichever is decided) are weighted by a group of decision makers—preferably the public or wildlife commissioners, but occasionally by wildlifers themselves (on the assumption, now proven false, that they "know" public desires). The top or most important resource or species is assigned a value of 1000. The importance of all other manageable species is assigned relative to this. Note that timber is included in the list. In some areas this may be cord wood, naval stores, or something else, but a type of dominant forest yield is listed. (Choose any unit such as 1000 board feet = 2.35 cubic meters.) This is weighted relative to the wildlife species. Yields can easily be weighted relative to one another because they are one type of thing, by definition; they are "priced" in the same units. They are managed as a set; the decisions to be made do not include leaving out one or two. (To do so would be to deny that they are objectives. A zero-weighted objective is a nonobjective; it cannot be included in the set.) Weighting by secret ballot and then taking the median (the value assigned by the most people) is a reasonable way to proceed, as is open discussion and consensus. Where consensus seems impossible, I suggest a group assigning, during discussion, three sets of weights, one for the "preservationist" public, one for the "meat-hunting and high-percentage hunting" public, and one for the "trophy-hunting" public. These might appear for the public in some management unit as in Table 9-1. The remainder of the approaches can be tried in the wildlife manager's mind, assuming these weights are true. The manager makes three simulations of the situation, seeing where the values would lead to significantly different decisions, and what percentage of the decisions would have about the same effect, no matter what the weights.

For nongame management, alternative means can be used for weighting species (for example, conspicuousness, abundance or rareness, kilograms of usable meat produced per hectare per year, or contributions to known ecosystem interactions). These can be listed along with the game species objectives. (See objective weighting in Chapter 5.) It is difficult to weight a unit of game relative to a unit of appreciation of rareness, but when these are listed as specific desired outputs (one species may be listed several times with different output units), then relative importance can be assigned (This method brings the weighting into the open and allows corrective feedback and full expansion for all interested parties.)

Next, the wildlife manager converts this table into a normalized version. All values add to 1.0, allowing better comparisons to be made and signifying the unity of the set of objectives. See Table 9-2. The equation is merely

$$P_i = \frac{W_i}{\Sigma W_i},$$

where P is the proportion of the ith weight among the sum of all weights.

Table 9-2 shows the relative importance of different resources to three publics, or select user groups. By comparing these, levels of conflict can be estimated, agreements noted, and where differences occur, comparisons made between accomplishments and complaints. Other uses will be demonstrated later. Ideally, this three-column "bracketing in" of objective weights will only be done for a few years and then one set selected. Hereafter, I shall use only the center column as if it had been selected by a wildlife commission or other representative group.

Next, the wildlife manager sizes up demand for each of the resources. This too is difficult, and an economist's help may be needed. The typical means are to make projections of licensed hunters and the average time they spend hunting (or otherwise using) each of the species. The product of hunters and time spent

TABLE **9-1**

Hypothetical sets of values assigned to wildland resources.

Resource	Preservationist	Public	
		Meat-hunting and high-percentage hunting	Trophy-hunting
Animals (per hectare)			
Black bear	1000	700	1000
White-tailed deer	400	1000	200
Cottontail rabbit	200	900	10
Ruffed grouse	500	100	100
Eastern wild turkey	990	50	1000
Timber (thousands of bd ft)	600	100	50

TABLE **9-2**

A normalized version of the species objective weights in Table 9-1.

Resource	Preservationist	Public	
		Meat-hunting and high-percentage hunting	Trophy-hunting
Black bear	0.27	0.24	0.42
White-tailed deer	0.11	0.35	0.09
Cottontail rabbit	0.05	0.32	0.004
Ruffed grouse	0.13	0.04	0.04
Eastern wild turkey	0.27	0.02	0.42
Timber	0.16	0.04	0.02
Total	1.0*	1.0*	1.0*

*Approximate due to rounding error.

is thus the user-days likely to be spent. New ways of assessing demand are needed, particularly of integrating other factors such as custom, supply, and urbanization of the hunter.

Based on various graphical or mathematical projections, it may appear that in 20 years 100,000 person-days of bear hunting recreation will be needed. What is

TABLE **9-3**

Hypothetical computation of the manager's weighted deficits.

Resource	Normalized weights of importance	Deficit	Weighted deficit	Managerial needs
Black bear	0.24	50,000	12,000	0.38
White-tailed deer	0.35	20,000	7,000	0.22
Cottontail rabbit	0.32	0	0	0
Ruffed grouse	0.04	0	0	0
Eastern wild turkey	0.02	10,000	200	0.01
Timber	0.04	300,000	12,000	0.38
Total	1.00*		31,200	1.00*

*Approximate due to rounding error.

produced naturally, or by the present system without the manager's investments? Perhaps the answer is 20,000. The deficit is 80,000 person-days, which must be supplied (or effort made) by the manager. (The wily manager will check to be sure 100,000 does not exceed a natural or biological maximum or threshold. If so, the amount will be reduced accordingly.)

Risk levels are assigned to each species. These, roughly speaking, are expressions of how wrong a manager can be without major disruption in the system. The higher the risk, the more precise must be the achievements to make up any deficits detected.

After the normalized weights (Table 9-2) and the deficits have been calculated, a table of weighted deficits can be constructed (Table 9-3). Such a table can be a first step in allocating funds and managerial power and assessing the appropriate mix of inter-species efforts for a forest, as well as a basis for feedback in analyzing whether efforts are being expended properly. The managerial needs in the last column of the table have a variety of uses. These are not themselves the basis for allocating funds, for the cost of producing a rabbit-day is not the same as the cost of producing a bear-day.

Now the manager can begin to evaluate how to make up the weighted deficit. In some species there may be no deficit. The objectives are obtained free of charge, as a gift of nature. Any further investments (of which there have been many) are misallocations of resources. To overproduce is to utilize money (or other resources) probably needed to overcome some production deficit elsewhere.

The Costs of Game Management

In the preceding discussion it was assumed that wildlife *was* to be managed. For those in doubt, the profitability of the decision to manage forest wildlife can be gauged relatively easily from the *stumpage value* for a mature forest. Stumpage is the price bid or paid for wood per land unit. It is based on a calculation of how much profit can probably be made if the wood is sold for X price and costs are Y (roads, transportation, labor, supervision, insurance, interest, and so on). As it is a synthetic variable, it can be meaningfully compared with the worth of a unit of wildlife, typically also a synthetic variable, comprising site factors, transportation, and so on. The stumpage value is set equivalent to the weight assigned timber (for example, 0.04 in column 2 of Table 9-2) and the opportunity cost approach (Chapter 1) used to value wildlife relative to timber. The bear-timber or turkey-timber relations are most conspicuous, for both typically require, for at least part of their year, mature timber stands.

Various management practices have changing yields over time, as seen in production curves. Costs are incurred to initiate a practice, and some practices have continuing costs. It is possible to estimate a *cost curve* for a practice as shown in Figure 9-2. These investments in maintenance or operation are directly related to the production curve concept described previously. A spike cost curve exists for a wildlifer's car, for which no gasoline or oil funds are provided. The declining usefulness of the car is largely a function of rusting (a type of cost). A car with initial cost and continuing operating costs (Figure 9-2) would have a reasonably stable but declining production function and an increasing cost curve, and both production and cost become zero when the car is sold or recycled.

The wildlifer tries to choose practices with the highest mean production-per-unit-cost over the duration of the investment. These choices are complicated by such factors as the timing of yields (for example, a forest is cut at the end of a rotation period even though potential yield or ecosystem production has been occurring during that time) and appropriate discount procedures and rates. These topics, beyond the scope of this chapter, are treated in forest management textbooks.

Another of the wildlifer's decisions, after the preliminary decisions about the efficiency of various practices, is how to overcome the perceived deficit. The wildlifer recognizes that some inefficient methods may have to be used in order to achieve a high degree of effectiveness. To strive for production *or* for efficiency, alone, is likely to be a suboptimal strategy. Effectiveness is the key.

Concern with effectiveness implies using the concept of production functions in Chapter 2 and the aggregate curve of Chapter 4. There are six resources, each weighted. There is a desired level for all of them. An aggregate weighted

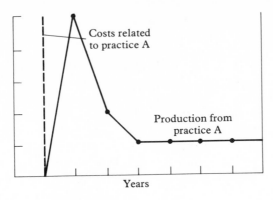

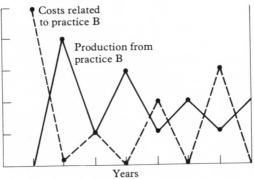

FIGURE **9-2**

Which is more *efficient,* practice A or practice B?
Production over time must be related to costs. Where
yields are experienced annually (for example, ruffed
grouse "flushings"), practice A will be better. The
mean production-to-cost ratio for A is 2.4; that for B
is 1.3. The total production from B is higher than from
A. Questions of effectiveness of A or B can only be
answered relative to whether the production was
desired and whether there was a deficit.

production curve can be developed for them as shown in Figure 9-3. The
production curves will differ with different practices. Much work needs to be
done to improve knowledge of such curves, as well as cost estimates for such
practices. The selected practices are then scheduled (Figure 9-4) so that their
production will overcome the deficit just as precisely as possible.

Foresters continue to argue over area control and volume control of timber
harvest. (See the *Journal of Forestry.*) They debate whether to set cutting quotas
in terms of volume of wood to be removed or acres of land from which the wood
will be taken. Neither will be satisfactory for wildlife management; subop-

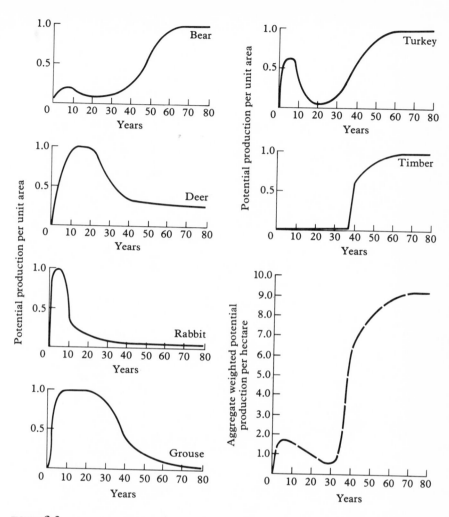

FIGURE **9-3**

Individual estimated production curves for all resources being discussed. The aggregate weighted potential production curve is shown last. Each point on an individual curve is multiplied by the resource weight (Table 9-2) and the best estimate available of the potential animal density in hectares (1 acre = 2.471 hectares). Timber is expressed, for example, as 1000 board feet per acre (205.9 cubic meters per hectare). Note in the aggregate curve that for the species being considered and the weights available for *this* forest, short rotation or early-age forests are not likely to achieve the objectives very well. A forester-wildlifer conflict would not be unusual in such a situation.

timization, both in unstable game populations and user satisfaction, is likely. The approach just discussed subsumes both arguments and provides a means of stabilizing wood profits simultaneously with wildlife objectives, in a system

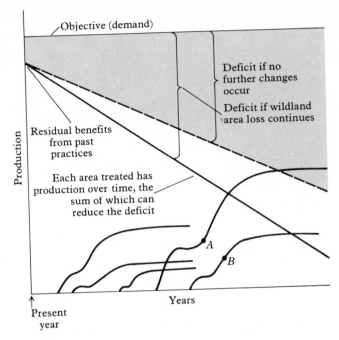

FIGURE **9-4**

By scheduling and appropriate control of the areas treated, the total production can be made to equal very nearly the objective, over time. The five curves on this graph represent production on five areas of different size. Curve *A* is from a larger tract than *B*.

amenable to site-quality and cost differences (see Figure 2-18), economic theory, yield curve data, adjustments in site quality for interspersion and justaposition, and basic ecological theory.

The complexity of the proposed procedure, outlined in Figure 9-5, is evident. Problems in management have occurred largely because of a left-out step, inadequate knowledge, improper estimates, or improper integration and processing of these steps. Computer systems are available to help the wildlifer or agency achieve better integration of the various steps. It will never be possible to eliminate all risks, errors, or problems. It seems reasonable, however, to try to minimize them.

Bear Management

It is unlikely that *bear* will be a wildlife manager's objective. Days of quality bear hunting may be an objective. A bear "produces" such days, which can be estimated as follows: There are 10,000 bear hunters. Each spent an average of 8

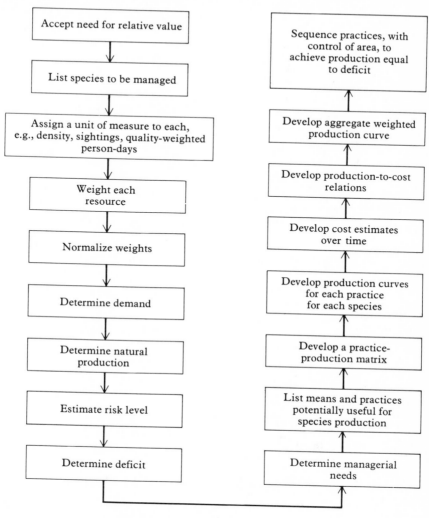

FIGURE **9-5**

An outline of an approach to forest wildlife management.

quality-weighted days (as determined from questionnaire responses) in hunting bear. There were 200 bear harvested. Each bear is equivalent to or "produces" 400 bear-hunter days of recreation. Then the questions become: How to produce bears at reasonable costs? and How to increase quality weights for bear-hunting days experienced?

The techniques and approaches used in bear management will vary by area and situation, but they will tend to be selected from, or be improvisations on, the basic methods cited here.

Passive management relies on two broad approaches:

1. Reserve old-growth or climax forests. Wilderness-like reserves or a timber rotation scheme that perpetuates a constant large area of very old trees is needed.

2. Establish sanctuaries or low-disturbance areas, making them off-limits or use-restricted in cubbing season and prior to denning during critical food-gathering seasons.

Active management involves manipulation of population dynamics and structure, habitat, and hunting practices. The assumption is that a stable or increasing population is needed. Reducing the population is also management, but, in the case of bear, far easier than increasing it.

Manipulating Population Dynamics. Bear populations can be increased by limiting mortality, increasing survival, or increasing natality. Mortality is limited by:

1. Limiting weapons used.
2. Limiting hunters through quotas.
3. Limiting hunters through license fees.
4. Limiting hunters through news releases and education.
5. Restricting dogs used.
6. Restricting hunters in party.
7. Restricting number of vehicles used.
8. Restricting radio use in chases.
9. Restricting younger (small) bear kill.
10. Restricting bear kill per individual in a 5-year period or lifetime.
11. Establishing quotas and closing the season when the quota is "checked in" or when the kill will be reached based on projected rate of kill.
12. Artificially restricting length of season (not based on quota).
13. Influencing hunter density by assigning territories, under permit, or by education.

Survival can be increased by:

1. Intensifying law enforcement, as appropriate.
2. Reducing auto speeds to reduce bear accidents.
3. Increasing food supply (total).
4. Increasing food supply (summer, autumn).

5. Increasing food supply diversity.
6. Increasing food quality (species-specific timber operations).
7. Reducing stresses from roads and habitations (See Figure 9-6).
8. Reducing conflict with sheep and apiaries (buy nonbear-conflict easement on land use; pay damages; encourage viewers whose use payments exceed income from sheep or bees).
9. Reducing conflict situations of dependence on and use of dumps.

Natality can be increased by:

1. Learning seasonal differences in behavior of sexes and modifying area use and hunting zones to minimize female kill.
2. Emphasizing larger animals as yield (in order to protect younger female animals, which may take 3 years to mature).
3. Restricting hunting and disturbance (such as logging) during breeding season.
4. Reducing strange males in vicinity of females at breeding season by protecting territorial markers, avoiding moving "bad" bears during this time.
5. Doing selective cutting and forest management to maximize energy readily available at ovulation periods with small feeding area (to reduce energy drains).
6. Maximizing mast crop (nuts, seeds and fruits eaten by animals) by maintaining mast tree diversity, protecting mast producers in frost-free areas, and stabilizing production of highest-quality (energy-protein) food supplies.
7. Preserving den areas.
8. Protecting den areas.
9. Developing water supplies near den areas.
10. In some areas, creating den spots, such as dispersed log piles, as shown in Figure 9-7. (Bear frequently den beside large downed logs with a depression or overhang. There is much to be discovered about the ecology of the den site, including size, shape, orientation, wind, and other factors.)
11. Reducing bear access to dumps, agricultural and forest pesticides, and toxicants.
12. Planting fruit and mast-producing trees.
13. Maintaining old home sites.
14. Managing a few areas for high rodent populations.
15. Managing a few areas for high amphibian populations.

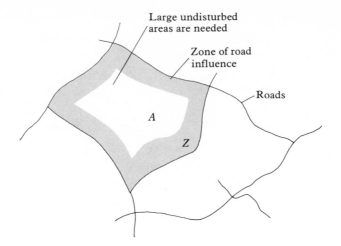

Large undisturbed areas are needed

Zone of road influence

Roads

A

Z

FIGURE **9-6**

The zone of influence concept can be used in bear management. Relative production of areas can be explained in part by the *A/Z* ratio. The higher the ratio of area *out* of the zone of disturbance (*A*) to the area *in* it (*Z*), the greater is the production potential of the area.

Manipulating Population Structure. When large, suitable islands of habitat exist, in which conflicts between bear and humans are unlikely, and bear are not already present or have been extirpated, then introductions can be attempted from other areas. Bear are wanderers and have returned over 60 miles (airline) to areas from which they were trapped. As with most other mobile forms, if good habitat exists, it will usually be filled without the manager's effort. However, the rate can be influenced.

Bear are not conspicuously sexually dimorphic. There is no way to hunt "only females." But behavioral studies of sex ratio by day of the season may permit sex ratios in the harvest to be shifted. That is, seasonal conspicuousness may make possible sex-biased harvests. Undoubtedly, sexes have different movement patterns (for example, high or low attitude), which may influence kill and thus residual sex ratios.

Age ratios in bear can be determined best by molar or canine annuli (rings). Eye lens weight has also been used. The heavier the formalin-fixed, dried lens, the older the bear. Commerical aging service is available and some states have their own capabilities. Age is difficult to determine—impossible for the hunter. Only by gross age-weight relations can age structure be influenced. Perhaps young bear have behavioral traits that could be used to so bias hunting kill as to allow animals to reach reproductive age.

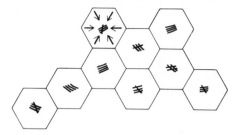

FIGURE **9-7**

Massive piles of three to five whole trees felled together or pushed with a bulldozer into a group can provide den sites in high-intensity managed forests without rock dens. Regional studies of distances between known dens will improve the estimate of an appropriate distance between such sites, perhaps 4 km.

Densities are largely a function of carrying capacity, which depends on available net energy, contiguous food and water supplies, diverse and stable food supplies ample to build fat stores before winter, protection from over-hunting, and avoidance of conflict situations and damage. Analyses can be performed to determine whether destruction of conifers by bears represents injury or damage. Maximum regional bear densities should be sought to establish realistic achievement targets. The rate of loss of bear habitat or potential bear habitat should be plotted and reported regularly to alert people of the impending threats to a largely wilderness animal from increasing land-use intensities. The bear will lose. Its value (Table 9-1) will increase as its abundance diminishes.

Since bear do not recognize state boundaries and do roam widely, efforts at interstate cooperation in regulation, studies, and coordinated management should be made. Since large amounts of federal tax dollars are now used to manage all wildlife and since species like bear, elk, and cougar have large home ranges, increasing use should be made of regional management, various interstate laws, and regional research teams to improve their management.

Increasing Quality of Bear-Hunting Days. The identical number of bear can produce different bear-hunting days of use over a few years. The difference is in (1) the number of users, (2) the days spent, and (3) the quality attached to each day. These three must be balanced, since, for example, increases in (1) may cause significant decreases in (3). The wildlifer (and the ecologist-biologist concerned with producing bear) must *simultaneously* confront the sociological, economic, and recreational problems and achieve an optimum balance among them.

A number of methods are available for increasing quality bear-hunting experiences:

1. Promoting the sport of bear hunting.

2. Increasing emphasis on seeing bear sign, observing bear from blinds, and photography.

3. Preparing maps, booklets, and trails.

4. Setting seasons to avoid bad weather.

5. Improving access, where appropriate, and exit routes.

6. Requiring team hunts to avoid difficulties of removing a bear from the back country.

7. Encouraging camps and camping.

8. Making records or successes better known, thereby increasing the prestige of hunting.

9. Reducing use of radios and other means that reduce "fair chase."

10. Requiring quick kills and reducing baiting, bear-dog encounters, and other hunt perversions.

11. Requiring hunters to pass tests of eyesight, strength, and knowledge of bears and their ecology before being licensed to hunt bear.

12. Listing, licensing, and encouraging quality taxidermy of bear; encouraging proper care of the kill.

13. Encouraging proper meat handling, processing, and cooking.

14. Encouraging bear-hunting clubs to heighten *appreciation* of the hunt and the harvest and to emphasize pre- and post-hunt experiences.

Each one of the procedures listed can be evaluated in terms of how many *extra* bear (or bear-days) will be produced. This is difficult; it requires imagination and innovation. But an estimate can be made, as follows:

1. Forest practice X will double the mast crop (the acorns, seeds, and other fruit eaten by wildlife). The practice will be used on 10 percent of the area. The total area supports 100 bear. The area on which the practice is used produces 10 percent, or 10 bear. The support is only for 3 months (0.25 years). The support is thus for 2.5 bear-years. The use of practice X may potentially *increase* bear production by 2.5 bear years. What is the cost of implementing practice X? $5000. The cost of practice X is $2000 per bear-year.

2. The manager decides to "build" dens of pushed-together felled trees. If 5 percent of the dens are used, and if each increases the cub survival by one

TABLE **9-4**

A practices-production matrix. A +
represents a positive change, 0
represents no or unknown change,
and − represents a likely loss or
detrimental effect on the population.

	Species			
Practice	A	B	C	D
1	+	+	0	+
2	+	+	−	0
3	+	0	0	0
4	0	0	+	0
5	0	0	+	+

bear, one-fourth of which are harvested, and each den costs $500, then the
cost is computed:

$$\frac{\$500}{(1 \times 0.05)(1 \times 0.25)} = \$40,000 \text{ per extra bear produced.}$$

The price may sound high, but compute labor, transportation, equipment,
planning, mapping, wood preservative, hand labor, and in some cases lost
timber value. Full accounting (even estimated) is rarely done in wildlife
management (or forestry). If it were, and feedback applied, practices would
change drastically.

One practice, such as clearcutting or burning, can have various effects on
several species. Often techniques are selected that will influence several species.
(This increases the production-to-cost ratio.) A table such as Table 9-4 is useful
for evaluating the potential impact a particular practice will have on the mix of
wildlife being managed. Whether a positive cancels out a negative can only be
determined by a production-to-cost analysis.

Everything a manager does has a production function. A booklet on laws may
be good for a year. It was produced to achieve certain objectives over some
period. The 1-year production is a spike or point on a curve. A corn planting for
bear also has a spike production curve, but an apple orchard has a curve like
that shown in Figure 9-8. By evaluating the production and cost as shown in
the above examples, the long-term production and cost of each practice can be
computed. Production over the years, although not regular, tends to make the
practices with the longer-term curves more cost-effective.

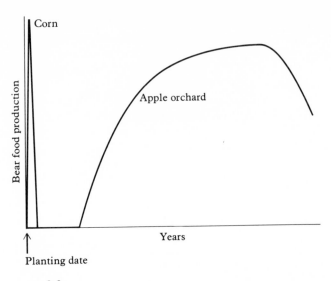

FIGURE **9-8**

Two production functions of activities designed to provide bear food. A corn planting has a spike function. An apple orchard has a curve like that shown. The orchard curve varies with variety and other factors. Young trees do not produce apples; old trees lose productivity.

Deer Management

There is much too much written and known about deer for a small section of a chapter to be very meaningful. The white-tailed deer is the most popular big game animal in North America. It attracts large numbers of hunters, many of whose license fees support other wildlife management. However, it can also be a terrible pest in the forest; uncontrolled, it can destroy forest reproduction. In the western United States it is highly dependent on streamside vegetation and the winter range—in some areas less than 10 percent of the summer range. The annual migration to the lowlands can cause extreme densities on winter range, massive range damage, and a host of associated population-nutrition-stress-disease relations. The situation is equally bad in parts of the northeast, where deer "yards" are found. These areas, often white cedar groves, are the equivalent of the western winter range. The situation is not as conspicuous in the southern part of the United States, but seasonal changes in movement and feeding (that is, in energy relations) do occur.

The chaining within a scenario might appear as follows: bucks-only season passed over wildlifer's objections; bucks-only season; large residual population; high winter mortality; moderate winter range damage; migration to summer range; large fawn crop; high survival; severe snows; unusually great winter range densities; destruction of forest understory including all reproduction; erosion; increased sedimentation; reduced quality of salmon redds (spawning areas); citizen distress over starving deer; citizens agree to either-sex season; bad weather restricts hunter kill; larger numbers than ever return to winter range; starvation excessive; erosion control using vegetation thwarted by deer; range destroyed for 30 years; kill being down (due to weather), organized sportsmen insist season be closed to protect "the declining deer herd"; season closed; herd further reduced by starvation; erosion accelerates; cattle range losses occur; fishery eliminated; hunter success declines further; commissioners are replaced; winter feeding is proposed; land for growing grain is purchased with license fees; and on it goes. Every community has an only slightly different story to tell.

The means required to stop this mismanagement of resources are:

1. Good data from inventory and research on habitats and populations.
2. Brave (often bold) wildlifers with a desire for aggressively communicating their knowledge.
3. Communication and education experts.
4. Supportive legislation and legislators.
5. Authority (and accountability) for resource control.
6. Resources and authority to modify the deer population as needed.
7. Resources to modify the habitat.
8. Support services (techniques and practices, administration, research, operations, education, communication) from agency and entire field of wildlife management.
9. Supportive organizations and individuals with knowledge and political power.
10. Feedback showing program effectiveness.
11. Improved decision-making tools and assistance.

Deer management is dependent upon manipulating succession to produce forage (see the f^7 law in Chapter 4). It is expensive to manipulate succession. It is expensive to maximize deer. This objective can be approached by manipulating population structure and dynamics, habitat, and hunting practices.

Population. In some areas of the United States deer are pest species, and there the objectives will be to reduce their populations without eliminating them. Elsewhere stability is desired. In some areas either stability or increases may be desired. Students in the past have been frustrated by the ambiguity of wildlife management. "Tell us what to do to manage deer!" The answer is always: It depends on the objectives and the situation. Often the answer is do nothing and see that nothing continues to be done.

The following is a list of ways to increase deer. The converse recommendation will usually decrease the population or explain why one is low. Ways of modifying population structure and dynamics include:

1. Manipulate season length, starting day, starting and closing times.

2. Establish a flexible closing date so that the season can be closed when the computed desired harvest has been taken. (Note that this includes the possibility of closing the season entirely, as well as multiple opening days.)

3. Restrict effectiveness of weapons (type, number of shots, scope), thereby reducing harvest per unit time spent.

4. Regulate sex, age, and number of deer to be taken in a season.

5. Minimize disturbance during fawning period.

6. Minimize disturbance during breeding period.

7. Improve population density estimates.

8. Maximize a set of condition indices such as weight and antler development.

9. Minimize stress and crowding to minimize disease-related mortality, parasite effects, and reductions in natality.

10. Minimize domestic dog predation by leash and collar laws and dog licensing.

11. Minimize fawn pick-ups by citizens (rearing success is low, and hazards are great with adult pet survivors in breeding season).

12. Where deer are exterminated, stock deer from nearby populations.

13. Resist introductions of exotic deer.

Habitat. Deer are a function of their habitat. The more supportive, the more energy-rich the habitat, the greater will be the population. When the habitat is treated in the following ways, deer populations are likely to be increased to an upper level (probably about 5 acres per animal) that will be set by crowding stresses and forage availability. One deer per 30 acres is a better than average density.

1. Minimize toxicants and pollutants in deer habitats.

2. Acquire habitats likely to produce long deer seral stages, those likely to be easily operated or to have a short rotation, those with low energy drains on deer (snow, elevation, or other hardship factors).

3. Diversify food supplies over area, season, and year, by interspersion and juxtaposition.

4. Provide food by means of timber cutting, taking into account size, orientation, and shape of timber cuts.

5. Provide food by slashings, care and management of high mast yield forest stands, and food plantings in select areas.

6. Preserve winter range, protecting it from development, alternative uses, and disturbance.

7. Provide winter cover proximal to winter food.

8. Provide poacher or visual cover, especially near roads.

9. Prevent roads from being rutted by hunter use when road bed is wet.

10. Study needs of local deer population for salt and water. Provision of salt licks and watering holes may benefit deer watchers more than the animals themselves, but this is a legitimate basis for allocating funds.

11. Develop active habitat mixes (cuttings, plantings, research plots, orchards, ponds) likely to be seen readily by resource users.

12. Use screenings and waste grain to seed down logging roads, mine scars, and other areas to produce deer forage and reduce erosion.

13. Maximize the area in the zone of influence of roads and trails for deer hunters.

14. Make habitat developments only within, or within one cruising radius of, the zone of influence.

People. Assuring that produced animals can and will be harvested, that waste is reduced, that maximum benefits are derived from the limited resource, and that opportunities are provided for many types of users to benefit from the resource are all needed along with population and habitat manipulation. The following are examples of ways people's behavior can and must be modified to achieve deer management objectives:

1. Disperse hunters by roads, trails, mass transit, signs, and maps.

2. Conduct staggered hunts.

3. Utilize permits and fees to regulate hunting pressure.

4. Provide information on success and areas where hunting will be beneficial to the population.

5. Provide continual education (see Chapter 5).

6. Conduct target practice and provide sighting-in ranges.

7. Closely license hunters.

8. Provide camp sites and encourage group hunting.

9. Differentiate opportunity areas by party size, weapon used, or type of equipment.

10. Minimize accidents and landowner-hunter conflicts.

11. Minimize land posting.

12. Encourage formation of land cooperatives.

13. Explain how area density and probable success will change, using the production curve approach.

14. Maximize law enforcement effectiveness.

Deer populations are very sensitive to particular practices, such as the bucks-only hunting law. Even more influential at the international scale are timber import-export laws. These influence the timber cut quotas of national forests and commercial forests, the rotation, the acres cut, and thus the food produced. A change in a cut quota, which is carried out on the land in about 2 years, makes its effects felt on deer populations nationwide in 8 years and continues to influence them for almost 20 years more. The forest wildlife manager should not lose sight of the scale of management and its significance. A highway will destroy 36 acres of deer yard per mile; pulp technology, such as whole tree chipping and root extraction, can alter rotations and understory (thus food) quantity and quality; and energy plantations (wood grown for fuel or biochemical processing) will have more influence on deer than all the deer managers who have ever lived. Anti-hunting laws and gasoline shortages can significantly change people's interest in deer and can convert the wildlife manager's role into that of controlling range and crop damage. With prospects for increasing acreages of deer seral stages and reduced deer harvests, the managerial problem looms immense. It is essential to see these environmental and human problems as a part of deer management and to participate actively in decisions, articulating consequences of such mega-acts on the deer populations of the nation.

Grouse Management

How to increase grouse is fairly well known. The manager should develop edge, cover, mast, high-insect areas for broods, dusting sites, conifer-hardwood mixes, and specific seral stage. He should not try to stock grouse. The seral stage with the highest food protein levels has the highest grouse densities. Aspen (*Populus tremuloides*) seems to be a dominant member of many grouse-productive committies. Seasonally high protein is critical. Forest managers should cut only on those aspects (directions the slopes face) on which preferred grouse food will re-seed, protect seed trees, use prescribed burn to encourage poplar and birch re-growth, and exercise their silvics knowledge to achieve conifers on north slopes with proximity to streamside conditions, edge, and grassy spots (road and trail edges). Predator control with ruffed grouse management is worthless; it seems as likely to augment egg or nest depredators as it is to remove predators of adults or young.

The ruffed grouse is a much studied bird about which little is known. The species is very difficult to study, population densities are low, and sample sizes are expensive to obtain, variable, small, and destructive. (The sampled birds are not often returned to the population.) Nevertheless, research is needed to aid the manager in decision making. It must be long-term, well-planned research, independent of changing personnel and designed to yield practical conclusions. The approach (as for select other species) is to analyze all that is currently known about the species and to develop a computer simulation to study those factors to which, if the *real* number were known, the grouse population would be most sentitive. Of all the things that could be known or asked about the grouse, which are essential knowledge, and which will contribute the most to population predictions? These analyses can now be made. Once the critical factors are determined, a system can be set in motion to collect the data over time. Analyses would be made automatically by computer every four to five years or when a prescribed sample size was reached. Various observers would perform part-time data collection. Either such systems will be created or wild-lifers will continue to write: "An inadequate sample size prevented a conclusion being reached. More research is needed."

Rabbit Management

Rabbits are widespread and a popular farm game animal. They occur in high densities in young forests and recently cut stands and in low densities in old forests. They are rarely hunted in forests, partially because a clear shot is almost impossible. In a young pine stand or among slash and treetops a glimpse of them is rare even though dogs may be very busy on their trails.

The rabbit generally represents an interesting forest creature—an extra set of tracks in a snow; a buffer species to fox, hawks, or owls; a parasite reservoir of interest and importance; and an influence on forest regeneration, through its activities of stem girdling and tip injury. The rabbit also presents a potential game animal, which can be "marketed" by special seasons and special events, by providing data on densities, and by brush-hogging or chain-dragging habitat strips to increase both habitat suitability and rabbit conspicuousness.

Turkey Management

Throughout this chapter I have refused to repeat the adage that effective management requires population census or estimates. The eastern wild turkey illustrates the fact that a census or estimate does not have to be made. The reasons are presented in Chapter 2. The turkey has been managed effectively with hardly any estimate of population size, certainly not of density. It varies annually by 50 percent of the long-term mean. It has provided increasing harvests in many areas. It has been widely transplanted. The turkey is said to need at least 2000 hectares (about 5000 acres), but this is meaningless because no one specifies flocks or flock sizes. Flight patterns are erratic, and a frightened bird will readily soar several miles across a valley. The bird changes sites and feeding patterns regularly. With a brood it will frequent one side of a mountain for weeks, then disappear. Is the density 10 per 50 hectares, or is it 10 per 2000 hectares because during the year the bird flies to points which, if roughly encircled, enclose about 2000 hectares? There is no good answer.

The wild turkey, perhaps more than other species, requires spatial diversity. It needs insect-producing areas for its broods (90 percent of their diet). It needs edge for nesting. It needs mature forest mast and invertebrates, mast diversity, and seasonal food diversity. It needs in-depth protection from human disturbance during nesting, as well as from grazing animals and domestic dogs. It needs protection from domestic turkeys to avoid reduced wildness and introductions of white feathers into the breed. It needs the protection of well-conceived and enforced laws. Foods can be planted, strip clearings made, patches retained in agricultural clearings and orchards, and a high degree of interspersion maintained. Turkey management requires a regional view, an intensive use of the production curves, a regard for juxtaposition, especially subsequent range for young broods. Feeding of turkeys in winter should be avoided because, among reasons given earlier, disease risks are high. Free water in pond, stream, or spring are said to be needed, and their dispersion, based on a zone of influence criterion, can improve the range or be one factor in explaining range-density differences. Harvests of 20 to 40 percent can be sustained annually. Crippling loss can be reduced by controlling time of hunting, licensing of hunters, and education.

Increasing monocultures, large-scale clearcutting, and coalition of farms all work against the habitat diversity required for turkeys. Land use intensification of all types works against turkeys. Powerlines raise an interesting question of the effect of such land use on turkeys. A powerline through a turkey range would require a right-of-way swath about 65 meters wide. It would require removal of mast-producing trees and grape vines, but it would also also create edge, vegetative diversity, and alternative food supplies, particularly for broods. Is a powerline good for turkeys? The answer can only be stated relative to (1) habitat types, proportions, and distribution already in existence and the significance of losing mature stands versus adding cleared strips, and (2) the importance of turkeys vis-à-vis all of the other species influenced by the same land use change. Consequence tables, such as can be produced by using production curves, are a vital link between wildlife managers and land use planners and those who develop environmental impact statements. Such tables can permit a proper comparison of estimated desired wildlife resource benefits before and after the right-of-way is cleared.

Research and Long-Term Management

The more one knows about forest wildlife management, the more evident it becomes that the timber harvest decision is the dominant decision. It affects areas, over time, in a very profound way. Forest wildlife is thus largely in the hands of foresters. There are needs for interdisciplinary experts who can improve the exchange of knowledge between these two (and other) disciplines. The demands for wildlife, once well articulated, will generate the power to achieve them. By whom is not important.

The wildlife manager must learn much more about disease, parasites, energy relations, and predation in order to assess the starting point of management and to appraise properly the limits imposed by the natural system. Knowing these limits, the manager can perform realistically, to achieve reasonable goals. To do so will mean to focus on population densities as produced over time on various sites. This will require studying densities on known-age sites as well as starting studies for controlled, long-term analysis. It will also require studies of large areas with efforts to control variables and to factor those variables that contribute to differences in densities and production.

Because the forest ecosystem is such a slow-moving system (relative to a wildlifer's career years), it is evident that new long-term planning and management systems must be designed and maintained. Such systems can provide transition between managers, minimize loss of dates and information, reduce duplication, and maintain balance between the benefits to be derived from carrying a management strategy to completion over 100 years and the benefits to be derived from a new idea, evidence for discarding the existing strategy, or a manager's personal ambition. (There are weighty questions of professional ethics regarding the responsibilities of a wildlife manager to carry out the plans for forest wildlife put into operation by former managers.) Long-range planning and management systems are not now available except in primitive turning-over-the-files rituals. They will probably emerge as regional computer systems, highly dependent on computer mapping, visual display of data, and remotely sensed land use data (Fales 1969).

Study Questions

1. List the predominant forest game species in your area.
2. List the nongame species potentially manageable.
3. Describe likely differences between single-species management, multi-species management, and multiple-use management.
4. Write a paper, based on a study of the literature, on the various meanings of multiple use and how these interpretations can influence wildlife resources.

5. How do the various scales or levels at which forest wildlife management is practiced differ?

6. What are optional ways to value forest game? (See Chapter 1.)

7. Why are *relative values* usually suitable for forest wildlife?

8. What is the scientific name of the ruffed grouse? The white-tailed deer? The mule deer? (See Chapter 1.)

9. Select a set of species and you or the class weight them, then normalize the weights. What is meant by bracketing the weights?

10. What is the significance of emphasizing person-days of quality-weighted bear-hunting opportunity rather than bears produced?

11. List ways of producing bear.

12. What are means for increasing quality of hunting days for bear? For deer? For forest bird watching?

13. What is a practices-production matrix?

14. How is the deficit overcome between demand and present system production?

15. What is an aggregate production curve? How is it developed?

16. List in sequence the major steps of the forest wildlife management procedure (Figure 9-5). Does the procedure differ significantly for other wildlife?

17. What are means for increasing deer? For reducing crop damage?

18. What are means for improving forest wildlife research?

19. Are powerline rights-of-way good for turkeys?

20. Should a forest wildlife manager taking over a forest from another manager be compelled to follow the plans already in operation? To what degree? Why? What are the ethical dimensions of the question? Discuss the question with classmates, your instructor, and wildlifers.

Selected References

Allen, W. R. III and J. M. Collins. 1971. A modified cryostat technique for tooth sectioning. *J. Mammal.* **52**(2):471–472.

Asdell, S. A. 1964. *Patterns of mammalian reproduction,* 2nd ed. Cornell University Press, Ithaca, NY.

Beckwith, S. L. 1954. Ecological succession on abandoned farmlands and its relationship to wildlife management. *Ecol. Monog.* **20**:349–375.

Berner, A. 1969. Habitat analysis and management considerations for ruffed grouse for a multiple use area in Michigan. *J. Wildlife Management* **33**:769–777.

Black, C. T. 1953. Fourteen-year game harvest on a 1500-acre Michigan farm. *Trans. N. Am. Wildlife Conf.* **18**:421–438.

Bump, G., R. W. Darrow, F. C. Edminster, and W. F. Crissey. 1947. *The ruffed grouse: life history, propagation, management.* New York State Cons. Dept., Albany.

Byrd, M. A. 1956. Relation of ecological succession to farm game in Cumberland County in the Virginia Piedmont. *J. Wildlife Management* **20**:188–195.

Cheatum, E. L. and C. W. Sereringhaus. 1950. Variations in fertility of white-tailed deer related to range conditions. *Trans. N. Am. Wildlife Conf.* **15**:170–189.

Crawford, W. T. 1950. Some specific relationships between soils and wildlife. *J. Wildlife Management* **14**(2):115–123.

Dahlberg, B. L. and R. C. Guettinger. 1956. *The white-tailed deer in Wisconsin.* Tech. Bull. 14, Game Mgmt. Div., Wisc. Cons. Dept., Madison. 282 p.

Dalke, P. D. 1942. *The cottontail rabbits in Connecticut.* Conn. Geol. Natural Hist. Survey Bull. 65. 97 p.

DeWitt, J. C. and J. V. Derby. 1955. Changes in nutritive value of browse plants following forest fire. *J. Wildlife Management* **19**:65–70.

Dorney, R. S. 1966. A new method for sexing ruffed grouse in late summer. *J. Wildlife Management* **30**(3):623–625.

Edinister, F. C. 1947. *The ruffed grouse.* Macmillan, New York.

Fales, R. R. 1969. *Some applications of computer-generated maps to wildlife management.* Unpub. M.S. Thesis, Virginia Polytechnic Institute, Blacksburg viii + 83 p.

Fay, F. H. and E. H. Chandler. 1955. The geographical and ecological distribution of cottontail rabbits in Massachusetts. *J. Mammal.* **36**(3):415–424.

Gates, C. E., W. H. Marshall, and D. P. Olson. 1968. Line transect method of estimating grouse population densities. *Biometrics* **24**(1):135–145.

Gavitt, J. D. and R. H. Giles, Jr. 1972. Simulation studies of quail hunting success associated with ecological succession on planted pine stands. *Proc. First National Bobwhite Quail Symposium,* Stillwater, OK. pp. 343–349.

Giles, R. H., Jr. (Ed.). 1971. *Wildlife management techniques,* 3rd ed., revised. The Wildlife Society, Washington, DC. vii + 633 p.

Giles, R. H., Jr. and A. B. Jones III. 1974. HUNT I and II. Computer-based deer management units for university and in-service education. *Proc. S. E. Assn. Game and Fish Commissioners.*

Giles, R. H., Jr. and J. M. Lee, Jr. 1975. When to hunt Eastern gray squirrels. In *Forest resource management: decision-making principles and cases,* ed. W. A. Duerr, D. E. Teeguarden, S. Guttenberg, and N. B. Christiansen. (Vol. 2, Chapter 49). O.S.U. Book Stores, Corvallis, OR.

Giles, R. H., Jr. and T. D. McKinney. 1967. Feeding deer to death. *National Wildlife* **6**(1):46–47.

Giles, R. H., Jr. and N. Snyder. 1970. Simulation techniques in wildlife habitat management, p. 23–49. In *Modeling and systems analysis in range science,* ed. D. A. Jameson. Range Science Dept., Sci. Series No. 5, Colorado State University, Ft. Collins. 134 p.

Graf, R. L. and R. H. Giles, Jr. 1974. A technique for delineating optimum deer management regions. *Proc. S. E. Assn. Game and Fish Commissioners* **28**:581–586.

Grange, W. B. 1948. *Wisconsin grouse problems.* Wisc. Cons. Dept., Madison. 318 p.

Grange, W. B. 1949. *The way to game abundance, with an explanation of game cycles.* Charles Scribner's Sons, New York. xviii + 365 p.

Halls, L. K. (Ed.). 1969. *White-tailed deer in the southern forest habitat.* Proc. of Symp., Nacogdoches, TX. 130 p.

Hamilton, W. J. and K. E. F. Watt. 1970. Refuging. *Ann. Rev. of Ecology and Systematics.* 1:193-214.

Haugen, A. O. 1942. Life history studies of the cottontail rabbit in Southwestern Michigan. *Am. Midland Naturalist* 28(1):204-244.

Hayne, D. W. 1949. Calculation of size of home range. *J. Mammal.* 31:1-18.

Herrero, S. (Ed.). 1972. *Bears—their biology and management.* International Union for the Conservation of Nature, Morges, Switzerland.

Hewitt, O. H. (Ed.). 1967. *The wild turkey and its management.* The Wildlife Society, Washington, DC. xiv + 589 p.

Hoecker, S. W. 1976. *NATAL: A computer-based educational unit on white-tailed deer bioenergetics.* Unpub. M.S. Thesis, Virginia Polytechnic Institute, Blacksburg. vi + 163 p.

Jonkel, J. C. and I. McT. Cowan. 1971. Black bear in the spruce fir forest. *Wildlife Mono.* 27:5-57.

Korschgen, L. J. 1966. Foods and nutrition of ruffed grouse in Missouri. *J. Wildlife Management* 30(1):86-99.

Lobdell, C. H. 1971. *A deterministic model for evaluating long-term effects of wildland management decisions on public benefits.* Unpub. M.S. Thesis, Virginia Polytechnic Institute, Blacksburg. x + 94 p.

Lobdell, C. H. 1972. *MAST: A budget allocation system for wildlife management.* Ph.D. Thesis. Virginia Polytechnic Institute, Blacksburg. 227 p.

Lobdell, C. H., K. E. Case, and H. S. Mosby. 1972. Evaluation of harvest strategies for a simulated wild turkey population. *J. Wildlife Management* 36(2):493-497.

Lord, R. D. 1963. *The cottontail rabbit in Illinois.* Ill. Dept. Cons. Tech. Bull. 3, 94 p.

Madson, F. 1969. *Ruffed grouse.* Winchester-Western Div., Olin Mathieson Chem. Corp., East Alton, IL.

Moen, A. N. 1973. *Wildlife ecology.* W. H. Freeman and Company, San Francisco. 458 p.

Palmer, W. L. and C. L. Bennett. 1963. Relation of season length to hunting harvest of ruffed grouse. *J. Wildlife Management* 27(3):634.

Peterle, T. J. and L. Eberhardt. 1959. Is the Lincoln index reliable for cottontail censusing? *Trans. N. Am Wildlife Conf.* 24:261-270.

Rayburn, E. B. and R. H. Giles, Jr. 1975. Energy balance as a criterion for acquiring deer management areas. *Proc. S. E. Assn. Game and Fish Commissioners* 29:481-492.

Roseberry, J. L. and W. D. Klimstra. 1974. Differential vulnerability during a controlled deer harvest. *J. Wildlife Management* 38(3):499-507.

Rusch, D. H. and L. B. Keith. 1971. Seasonal and annual trends in numbers of Alberta ruffed grouse. *J. Wildlife Management* 35(4):803-821.

Russel, K. R. 1966. Effects of a common environment on cottontail ovulation rates. *J. Wildlife Management* 30(4):819-827.

Schorger, A. W. 1966. The wild turkey: its history and domestication. University of Oklahoma Press, Norman. xiv + 625 p.

Siegler, H. R. (Ed.). 1968. *The white-tailed deer of New Hampshire.* Survey Rpt. 10, New Hampshire Fish and Game Dept. Concord. 256 p.

Smith, V. G. 1928. Animal communities of the deciduous forest succession. *Ecology* 9(4):479–500.

Sweeney, J. R , R. L. Marchinton, and J. M. Sweeney. 1971. Responses of radio monitored white-tailed deer chased by dogs. *J. Wildlife Management* 35(4):707–716.

Sweetman, H. L. 1944. Selection of woody plants as winter food by the cottontail rabbit. *Ecology* 25(4):467–472.

Taylor, W. P. (Ed.). 1956. *The deer of North America—their history and management.* Stackpole Books, Harrisburg, PA and Wildlife Management Institute, Washington, DC. 668 p.

Teer, J. G., J. W. Thomas, and E. A. Walker. 1965. *Ecology and management of white-tailed deer in the Llano Basin of Texas.* Wildlife Mono. No. 15, 62 p.

Walters, C. V. and P. J. Bandy. 1972. Periodic harvest as a method for increasing big game yields. *J. Wildlife Management* 36(1):128–134.

Walters, C. V. and J. E. Gross. 1972. Development of big game management plans through simulation modeling. *J. Wildlife Management* 36(1):119–128.

Watt, K. E. F. 1968. Ecology and resource management. McGraw-Hill, New York. 450 p.

Wilder, E. H. 1969. Walking trail development for hunters of the Nicolet National Forest. *J. Wildlife Management* 33(4):762–768.

PART III

EXAMPLES AND APPLICATIONS: PEOPLE

Chapter 10

Wildlife Law Enforcement

A giant wildlife law enforcement effort is expended annually across the United States. It is carried out by 5800 employees, whose deep personal commitment to wildlife conservation motivates them to work long hours, often under unpleasant or dangerous conditions, for relatively low salaries (see Sigler 1972). These men and women are aided by thousands of assistants and special enforcement personnel who work without pay. The law enforcement effort is a vital part of wildlife management. Yet it has little theory, virtually no basis in research, and only primitive evaluation.

The purpose of this chapter is to sketch how a wildlife law enforcement system can be developed. A systems approach may help reduce conflicts between enforcement agents and biologists by enabling each wildlife subsystem to see its role more clearly, achieve its goals more precisely, and be rewarded more rationally and equitably than at present. Law enforcement agencies spend about one-fourth of wildlife agency operating budgets (Morse 1972), and pressures for economy and more rational budget allocation will surely increase.

A *context* is needed to design a wildlife law enforcement system. At present there is little conceptual basis, no dialog, no research, and few authorities for doing so. There is little useful law enforcement literature; parallels are difficult to find. Even the causes of crime are poorly understood.

There is no coherent organization theory for wildlife law enforcement. Attention is easily drawn to the game warden, conservation officer, resource officer, wildlife protection agent, or ranger, as this agent is variously called. (In this chapter, the term "agent" will be used throughout.) This focus on the individual agent confuses the image of enforcement, for most agents participate in education, surveys, some management, gun safety instruction, and other activities, in addition to law enforcement. The agent is largely unsupervised and tends to adapt personal interests and abilities to the local situation, to the perceived problems, and to the perceived reward system within the agency. Solitary performance tends to create a very diverse group of people, each person working toward ambiguous goals, each in a unique way.

When attention is focused on the agency, and not the agent, the image may be blurred even more by budget overlaps and program interactions with other divisions or agencies. Land acquisition for wildlife invariably involves changes in laws affecting property. Management can congregate game or fish and increase poaching opportunities; trespassing problems can increase; an agent may be required to monitor water quality (an activity related to fish kills and pollution), but what agency should be doing the work? Similar questions occur at the blurred departmental boundaries. (It might be observed that organizations have ecotones and edge effect. A larger amount and variety of work get done at the edges as a result of cooperation, but, as in ecosystems, the energy and related costs are higher per unit produced at the edge than in either adjacent unit.)

The wildlife law enforcement context is made hazy by other law enforcement work and by the courts. In some states, agents have total police power, in others only the authority to enforce game and fish laws. The courts handle "laws," "ordinances," and "regulations" (hereafter called laws) differently, and conviction, dismissal, and appeal rates vary widely among the states (Morse 1972).

Game Laws

There is a developing hypothesis that game laws—violations of which are misdemeanors—are taken less seriously than other laws (with perhaps the exception of minor income tax evasion, excessive highway speeds, and some types of pornography sale). Poaching may be considered more like "stealing bases" than stealing a public resource. Wildlife laws also vary widely. Certainly some variability is expected; some is highly desirable. Model laws can reduce variability, but in a dynamic society, such models may be outdated before they are printed. A static standard for a dynamic system can only result in conflict.

Except for model laws (see Conservation Dept., Winchester-Western Division, Olin 1972) there are no baseline concepts for wildlife laws. Basic criteria can provide an alternative to the need for developing a model code. They provide the reference points for formulating law, for making fundamental tests for proposed laws, or for evaluating existing laws. There are nine such criteria for strengthening wildlife agency legal policy and providing further context for the enforcement agency (Giles 1974).

1. A need for the law must be clear to the public and to professional wildlife resource managers. This need should be well articulated and should express the expected long-term net public benefits from having such a law. The need for a law is rarely established by a mere chance event.

2. The objective or intent of the law must be explicit. It must order some particular action or attempt to prevent it. Laws are only one way of achieving user objectives from resources. The objectives of laws must be narrow enough to enable their effects to be recognized. The theoretical question must be asked: If the law were perfectly enforced, what changes would actually occur? The best-intended laws may not be enforceable. Even perfect enforcement may not achieve the desired change.

3. The cost of enforcing a law should not exceed the estimated net social good resulting from compliance with that law. Total costs of enforcement can be readily quantified. Net social good is much more difficult to assess, but rough estimates may allow program effectiveness to be evaluated in such terms as "perhaps a ratio of estimated costs to benefits of ten times may be a bit too high."

4. Counterintuitive (and counterproductive) results of the law should be anticipated by as many techniques as possible, including conferences, task forces, and computer simulations. To take a glaring example, hunting laws that are too detailed or very time- and site-specific may create frustration for hunters or fear of unintentional violation, with possible lengthy court involvement for minor infractions. Such laws may even cause some people to give up hunting. A well-intentioned law formation effort may thus result in a net loss of quality recreational benefits.

5. The law must be directed at ensuring the existence of a species or species group at or above all minimum thresholds for survival. Other stipulations for the use or management of the resource are purely a function of demands or needs articulated by resource users. Such stipulations represent modifications in the benefits derivable from a resource.

6. A wildlife law should maximize an index to net present worth of units of the resource and minimize the annual variance in the resource opportunity for the users (within the constraints of Number 5 above).

7. Past laws (or lack of them) establish precedents or stability in a system. Great disruption in a system is usually undesirable. Counteractions to some laws have produced results worse than the problem the law was intended to correct. Thus, one criterion for a wildlife law is that it must not directly reverse an existing law or condition without the relevant agency generating public

commitment to the new law. The implication is that initiating or changing laws must be preceded by planning and education.

8. A wildlife law should result in likely positive change for the resource or resource users. Harvest regulations may have no effect on game populations or have no significant effect in increasing resource utility to large percentages of resource users (McFadden 1969:140). Questions of scientific substance must be asked of proposed regulations. For example, does weapon type X significantly change the vulnerability of species Y or age-class Z? Is a law justified in protecting Y or Z by regulating X? Time and method of game and fish harvest are examples of restrictions that have often been approved without prior evidence of real population protection or hunter safety.

9. A wildlife law should minimally impose limited group moral codes or philosophical preferences on resource users. Kennedy (1970) and others have demonstrated that significant differences exist between public desires for wildlife and the wildlife specialist's perception of their desires. Various aspects of hunting or fishing that are morally distasteful to small segments of the public or to agency personnel—for example, conspicuous car-top display of the kill, or crippling losses, which could easily be reduced by requiring marksmanship qualifications for licenses—could be controlled by laws. These laws can often have a more profound impact upon high-quality person-days of hunting or fishing than any habitat crew, administrator, researcher, or even the impact of some mega-facility on the landscape.

Theories of Crime Causation

A theory of law violation (1) imposes a basic order on acts of wildlife law violators, (2) forms the basis for initiating research toward predicting individual or population behavior, (3) opens avenues for creative control methods, and (4) helps establish concepts of maximum or potential control. McCormick (1971) said, "Law enforcement administrators in the 1970's will be increasing their capacity to find the causes of violations rather than seek only increased capacity for violator apprehension and control."

There are four current theories of wildlife crime causation: the *transactional analysis, hedonistic, differential association,* and *alpha-person* theories.

Transactional Analysis. The transactional analysis (TA) game of "cops and robbers" described by Berne (1964) offers a provocative theory of wildlife crime causation. Further work is needed to describe the phenomenon based on Berne's insights and related ones. The game equivalent to "cops and robbers" is the "poacher and warden" game, played only secondarily for material gain but primarily for the thrill of the chase, the getaway, and the pleasure of telling tales and making boasts to peers. The agents, as father or authority figures, seek the poacher. The suspense is real; there is always someone to play (by law); people do get caught. Berne (1964:133) concluded: "It soon becomes clear that being found is the necessary payoff." (Compulsive poachers do not play this game: These professional poachers are eventually caught, but their gains so far exceed the likely losses—that is, the fines are so small, relatively speaking—that it is rational for them to continue to poach.)

Berne's analysis is useful in describing at least three types of poachers: the *accidental* violator (which Berne says is never truly accidental); the *game player*, who enjoys the game and needs to be caught to experience payoffs; and the *compulsive* or professional poacher, who does not need to be caught and rarely is. Berne (1964:136) observed: "The fact is that tools [of psychological research] have so far not yielded one single solution to any problem in criminology. Researchers might therefore be better off discarding the old methods and tackling the problem freshly. Until C & R [the cops and robber game] is accepted not merely as an interesting anomaly, but as the very heart of the matter in a significant percentage of cases, much research in criminology will continue to deal with trivialities, doctrines, peripheral issues or irrelevancies."

Hedonism. The hedonistic theory of crime conceives of crime resulting when an individual calculates that the pleasures obtained from committing a crime exceed the pain or negative aspects of being apprehended and punished. "Pleasure" or "benefit" is the fundamental triggering mechanism. The theory is symbolized as:

$$\text{Crime} = \text{Pleasure}/\text{Pain} \geq 1.0,$$

or $$\text{Crime} = \text{Pleasure} - \text{Pain} \geq 0.$$

The hedonistic theory is intuitively appealing and can be tied to much decision theory and to concepts of rational or economic human behavior. Pleasure and pain are analogous to benefits and costs. The theory seems to explain much criminal behavior, but it cannot explain why everyone is not a wildlife law violator given the low probability of fines or lasting social disfavor.

Differential Association. According to Sutherland's differential association theory (Sutherland and Cressey 1970), criminal behavior is *learned* through interaction with, and communications from, others, particularly intimates. The learning includes both techniques of committing the crime and the specific directions of motives, drives, rationalizations, and attitudes. The latter are determined by the group's definitions, favorable or unfavorable, of various laws. A person becomes delinquent because of an excess of definitions favorable to violation of law over definitions unfavorable to violation of law. These differential associations may vary in frequency, duration, intensity, and priority. The process of learning criminal behavior by association with criminal patterns involves all of the mechanisms that are involved in any other learning.

Deer spotlighting illustrates this theory. It is typically done by a group of people and tends to be very socioeconomic class-specific. Drinking was found to occur in 33 percent of the incidents in Virginia, which suggests that poaching was considered a social event. It is seen by many as a means to gain excitement in a relatively humdrum life. In family, social, or work groups, the desirability of violating game laws could easily exceed the undesirability of doing so. The latter is largely uncommunicated except through sportsmen's magazines—not likely to be the reading matter of poachers.

Kaminsky (1974) described the poacher's redefinition of legal codes as unfavorable. "These redefinitions provide direction to the learner's motives, drives, rationalizations, and attitudes. In many groups in society, individuals are surrounded by people who define the legal codes as rules to be observed, while in others they are surrounded by those whose views are favorable to the violation of the legal codes. In American society, in general, these definitions are almost always mixed. The consequence of this normative pluralism is cultural conflict in relation to the legal codes. When a citizen is caught, [then that] produces conflict. When he sees around him more attitudes supporting spotlighting than rejecting it, he may violate the law."

According to the differential association theory, a person who becomes delinquent has received more encouragement for violating the law than discouragement. Even when poaching alone, this person is violating the law as part of a group associated with criminal patterns and isolated from anti-criminal patterns.

The previous three crime causation theories can be illuminated and unified under a concept of human homeostasis called the alpha-person theory.

Alpha-Person Theory. People cannot simply be classified as criminal or non-criminal. Their concepts, life styles, and individual actions fluctuate. The limits of criminality are set socially. The same group of people with stable behavior can become criminals overnight by a change in a law. People act to achieve multiple objectives, including pleasure, money, recognition, and group acceptability. If their *only* known alternatives for achieving their objectives are readily classified as crimes, then it is likely these people will always be judged to be criminals, even if a few laws change (that is, alternative acts are reclassified, which can be perceived as a lowering of the legal code line in Figure 10-1). I call these *delta* (Δ) people, to avoid the connotations and stereotypes of "criminal." It seems likely that their performance pattern can be changed. Whether sufficient change can occur to allow *all* to exceed the criteria seems

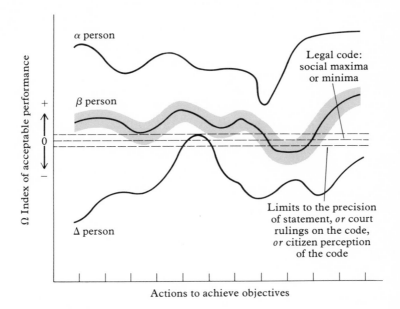

FIGURE **10-1**

Theoretical performance of three types of people relative to the minima or maxima criteria of the legal code. The Δ person habitually engages in criminal behavior; apprehension is nearly certain. The β person violates certain laws: apprehension is probabilistic. The α person violates no laws. All nonpathological people can be described relative to these types along a continuum.

unlikely, but perhaps enough change can occur so that only a few undesirable behaviors will remain, they can be isolated, and society can be protected from them.

The *beta* (β) person lives a relatively homeostatic life. The actions the person elects are consistently near the 0 value of Ω (omega) in Figure 10-1, but generally on the positive side. The person is perceived to be law-abiding. Because the behavior is so regular, so homeostatic, any change of behavior (whether due to an energetic imbalance, an injury, or a social encounter) can result in a criminal act. Similarly, a change by society, family, or courts in Ω, that is, in the notions of the acceptability of certain illegal actions, can result in this person becoming a violator.

Whether the violator is apprehended or not reflects the coincidence of two probability functions in time and space—the agent and the violator. The poacher is probably a β person, though there are undoubtedly Δ poachers (for example, market hunters). If there are 9000 spotlighting violations in a state of 4.5 million, the α people (nonviolators) and β people for this violation comprise 99.998 percent of the population.

TABLE **10-1**

Expected payoffs are calculated by individuals, and actions are usually taken that will maximize those payoffs. Two representative risks (0.8, 0.3) are examined. Relative units of benefit (estimated total) are given for the two actions. In the hypothetical situation of this table, the person would violate the law at **.

Situation	Peer pressures			
	Anti-violation		Pro-violation	
Risk of apprehension	0.8	0.3	0.8	0.3
Violate	300	300	1000	1000
Obey law	600*	600*	100*	100*
Payoff				
Violate	60	210	200	700**
Obey law	600	600	100	100

*There is zero risk of apprehension for obeying the law, thus the payoff equals the expected benefit.

People's expectations are largely culturally imposed. Merton's (1968:186) quest was "to discover *how some social structures exert* a definite pressure upon certain persons *in the society to engage in nonconforming rather than conforming conduct.*" Expectations can be arrived at individually, from the media, or from peers. Peer pressures can be analyzed in terms of personal energy required to achieve group homeostasis. "Evil companions" can exert such pressure; the individual will maximize the expected payoff from an act. Behavior is not consistent because perceived risk, estimated payoff, and peer pressures vary. There is some evidence that the calculations in Table 10-1 are being made, informally, of course, in the minds of would-be criminals. Expected payoffs from an act are computed from $(1.0 - \text{Risk}) \times (\text{Expected benefits of all types})$. Note in Table 10-1 how close the maximum expected payoff of crime (700) is to obeying the law. Inflating the risk, reducing direct rewards, could have changed the decision and negative peer pressure by small amounts. (Further analyses should be made of this behavior using game theory. See, for example, Luce and Raiffa 1957.)

The disparity between attainment and expectation is called frustration. It has a gradient (see Figure 10-2). A person in extreme hunger, that is, in a

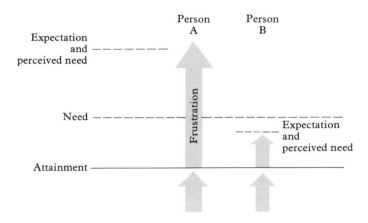

FIGURE 10-2

Homeostatic conditions exist when need, attainment, and expectation
approximately coincide. Peer pressures can inflate expectations, producing
frustrations that are relieved by criminal acts. Person A is more likely to
commit a crime than person B.

marginal state in which energy or other life support is needed not just in ample
quantity but in appropriate sequence and within the requisite time, demonstrates the fact that "needs" have quantity (including capital or threshold
amounts), quality, and rate dimensions. With such need (in which the risk of
failing to secure them is very high) certain criminal acts will be committed that
would not be committed under other conditions.

A lesser need combined with relaxed or inefficient law enforcement (real or
perceived) may result in the same decision among alternatives. Ignorant people
have fewer alternatives than do the informed; the alternatives are culturally
imposed, that is, by peers. (Certain groups would never appeal a conviction;
certain others do not shoot firearms, thus limiting their alternatives; others do
not eat meat; some cannot or will not read; others would never consider asking
an agent a question by phone.)

Omega, Ω (Figure 10-1), represents 1.0 or the legal code minimum acceptable
performance. S_i is the probability of perceiving Ω correctly. S_i is an overall
estimate based on past performance and is an expression of likely risk-taking
behavior. Such behavior is a sociological and economic characteristic and can
be predicted for classes of people. "Ignorance is no excuse," but if reading or
researching a problem is frowned upon by peers (a force as real as a member of
the group removing a code book from a person's hands), then the code is not
known and violations are likely. The decision maker evaluates, based on per-

sonal values, the level of benefits, N_i, potentially available from an illegal act, i (N_i ranges from 1.0 to 0.), and then subtracts p percent (for example, 5 percent) of doubt about the assessment at the time. N is under the influence of expectations. The felt intensity of this need is expressed as Z_i. A weight of 1.0 represents absolute and essential need, such as food for a starving person. Whether a person truly needs something or not is largely irrelevant; *perceived* need at some time and place and the intensity of that need are relevant to the decision to act. All acts are assumed to follow decisions made, except in people in pathological states or under the influence of drugs.

The likely maximum or potential production or yield, Y, for each alternative act i, is multiplied by a similarity index, K_i, of Y to N ($1.0 > Y_i > 0$). K_i is the probability of each alternative action meeting the decision maker's personal needs. It is an expression of substitutability. The product is then multiplied by the probability of apprehension, A_i; the probability of an unpleasant agent-violator contact, V_i; the probability of peer plaudits (or at least acceptability) if convicted, Q_i; and the effectiveness of the courts, C_i. For example, a lenient court can be conceived as having an effectiveness index of 0.6; a harsh court may have an index of 0.9. C_i approximates a perceived probability of a conviction. The decision to choose an alternative will be influenced by this coefficient. Each decision by any person is then based on the law obedience criterion, which is: Will Ω be greater than 0? The answer lies in the equation

$$\Omega_i = S_i\{[N_i(100 - p)/100]Z_i - Y_iK_iA_iV_iQ_iC_i\}.$$

The Ω value is manipulated in the n-dimensional space of the decision maker's mind. The interactions of the physiological and psychological state of the potential violator, society, the courts, and the enforcement agency are all accommodated. Subtle shifts in several factors or a major change in one factor in the above equation can shift Ω to either side of zero. These changes collectively move the person into or out of deciding to commit a criminal act. When Ω is less than zero, the person commits a crime; when Ω is greater than zero the person acts within the law. When Ω is *equal* to zero, a very low probability, the person waits a millisecond and re-evaluates Ω, or at least parts of it.

There are law-abiding citizens, *alpha* (α) people, who do not need to make these decisions all of the time. They are rarely tempted. They have decided in advance not to commit any crime if they can help it. They automatically rate A and V as very great ($\cong 1.0$), Q as very low ($\cong 0$), and C as very high. Rather than waste energy in the calculus of Ω, they discard most law violation alternatives and attempt to stay "well within the law."

This theory provides a rational basis for explaining crime. It is consistent with observed criminal behavior and inclusive of known crime causation theories. It provides a basis for analyzing acts, predicting performance, and designing systems to influence controllable variables or at least to explain changes that *do* and *will* occur, no matter what investments are made in law enforcement agencies, court efficiencies, or educational tools.

Morris (1972:40-41) despaired at the general crime rate increases even after several major crime commission reports and hundreds of recommendations had been made for improvement. "Over all," he said, "the criminal justice systems—federal and state—still resist change." He recognized that there are "considerable political vested interests in preserving the present inefficiencies," but added:

> What we ought to do now is consider the lessons to be learned from five years of experience with reasonably designed well-financed failure. It would seem that levels of planning, programming, and financing have been insufficient to cope with the complexity and intractability of the criminal justice systems of this country. Perhaps the type of sporadic reform that has been pursued is tokenism, merely reshuffling relatively discretionary authority among police, prosecutors, courts, and corrections with little effect. Perhaps the time has come to plan a quite different and much more comprehensive approach to the control of crime and juvenile delinquency in this country, without abuse of human rights.

A theory of wildlife crime causation is fundamental to a quite different rational and comprehensive approach to controlling and reducing wildlife crime. Perhaps the theory will also be useful in dealing with other types of crime.

Agency Objectives

Wildlife management is a system composed of many interrelated variables. It is known from the principle of limiting factors that the strength of a system is only as great as the strength of its weakest part. Agency goals have not previously been precise enough for effectiveness studies to be conducted; the criteria for the weakness of parts of a wildlife agency have been missing. Enforcement may be a limiting factor in the wildlife management system of the future. However, it need not be.

Objectives are absolutely essential for the design, analysis, and evaluation of all wildlife management activities. Without them there is no direction, no destination, no criteria for goodness or optimum performance.

First-order objectives, also called goals and occasionally even policy, are the broad statements of what an agency should be. They provide general guidance and direction but rarely provide the basis for determining whether a program is good or an agency performing well. Second-order objectives specify what an agency should do. These are fundamental criteria for designing and evaluating execution of the design for a law enforcement agency or any other wildlife program. Third-order objectives specify acts to be carried out—for example, to make three arrests for spotlight poaching of deer. Whether or not they are achieved does not affect the first- and second-order objectives. Fourth-order objectives, usually called policy, specify how all of the above will be performed—for example, safely and efficiently. It is easy to formulate these so they sound like second-order objectives—for example, to maximize the agency's safety record.

Failures at past efforts to express agency objectives have resulted from trying to simplify and generalize them. There is no single objective other than *to maximize the achievement of a weighted set of objectives.* Other failures have resulted from choosing between two conflicting objectives. The approach proposed herein requires objectives to be stated but then allows such objectives to be weighted and actions to achieve *all* balanced out. An (admittedly extreme) example of conflict may be useful. Obviously, the best way to minimize arrests (as evidence of a good crime prevention program) would be for all agents to stay at home! To maximize arrests (as evidence of abundant, vigorous field work and many public contacts) the agents' strategy would be to promote complex laws, hide the law books, suppress education, and write "tickets" for every possible violation of the most insignificant type. Of course, neither tactic is desirable. The agent can better balance education and apprehension efforts if these two objectives are stated *simultaneously* and weighted.

First-Order Objectives. Wildlife law enforcement has the following first-order objectives:

1. To prevent wildlife populations, particularly endangered, migratory, and breeding populations, from becoming extirpated in an area.
2. To protect the ecological health of habitats, especially from conflicts of land users.
3. To assure that desired, calculated harvests are achieved.
4. To regulate the rate of exploitation of wildlife populations.
5. To assure each licensed person an equal opportunity to pursue fish or game.
6. To maximize the opportunities of all citizens, licensed or not, to experience benefits from wildlife.
7. To assist in balancing user satisfactions with expectations.
8. To balance the allocation of the resource to the users, properly weighting special group interests and influence (for example, hunting clubs, anti-hunting lobbies), preventing exploitative groups from forming, and minimizing private interests' preying on the public "capital."

9. To ensure stable agency income, consistent with agency objectives, by encouraging the user to pay through licenses and fees.

10. To protect commercial interests (for example, crops and orchards) from wildlife.

11. To protect property, landowners, and hunters from the hunter.

These first-order objectives can help clarify the context of enforcement.

Second-Order Objectives. Ritter (1975) and I have analyzed second-order wildlife law enforcement agency objectives. We operate from the theoretical base that effective wildlife management is the superstructure, management of people one of the basic components of such a management system, and law enforcement a strategy in the management of people. The wildlife law enforcement agency is now the major functional basis for executing this strategy.

A wildlife law enforcement system is conceived and operated by an agency, but the system includes the public, the media, the courts, other agencies, and so on. A wildlife law enforcement agency, although an entity in itself, is the sum of the production of the individual agents (see the concept of aggregates in Chapter 4). Many organization theorists would argue that because of its various interactions the agency is greater than the sum of its parts. It may be, but measurements of these interactions would be difficult to obtain, and, for the most part, once they were obtained they would be of analytical value only. No regional or federal group, for a very long time, will manipulate state wildlife law enforcement agencies! In other words, the relevant context of wildlife law enforcement is the state agency.

The aggregated-agent concept seems the most meaningful way to view the state agency. There is little point in, and no basis for, comparing the effectiveness of state agencies. Furthermore, communications systems, insignia and uniforms, educational media and publications, personnel, legal counsel, data processing, training, and other benefits and services associated with an agency are all spread among the agents. Collectively, these are a potent force. They are a multiplier, a coefficient for raising the overall objective achievement of all agents. Average annual increases in agent performance can reflect the work of the "main office" or the agency per se.

Ritter (1975) developed a computer program to assist states in articulating their objectives and, using various weighting techniques such as those described in Chapter 5, arriving at measures of agent performance. This system enables agents to analyze their own performance, to compare their effectiveness with others', to redirect their efforts toward objectives, and to experience the pleasure and rewards of contributing to overall system improvement as measured by the sum of the agents' performance on a large set of objectives.

Typical second-order objectives might be to maximize compliance rate per unit of cost; to maximize the arrests per reported crime; and to maximize conviction rates for violators of the most significant wildlife resource laws.

One important aspect of Ritter's system is that it is value-free. Each state may assign weights to objectives, including a zero weight, which can exclude an objective. General systems can be created that provide the analyses for decision makers, leaving for them the most human of activities—the dynamic assessment of values.

Measures of Second- and Fourth-Order Objectives. Ritter (1975) developed several means to measure objectives. Nine of these are geared to statewide analysis, reflect on all agents and the agency, and are conducted only periodically.

1. *Agent politeness scale.* Sportsmen assess the politeness of warden contacts on a scale, say, of 0 to 100.

2. *Law complexity scale.* Sportsmen evaluate the complexity of a set of laws or one law on a scale of 0 to 100. In a way this measures performance of the legislative process.

3. *Arrest-to-violator ratio.* People in a well-designed sample are asked if they have violated game laws (V) and second, if they were detected by agents and arrested or given tickets (A). The A/V ratio is likely to be small but should approach 1.0 as the agency becomes more effective.

4. *Public cooperation coefficient.* A coefficient of public cooperation (C) is calculated, where C = Number of respondents who say they would report a violation (r) ÷ Total who were asked the question (R). The objective is to maximize this coefficient through education and incentives (Beattie 1976).

5. *Percentage of violators.* The percentage is figured of respondents to an anonymous questionnaire who admit to ever having violated a game law. The objective is to reduce this percentage.

6. *Percentage of specific violators.* The percentage is figured of respondents to an anonymous questionnaire who admit to ever having violated a specific set or type of game laws or admit to having committed more than a certain number of violations. A refinement is to include a specific period.

7. *Sportsman satisfaction index.* A measure is taken of the percentage of sportsmen respondents feeling their enjoyment of hunting or fishing was impaired by agents' inspection. The index (S) is

$$S = s/T,$$

where s is the total number of those who answer in a questionnaire or interview that inspections spoil the pleasure of hunting or fishing and T is the total respondents. There is likely to be an interaction between S, the warden politeness index (Number 1), total contacts, and contacts per unit time afield.

8. *Hunter safety index.* A standard index is employed to measure the rate of reduction in hunting accidents and fatalities.

$$a = \frac{\text{Accidents in year } t}{\text{Accidents in year } t - 1}.$$

9. *License sales index.* Standard indices of numbers and income are employed to maximize both (as in Number 8).

Measures of Objectives for Individual Agents. Another type of measure provides detailed analyses of individual agent effectiveness. Ritter (1975) developed a computer system for employing any of the preceding indices or the following ones for assessing individual objectives, their weights, and data.

1. *Compliance rate.* Compliance $(C) = 1.0 -$ Arrests/Inspection (McCormick 1968). An assumption is required that inspections generally represent an unbiased sample of all sportsmen. If so, the proportion of violators in the sample should reflect the proportion of violators in the total population of sportsmen. Some agencies are unwilling to accept "reported inspections" since there can be no audits. This, in part, is the reason why multiple objectives are needed and why one such as "maximizing the compliance rate" can be given as much or as little importance in evaluating an enforcement system as the evaluators desire. The agency objective might be to prevent it from falling below some number, say 85 percent. See Box 10-1.

2. *Weighted compliance rate.* Like the method just described, this method employs the administrators' or agents' median weights for each violation, in terms of its seriousness. Compliance with different laws is not equally important for agency performance (for examples, waterfowl baiting versus failure to sign a duck stamp). See Box 10-1. Wardens with constituents who commit fewer of the more serious violations, or who are caught less, will have the higher rates of compliance.

3. *Conviction rates.* Conviction rates measure convictions per arrest. The minimum cost or effort per conviction is desired. One method is to convict as high a percentage of arrests as possible. This may be achieved by making fewer arrests but only those that will bring sure conviction. Agents generally have very high conviction rates. Some locales have judges that lower the agent's score; others raise it. It is clear that multiple objectives are essential. Compliance rate is supportive of or may be balanced with this measure.

4. *Weighted conviction rate.* The weighted conviction weight parallels weighted compliance, outlined in Number 2. The purpose is to give an agent more credit for gaining convictions of those who commit serious violations than for convictions of those who commit trivial ones. See Box 10-1.

Box 10-1. Computation of the Adjusted Inspection Rate, Weighted Compliance, and Weighted Conviction Rate

Because of the potential problem of inaccurate recording or outright falsification of the number of inspections made of sportsmen or potential violators—particularly as compliance rates and similar statistics become more critical as measures of competition—some method is needed for assessing the effectiveness of inspections. Ritter (1975:120) suggested that the largest rate of inspections per hour for any agent for the past 5 years be determined and that this be assumed to be the maximum rate possible. Those reporting more than this amount would be required to substantiate their figures. Another method would be to assume some time required (for example, 2.5 minutes) for each mile driven (M), calculate the hours driven in a patrol car, subtract this from total work hours (T), and calculate the likely inspections per hour (I^*). That is, $I^* =$ Inspections/$[CT - (2.5\ M/60)]$. The largest value of I^* observed in the last 5 years would be used as the maximum inspection rate.

The weighted compliance (WC) is

$$WC = 1.0 - \left(\sum_{j=1}^{N} (W_j A_j)/I \right) \Big/ W_{\max}$$

where W is the violation weight, $W_{\max}$ is the maximum weight assigned, A is arrests, N is the number of violations, I is inspections (I^* may be substituted), and J is the specific violation type from the first to the Nth one. The weighted conviction rate (WCR) is

---

5. *Dollar-weighted arrest.* A measure of cost-effectiveness is needed. The dollar-weighted arrest (DWA) is computed as

$$DWA = \sum_{j=1}^{N} (W_j A_j / T_j P),$$

where T is the estimated arrest time in hours, P is the agency cost in dollars per hour, and the other variables are as previously listed. P can be a constant, such as eight dollars, (McCormick 1969), or can be based on an individual agent's pay scale and operating expenses. The objective is to maximize DWA—for example, by spending more time on serious violations, working on violations requiring less time per arrest, and having more highly paid agents spend time very wisely in order to be cost-effective.

$$WCR = \left(\sum_{j=1}^{N} W_j C_j \Big/ \sum_{j=1}^{N} A_j\right)\Big/ W_{\max}$$

where $N, j, W,$ and A are the same as before and C is the number of convictions. If no arrests are made for a particular violation, the weight for that violation is not entered.

Ritter (1975:106–107) suggested a modifier for the number of cases (for example, one agent makes 2 arrests and gains 2 convictions, another makes 33 and gains 29, making the first agent appear by this measure the more effective). He suggested a modifier of the index, that is, subtracting M, where $M = (1/\text{number of cases})$. The $WCR^* = WCR - M$. In the first example the $WCR^* = 1.0 - 1/2 = 0.5$; in the second $0.88 - 1/33 = 0.85$.

Compliance rate computations must be used only with extreme care because:

1. Hunter contacts may not be representative of the population; they are likely to tend toward "suspicious characters" and to be fewest, relatively, where populations are highest.
2. Multiple contacts of the same hunters are not accounted.
3. Warnings, even though violation is evident, are not accounted.
4. Violation rate per day per hunter over a season is not accounted.
5. Reported inspections may be altered by agents.
6. Between-year factors may change, making between-year comparisons spurious.
7. Violation types are not accounted. Compliance may be high for low-importance laws, low for high-importance laws.

6. *Inspections per hour.* Reported inspections per hour is a gross index to contacts with sportsmen, held to be highly desirable. The greater the contacts, theoretically, the greater the agent's "pressure," and the greater the deterrence. Also it has been said that contacts improve public relations. Hasty inspections can be counterproductive of such relations, but this can be estimated by the agent politeness scale. Reported inspections can be adjusted as shown in Box 10-1.

7. *Inspections per person per hour.* The number of inspections per person in the patrol area per hour is an index that reduces apparent differences between agents' performance in sparsely and densely populated areas. The inspections can be reported by total sportsmen (but these are rarely known) or total population in the area. The best estimate of the target population to be inspected is needed.

8. *Inspections per person per square mile.* An area expression can be devised as in Number 7 above. The agents in more densely populated areas should be able to make more inspections than others since travel time between sportsmen is less.

9. *Game kill.* Game kill is an index that implies that game increases (for example, in deer or wild turkey) are a direct function of law enforcement. Certainly enforcement is one factor, but there are major complications. A deer management objective may be to stabilize or increase the legal kill per rural acre in a county. (The acreage is specific to approximate deer range.) Or, it may be to maximize kill per quality-weighted acre. (Quality-weighted refers to some best local measure of site quality, habitat potential, or carrying capacity.) These expressions may work well in many regions, but law enforcement agency effectiveness can hardly be judged satisfactory in areas where there is high forest or agricultural damage. Increasing deer kills are looked upon as a sign of a growing herd, but a reduced herd may be desired. The objective can be expressed as achieving stabilization in 85 percent of all counties between two expressed levels of deer kill per quality-weighted acre per hunter. Another approach would be to design a system to enable a county to achieve a high ratio of actual-to-potential game harvest. Around such an objective, coordinated interdivision cooperation and total wildlife agency direction could be solidified.

10. *Illegal kill ratio.* The objective is to minimize the ratio of known illegally killed animals to the total legal kill. Since illegal kills are very poorly known without studies like those of Vilkitis (1968), this objective is likely to be given a low weight of importance.

11. *Arrests per road acre.* Agents in areas with more roads have a higher probability of making arrests than those in roadless counties, other things being equal. A measure is needed of how easily an agent can cover an area of responsibility. Kaminsky (1974) found that the average field depth (for deer spotlighting) was 156 m (171 yards) in Virginia. This was used as one-half the width of the zone of influence of roads. The road acreage (RA) is equal to (miles of road $\times$ 5280 ft per mile $\times$ 3 ft per yard $\times$ 171 yards $\times$ 2 sides of the road)/43,560 ft^2 per acre). The only variable is miles of road (available from highway commissions), and thus the expression could simply be arrests per mile. However, if detailed adjustments were made for road types and field widths and sides of roads in sections of an agent's area, the details would justify computing arrests per road acre. Terrain factors of slope and noise travel distance can also be added to modify the road acre concept.

12. *Crime rate I.* One crime rate is expressed as arrests per 1000 people in an agent's county or area. The objective is to minimize the rate. (The evident way is for the agent to stay at home or hike the backcountry.)

Box 10-2. Computation of an Official Crime Rate

An official crime rate (*CR*) is the crimes known to the agents per 1000 people. It is expressed as

$$CR_t = (A_t + C_t) + (O_t/P) \times 1000,$$

where A_t is agent reported violations and arrests from patrols, C_t is citizen-reported violations, and O_t is other reported violations (such as by agencies). *P* is the area total population. All are expressed as at some time, *t*. The objective is to minimize *CR*.

---

13. *Crime rate II.* Another crime rate is expressed as reported violations *and* complaints, whether arrests are made or not, per 1000 people. Incident reports are strongly recommended. The objective, of course, is to minimize the crime rate. See Box 10-2.

14. *Arrests per crime rate II.* The objective is to maximize *Z* where $Z =$ Arrests/1000/*CR*II.

15. *Arrests and assisted arrests per hour.* Better than total arrests (but not much), this index is part of the most prevalent measure of agent effectiveness (though roundly disclaimed as such). This measure is merely the total arrests in a period (a month or a year) divided by the total hours an agent worked. When agents work together, only one makes an arrest. Some states allow agents to report time spent assisting another agent in an arrest. Often there is no way to assess which agent did the most work or to allocate credit fairly for the arrest.

16. *Weighted arrests.* Supervisors sometimes complain that agents seem to make petty arrests to fill some unofficial arrest quota. When arrests are weighted for importance, the agent who makes petty arrests will not score as well as one who works on more important cases. Each agent can work out a personal optimization between time, arrests, and importance. See Box 10-3.

Using the objective weighting approach (Chapter 5), a computer program was designed to allow all of the above objectives to be weighted and a total score of multiple objective achievement computed. The best score of any agent is assigned a value of 1.000. Other scores are printed relative to that score. Agent scores can be compared or grouped and compared by district and between periods.

Box 10-3. Computation of a Weighted Arrest Rate

A better measure than arrests, weighted arrests (WA), is computed as

$$WA = \sum_{j=1}^{N} W_i A_j \bigg/ \sum_{j=1}^{N} W_{\max},$$

where W is the violation weight, $W_{\max}$ is the maximum weight for each violation, A the arrests for that violation, and N the number of violations.

Because agents often work together, and both should get some "credit" for an arrest, then A^*_j reported as an assist can be substituted in the above equation for A_j. Assists will also be judged on the basis of performance on important cases.

There is always a way to "beat" any system, but when objectives are well articulated, when they tend to be interactive and counterbalance one another, and when flagrant cheating is prevented, efforts to beat the system typically result in heightened achievements of objectives. Other reasons for all of the above are improved justification for programs and budgets, improved comparison of various strategies of enforcement, a basis for pay raises and promotions, and an answer to the simple question, "How am I doing?"

Reports, Facilities, and Agent Selection

Objectives tend to specify what inputs to a system are needed. The thousands of agent-hours spent on weekly reports can be reduced by simplified forms and more computer assistance, freeing the agents' time for primary duties. The importance of setting clear objectives becomes evident when past reports and summaries are scrutinized in light of the real needs.

McCormick (1969) reported the deficiencies in the familiar "stereotype law enforcement reports" and the difficulties "in determining exactly what the data mean." He advocated the concept of an acceptable level of compliance as the basis for evaluation. "What do you do with these numbers?" asked of wildlife law agencies often produces blank stares or nervous head scratching. The real question is: How can we collect the least possible amount of data that will supply us with the most information needed (but no extras) to achieve our objectives? The answers are hard. Agents in the past have asked these questions and designed forms to collect data so that when enough were available a "really good" analysis could be done. Usually the analysis was not well planned or not scheduled, and data have continued to collect because no one was willing to decide to stop. There is much evidence that files can be cleaned, input systems redesigned, and significant outputs achieved at the same or less cost than now incurred. With regional cooperation, computer systems for such data will not have to be redesigned for every state or federal agency (Giles 1974, Giles et al. 1971, Giles and Ritter 1974, Ritter 1975).

Representative inputs needed for each agent and area are:

1. The human population's sex, age, and race ratios and socioeconomic status.
2. Numbers of hunters, fishermen, and other resource users.
3. Proportions of convicted violators in the above classes.
4. Total area.
5. Area within agent's normal searching ability (visual and auditory).
6. Road mileage (segments with maximum speed).
7. Trial mileage (average distance from office to court).
8. Coordinates of arrest sites.
9. Characteristics of arrest (species, number, time, and equipment).
10. Characteristics of violator and others associated with an arrest (age, if drinking).
11. Events leading to arrest (tips, chance, miles driven, time spent, air surveillance).
12. Court action (time, disposition, fine, costs, appeal).
13. Persons contacted and activity.
14. Evidence of violations observed but no case made.

The above are types of data inputs to the system. Other systems inputs are funds, manpower, facilities, and citizen involvement.

The character of the agent is critical to the effectiveness of an agency. Applications for jobs exceed many times the nearly 900 agents' jobs available each year. Research is needed into the psychology and value systems of agents. Comparative studies with other law enforcement agents are needed as well as the relative differences between agents and the groups such agents typically contact. The intent of such studies would be more rational selection of agents for special tasks or areas and better understanding of public or group reaction to the agents' performance. The educational needs of agents should be studied to discover how agents can be enabled to achieve their potential. A special input needed is the attitude and expertise that new systems-oriented employees can bring or that agents can gain.

"More" is not a convincing answer to a question about needed agency facilities. Optimum system design of radio, vehicle, housing, and storage facilities is a constant concern of the operations research expert. Aerial surveillance and aerial photography are facilities that may be used. Techniques such as the precipitin test for meat and blood identification (Brohn and Korschgen 1950), crystal structure (Jackson 1958) and paper chromatography (Jackson 1962, Brunetti 1965) for meat identification, and electronic sensors and observation equipment are special inputs to the system.

Enforcement Measures

Enforcement measures can be analyzed as *active* or *passive* and *continuous* or *instantaneous* (see Figure 10-3). Enforcement involves *apprehension* with warning or conviction; passive enforcement involves *prevention* and *deterrence*.

Passive Measures. *Prevention* starts with agents preventing undesirable laws from getting in the books. From there, prevention usually becomes a task of information and education. The emphasis is clearly on the law-breaking behavior, and thus educational objectives are very easy to state and educational program effectiveness easy to measure. A wildlife agency should have directed educational programs. Currently it is considered practical for the same agent to conduct educational programs for different agency divisions—for example, to sell habitat management as well as instruct hunters on why and how to avoid violating game laws. However, it is difficult enough to be a good educator, even about a topic on which a person is an expert. It is time wildlife agencies recognized the advantages of specialization. I do not propose that divisions stop cooperating and aiding each other. I advocate that they educate to achieve behavioral objectives peculiar to their own divisions and coordinate their efforts with those of other divisions.

When a wildlife law is a good and just one, it would seem in the best interest of everyone to abide by it. How individuals calculate their "best interest," however, is a complex psychological and economic calculus. An exciting challenge to the behaviorist and educator is to find ways to resolve conflicts between "best interests" outside of the legal system. People and animals both respond best to positive reinforcers of good behavior. However, negative action, punishment of a sort, can also result in desired behavior. The fear of punishment, whether of merely an unpleasant experience or of fine and imprisonment, is *deterrence*. This is a passive theoretical basis for enforcement. There are no studies in wildlife management (and they are needed) of whether the agent's presence truly deters law violation. The hypothesis to be tested formally can be usefully stated as: When the net personal benefits of living within the guidelines of the

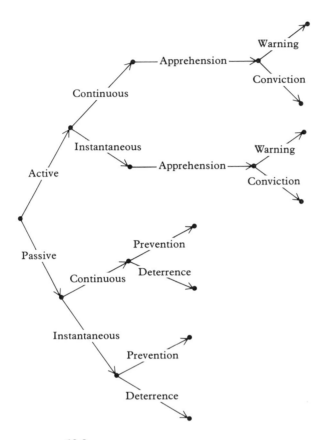

FIGURE **10-3**

The major components of the enforcement process and the
alternative pathways that can be taken by agent and agency in
action and policy.

law are at (or are perceived to reach) zero, or when they are vague or imper-
ceptible, the presence of a negative force (the agent, representing the risk of
punishment) can make the net benefits appear to be positive, thus resulting
in most normal people obeying laws.

The usual deterrents are:

1. Embarrassment.
2. Time in court and legal fees.
3. Conviction on "record," which may influence employment opportunities.
4. News releases or public display of arrests and convictions.

5. Required attendance at special schools.

6. Fines, animal replacement costs, and court costs. Christiansen and Folkman (1971), having studied the characteristics of people who start fires, observed, "When fires are started by these individuals and damage costs are charged against them, they avoid paying these costs about half of the time. A more vigorous and skillful program of investigation and prosecution is suggested if such action is to have the desired deterrent effect. The lesson that an individual is likely to be caught, prosecuted, and pay for a fire he starts will then not be lost upon others living in the community."

7. Confiscation of cars, boats, and weapons involved in a violation.

8. License revocation for short or long periods and denial of future license purchases during a revocation period.

9. Work details relating to animal propagation or habitat improvement.

10. Jail.

In the future, education may be able to replace, to some extent, the threat of apprehension. Menninger (1968:55) asserted that with all programs the secret of success is the replacement of a punitive attitude with a therapeutic attitude. He remarked,

> The public will grow increasingly ashamed of its cry for retaliation, its persistent demand to punish. This is its crime, *our* crime against criminals—and, incidentally, our crime against ourselves. For before we can diminish our sufferings . . . we must renounce the philosophy of punishment, the obsolete, vengeful penal attitude. In its place we would seek a comprehensive constructive social attitude—therapeutic in some instances, restraining in some instances, but preventative in its total social impact.

Massive opposition to this philosophy, based on opinions that punishment is necessary for deterrence and that violators should pay the price for their crimes (revenge), does not make the therapeutic approach less appealing. The concept that must be challenged is that of criminal law itself, which Sachar (1963:39) said has the objectives of: (1) "the affirmation of the ethical absolutes of society," (2) "the moral condemnation and punishment of those who violate these absolutes," and (3) "the reduction of the number of criminal acts within society" primarily through "the penalty system of deterrence and correction." He, too, argued that there are major alternatives to punishment.

Active Measures. *Apprehension* of violators requires better studies of attitudes and behavior. Vilkitis (1968) did a study of poacher psychology in which he compared hunters convicted of game violations and law-abiding hunters in the state of Idaho. (Also see Amidon 1968.) Shafer et al. (1972) have compared the violators and the nonviolators among New York deer hunters. Studies are needed that will permit crime rate predictions as a function of age and sex distribution in the population, of changes in income and discretionary funds, of education, and of urban versus rural origins. Attitudes toward laws, agents, the courts, and wildlife must be determined. The psychological impact of conviction, fines, and publicity must be known. It is conceivable that by knowing the dynamics of the human population of a state it will be possible to project the future sex, age, and education of the population, and to estimate probable associated crime rates in each group and in the total group. Such statistics are essential since even if an agency could *double* its effectiveness within a certain period of time, during the same time the dynamics of the population might increase the enforcement problem *four* times. Those granting agency support funds could claim that the agency performance had slipped by a half!

There are two major types of violations: *continuous* and *instantaneous,* or discrete. The best examples of the former are possession of an improper license or gun, and waterfowl baiting. These are subject to detection over a period of time. The presence or inspection by an agent is like a sample from a continuous distribution. The probability of detecting such violation types is much greater than the probability of detecting the instantaneous type, such as the act of spotlighting a deer. These types of violations should be reported separately and arrest and conviction rates then reported together only with appropriate weighting factors.

The probabilities of being arrested for a violation are high if a resource user is "checked." The number of hunters checked in Virginia in 1970 was 83,152, of a total of 273,917 (30 percent). Of those checked, 2975 were considered by agents to be in violation of the law. Thus, in general, there is approximately a chance of 3 in 100 that if an agent is encountered, the experience will be unpleasant in some respect for the resource user. In California, the chances seem higher (McCormick 1968). Game laws are notoriously complex, and many violations are due simply to oversight or misunderstanding. The probabilities of being 100 percent within the laws governing land, county or parish, permit, weapon, licenses, ammunition, garb, and season are indeed small. There are, of course, deliberate violations. The question remains: Is it in the best interest of the total hunting population to cloud the hunting experience with the negative aspects of the potential enforcement agent encounter? Surely the answer is "yes," but the next question, one remaining for research to answer, is: How much?

More knowledge of violation rates is badly needed. (See Box 10-4.) Time, location, and group characteristics need to be developed so that search and stake-out strategies can be improved and apprehension probabilities increased. For example, Kaminsky (1974) found most arrests for deer spotlighting were made on Saturdays between 10 PM and 11 PM. Nearly 56 percent of all apprehensions were made between 8 PM and midnight. Most arrests for spotlighting were made in November. Arrests began to increase in October and decreased

Box 10-4. Methods for Computing Violations

License-Purchase Violations

Michael Kaminsky, in an in-house communiqué of the New Jersey Division of Fish and Game, described how to compute the magnitude of failures to obtain proper hunting or fishing licenses.

He assumed that (1) the agent inspects a random sample of hunters for licenses, (2) the agent will make a negligible percentage of duplicate inspections, and (3) all hunters are not inspected by conservation officers. Some individuals may hunt their entire lives without being inspected, whereas some few individuals may be inspected a dozen times every season.

He observed that in Virginia, in 1969, an average of 24.0 license inspections per violation were required. Thus, one hunter in 24 or 4.2 percent of the total number of hunters were in violation of the law. During the same year, 539 summons were written for hunting without a license. A total of 3142 hunting violations were prosecuted that year. Therefore, 17.0 percent of all hunting violations were for hunting without a license. Since 4.2 percent of the total number of hunters were in violation of a game law, and 17.0 percent of these were hunting without a license, then 0.7 percent (that is, $0.170 \times 0.042 = 0.007$) of the total number of hunters were hunting without a license.

Total hunters = Licensed hunters (L) + Unlicensed hunters (X).

It was established that 0.71 percent of the total number of hunters $(X + L)$ hunt without a license. Therefore:

$$0.007(x + L) = \text{the number of unlicensed hunters, or } X$$
$$0.007L = 1X - 0.007X$$
$$0.007L = 0.993X$$
$$0.00705L = X.$$

When L is 273,917 licensed hunters, as was the case in Virginia in 1969, then $X = 1931$ hunters without licenses. Since 539 summons for this violation were written, the conservation officers apprehended 27.9 percent of those hunting without a license.

In-Season Violations

Dahl (1972) explained a violation analysis procedure as follows: A total 74,844 contacts by agents of big game hunters were made in one year. Agents therefore contacted 11 percent of the 671,783 licensed big game hunters. Of those contacted, 2,229 or 3.0 percent were found to be in violation of game laws and were arrested. (Warnings were also given but these must be analyzed separately.)

The average big game hunter in the state spends 6.2 days afield during the season. The agent is assumed to make one contact during a person's 6.2-day hunting period. Total use-days are estimated (that is, $671,783 \times 6.2 = 4,165,055$ use-days). Assuming:

$$\frac{\text{Total violators}}{\text{Total hunters}} = \frac{\text{Violators among those checked}}{\text{Total hunters checked}},$$

and making simplifying assumptions, it is estimated that a minimum of 124,952 violations were committed by big game hunters during the season:

$$\text{Total use days} \times \text{Violation rate} = \text{Violations}$$
$$4,165,055 \quad \times \quad 0.03 \quad = \quad 124,952.$$

Pursuing this example further, 17.9 violations occurred per 100 big game hunters expending 6.2 hunter-days use ($120,787 \div 671,783 = 17.9$). 1971 Michigan big game hunters could be said to have an 82.1 percent rate of compliance. If warnings were included, the analysis would be

$$4,165,055 \text{ total hunter-days use} \times 0.076 = 316,544 \text{ violations.}$$

Out-of-Season Violations

Vilkitis (1968) studied out-of-season big game poaching in Idaho, then retested the methods in Maine. First he defined:

violation = an offense against existing fish and game law. One violation produces one set of evidence.

arrest = an agent legally arrests a person when enough information is available to prosecute an alleged violator.

incident = positive evidence of a violation is available but information is insufficient for an arrest.

violation simulation = an act performed by a specially authorized agent of the state to duplicate, in every way possible, a violation.

He employed our earlier rationale that the total number of violations (I) for the study period was related to the total detected violations (either arrests M_a or incidents M_b) in that time, in approximately the same way that total violation

Box 10-4, *continued*

simulations (C) were related to total simulations reported (R) by enforcement personnel.

Thus:

$$I = \frac{M_a C}{R} \quad \text{or} \quad \frac{M_b C}{R}$$

depending on the data being studied. The reader will readily see the similarity to capture-recapture methods of population estimation. An unbiased estimate is achieved (Bailey 1951, Chapman 1951) by

$$I = \frac{(M + 1)(C + 1)}{(R + 1)} - 1,$$

where $3MC$ must be greater than I to insure the arrests or incidents include at least one "marked" sample (a violation simulation). The approximate percentage of bias of the estimate, B, is

$$B = 100e^{-(M+1)(C+1)/I}$$

(Robson and Regier 1964:216), where e is the base of the natural logarithm. In Idaho the violation simulator simply displayed a legal collecting permit to the arresting officer. In Maine, the simulator waived trial in the lower court and postponed the superior court hearing to a date after field research was to be completed. The simulator dressed and acted as much like a poacher as possible. The violation simulations were performed with collected animals. Eighty-one were achieved with 15 animals. Shots were fired, and evidence of blood, hair, hides, and drag trails was left.

Using the above equation, Vilkitis computed in an unpublished manuscript the illegal closed-season big game kill in Maine as

$$I = \frac{(136 + 249 + 1)(81 + 1)}{1 + 1} - 1 = 15,825$$

and concluded this to underestimate I by 13.95 percent ($e^{-2.0} = 0.1395$) since no arrests were made for violation simulations. Recording the incidents was a new requirement for agents and minimally done, and $3MC$ was not greater than I. The unbiased estimate was 18,033 big game animals, 0.56 of the legal kill. When the same approach was used and 49 violation simulations were committed at night, the magnitude of spotlighting was estimated at 20,199, also considered an underestimate. The unbiased estimate was 27,780.

Vilkitis developed an equation (needing further tests of assumptions) for estimating the illegal kill:

$$\text{Illegal kill} = 122.9 \times \text{Closed-season arrests.}$$

He used this equation to estimate illegal kill in Maine, then computed the apprehension rate. It was 1.1 in Idaho, 1.2 in Maine. The above studies (or their alternatives) need not be conducted every year.

Stork and Walgenbach (1973) used the above simulator concept to study fishing law violation in a large California lake. By placing varying numbers of known violators (simulators) around the lake, and finding out the number of agent-hours spent in each area, contacts, arrests, and warnings, they could estimate the effectiveness of law enforcement. They noted percentage of arrests per contact, enforcement hours spent per arrest, and hours per contact. Insufficient data attributed to weather and other factors limited their conclusions.

Waterfowl Violations

Martinson et al. (1967) reported on using hunter-submitted waterfowl wings to obtain minimum estimates of kill of illegal species (such as during a special teal season).

Carney and Smart (1964) reported on spy blind analyses. A spy blind is used on waterfowl areas. An agent stations himself in a blind, observes hunter behavior, and compares it with hunter reports of that behavior.

after January. All spotlighting was done from public roads over private fields. Violations occurred about 1 mile from occupied houses and an average of 19 miles from the agent's home. Without other information or leads, agents should be especially alert for late-model sedans carrying three males in their late twenties on rural roads on November evenings after 8 PM.

Feedback and Feedforward

Carter (1973:693), though describing national science indicators, could have been speaking of law enforcement system indicators when he noted that indicators are the basis for identifying a system's strengths and weaknesses and "for charting its changing state." The indicators (1) provide an early warning of trends that might weaken the system and reduce its capacity to meet resource user needs, and (2) assist in setting priorities and allocating resources.

There are needs for sequential development of indicators of (1) inputs (the resources used), (2) outputs (measures of achievements), and (3) input-output relations (measures of the effectiveness and productivity of the system). An evolving set of indicators, with feedback monitoring itself, in an experimental environment of continuing exploration, refinement, and testing of prospective indices can significantly improve wildlife law enforcement systems. Computer-generated reports of system performance measures will be the primary feedback. These reports to each agent can be enough feedback to cause major, almost overnight changes in wildlife law enforcement practice.

Each part of the wildlife law enforcement system has special feedback needs. *Input* can be improved by:

1.   Data studies that provide coefficients and equations for better handling of collected data.

2.   Improved input formats, reduced copies, reduced mailing, reduced chances for loss.

3.   Data protection.

4.   Link-ups with other data systems (for example, computer mapping).

Processes can be improved by feedback aimed at wildlife laws. The relation of the law to the recreational outputs of the agency is underlined by such questions as: Should law A, which will result in the harvest of 100 raccoons but generates 5600 additional hunter-hours of recreation, be passed? Law B will ease enforcement, increase convictions, and reduce deer kill, but should it pass when it is difficult for hunters to understand, and thus may reduce the pleasure or benefits experienced from the hunt? Where should the agent devote most time—to enforcing a squirrel regulation that has no measurable or significant effect on future squirrel populations, or to investigating market hunting? Wildlife agencies will discover in the future that a particularly useful and powerful formulation of wildlife objectives is in terms of maximizing the sum and minimizing the variance of the net quality-weighted person-days of hunting or fishing (that is, the utility function). The enforcement system can participate effectively in achieving such an objective.

Other law enforcement processes can be improved by feedback. These include analyzing data, allocating manpower, cooperating with other educational and enforcement groups, using computer-aided search and patrol strategies, investigating reports, making court appearances and presentations, and engaging in periodic inter- and intra-agency personnel exchanges.

The *feedback* component itself can benefit from the following types of feedback:

1. Supervision.
2. Periodic checks of diaries and reports.
3. Use of spy blinds, in which agents concealed near hunting blinds record all shots, time of day, ducks killed, and other relevant data, and later query hunters as they are checked out of the hunting areas to discover any discrepancy between actions and reports. The results provide a means for adjusting data obtained from hunter questionnaires elsewhere. Hunters typically report only about 60 percent of their kill (therefore reported kill/0.59 = actual kill). They remember the time of kill very accurately, but only report 55 percent of cripples (thus, there are about 0.25 cripples for every bird bagged).
4. Use of interviews to supplement questionnaires. Hesselton and Maguire (1965) used an approach similar to that of the spy blind to estimate the bias in the reported deer kill. They compared the reports of agent-checked hunters with actual data on the same hunters. Only 78.4 percent of the deer were reported. Questionnaires such as those used by Barick (1969) can provide "ball park" figures, but pooled estimates are dangerous for some uses.
5. Use of computer search strategies, as in military warfare (for example, Howland et al. 1971) to increase the probability of encounters between agent and "the enemy."
6. Periodic assessments of agents' performance and capabilities, including (a) public promotions and awards, emblems, or insignia, (b) educational evaluation reports, (c) periodic certification and relicensing of agents, (d) periodic complete medical examinations, (e) periodic psychological tests, (f) comparisons of main office performance with agents' performance (an evaluation of the potentiating effect), and (g) agency overview teams (interstate exchanges and federal reviews) employed periodically to inspect and consult with agents and agencies.

Output, or actual achievement, can be assessed by:

1. Periodic committee analyses of objectives.
2. Periodic general public hearings.
3. Periodic public questionnaires.
4. Periodic tabulation of complaints and periodic performance analyses to determine if alternative objectives are being articulated through action.

Feedforward approaches to be used in the agency include encouragement of scenario writing, the addition of a "future" dimension to educational programs for advanced agents (Coates 1972), sending of select agents to future-oriented conferences, and employment of long-range computer simulations of populations, crime rates, and agency dynamics. The wildlife law enforcement agency can become a sophisticated arm of the total practice of wildlife management, all the while maintaining a personal, friendly, pragmatic attitude, which is right for most of the people and for the land.

Study Questions

1. List some of the major factors that influence wildlife law enforcement.
2. Compare the topics of Sigler's book on wildlife law enforcement with the topics presented in this chapter.
3. Approximately what percentage of a wildlife agency budget is spent on law enforcement? In your state?
4. What are the major criteria for wildlife laws?
5. What are ten major first-order objectives of wildlife law enforcement agencies currently? Discuss which should be objectives. Weight them using a scale of 0 to 100. Compare your weighting with others.
6. Conduct an experiment. Have half the group weight the objectives independently, then take the mean or modal weights. Compare this statistic with those determined by group processes and discuss the weights to be assigned.
7. Is it reasonable to assume the effectiveness of the agency is the sum of the effectiveness of its agents? Will this under- or overestimate the action? How can this be adjusted to be made more accurate?
8. From the nine measures of statewide objectives presented (and others), design an efficient and effective system of assessing achievement of objectives that you can justify before a group of your colleagues.
9. Select from the individual objectives a minimum set under which you would be willing to work. Weight their importance or how much they should contribute to your salary and promotions.
10. Evaluate arrest rate as a criterion of agent effectiveness.
11. Debate or write an essay on: The agent as educator: Is the agent's sole purpose to achieve law enforcement agency effectiveness?
12. List ten major law violation deterrents.
13. How would you prove or otherwise *know* the reality of deterrence?
14. Why are demographic analyses essential to all law enforcement agencies?
15. Using hypothetical data, compute at least one estimate of the number of unlicensed hunters.

16. Describe the violation-simulation approach to estimating illegal kill. Give the basic equation. If there are 600 detected violations, 50 simulations, and 4 reported simulations, what is the illegal activity?
17. What is a spy blind? Why is it used?
18. Give examples of feedback.
19. Describe the transactional analysis game of "cops and robbers." Is it a reasonable model of wildlife crime causation? What are some alternatives to this approach?
20. What is the hedonistic theory of crime causation?
21. What is the differential association theory of crime?
22. Describe in detail, with diagrams, the alpha-person theory of crime.
23. Is the poacher a β or Δ person?
24. What variables influencing Ω would an agent be able to influence?
25. If the dread Agents' Virus (hypothetical, of course) epidemic struck within your state and all agents were hospitalized for a year, what would be the consequences to game populations? To hunter benefits? What if the Violators' Disease struck?

Selected References

Amidon, P. H. 1968. *New York deer hunters: a comparison of deer law violators and non-violators.* Unpub. M.S. thesis, State University College of Forestry, Syracuse University, Syracuse, NY. ix + 143 p.

Bailey, N. T. J. 1951. On estimating the size of mobile populations from recapture data. *Biometrika* **38**:293–306.

Barick, F. B. 1969. Deer predation in North Carolina and other southeastern states. In *White-tailed deer in the southern forest habitat,* ed. L. K. Halls. Proc. of Symp., Nacogdoches, TX.

Beattie, K. H. 1976. Evaluative criteria used in anti-poaching campaigns. *Wildlife Soc. Bull.* **4**(1):29–30.

Berne, E. 1964. *Games people play.* Grove Press, New York. 194 p.

Brohn, A. and L. J. Korschgen. 1950. Precipitin test—a useful tool in game-law enforcement. *Trans. N. Am. Wildlife Conf.* **15**:467–476.

Brunetti, O. A. 1965. The use of paper chromatography in game law enforcement. *Proc. Western Assn. Fish and Game Commissioners* **45**:281–284.

Carney, S. M. and G. Smart. 1964. *Comparisons between hunters' reports and spy-blind observations during the 1961-62, 1962-63 and 1963-64 hunting seasons.* Admst. Rpt. No. 44, U.S.D.I., Fish and Wildlife Service, Migratory Bird Population Station, Laurel, MD. 10 p. Mimeo.

Carter, L. T. 1973. Land use law (I): Congress on verge of a modest beginning. *Science* **182**(4113):691–693.

Chapman, D. G. 1951. Some properties of the hypergeometric distribution with applications to zoological census. *University of Calif. Publ. Stat.* **1**(7):131-160.

Christiansen, J. R. and W. S. Folkman. 1971. *Characteristics of people who start fires . . . some preliminary findings.* USDA Forest Service. Res. Note PSW 251. 5 p.

Coates, J. F. 1972. The future of crime in the United States from now to the year 2000. *Policy Sciences* 3(1):27–45.

Conservation Dept., Winchester-Western Division, Olin. 1972. *A law for wildlife: model legislation for a state nongame wildlife conservation program.* Olin Corp., East Alton, IL. 20 p.

Dahl, G. M. 1972. *Procedure for evaluating law enforcement effort.* In-house document, dated 12-6, Michigan Dept. of Natural Resources, Lansing. 8 p.

Gardner, J. W. 1969. Responsible versus irresponsible dissent. *Science* 164(3878):n.p.

Giles, R. H., Jr. 1974a. Criteria for wildlife laws. *Wildlife Soc. Bull.* 2(2):68–69.

Giles, R. H., Jr. 1974b. Wildlife law enforcement research needs (1971). In *Readings in Wildlife Conservation*, ed. J. A. Bailey, W. Elder, and T. D. McKinney. The Wildlife Soc., Washington, DC, pp 557–561.

Giles, R. H., M. Kaminsky, and J. McLaughlin. 1971. Wildlife law enforcement research—the context and the needs. *Proc. S. E. Assn. of Game and Fish Commissioners* 25:677–687.

Giles, R. H. and A. F. Ritter. 1974. A proposal for a regional law enforcement research program. *Ann. Conf. S. E. Assn. Game and Fish Commissioners* 28:740–745.

Hesselton, W. T. and H. F. Maguire. 1965. *Report on percentage of hunters reporting the deer they take—1964.* A separate report, PR Project W-89-R-9, Job VII-C, Albany, NY. 4 p. Mimeo.

Howland, D., H. D. Colson, and C. R. McLean. 1971. *The analysis of tactics.* Project Nonr-495(28) RR003-11-01. Task No. NR 276-003. Office of Naval Research, Dept. of the Navy, Arlington, VA 22217.

Jackson, C. F. 1958. *Suggested methods for identifying the meat of the white-tailed deer.* New Hampshire Fish and Game Dept., Tech. Circ. No. 165. 9 p.

Jackson, C. F. 1962. *Use of paper chromatography in identifying meat of game animals.* New Hampshire Fish and Game Dept., Tech. Circ. 19. 15 p.

Kaminsky, M. A. 1974. *Analysis of the spatial and temporal occurrence of deer spotlighting violations in Virginia.* Unpub. M.S. Thesis, Virginia Polytechnic Institute, Blacksburg. x + 110 p.

Kennedy, J. J. 1970. *A consumer analysis approach to recreational decisions: deer hunters as a case study.* Unpub. Ph.D. Dissertation, Virginia Polytechnic Institute, Blacksburg. 182 p.

Luce, R. D. and H. Raiffa. 1957. *Games and decisions: introduction and critical survey.* John Wiley and Sons, New York. 509 p.

Martinson, R. K., E. M. Martin, C. F. Kaczynski, and M. G. Smart. 1967. *1966 experimental September hunting season on teal.* Admin. Rept. No. 127, Migratory Bird Population Station, Laurel, MD.

McCormick, J. B. 1968. *A procedure for evaluating the effectiveness of wildlife law enforcement.* 48th Proc. Western Assn. of State Game and Fish Commission, Reno, NV. Mimeo, 12 p. and appendices.

McCormick, J. B. 1969. *Trends in wildlife law enforcement: program management, a "systems" concept.* Assoc. of Game, Fish and Conserv. Comm., New Orleans. Mimeo. 9 p.

McCormick, J. B. 1971. *Wildlife law enforcement and the challenge of the 1970's.* Paper before a joint meeting of the Am. Fisheries Soc. and the Wildlife Society, Sacramento, CA. Mimeo. 8 p.

McFadden, J. T. 1969. Trends in freshwater sport fisheries of North America. *Trans. Am. Fish. Soc.* **98**(1):136-150.

Menninger, J. 1968. The crime of punishment. *Saturday Review,* September 7, pp. 21-25, 55.

Merton, R. K. 1968. *Social theory and social structure.* The Free Press, New York. xxiii + 706 p.

Morris, N. 1972. Reforming the criminal justice system. *Center Magazine* **5**(6):40-41.

Morse, W. B. 1969. Law enforcement. *The Wildlife Soc. News,* No. 119. p. 51.

Morse, W. B. 1971. Law enforcement—a tool of management. In *A manual of wildlife conservation,* ed. R. D. Teague. The Wildlife Soc., Washington, DC. x + 206 p.

Morse, W. B. 1972. Wildlife law enforcement. *Proc. Western Assn. State Fish and Game Comm.* **52**:118-137.

Ritter, A. F. 1975. *Objectives and performance criteria for state wildlife law enforcement agencies.* Unpub. M.S. Thesis, Virginia Polytechnic Institute, Blacksburg. xii + 199 p.

Robson, D. S. and H. A. Regier. 1964. Sample size in Petersen Mark-recapture experiments. *Trans. Am. Fisheries Soc.* **93**(3):215-226.

Sachar, E. J. 1963. Behavioral science and criminal law. *Scientific American* **209**(5): 39-45.

Shafer, E. L., Jr., P. H. Amidon, and C. W. Severinghaus. 1972. A comparison of violators and nonviolators of New York's deer-hunting laws. *J. Wildlife Management* **36**(3):933-939.

Sigler, W. F. 1972. Wildlife law enforcement, 2nd ed. Wm. C. Brown Publishers, Dubuque, IA. xxviii + 360 p.

Stork, D. F. and F. Walgenbach. 1973. An evaluation of public compliance with wildlife regulations and the associated influence of law enforcement. *Proc. Western Assn. of State Fish and Game Commissioners* **53**:81-95.

Sutherland, E. H. and D. R. Cressey. 1970. Criminology, 8th ed. Lippincott, New York. 659 p.

Vilkitis, J. R. 1968. *Characteristics of big game violators and extent of their activity in Idaho.* Unpub. M.S. Thesis, University of Idaho, Moscow. 202 p.

Vilkitis, J. R. and R. H. Giles, Jr. 1970. Violation simulation as a technique for estimating illegal closed-season big game kill. *Trans. N. E. Sect. Wildl. Soc., N. E. Fish and Wildl. Conf.* **27**:83-87.

Chapter 11

Administration and the Agency

Wildlife agencies were created in the mid-nineteenth century, and only by 1910 did every state have one. This relatively slow development reflected the minor nature of the early problems of wildlife management and the low citizen involvement in such problems. Wildlife problems have grown rapidly, but public involvement has not. In the years since 1910, within the lifetime of many observers, the field of scientific wildlife management has evolved. That evolution has been shaped by the agency framework, molded by state and federal bureaucracy, and formed by the unique policy and peculiar intellectual set of relatively few people. Some will see the year 1910 as evidence of how youthful wildlife management is. Others see that date as evidence that enough time has passed to have evolved powerful organizations, administrative theory (for example, Simon 1957), useful organizational structure and function, and a management discipline appropriate to an interest that annually spends over a hundred million public dollars. Yet the current quality of American wildlife administration is unacceptable, whether judged in terms of organizational theory, public aspiration, or scientific fact.

Wildlife agencies started as employment agencies for game wardens and as producers of quasi-commercial pheasants and fish. They were largely a bevy of jobs for political patronage, usually controlled by a state governor. It is a wonder that such organizations persisted. They were hardly organizations in any formal sense. Wardens changed with the political wind. As Gutermuth (1971) said about that deplorable system, "in those cases where it did work, the incumbent commissioner usually was a man of exceptional ability with the political influence or good fortune to stay in his post long enough to learn his job."

Organizational Structure

The *one-commissioner system* lasted only through the 1930's. This dictatorial form of operation is very efficient, but in a public agency, if sufficient attention is not paid to public values, it can very easily be ineffective. In the one-commissioner system, the commissioner had great power and administrative discretion in hiring and firing, promulgating regulations, and distributing funds (Gutermuth 1971) and was thus under great pressure to give favored jobs, alter regulations, and stock game and fish on demand. Benevolent dictators are difficult to find. Most are vulnerable to political and other enticements. The one-commissioner system operated well where there were few political party shifts. However, political pressures on administrators could mean that a good idea for administering a public agency would probably not work very long. Program stability was always in jeopardy under the commissioner system, for the commissioner might die or retire or simply be removed by a governor. Budget allocations for the wildlife agency were hard won from the legislators, further compounding political pressure. (At that time most license fees entered the general treasury and were not readily available to the wildlife agency.) The commissioner system is an evolutionary step from *tradition* to *charisma* (Toffler 1970:113).

Charisma was not enough to satisfy sportsmen, who were well aware of payoffs, inequities, and program instability. They were able, through legislative and political work of their own, to help the agency retain license fees by passage of the Pittman-Robertson Act and to establish a *commission* form of agency administration. This, a faltering evolutionary step toward *bureaucracy,* may be followed one day by the *rational adhocracy* (Toffler 1970:113) described later in this chapter.

The *commission system* is now widely used (90 percent of the states in 1971). See Figure 11-1. Most state commissions are based on the Model State Game and Fish Administrative Law formulated in 1934. This system seems to work, for it has been widely adopted.

Commissioners are appointed by a governor and have staggered terms, so one governor cannot quickly change an entire commission. Whether a commissioner is a representative of the people of one region or the whole state varies by state and the progress of the ongoing debate. The commission employs

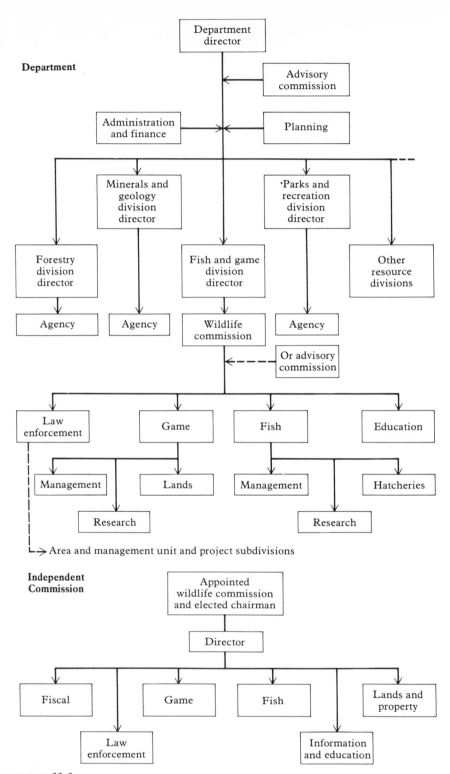

FIGURE **11-1**
Typical wildlife organization flow charts.

a staff, typically headed by a director. Divisions are created. (See the Independent Commission, Figure 11-1). The commission then, typically acting on the model of an industry's board of directors, hires and fires, sets policy, enters into legal contracts (such as for land purchase), and establishes game and fish regulations, but leaves the daily operations to its staff. It often seeks advice from its staff and may rely upon staff heavily, in some cases approving major land purchases after only one or two questions. There is a fine line between setting policy and becoming involved in the daily affairs of management. Commissioners have a tendency toward the latter, managers toward the former. It is easier to get a manager to retreat than a commissioner. Effective leadership can reduce the inefficiencies that typically occur with the crossing of this gray line. The commission disperses political pressure, allows broad representation of users, provides more information and experience to be brought to decisions, and dilutes the risks that must be taken in all decisions. A short-term homeostasis can occur.

Just because the commission system has seemed to work does not mean it is the best form of wildlife agency administration. Idolatry occurs in many forms: homage to leaders, books, concepts, management practices, and administrative structures. There is a tendency to universalize structure. Structures are easy to learn; political games are easily played. A winning strategy, once developed, wins widely. But how long can uniform systems persist? Diversity and stability of agencies are intricately related. Without diversity, exploratory structures, and a national dynamic, the uniform adoption of a commission system is a design for crisis. An alternative will be discussed later in this chapter.

A third organizational form that has been employed with some success is the *departmental system*. See Figure 11-1. Within states, agencies are grouped by a resource name, such as forests or fish and game. These are called departments and may have general overview councils or commissions (such as an environmental council) and specific advisory councils (such as the citizen advisory board to the wildlife department, also occasionally called a commission). In a department the division head is a state employee, directly responsible to the department head. The department head, depending on state law, may be appointed or may be a civil servant. Various departments (for example resources, commerce, health) then comprise the governmental management structure. The reader should be aware that these descriptions are generalizations. It is likely that now each state organization is unique. It will be valuable for political scientists to establish criteria for assessing these structures, to provide guides for improving agencies responsible for resource management, and to provide tools for predicting when resource abuse will occur as a result of the intrinsic phenomena of the organizational structure.

The departmental system is created with the high intent of integrated action, coordination, and reduced duplication of service and more uniform recommendations. Few of these hoped-for consequences have been realized and a new problem has arisen. In states where there are departments, there is no longer design competition between agencies (such as in what land use will produce the most intensive benefits, what agency has the highest B/C ratio for ponds constructed for various purposes, what administrative procedures and reward systems are most effective). All resource agencies fly under the same flag. *Loyalty* becomes a substitute for *authority*, an inadequate basis for rational management. There is more uniform control; there is no need to compete, except at the personal level or at empire building.

There have been real and persisting problems for the wildlife group in the large environmental or natural resource agency. The wildlife commissions in some states retained their authority. In others, they kept their name but lost their power. They became strictly advisory. In some states where wildlife agencies had complete control over a budget, reorganization occurred and they became part of a larger department where funds had to be won in competition with other divisions such as parks, forestry, and ocean fisheries.

The wildlife agency usually has a relatively large budget from license sales and is not subject to legislators' whims or political shifts. However, if the wildlife agency does not watch out, a forestry agency's new road may be called wildlife habitat; a new water-control project called fish habitat; or a picnic area be paid for by license funds and called a hunter campground. The potential open vent in departments is the "wildlife planner," who may do everything but wildlife planning. Of course, projects that provide multiple benefits are desirable, but blatant misuse of wildlife funds should be guarded against by sportsmen and federal inspectors.

The problems outlined in previous chapters have grown within the dominant administrative structure called the commission system. Some try humor as a salve: the system may be no good, but it's all we have. Others try to analyze the problems and design new systems that will be dynamic and responsive to the needs of wildlife resource users.

The major challenges to wildlife and related organizations arose in the early 1970's when the environmental movement gained momentum (Haskell and Price 1973). Former organizations were deemed inadequate. Massive reorganizations occurred. New super-departments of the environment, natural resources, and ecology emerged. Agencies are now structured in many different ways. Ackoff (1974:50–53) suggests a circular organization with much inter-group representation on higher decision-making boards within the agency. The present diversity gives the appearance of a grand experiment. The samples are so few and variations so great that no conclusions on which are "best" are possible. The determining factors will be: (1) budgetary constraints in federal and state law that prevent change, (2) political power, and (3) a sense of public "quiet" and acceptance, purely pragmatic. The dominant structures tend to appear as in Figure 11-2.

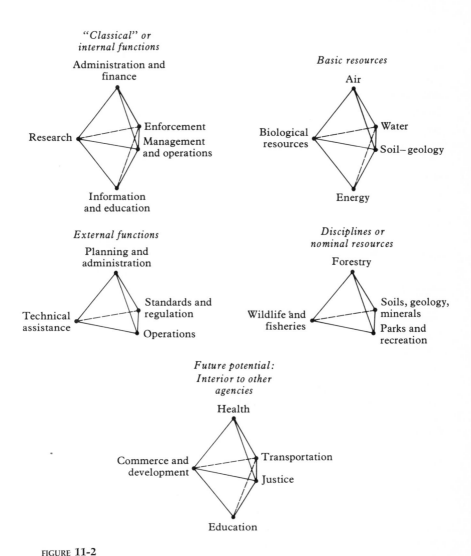

"Classical" or internal functions

Administration and finance

Research — Enforcement / Management and operations

Information and education

Basic resources

Air

Biological resources — Water / Soil–geology

Energy

External functions

Planning and administration

Technical assistance — Standards and regulation / Operations

Disciplines or nominal resources

Forestry

Wildlife and fisheries — Soils, geology, minerals / Parks and recreation

Future potential: Interior to other agencies

Health

Commerce and development — Transportation / Justice

Education

FIGURE **11-2**

Many natural resource and wildlife organization structures are developing to meet new demands. Organizations need to grow to handle all relevant matters, but as they grow, coordination difficulties and administrative costs increase.

Organizational studies suggest that a decision maker's "span of management" should include no more than seven people or groups (Ackoff 1974:52). Beyond a few such guides, there is little upon which to base the design of an optimum organization. An organization should be seen as a means to achieve objectives.

Each unique set of objectives should probably require a unique organization. No one design will be optimal; one pattern for all states will surely be sub-optimal. After years of amateur efforts at analyzing organizational structures, vying for newsworthy wildlife practices, trying for records in game farm production or questionable annual kill figures, and even occasionally hiring efficiency consultants, wildlife resource agencies now seem no closer to arriving at a conceptually satisfying operation than European businesses are to achieving the power of the large American corporation.

Students of organizational theory repeatedly observe that *people* and *purpose,* not organizational *structure,* determine agency success. But optimal organizations can enable such people to achieve their purposes efficiently. Why is organizational change so popular? It is very clear. New leaders bring new objectives. Reorganization is an initial show of power and a practical means by which new leadership can be exercised. Alternative interactions or processes are seen and tried (even if previously tried and rejected, because there exists a new system). Old failures can be blamed on the old organization (even if the personnel remain the same). Organizational structure can also be a blocking or holding action against larger-scale reorganization, legal actions, or the personal wrath of some magnate. Organization creates opportunity; it does not make decisions, originate ideas, or take risks.

Reorganization will continue. It can be expected and it is normal. Neverthe-less, it may produce delays, waste, and morale and other personnel problems. Unless there are great benefits expected, the costs may be excessive. An or-ganization may rationally remain inefficient if the costs of change exceed the likely benefits. Gradual reorganization is almost impossible because of estab-lished interactions between parts of the organization. The complexity of most organization prevents removal of a part without major disruptions. Parts can be added more readily, and interactions will then grow slowly. Because reor-ganization is a part of public organizational life, personnel and agencies should prepare for it. This can be aided by (1) continual study of advances in ad-ministration science and organizational theory, (2) improved personnel capability and experience records, (3) centralized data systems, and (4) continual close cooperation and liaison with related agencies.

Improving the Wildlife Commission

The wildlife resource, for the most part, is the legal property of the states. Thus a public commission for its regulation was quite logical. The problems began long ago and have increased, for game, although legally a public resource, is de facto a private resource. Landowners control access. Birds on their land, having been fed by their grain, housed in their coverts, and having damaged their crops, are *their* birds. Regulations now only restrict the time of legal harvest by the landowner—a modest effect.

Why should game be managed by a civil service agency? Only recently has the question had relevance, for now it is becoming clear that there are two types of resources—public and private. Those to be managed for the public (for example, those on U.S. Forest Service lands) need public controls, as exerted by commissions or other means of bringing public values and desires into complex decisions. Who the decision maker will be is the critical issue. In the private sector, the decision maker's identity is clear. In the public sector, decisions about wildlife resources are ordinarily entrusted to a commission. Each decision is reached with the strike of the gavel; *the* decision maker is the group.

Selection of Commissioners. Wildlife commissioners should perform the same type of duties as the board of a corporation. Typically, they do not. At present the wildlife commission is intended to reflect the wishes of the people. However, there is no longer the need for this role that there once was, for it is far better handled by the methods detailed in Chapter 5. There are certain issues that will arise, however, for which public sampling has not been done or cannot be done swiftly. Of course, the commissioner's role of mirroring the public's wishes in such situations is important and probably irreplaceable. However, this primary role requires great attention to how commissioners are selected to achieve that objective.

Currently, commissioners are selected or appointed from regions—often on the basis of area alone, without regard for population density. Commissioners should be chosen, not to represent areas, but to take responsibility for achieving statewide or nationally optimal resource benefits. Regionalism produces suboptimization. State agencies must "operate" the entire state system, not the additive and noninteractive, and often arbitrary, regions of the state. There is no conscious effort (other than wishfully asserting that a commission represents a cross section of society) to "sample" proportionately from the population either by sex, race, age, user types, employment, or income. Political affiliation is an evident criterion, but its bearing on the benefits received from the wildlife resource seems obscure. If representation is not the objective, then these criticisms are irrelevant. However, the assertions by agencies and the claims in reports of the Wildlife Management Institute staff, who have consulted about wildlife agency administration with over 35 state and provincial agencies, suggest that the criticisms *are* relevant.

Commission membership stipulations must be more explicit. Small commissions being desirable (5 to 15 members), intermediate groups of "representatives" are needed for achieving reflections of public desires. These temporary groups (of less than 200) would be contacted infrequently as needed for critical issues where public desires are paramount and commissioners have inadequate knowledge of such desires.

It is almost pointless to advocate strong, independent commissioners who detest vested interests, to praise ecological statesmanship and decry weak leadership at times when risks must be faced. It is almost pointless, but not quite. These are the bold, basic, and not very precise concepts that have inspired people in the past and may yet do so.

The experience or knowledge of commissioners should include broad business or administrative principles. Commissioners running a wildlife commission must have credentials. It takes more than being a Sunday driver to run the General Motors Corporation. It takes much more than liking the product to maximize the benefits of a resource to a citizenry.

Staggered terms for commissioners can provide continuity and stability. They tend to allow, even encourage, responsibility for decisions being passed from one commission to another. They reduce the opportunities for one governor to "stack" a commission. The trade-off between program stability and innovation is difficult. Theoretically, in a properly functioning democracy it would be best to allow the elected governor to appoint all commissioners, for they would reflect the desires of the electorate in that period. It is evident, though, that this is more theoretical than realistic. Program stability through staggered terms is a functional approach. The costs are (though not necessarily) lagging theory, policy, and practice. The commissioners, not the organizational structure, determine the group dynamics. Those who prefer personal peace are far more conspicuous than those ready for the perils of progress.

There should be no compensation for service for commissioners (other than expenses). The role is one of public service, not a supplementary job (Gutermuth 1971) as it is for highway or boxing commissioners.

A full-time, professionally qualified civil servant is needed to direct the wildlife agency. This administrator is responsible to the commission for the complete operation of the agency.

Commissioners' Responsibilities. The commissioners' responsibilities are those of (1) setting policy, (2) establishing budgets, (3) allocating money, (4) accepting endowments, and (5) entering into contracts.

One typical responsibility is the setting of hunting or fishing seasons and other game and fish laws. This is as it ought to be. Game and fish laws are not biological decisions. They are complex decision sets, only a few components of which are biological. The proper integration of these objectives, values, constraints, and phenomena is the commissioner's responsibility. Wildlife laws are too important to be left completely to biologists.

Wildlifers have argued for years (and have included in the objectives of The Wildlife Society) that more biologically sound decisions should be made. The role of the wildlifer—and it is a key role—is to present clearly and completely to the commissioners an expert interpretation of the consequences of deciding between three or four major strategies or policies. The wildlifer is ancillary to the commission. Like an engineer appearing before a board, the wildlifer will have screened many alternatives and selected the evident best three or four—possibly with the help of computer simulators or optimization programs. The alternatives presented will be the ones between which the decision will be most difficult. The biologist of old typically advocated *a* policy or *an* alternative, fully expecting truth to win out and rationality to prevail. This was an over-simplification, which failed to recognize or come to grips with the complexity of the average commission decision. The fact is that decisions are rarely made; alternatives are rejected.

The wildlifer's winning strategy is to make the alternatives to correct action as undesirable as possible. The wrong alternatives are far more readily recognized than those that are right. The wildlifer's role is best practiced when three distinct and conspicuously different alternatives are presented, all of which have the same natural resource benefit-producing potentiality. Another strategy is to make the scientific reports about recommendations have broader perspective, encompass wide aspects of the problem, and involve many specialists, interactively. The wildlifer should bring to the commissioners a detailed integration of all of the significant population, habitat, and people facts available.

Wildlifers have typically been expert biologists but poor salesmen. After making the presentation requested by the commission, with any necessary clarification, the wildlifer is out of the picture (just as an engineer will not be the exclusive participant in an industrial decision, but must vie for full hearing with the presentations of labor, personnel, transportation, and marketing experts). The commission must decide. *It* is the decision maker, not the wildlifer. Far too often the wildlifer will be held responsible for an adopted recommendation. This misguided soul will often accept the burden. If the weather or unpredictable events make the decision improper, the biologist shoulders the burden. Would that every board could so easily divert the wrath of its stockholders! The average wildlifer, unschooled in politics, does not recognize the tremendous difference in a 90 percent opinion by biologists and a counter 51 percent opinion among commissioners. The difference is 39 percent, but that ignores political power. Percents, like objectives, can be weighted. *Who* casts those 39 percent of the votes is the basis of decision-making power. The wildlifer must stick strictly to the role of professional advisor. An advisor must take responsibility for *advisory* decisions (a subset of the infinite set of alternatives, presentation, and advocacy). However, an advisor should not, need not, and must not take the responsibility for making the final decisions. Such decisions are beyond the advisor's expertise, education, and job description, and careful interpretation of most state statutes reveals that they are illegal. The wildlifer has too often confused science with morality. To become all "scientific" is to become ethically neutral. To advocate a moral stance is to join the ranks of the average citizen. The wildlifer must do both, but must distinguish clearly between these roles.

The wildlifer should present alternatives as early as possible to encourage dialog. Years ago when everyone could be a generalist, and everyone could (and would) attend a town meeting, public hearings were an effective mechanism. They are no longer effective. They serve no function in developing consensus or expressing value, and there is inadequate time for an agency to explain to the public the intricacies of even a modestly complex wildlife issue. New methods must be employed. The present "public hearing" usually convinces the public that the agency has listened, that it has not heard, and that it is going to do exactly what it planned to do before the hearing.

The commission must not dabble in agency operation. The director must guard the agency against such infringement. Similarly, the commission must guard against legislators dabbling in commission affairs. Legislators can be the worst sort of barber-shop biologists. Instead of being compelled by the tough issues of social welfare, environmental degradation, and human health, some are invariably diverted by such questions as how many barbs should be allowed on a fish hook, or whether a raccoon hunter can carry a side arm at night.

Cliques readily form within commissions. The larger the commission, the more probable it is that these cliques will form. These must be resisted and strong leadership exerted to nullify or break them.

Educational sessions are needed for all commissions. It is ineffective and unrealistic to depend on all members learning all they need to know about the resource and its management in the course of general business. These sessions should be brief and intensive. Commissioners, like society, will veto any idea or proposition they do not understand. The veto, uninformed, is nondiscriminating. The educational program must contain harder problems than those encountered in the past.

Commissions must announce their successes and display in clear terms the social good they achieve. This is essential for desirable public relations. On the other hand, it is absurd to announce with pride successes in avoiding obstacles of the agency's own creation. It is similarly absurd to exalt in winning at a *policy of inadvertence,* to roll a natural resource snake-eyes every few years. Much commission time is spent in such action as a result of an inept staff, the commissioners' own decisions, or their nonpolicy.

There is a recurring bit of lore in wildlife agencies that the game warden (by whatever name) is "the commission" to the person on the street or in the field. If this agent provides the only image, the commission deserves that image. By better publicizing successes, by exercising firm employee policy, and by better articulating for the public the role of agent and administration, it is possible to convert the image of the commission from the authoritarian uniformed personage to a successful, vigorous, serious and sophisticated generalship bent on resource optimization.

When commissions approve an appropriate salary and wage scale and yet find their wildlife managers moving to other states, they should suspect that the decisions they have reached are resulting in actions diametrically opposed to current knowledge and thus wasteful or ineffective. The sophisticated wildlife manager will recognize that there are other elements of decisions that have not been stated, and perhaps cannot be. However, when conspicuous resource abuse occurs because of a commission's decision, after unsuccessful efforts to prevent such reoccurrence, it would seem to me to be the wildlife manager's responsibility to move or take other bold action.

Because public demand and the public's best interest may not be synonymous, it is a major commission responsibility to establish constraints. Public pressure can thus be accommodated within the limits of policy or even laws (for example, the earliest opening and latest closing date of a hunting season).

No commission can stand the damage to its public image caused by improprieties in commissioner or employee use of funds, equipment, guide services, or game. A friend of one New Mexico commissioner was apprehended after illegally passing a big game checking station. The stations are now called "voluntary game research stations." Such culpable behavior can counteract thousands of dollars and many years of creative public relations effort. It is cost-effective to make outright payment of such benefits to commissioners and employees rather than to allow them to increase the credibility gap of the public agency.

Commissioners must be aware of the recent tendencies of technological successes to raise public expectations beyond any agency's ability to meet them. The commission's (and its staff's) role will be to announce targets, to explain *beforehand* why certain goals cannot be achieved, and to manage *expectation* along with *production*. It is all too easy for the public to transfer technological success to ecological and sociological success. The rate phenomena are quite different, and this difference must be communicated. If not done, the results are oversimplification, overexpectation, and then grave tensions.

Improving the Wildlife Agency

There is a need to create within agencies a concept of resource managers, not as thinkers only, or as doers only, but as *rational doers*. Intellectual communities must feed themselves—read rapaciously, ask questions incessantly, and look to theory for the models for what they must do. It takes strong people to advance new ideas. When ideas seem to be rejected or ignored, stresses occur. An agency should welcome ideas from all its employees and recognize that it needs these ideas in order to excel. How dare a manager talk about being an applied ecologist while denying the interactions of ideas! The intellectual environment must be such that all ideas are fair game; none can be restricted to a particular person or group. Surely the most knowledgeable employees will be sought out for the development of an idea, but *inthink* should be avoided.

Oldthink, too, should be avoided. There needs to be an attitude, within limits of course, that if something has been done one way in the past, it should be done differently now. Why something *cannot* be done is a final question, not a first question; such questions can be suppressed for good gains. Many people are defensive about good ideas of the past. But there have been significant changes both in the problems and in the solutions. It is no discredit to have a good idea replaced. Obsolescence is not bad; retaining the obsolescent is bad. A widely used idea or technique may have been the answer to a question, but the question has probably changed. Bureaucracy founders mostly on its inability to adapt to change.

The Organizational Environment. There is a significant body of literature and expertise in personnel management. Although salary checks, employment and travel forms, and insurance are nicely handled in most wildlife agencies, too little attention has been given to those types of activity geared to bringing out employee potential, minimizing complaints, predicting employment needs, and scheduling educational and professional improvements. There is an unexploited opportunity for expert *personnel management* in an environmental agency.

In the push for efficiency, employee motivation is often neglected. When an employee fails to gain recognition, the agency is courting inefficiency. It is appropriate for a wildlife agency to recognize ideas and work even to the point of "overdoing" it relative to other agencies. Even committee reports should have members' names included somewhere, rather than just the chairman's name being used.

Flexible organizations are needed. Most administrators have wall charts that show organization and salary scales. Such charts may have a legitimate purpose, but problems are bound to arise that cannot be met by the existing organizational structure. Problems are now too complex, dynamic, and instantaneous for any agency to have all the manpower it needs to attack *any* problem that arises. Agencies typically can solve problems that no longer exist. Some agencies have responded to problems by hiring people for several years and then being burdened by them once their specific tasks are completed. Employment ceilings prevent certain important problems from being solved. Problems often interpenetrate the domains of several agencies. Supra-agencies are needed, coalitions of personnel willing to and compelled to cross the bureaucratic boundaries for the general good. These small groups or task forces, or the larger supra-agency, constitute the *adhocracy* described by Toffler (1970:113). "We are . . . witnessing the arrival of a new organizational system that will increasingly challenge and ultimately supplant bureaucracy. This is the organization of the future." The future has arrived since his writing. The well-selected consultant, attacking a well-defined job having specific required outputs, will pay off abundantly. The effectiveness of such consultants could be magnified by having them work with an in-division standby task force or "assault group" of para-ecologists. Using such in-division groups and consultants should become a normal practice of the agency's social ecology.

Within agencies there are needs for feedback mechanisms. One need is an *ombudsman*, a person of top intellectual and moral caliber with investigative and advisory authority. The ombudsman's job would be to study the agency itself, criticize performance, hear grievances, make suggestions for improvements, ask questions of efficiency and effectiveness, and suggest means for obtaining answers.

Environment influences employee performance. Heat, light, and humidity are important, but even more important are the influences of "taste." Unsophisticated, slovenly, tasteless office and lab facilities degrade both public image and performance criteria. These are interactive.

A necessary ingredient of the organizational environment is a bit of *magic*. Some of it is present in a few agencies. Magic is that sense of a glad, bold commitment; of a land and a cause worth working for; of the chance for spectacular success; of risk taking that goes along with being far out in front; of having an approach that is right for the day—perhaps the only hope. Such magic is sensed by everyone. It can be cultivated. It is part of the environment needed by strong men and women to attack a Herculean task.

The Role of Women. With conspicuous exceptions, there are few women in professional wildlife resource management. There are of course brilliant secretaries throughout wildlife agencies—women who virtually run many offices. There are also women writers, spokesmen, legislators, and lobbyists who play essential roles in effective resource management. Title VII, the Equal Pay Act of 1963, presidential orders, and recent labor acts notwithstanding, sexual discrimination in the wildlife agencies is worse even than racial discrimination.

Women do have a place in wildlife management, contrary to what present employment practices would suggest. Wildlife work is not a man's specialty. Many women have strong biological and ecological interests; many study quantitative sciences; many are concerned about public education. Nationwide, annual experiences with the Christmas bird counts and many university field trips abundantly attest that women can do vigorous field work in mixed groups under adverse seasonal conditions. Women's physical strength and stamina differ widely, as do men's. Weak women, like weak men, will rarely apply for strenuous jobs. There are strenuous as well as nonstrenuous wildlife jobs; they cannot be classified on the basis of maleness.

The ability of women to work outdoors is clearly not a bona fide occupational qualification. Even if it were, there are many who are qualified. There are many non-outdoor roles that women can fill in wildlife management. Most aspects of research are suitable. Physiological and nutritional studies of wildlife, mathematical and computer-based ecological modeling, developing aids to management decision making, and pathology and epidemiology are appropriate for those uninterested in field work. There is a wide spectrum of employment possibilities ranging from research directors to clerks. Since evidence of women in higher-paying categories of wildlife management is lacking, a spectrum of starting jobs or activities for women with university educations in wildlife management is likely to be instructive.

The list, not differing from one for men, includes education specialists; youth conservation camping directors; executive secretaries for agencies, foundations, museums, and field stations; staff members of surveys and planning groups; illustrators of management and technical reports and presentations; developers of TV and mass media communications; public school conservation advisors; interpretative specialists; area receptionists and group leaders; data processors and analysts; editors for technical and scientific publications; wildlife photographers; systems analysts; taxonomists; museum or special-collection curators; research and law enforcement laboratory technicians; and state and federal wildlife biologists. The list is not complete; it is as long as there are job descriptions for men. The list is convincing that there is opportunity.

Whether the opportunity is real is yet to be decided. This opportunity is a decision and little more. It depends on whether a male-controlled, relatively closed shop will open its doors to allow the best people available within the population, male or female, to gain an education and then to apply their minds and skills creatively to wildlife resource problems.

There are real problems for women who would do graduate work in wildlife management. There are less than a thousand women graduates a year in fields related to wildlife management. Finances are the major barrier to graduate study. Only one-fourth of the women, compared with almost half of the men, enrolling in graduate school receive stipends. The other major barrier is family responsibilities. But these barriers can and will be overcome by a combination of forces now working in society and by the following changes in the field of wildlife management:

1. Public wildlife agencies must open their doors to qualified women university graduates in wildlife management. Agencies must let this policy be known to universities.

2. Universities must cease to discriminate against women graduate students in wildlife management. Part of their reluctance to enroll women is the belief that there are no employment opportunities.

3. Part-time matriculation in graduate programs must be offered as an option for women with families who wish to pursue advanced studies in wildlife management. Campus-linked self-study or programmed-learning opportunities should be made available.

4. Wildlife agencies, universities, and organizations must provide opportunities for part-time employment for women graduates. Many tasks such as computer programming of ecological problems and taxonomic work do not require full-time employees. Teaching on a part-time basis is now done and can provide opportunities for women with family responsibilities. Planning is an effective use of women with strong skills but also with family responsibilities.

5. The Wildlife Society, universities, and other resource organizations could provide information on opportunities for women to deal meaningfully with problems of the wildlife resource.

6. Evident discrimination in the granting of graduate support or stipends to women must cease. *Additional* special stipends and special allocation of funds need to be sought to help overcome past imbalances. It is instructive that continuous graduate enrollment for women is more than twice as likely to occur when they receive stipends as when they do not. Special funds are needed to enable mothers to complete their graduate programs. If university child care centers are not provided, allowances are needed. These funds will tend to prevent the high drop-out rates of mothers in graduate school programs.

The role of women in wildlife management is now only dimly seen. For a while, it will take brave women to venture into this male-dominated territory, and it will take male colleagues to support and encourage their venture.

Associates. Internal forces may stimulate change in wildlife institutions. But external forces are needed before wildlife institutions gain sufficient momentum for truly significant change and development. One major external force will be the appearance of self-conscious, profit-making wildlife organizations.

Such organizations, hereafter called *associates,* will provide needed services for people in study and management of, and education related to, the wildlife resource. Their composition will usually be of groups of associates, subcontractors, and specialists called into jobs as situations dictate. The peculiar strength of the associates will be their ability to bring to bear on a problem more resources of the highest caliber available, more quickly, with greater assurance of payoff, and with less red tape than any existing public land management agency. The permanent staffs would be small or nonexistent; capital investments would be minimal; no self-perpetuation or make-work situations would be necessary.

The opportunities and needs for the following services and functions in wildlife and related ecological, environmental, and natural resource fields become more evident daily: environmental impact reports, legislative advisory reports, resource "audits" by a disinterested third party, field surveys and analyses of habitat potentials, state-of-development technological reports for researchers and managers, bibliographies and literature reviews, problem scenarios, and organizational analyses.

To the just mentioned activities envisioned for the associates would be added many of those common to the consulting forester—that is, aerial photo services, land surveys and maps, land valuation, and retainer management and supervision. In addition, managerial activities may include computer-based simulation and decision systems, computer-generated management maps, specialized land treatment services, inventories and data tabulation services, advanced cost-accounting and program-planning systems, problem-specific allocation models and solutions, and custom-packaged population estimators and evaluators. The need for managerial prediction could be readily met by the specialists and the tools of such associates. Special services could be provided for shooting preserves. A particularly valuable service would be that of providing aid in bridging the gap between the client and other service groups such as large-scale computer software companies. Unique advantages could be supplied for clients by such a group in (1) serving as a sounding board for new policy, (2) making analyses of the group dynamics of staffs, and (3) working with agency task forces. A possible hatchet man role may be a very influential activity for governmental wildlife groups. The expertise and high reputation of the associates may make them the only institution capable of filling the void left by the dissolution of the credibility of agencies and authorities.

Educational and social engineering functions of associates would profitably be those of ghost writing speeches, developing publications on contract, giving lectures, operating computer-based training games and management decision-making simulators, publishing a management-oriented bi-monthly, preparing training program texts, providing professional editorial services and art work, conducting tours for legislators, engineering problem-specific public attitudinal changes, and solving specialized wildlife law violation problems. An elite, well-trained and rehearsed cadre using the best in educational technology could present highly efficient post-graduate education and in-service training programs.

There are few such groups. Many broad environmental consulting firms exist. There are a few successful wildlife consultants. Many have not succeeded because they could not stabilize a suitable income within their limited capabilities and interests while working within relatively small regions. Even state wildlife agencies do not have the diversity of interests or activities to sustain professional manpower in all the areas listed. A principle that is well known to ecologists—the more diverse the environmental complex, the more probable its stability—applies to consultants, associates, and even to states. That the federal wildlife agency could long ago have supplied such a service pool seems apparent under the principle of "doing collectively what each cannot do alone." The states' traditional resistance to federal intervention in their affairs has been as much to blame as the narrowness of the federal agency's innovative spirit. No wildlife agency has all these capabilities within itself; no agency needs them all; no agency can afford them. A private group of associates for consulting in management and research would have the capability to augment its staff with specialists as problems arise, a capability few government wildlife agencies have or have exercised. The private wildlife organization would in no way relieve the administration or client of the prerogative and responsibility of decision making. It would, however, provide the alternatives and recommendations for the "best" decision and the essential steps both in planning and performance to achieve desired results.

No matter how glowing the talk of cooperation or how fat the files on coordination, it is extremely difficult to do interagency work. Overcoming personality problems is a monumental task, arranging for proper "credits" is deadly, and budgeting properly is enough to strain anyone's honesty. Imagine two agencies building a small wildlife pond on public land, agreeing to go 50-50. Both have a small, set amount of money allocated for the pond; both have included bulldozer rental and drainpipe purchases. No fiscal agent is willing to buy one-half a pipe; few have the authority to transfer funds from rental categories to purchase categories. By the time the operation is over, the "wildlife" manager has "managed" some books, "rented" some pipe, and consumed the time of at least two fiscal agents and two field people and their supervisors. The "administration" for such activities often costs the taxpayers more than the structure, and often there will be some potentially hazardous physical shortcuts due to budgetary constraints. Two agencies could contract with one of the associates to build a pond for them. The results would probably be an equally good or better structure for less money. The agencies' employees could make their essential contributions in site selection and design specifications to achieve explicit local wildlife objectives.

Associates could provide a voice for the public, unfettered by state and federal political concerns. Although the widespread acceptance of commission forms of wildlife agency administration has reduced political influences of a type, it has increased others. It cannot be fairly said that commissions, or the influence of laws relating to expenditures of tax funds from sporting arms and ammunition, have checked harmful political influence on wildlife resource management.

At the state level, for example, a biologist who has for 10 years been gaining acceptance for a particular beneficial type of hunting season that is nontraditional may lose professional esteem in a community after a commission opposes such a season. The credibility gap is very real when a wildlife biologist experiences not only a setback from such a decision, but also the full force of the agency's educational services in "selling" the new decision. The conscientious wildlifer can rarely speak out without appearing openly to criticize the wildlife agency. Agency loyalty and resource loyalty are often placed on the balance. Agency loyalty, of the two, is usually too heavily weighted—basically by fear of loss of a job, failure to gain pay increases, or increased work loads. Associates may serve as vocal third-party authorities that may provide better balance in decisions about what is the wisest use of the wildlife resource.

Wildlife workers have been notoriously low paid relative to similar workers. The employee supply is abundant; there is a buyer's market. The state or federal monopoly is further restrictive. The Fish and Wildlife Service has been reluctant to advance salaries for wildlifer managers—even to a level equivalent to U.S. Forest Service salaries. The willingness to work for low salaries is commendable, but a condition over which the employee should have control, not the employers. Competitive associates could have a profound effect on salaries, raiding the agencies for top people. Now that computer programmers can command higher salaries than game division chiefs, it is unlikely, as state hierarchies go, that essential programmers will be employed until upper levels are shifted. Associates could interview at universities, now rarely done by the wildlife agencies, and acquire the top people—both because of their organizational objectives and because of their ability to offer high salaries. A healthy competition between the agencies and the associates for personnel will surely develop to the advantage of the public and individual wildlifers.

The files of every game agency in the country are full of unfinished reports, unanalyzed data, and thousands of field reports that are the only visual or real representation of any outputs of thousands of dollars spent on research. The contractual nature of the work of associates tends to require completion reports and specified final documents. The agencies have had *control* over the entire process, but they have been unable or unwilling to exercise similar control over their own field work. There is almost no way to fire a salaried wildlife employee. Rarely would salaries be withheld; suspensions are unlikely. The only real "control" is personal badgering by a supervisor. Throughout the field, stalemates exist; the supervisors are tired, the badgered are numb or have moved to another state where there is a supervisor more tired than the last. Associates can clean up the research files, convert data to useful information, gain the rewards of past investments, and move on to neat, guaranteed-payoff, and well-planned contractual projects. New standards of performance can be set. The results, beside the financial benefits for the members of the associates, will be to liberate and encourage the good public servant who is already anxious for the needed change.

A Law of Effective Reform

Nicholas Johnson, attorney and member of the Federal Communications Commission, concluded that a law of effective reform of legal institutions was needed. Such a law (Giles 1969) can provide reform to those wildlifers who are willing to operate within and change the system or for those who will work effectively outside the system. The "law" is an alternative to those who would curse wildlife management or deny its existence. The law is not restricted to legislative reform but provides the rational mechanism for challenging "established" concepts, "proven" practices, and other items under the topic of "that's just the way it is."

The law is needed since the classical wildlife protest is one that fails. Analyses show that vague feelings are presented rather than facts, that letters or testimony are not specific about who has done something wrong, or what legal principle has been violated, and give no remedy or appropriate alternatives. Gardner (1969) talked of such people. "The model of the ineffectual radical is the man or woman who spends a few brief years exploding in indignation, posturing, attitudinizing, oversimplifying, shooting at the wrong targets, unwilling to address himself to the exact business of understanding the machinery of society, unwilling to undergo the arduous training necessary to master the processes he hopes to change. . . . He never exposes himself to the tough tests of reality. He doesn't subject his view of the world to the cleansing discipline of historical perspective or contemporary relevance."

The pragmatic components of the law of effective reform are:

1. Understand the complex processes by which change normally occurs, by which change has been accomplished, and by which other options might be exercised.

2. Determine the factual basis for the conflict or grievance and the specific parties involved.

3. Identify the key points of leverage.

4. Assert the particular principle that indicates resolution or relief is due (for example, constitutional provision, statutes, regulations, court decisions, or policy).

5. Identify feasible alternative solutions.

6. Assert the precise solution or remedy sought (for example, the optimal solution, the desired statute, the precise policy statement).

7. Measure the results by real accomplishments and changes.

8. If the solution is less than satisfactory, re-initiate the aforementioned actions.

Failure to understand this law makes most legitimate protests ineffective. Use of such a law will produce profound effects even for the most meek.

The means exist for accomplishing changes in wildlife agencies and for guiding and maintaining a highly effective wildlife agency. The means is a systems approach.

Study Questions

1. Relate the commission to the departmental wildlife agency administration.

2. What is the most prevalent system of organization?

3. Write a scenario for your state or province describing wildlife administration under a law of wildlife ownership different from the present one (for instance, living wildlife soley the property of the landowner, not the state; internationally owned; or owned by a commission).

4. Describe the implications of a cadre of "rational doers" in a wildlife agency. What desirable changes might be expected? What problems encountered?

5. Examine any modern textbook on personnel management. What techniques and concepts do you think can be readily applied to the agency for which you work or with which you are familiar?

6. Give examples of agency feedback mechanisms.

7. What is meant when it is said that agencies need a bit of magic?

8. What is the role of women in wildlife management? What are their limitations? What are their strengths?

9. A dynamic *associates* group may be perceived as a threat to an agency. Why? How can the perceived threat be prevented by the agency? The associates?

10. What are future prospects for associates?

11. Analyze the law of effective reform as a general system.

Selected References

Ackoff, R. L. 1974. *Redesigning the future: a systems approach to societal problems.* Interscience Publishers, John Wiley and Sons, New York. ix + 260 p.

Gardner, J. W. 1969. Responsible versus irresponsible dissent. *Science* 164(3879):n.p.

Gilbert, D. C. 1971. *Natural resources and public relations.* The Wildlife Soc., Washington, DC. xxiv + 320 p.

Giles, R. H., Jr. 1969. Law of effective reform. *Wildlife Society Newsletter.* No. 124:47.

Gutermuth, C. R. 1971. *Role of policy-making boards and commissions.* Paper presented at the 7th Annual Short Course in Game and Fish Manage.; Colorado State University, Fort Collins, Feb. 9. Offset. 11 p.

Haskell, E. H. and V. S. Price. 1973. *State environmental management: case studies of nine states.* Praeger, New York. xv + 283 p.

Morris, W. T. 1964. *The analysis of management decisions.* Richard D. Irwin, Homewood, IL. 551 p.

Simon, H. A. 1957. *Administrative behavior,* 2nd ed. *The Free Press,* New York. xxxix + 259 p.

Toffler, A. 1970. *Future shock.* Random House, New York. 505 p.

Index

abiotic environment, 171
abomasum, 180, 181
abortion, 77
abundance, 17
access, 123–125, 128, 129, 203, 252, 283, 284, 326
accidents, 67, 97, 99, 103, 322, 331
  hunting, 354
acid rain, 249
acids, volatile fatty, 186
Ackoff, R. L., 382, 383
acorns, 166, 326
acquisition. *See* land acquisition
activity, 176
adaptability, 167
added value, 19
adhocracy, 379, 391
administration, 303, 329, 346, 378–399, 381, 395
adreno-pituitary, 102
advertising, 6
age class, 68
agencies, 210, 211, 219, 220, 222, 224, 234, 249, 270, 281, 293, 329, 344, 352, 353, 355, 363, 364, 378–399
  supra-, 390
agency
  effective, 398
  improving the, 389
  objectives of, 221
  performance of, 215
agency, law enforcement, objectives, 353
agent, 323, 344, 357, 360, 361, 362, 373
age pyramid, 53, 54, 55, 56, 66, 73
  human, 363, 367
age ratios, 53, 69, 70, 79, 102, 178, 253, 324
aggregates, 152, 199, 214, 248, 252, 317, 319, 355. *See also* production functions and production curves
aging, fish, 290
agribusiness, 275

agriculture, 94
air, compressed, 288
aircraft, 42, 106, 124, 302
aircraft patrols, 42
air pollution. *See* pollution
Alaska, 276
Alberta, 264, 276
Alces americana, 9, 174
algae, 301
Allen, R. P., 39
allocation, 200, 212, 262, 278, 372
allowable harvest, 253
alphachloralose, 106
alpha people, 348, 352
American buffalo, 9
Amidon, P. H., 366
amino acids, 290
amphibians, 124, 323
amplitude, ecological, 244
amplitude, group, 216
anadromous fish, 282
analysis, 12, 95, 105, 119, 136, 216, 229, 252, 353
  definition, 32
  organizational, 394
analysis and design, habitat, 119–209
Anas discors, 262
Anas rubripes, 265
Anderson, D. R., 273, 276
Anderson, L., 106
anesthetizing drugs, 8
animals as environment, 129
annual food patches, 203
annuli, tooth, 324
antelope, 25, 103
anthrax, 107
anti-hunting groups, 16
Antilocapra americana, 9
antlers, 37, 101, 112, 116, 181, 330
apiaries, 323
apple orchard, 327, 328

400

Ontario, 265
opening day phenomenon. *See* phenomenon,
  opening day
opportunities, 27, 301
opportunity cost, 24, 27, 316, 317
optimization, 287, 305, 325, 353, 387
optimum population, 295
option demand, 23
orchards, 5, 227, 311, 327, 331, 334, 355
ordinances. *See* law and regulations
Oreamnos americanus, 9
orientation, 262
organic matter, 180, 301
organizations, 23, 382, 384, 390
organisms, as integrators, 191
organohalides, 249
ornithosis, 107
otters, sea, 284
outer-bound method, 44, 46
outputs, 12, 235, 372, 373
ovaries, 101
ovenbird, 132
overharvesting, 120, 254, 278, 292
overhunting, 325
overpopulation, 101
Overton, W. S., 42, 45
overutilization, 178
Ovibos moschatus, 9, 77, 244
Ovis canadensis, 9
ovulation, 102, 323
owls, 254, 333
ownership, 39, 284, 311
oxides, 287
oxygen, 285, 287, 300

palatability, 175, 255
Papageorgis, D., 233
paraecologists, 391
parallel worth, 19
parasite control, 106–107
parasites, 36, 37, 38, 96, 99, 106, 108, 330,
  333, 335
Parker, F. L., 85
parks, 121, 382
Park Service, 271, 300, 311
pathogen, 107, 108
pathology, 96, 392
patrol strategies, 372
pay, of wildlifer, 311, 396
Pearse, P. H., 23
peat, 250
Pecari angulatus, 9
peccary, 9
Pedioecetes phasianellus, 75
pelicans, 261
pellet groups, 44
pelts, 104, 249, 253, 313
pelvis, shape, 46
Penfound W. T., 247
penis ligaments, 46
Pennsylvania, 21
people, management of, 6, 210–239, 255, 331

people managers, education and
  employment, 222
peptic glands, 181
perch, 300
performance, measure of 304, 373
perimeter, 140–141
permit hunts, 123
permits, 19, 98, 101, 109, 121, 126, 269,
  310, 322, 331
permutations, 248
pest, integrated management system, 251
pesticides, 17, 227, 323
pests, 4, 19, 37, 91, 112, 136, 175, 251,
  268, 328, 329
  urban, 255
Petersen-Lincoln method, 45
petrels, 261
Petrides, G. A., 55, 70
pH, 300
pheasants, 5, 35, 75, 378
phenology, 161
phenomenon, opening day, 111–113, 302,
  304, 305, 330, 389
Philohela minor, 261
phosphate, 287
phosphorus, 300
photography, 77, 102, 108, 305, 326
  aerial, 132, 139, 248, 250, 364, 394
photosynthesis, 79, 246, 255, 276, 286,
  287, 301
physical utility, 16, 17
phytoplankton, 290
pike, 300
pine, 174, 198, 333
pintails, 266
Pittman-Robertson Act, 128, 379
placental transfer, 97
plague, 107
planimeter, 122
plankton, 301
planners, viii, 334, 382
planning, 124, 156, 161, 203, 204, 311, 313,
  327, 353, 392, 393
  long-range, 126, 335
planting, 173, 305
plant vigor, 177
platforms, observation, 256
plots, 164, 166, 168
plowing, 124, 199
"poacher and warden" game, 346
poachers, 79, 97, 138, 151, 160, 191, 203,
  331, 347, 348
  types, of, 347
poaching, 179, 227, 344, 348, 354
  timber, 309
points, 120, 135, 143, 151
point systems, 268, 269
poisoning, 38, 67, 255, 291
poisons, 99, 104, 167, 291, 305
policies, viii, 20, 220, 222, 265, 284, 310,
  311, 354, 378, 381, 386, 387, 392
policy of inadvertence, 388